The Emergence of Agriculture

This volume is the first in the *One World Archaeology Reader* series. It is a compendium of key papers by leaders in the field of the emergence of agriculture in different parts of the world, collected from the *One World Archaeology* series of books. Each is supplemented by a review of developments in the field since its publication.

The collection is introduced by a new review chapter on the latest concepts and methods developed to understand early agriculture to bring each article up to date.

Contributions encompass better known regions of early and independent agricultural development, such as Southwest Asia and the Americas, as well as lesser known locales, such as Africa and New Guinea. Other contributions examine the dispersal of agricultural practices into a region, such as India and Japan, and how introduced crops became incorporated into pre-existing forms of food production.

This book is intended for students of the archaeology of agriculture, and will also prove a valuable and handy resource for scholars and researchers in the area.

Tim Denham is a Monash and Australian Postdoctoral Research Fellow in the School of Geography and Environmental Science. His research focuses on early agriculture in New Guinea, with additional interests in environmental archaeology and archaeological theory. He has recently initiated a 6-year project investigating rockshelter and cave sites along a highland-to-lowland transect in a remote region of Papua New Guinea.

Peter White is Honorary Research Associate in Archaeology, University of Sydney. His lifetime research interest is the archaeology of New Guinea and Australia. He has edited the journal *Archaeology in Oceania* for more than 20 years. His recent publications include articles on Pleistocene animal translocation, Lapita pottery and writing for publication.

One World Archaeology Readers

The One World Archaeology Readers collect the most influential articles from the One World Archaeology series of books in thematic single volumes for student and reference use. Each volume features a new introduction which details the importance of the articles, explaining how they shaped the development of their subject.

The Emergence of Agriculture: a global view
Tim Denham and Peter White

The Emergence of Agriculture

A global view

Tim Denham and Peter White

Routledge
Taylor & Francis Group

LONDON AND NEW YORK

First published 2007
by Routledge
2 Park Square, Milton Park, Abingdon, Oxon OX14 4RN

Simultaneously published in the USA and Canada
by Routledge
270 Madison Ave, New York, NY 10016

Routledge is an imprint of the Taylor & Francis Group, an informa business

© 2007 Tim Denham and Peter White

Typeset in Sabon
by Keystroke, 28 High Street, Tettenhall, Wolverhampton
Printed and bound in Great Britain
by Antony Rowe Ltd, Chippenham, Wiltshire

British Library Cataloguing in Publication Data
A catalogue record for this book is available from the British Library

Library of Congress Cataloging in Publication Data
A catalog record for this book has been requested

ISBN10: 0–415–40444–4 (hbk)
ISBN13: 978–0–415–40444–0 (hbk)

ISBN10: 0–415–40445–2 (pbk)
ISBN13: 978–0–415–40445–7 (pbk)

Contents

Contributors

Catherine D'Andrea is an Associate Professor in the Department of Archaeology, Simon Fraser University, British Columbia, Canada.

Tim Denham is a Monash Research Fellow and Australian Postdoctoral Fellow in the School of Geography and Environmental Science, Monash University, Melbourne.

Jack Golson is Professor Emeritus of Archaeology in the Research School of Pacific and Asian Studies, Australian National University, Canberra.

David R. Harris is Professor Emeritus of Archaeology at the Institute of Archaeology, University College, London.

Christine A. Hastorf is a Professor in the Department of Anthropology, University of California–Berkeley.

Kharaiti L. Mehra can be contacted through the Indian Archaeological Society, New Delhi, India.

Deborah Pearsall is Professor of Anthropology and holds The Frederick A. Middlebush Chair in Social Sciences at the University of Missouri at Columbia, Missouri.

Dolores R. Piperno is Senior Scientist and Curator of Archaeobotany and South American Archaeology, Department of Anthropology, National Museum of Natural History, Washington, DC and Smithsonian Tropical Research Institute, Panama.

David Rindos was Senior Lecturer in the University of Western Australia at the time of his death.

Peter Robertshaw is Professor of Anthropology, California State University, San Bernadino.

Patty Jo Watson is Edward Mallinckdrodt Distinguished University Professor, Emerita, Washington University, St Louis.

Peter White is Honorary Research Associate in Archaeology at the University of Sydney.

George Willcox is a researcher with Archéorient, CNRS, University of Lyon II.

Daniel Zohary is Professor in the Department of Evolution, Systematics and Ecology, the Hebrew University, Jerusalem.

Preface

The World Archaeological Congress, as its name implies, encompasses archaeology world-wide. Since its first meeting in 1986, it has attempted to include archaeologists from around the world, as well as representatives of the communities within which they work. Both scientific and locally important results have come from these meetings, and many of them have been published, often in the *One World Archaeology* (*OWA*) series of edited books.

At the Fifth World Archaeological Congress (WAC5) in Washington, DC in 2003, the new President, Dr Claire Smith, pointed out strongly that nearly all WAC publications were produced in the First World, and sold at prices that only a few there could afford. Even academic libraries in many parts of the world would find them beyond their means, while students would never be in a position to own them. It is out of this concern that this book, which we hope will be the first in a series, has come.

The aim of the *OWA Reader* series is to bring together some of the papers on particular topics which have already been published in the *One World Archaeology* series, and to produce these in a form which will be within the economic reach of libraries, academics and even students in many countries. The core of the book is thus a series of reprints. To this we have added short updates, some by authors of the original papers and some by the editors. Our selection of papers for this volume has been guided by three principles: first, to focus on the development of early agriculture based on plants – a volume similarly focused on animals will hopefully be forthcoming; second, to include papers which give a good understanding of both the theory and practice of the topic; and third, to provide examples from as wide a geographic range as possible within the prescribed size limit of the volume.

The three *OWA* volumes drawn on here are:

Harris, D. R. and Hillman, G. C. (eds) (1989) *Foraging and Farming: the evolution of plant exploitation*, OWA 13, London: Unwin Hyman.
Shaw, T., Sinclair, P., Andah, B. and Okpoko, A. (eds) (1993) *The Archaeology of Africa: food, metals and towns*, OWA 20, London: Routledge.

Gosden, C. and Hather, J. (eds) (1999) *The Prehistory of Food: appetites for change*, OWA 32, London: Routledge.

The papers are reprinted with only minimal changes, which are largely confined to the updating of unpublished references, reformatting and minor editorial amendments. Thus, and to avoid confusion when referring to the original and reprinted versions, the radiocarbon conventions used in the original chapters are retained. In Harris and Hillman (1989: xxxiv) and the chapter from Shaw *et al.* (1993), bp, bc and ad refer to uncalibrated radiocarbon ages, whereas BC and AD indicate calibrated radiocarbon dates and calendric dates. Although in Gosden and Hather (1999) there is no explicit statement on the convention followed, BP was used for uncalibrated radiocarbon ages and BC and AD indicate calibrated radiocarbon dates and calendric dates. For most of the newly written updates, uncalibrated dates are prefixed by 'uncal.' and calibrated dates are prefixed by 'cal.'; only general age ranges and time periods are referred to without prefixes.

We are grateful for the efforts of President Claire Smith in the negotiations for this *Reader* series and we also thank Richard Stoneman of Routledge. Since the original papers were not available in any electronic form, preparation of the text required all the papers be scanned using Optical Character Recognition (OCR) so that minor editing and corrections could be made. This laborious task was carried out at the School of Geography and Environmental Science at Monash University by Kara Valle under the supervision of Phil Scamp. Gary Swinton and Phil Scamp of the same School diligently reproduced the figures for several chapters. The labour of scanning and graphics was kindly supported by funds from Graham Oppy (Associate Dean for Research, Faculty of Arts, Monash University), whom we heartily thank. We thank the various authors for permission to republish their works and for eagerly participating in the updating process; also Larry Gonick for the cartoon in David Harris' chapter. Finally, we thank our partners for their assistance and tolerance.

Peter White
and
Tim Denham

1 Early agriculture

Recent conceptual and methodological developments

Tim Denham

In this volume, key papers on early agriculture from previous *One World Archaeology* (*OWA*) volumes are reprinted (Harris and Hillman 1989; Shaw *et al.* 1993; Gosden and Hather 1999), together with brief updates that situate the original papers within their contemporary research contexts. However, there have been several major conceptual and methodological developments over the last 15–20 years, to which I draw attention in this introduction. These developments cluster around two inter-related themes: 'How we conceive agriculture' (conceptual) and 'How we investigate agriculture in the past' (methodological).

New conceptual directions

In this section I outline three conceptual viewpoints that have been developed over the last 20 years, but which are not represented by contributions to this book. These are the farming/language dispersal hypothesis proposed by Peter Bellwood and Colin Renfrew, the concept of 'low-level food production' proposed by Bruce Smith, and a 'post-processual' turn to the study of early agriculture illustrated through Tim Ingold's work.

The farming/language dispersal hypothesis

The farming/language dispersal hypothesis (see Bellwood and Renfrew 2002a), and a recent variant, the early farming dispersal hypothesis (Bellwood 2005), were proposed to:

> . . . account for the present distribution of some of the world's largest language families. . . . In short this proposes that some of these language families (such as the Niger-Kordofanian family (including Bantu), the Austronesian family, the Indo-European family, the Afroasiatic family, and several others) owe their current distributions, at least in part, to the demographic and cultural processes in different parts of the world which accompanied the dispersal in those areas of the practice of food

production (and of the relevant domestic species) from the various key
areas in which those plant and animal species were first domesticated.

(Renfrew 2002: 3)

Moreover,

> ... early farmers, by virtue of their healthy demographic and economic
> profiles, frequently colonised outwards from homeland regions, incor-
> porating hunter-gatherer populations and in the process spreading
> foundation trails of material culture, language and genetic distinctiveness.
>
> (Bellwood 2002: 17)

In summary, early farmers are considered to have spread outwards in a
'wave of advance' through demic (i.e. demographically-driven) expansion
from an agricultural homeland into adjacent areas occupied by 'hunting-
fishing-gathering' populations (Ammerman and Cavalli-Sforza 1984).
Consequently, and to varying degrees, the cultures, languages and genes
of farming populations replaced, or incorporated, those of non-agricultural
populations in newly colonised areas (see Bellwood 2005 for a global review).
This large-scale, comparative model was initially developed to understand
the distributions of Neolithic material culture, Indo-European languages and
genes across Europe (e.g. Ammerman and Cavalli-Sforza 1984; Renfrew
1987) and, in recent years, has been applied to disparate parts of the globe,
e.g. the spread of Austronesian language-speakers from Southeast China
or Taiwan, through island Southeast Asia and island Melanesia, and into the
Pacific (e.g. Bellwood 2001, 2005: 128–45). The farming/language dispersal
hypothesis has generated much debate; evidence has been marshalled in
support and critique for each region of the world to which it has been
applied (see papers in Bellwood and Renfrew 2002a).

In opposition to a model of demic diffusion, alternative perspectives
attribute a greater historical role to cultural diffusion and advance more
social and contextual interpretations to account for the spread of agriculture
and material culture in the past, as well as present-day distributions of languages and genes. From a cultural diffusionist standpoint, items of material
culture, language and genetic stock can move between interacting groups
without high degrees of replacement or absorption of one group (i.e. non-
farmers) by another (i.e. farmers). From a more contextual standpoint,
there is greater emphasis on understanding how people, languages and items
of material culture moved, were adopted and were transformed by communities in particular locales and on resultant transformations to those
communities. For example, Thomas (1996), among others (e.g. Price 1996;
Zvelebil 1996), has critiqued the application of 'wave of advance' models
to Northwestern Europe. He doubts whether a 'neolithic package' of shared
cultural traits ever existed (Thomas 1999: 14) and questions the ways in which
demic diffusionary models tend to represent non-farming communities as

passive historical actors who are generally replaced by, or incorporated into, farming communities as they spread. As Thomas states:

> ... the indigenous peoples of Northwest Europe were more active in the social and economic changes that took place in the fifth to third millennia bc than this perspective would allow. The mesolithic communities of Europe were already dynamic and changing societies, with a range of different sets of social relationships and economic practices, when they first encountered agriculturalists. So not only did the farming groups of Central Europe impose themselves upon or interact with foraging bands in a range of different ways, but the responses of those foragers will not have been uniform. Some may have been disrupted or assimilated, but it seems that many groups adopted aspects of the neolithic way of life in a fashion that was both novel and inventive.
>
> (1996: 312–13)

Advocates of the farming/language dispersal hypothesis have taken on board some criticisms, particularly with regard to specific regions, e.g. Northwestern Europe, and have clarified how periods of acculturation often accompany stalled demic expansion. However, they view some criticism as a function of analytical scale (Bellwood and Renfrew 2002b). The farming/language diffusion hypothesis seeks to explain broad-scale distributions in material culture, genes and languages that have emerged over thousands of years on continent-wide scales; from this perspective 'the irregularities of small-scale reality become "ironed-out"' (Bellwood 2005: 10). As an example, Renfrew perceives the need to more clearly distinguish 'between the life histories of individual languages and the rather different issues surrounding the life histories of language families' (2002: 470). Certainly the challenge for those seeking to understand early agriculture, as with conceiving the relationships between 'agency' and 'structure' in any element of social life (in the past or present), is to overcome dichotomous thinking and to conceive of how the cumulative effects of social practices at the community level relate to continental and millennial-scale cultural, genetic and linguistic distributions (Denham 2004). As Hodder (1999: 175) puts it with regard to archaeology generally: 'Rather than focussing on major transformations, it is possible to use archaeological data to gain an understanding of the indeterminate relations between large-scale processes and individual lives.'

Additional problems with the farming/language dispersal hypothesis stem from its genetic and linguistic bases. The hypothesis was derived to provide an historical process and time-depth to explain present-day genetic and linguistic distributions (following Ammerman and Cavalli-Sforza 1984 and Renfrew 1987, respectively). Archaeological data have been used selectively to verify or negate these processual and chronological frameworks. It is often hard for the non-specialist to evaluate differing genetic or linguistic evidence and interpretations, e.g. compare Oppenheimer and Richards' (2002) and

Hurles' (2002) accounts of the inferences that can be made from genetics about Holocene migrations across Island Southeast Asia, Melanesia and the Pacific. Certainly in many regions of the world, there are clear asynchronies among archaeological, genetic and linguistic data in terms of what they reveal about historical processes – as well as debate about the veracity of each body of work presented by archaeologists, geneticists and linguists (contrast Oppenheimer 2004 with Diamond and Bellwood 2003; Bellwood and Diamond 2005).

Despite these criticisms, the farming/language dispersal hypothesis has generated much interest in the fields of agricultural origins and the spread of farming communities, and has fostered much inter-disciplinary collaboration and debate.

Low-level food production: conceiving the middle-ground

Proponents of the farming/language dispersal hypothesis consider the independent transition to agriculture by pre-existing 'hunting-gathering-fishing' communities to have been a rare historical event. They consider agriculture and non-agriculture to be two distinct and separate lifeways, with few groups in the past or the present occupying the intervening middle-ground (Bellwood 2005). This claim is central to their hypothesis because those groups that did develop agriculture early and independently were afforded demographic advantages relative to non-agricultural groups.

In contrast to this view, many researchers consider there exists a continuum between 'hunting-gathering-fishing' and 'agriculture' in both the present and the past (Ford 1985; Harris 1989 [this volume]; Smith 1998a, 2001a). Indeed, there are great difficulties in trying to classify the lifestyles of many groups studied archaeologically and ethnographically as either 'hunting-gathering-fishing' or 'agriculture' (consider Hynes and Chase 1982; Yen 1989; Guddemi 1992; Roscoe 2002; Specht 2003; Denham 2005, for uncertainties in classifying Australian and New Guinean lifestyles). Consequently, there have been recurrent attempts to clarify terminology and to define the middle-ground of 'in-between' groups (see Harris 1989 [this volume]).

Bruce Smith has drawn on previous classifications by Ford (1985), Harris (1989 [this volume], 1996a, 1996b) and Zvelebil (1996) to reconceptualise the middle-ground. Multi-disciplinary research findings in different regions of the world, including Smith's in the Americas (e.g. 1992, 1998b), document diverse and numerous groups who actively and consciously engage(d) in various practices of food production – including cultivation of wild and domesticated plants – that fall 'in-between' foraging (hunting and gathering) and farming (agriculture). Smith (1998a, 2001a) terms the 'in-between' conceptual territory 'low-level food production' and differentiates this highly heterogenous category into 'low-level food production with domesticates' and 'low-level food production without domesticates'. Smith proposes neutral terminology and a tripartite division: food procurement, low-level food production (with and without domesticates) and agriculture (2001a: 27, 34). I will now examine these divisions.

Smith does not consider the mere presence of domesticated plants or animals in an archaeologically-derived assemblage to necessarily signify agriculture in the past. Although in Smith's schema domestication no longer defines the boundary between foraging and farming, it does remain a central concept:

> . . . because it represents such a significant level and form of intervention by humans in the life cycle of plant and animal species, and also because it is so clearly visible and recognizable across considerable spans of space and time.
>
> (Smith 2001a: 17)

Of most relevance here, Smith views the transition from 'low-level food production with domesticates' to 'agriculture' to lie along a cline from 30 to 50 per cent dependence upon the contribution of domesticates to annual caloric budgets. The cline accounts for the various societies who produce(d) food using a combination of wild, minimally managed and domesticated species in a variety of cultural and environmental contexts. Although no longer evidenced by the mere presence of domesticated plants or animals in archaeobotanical or zooarchaeological assemblages, respectively, agriculture in the past is defined in terms of 'a significant reliance on domesticates' (Smith 2001a: 18), i.e. a 30–50 per cent caloric dependence. The resultant temporal–developmental disjuncture between domestication and agriculture is highlighted by Smith with reference to his own research into early agriculture.

Smith has advocated a research methodology that utilises archaeobotany (principally macrobotanical remains) and the direct AMS dating of identified macrobotanical remains, in conjunction with comprehensive genetic finger-printing of modern crop plant distributions (Smith 2005; also see Erickson *et al.* 2005). Through this multi-disciplinary research, the present-day locations of wild progenitor populations of some key domesticated crop plants have been identified using genetics and compared to the locations of the archaeological sites containing the earliest evidence of domestication for these crop plants (Smith 1998a, 2001b; see Table 1.1). In several cases, these locations are near each other, whereas in others Smith considers the lack of spatial proximity to result from deficiencies in the genetic or archaeological data.

For each crop there is a considerable 'temporal–developmental gap' between the earliest occurrence of a domesticate and its incorporation into agriculture (Table 1.1). Thus, although archaeobotanical evidence suggests the presence of domesticated einkorn at Abu Hureyra at 9500 years ago, agricultural economies did not develop in the region until at least 3000 years later (Smith 2001a: 19; cf. Hillman 1996 and Willcox 1998). According to

Table 1.1 The consilience of archaeological and biological methods to the investigation of early agriculture, and evidence of domestication–agriculture time lags (sources: Smith 1998a, 2001a: 18–9, 2001b)

Crop plant	Earliest site	Date of initial domestication (years ago)	Distance of site to modern wild-progenitor populations (km)	Temporal 'gap' between domestication and agriculture (years)	References
Einkorn wheat (Triticum monococcum)	Abu Hureyra Syria	9500	200	3000	Hillman 1996; Heun et al. 1997; Moore et al. 2000
Squash* (Cucurbita pepo)	Phillips Spring USA	5000	60	4000	Decker-Walters et al. 1993
Maize (Zea mays ssp. mays)	Guilá Naquitz Mexico	6300	400–500	c. 2000	Benz 2001; Piperno and Flannery 2001

Note
* Summer squash lineage is being referred to here. The earliest presence of domesticated Cucurbita pepo dates to c. 10,000 years ago at Guilá Naquitz, Oaxaca, Mexico (Smith 1997), suggesting a domestication–agriculture temporal lag of 5500 years until the establishment of agricultural, village-based societies with maize-bean-squash economies by c. 4500 years ago (Smith 2001a: 19).

Smith's terminology, people were practising 'low-level food production with domesticates' for the duration of the considerable lag between initial crop domestication and the development of agricultural societies.

Smith's distinction between 'agriculture' and 'low-level food-production with domesticates' has now been clarified. Furthermore, the difference between the two types of low-level food production – with and without domesticates – is self-evident. The remaining terminological boundary within his schema, between food procurement and 'low-level food production without domesticates', can now be characterised.

The conceptual differentiation of 'food procurement' strategies, i.e. hunting-gathering-fishing, and 'low-level food production without domes-ticates' is complex and difficult. For Smith, previous schemas differentiated food-procurers from food-producers based on the nature of their practices; rather than there being a sharp boundary between the two lifeways, there were clines which attenuated in either realm (Smith 2001a: 29). However, Smith's clearest statement on the issue is ambiguous:

> As a result, any efforts to determine where exactly to place societies in this complex boundary zone of intensive food procurement and low-level food production is not simply a matter of ascertaining the presence or absence of certain forms of life-cycle-intervention activities on the part of humans, but rather should include consideration of the intensity, intentionality, species focus, and total range of such activities that are present in a group's economic repertoire.
>
> (2001a: 29)

Smith acknowledges that people in different regions followed diverse path-ways of food production, and, as a critique of teleological and deterministic arguments, he states that all types of food procurement and food production should be seen as 'stable solutions, as end points and destinations worthy of study in and of themselves' (2001a: 24). The middle-ground is not 'transi-tional'; it does not imply that people were inevitably developing from food procurement to low-level food production (and from 'without' to 'with' domesticates'), and on to agriculture. Rather, the middle-ground represents a diverse array of 'successful long-term socioeconomic solutions, fine-tuned to a wide range of local cultural and environmental contexts' (Smith 2001a: 34).

In evaluating Smith's schema, a major problem is his reliance on domes-tication as a grounding concept. Several issues remain unresolved in his consideration of domestication and how it relates to agriculture. Firstly, domestication in a plant or animal need not be marked by corresponding genotypic and phenotypic (i.e. morphological) changes. In some cases there may be good correspondences between genetic markers and morphological transformations, e.g. *Cucurbita* spp. (Sanjur *et al.* 2002), whereas in other species these correspondences are less clear (see Jones and Brown in press for a review).

Secondly, domesticated varieties of a species need not always be clearly demarcated from wild varieties, either in terms of the archaeobotanical record or in terms of extant species. For example, the differentiation of wild and domesticated rice in archaeobotanical assemblages has long proved problematic (Glover and Higham 1996: 431–3; see Crawford 2005 for a review). Additionally, many Pacific staples, as well as plants in other parts of the world, are characterised as 'semi-domesticated' (Yen 1985), or as having 'degrees of domestication' (Caballero 2004). Domestication is not an all or nothing event; rather, it can be a slow and on-going process even in cereals (Tanno and Willcox 2006). Indeed, genotypic and phenotypic changes may have been initiated in some plants and animals as soon as plants and animals were targeted by people (Hather 1996), and perhaps even incidentally.

Thirdly, the use of domestication within Smith's schema is problematic. Domestication is used to differentiate low-level food production with and without domesticates, even though Smith (2001a: 36) acknowledges that it may not be a good high-order distinction to differentiate societies of the middle-ground. Additionally, Smith grounds his definition of agriculture in terms of a 30–50 per cent caloric reliance on domesticates. Although morphological indicators of domestication may be visible in an archaeobotanical (macro and microfossil) or zooarchaeological record, the visibility of a social dependence upon domesticates is more difficult to quantify in archaeological records that are often partial and spatially and temporally fragmented (Harris 1995: 850; Yen 1998: 164).

In conclusion, Smith's schema is a major contribution to debates on early agriculture. However, it is also a product of a dominant intellectual tradition within archaeology – and especially within debates on early agriculture – namely, processualism. This intellectual tradition is now undergoing transformation, with implications for how early agriculture is conceived and studied.

A post-processual turn?

The 1980s marked a transition in the development of archaeological thought; the decade witnessed the emergence of a range of new (to archaeology at least) perspectives on how to interpret the past. These perspectives have become labelled as 'post-processual' and represent a critique of, and development from, the preceding 'processualism', or 'New archaeology' that had dominated Anglo-American archaeology for 20 years (see Hodder 2003 and Johnson 2000 for introductory reviews).

Until relatively recently, debates about the nature of agriculture, its origins and its diffusion remained isolated from broader conceptual developments within the discipline. Many of the principal participants in debates on early agriculture can still be situated squarely within functional, processualist traditions (e.g. Harris 1996a, 1996b, in press; Piperno and Pearsall 1998;

Smith 2001a; Bellwood and Renfrew 2002a; Renfrew 2002; Bellwood 2005). However, and particularly within the last decade, alternative – more post-processual – perspectives on how to conceive and interpret agriculture, particularly early agricultural practices, have increasingly come to the fore.

As a starting point, several authors have called for definitions of agriculture to be decoupled from the concept of domestication (Hather 1996; Spriggs 1996), just as other authors have decoupled agriculture from sedentism and other material cultural traits (e.g. pottery) (Thomas 1996, 1999: 7–33; Cauvin 2000; Denham 2006, in press). Most advocate more socially-oriented interpretations in which agriculture, domestication and production are not divorced from broader realms of social life (e.g. Hastorf 1998; Denham *et al.* in press; cf. Bender 1978). From this perspective, morphological and genetic evidence of domestication is not so significant for determining the presence of agriculture in the past. One such position has been eloquently argued by Ingold (1996: 21, 2000: 86), who defines agriculture in terms of 'the relative scope of human involvement in establishing the conditions for growth'.

In a thought-provoking essay, Ingold (1996, revised 2000: 77–88) un-ravels, challenges and rejects several historically received ideas that underlie orthodox, domestication-based conceptions of agriculture. For Ingold, these ideas are 'embedded in a grand narrative of the human transcendence of nature, in which the domestication of plants and animals figures as the counterpart of the self-domestication of humanity in the process of civilisa-tion' (2000: 77). Prominent among these ideas are a series of dichotomies that historically have permeated the distinction between hunting-gathering and agriculture (Figure 1.1; see David and Denham 2006).

Ingold's starting point is the division between collecting and production. A 'modern emphasis on production' attaches 'special significance . . . to the so-called "artificial selection" of plants and animals as the key criterion for distinguishing food-production from food-collection, and hence for determining the point of transition from hunting and gathering to agriculture and pastoralism' (Ingold 2000: 85). Ingold criticises this reliance on domestication.

For Ingold, the idea of domestication implies that people 'make' an animal or plant in terms of some preconceived end, i.e. it is teleological and implies

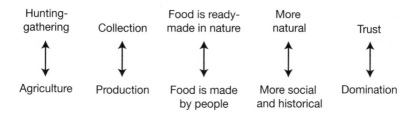

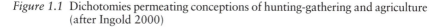

Figure 1.1 Dichotomies permeating conceptions of hunting-gathering and agriculture (after Ingold 2000)

some deliberate design. The relative duration and inter-locking of the life-cycles of people with animals and plants would seem to undermine the putative deliberateness of domestication except for the fastest growing species, e.g. annual and biennial plants and relatively short-lived animals. By contrast, given the lifespan of most species of tree is much greater than that of humans, the idea of planned intervention in the generation of domesticates is untenable. Ingold reorients the analytic focus from domestication, i.e. the production of genotypic and phenotypic variants, namely domesticates, to the 'conditions of growth', i.e. the practices people engaged in to grow plants and animals.

Further, he argues that the dichotomy between collection and production is the fundamental cause of problems in attempts to define agriculture and distinguish it from other forms of obtaining food:

> In terms of this dichotomy, human beings must *either* find their food ready-made in nature or make it themselves. Yet ask any farmer and he or she will say, with good cause, that the produce of the farm is no more made than it is found ready-made. It is *grown*. . . . [but] *what do we mean by growing things*? On the answer to this question must hinge the distinctions between gathering and cultivation, and between hunting and animal husbandry.
>
> (Ingold 2000: 85; emphasis in original)

As his argument develops, Ingold shifts the emphasis from 'making' to 'growing', and in doing so he seeks to undermine the most basic of all western dichotomies, that between nature and culture (see Levi-Strauss 1969 and critique by Derrida 1978). Ingold does not envisage a distinction between social and natural worlds; he does not consider that people 'make' or inscribe themselves on nature either through the construction of landscape or through plant and animal domestication. Rather, humans and the environment are mutually constitutive for the transformation of the world; they grow together in 'a single, continuous field of relationships' (Ingold 2000: 87).

If Ingold's perspective is adopted and applied to studies of early agriculture, the focus shifts from documenting genotypic and phenotypic changes in plants and animals to studying the degrees to which people establish 'the conditions for growth' as a means of distinguishing 'regimes of plant and animal husbandry' (Ingold 2000: 86). However, there are problems of application. Although in the example given by Ingold (2000: 85–6), garden cultivation clearly displays a greater degree of intervention than gathering plant foods, there is a lack of clarity in how the varying degrees of 'human intervention' are to be evaluated in more complex scenarios (such as those discussed by Smith 2001a).

Ingold's work marks a dramatic shift in the way agriculture is conceived. As yet, few studies have seriously attempted to directly apply his thinking to the study of early agriculture; although his ideas have tangentially informed practice-centred, contingent and more ambiguous interpretations of early agriculture and arboriculture (e.g. Denham 2004, 2006; Fairbairn 2005). As post-processual ideas continue to take hold in debates on early agriculture, the nature of agriculture and the methods used to study it in the past may change and diversify dramatically.

Methodological advances

Methods for the investigation of macrofossils, whether plant or animal, are well established (Binford 1981; Hastorf and Popper 1988; Stiner 1994; Renfrew and Bahn 2004: 275–316). However, over the last two decades there is an increasing realisation that macrobotanical assemblages at archaeological sites have been dominated by seeds, wood, and the hard pit stones and kernels of fruits and nuts. In discussions of early plant exploitation and agriculture for some parts of the world, this may have yielded an over-emphasis on seed-bearing plants, particularly the early domesticates barley, einkorn and emmer wheat, maize, millets, oats, rice and sorghum, as well as many weedy species, woody species and fruit- and nut-bearing trees. Species which yield little pollen under cultivation and which neither produce seeds, nor hard and woody tissues, have been under-represented; these species include most of the major root crops, as well as other starch-rich plants, such as bananas and breadfruit (Golson and Ucko 1994).

In this section, several key methodological developments in microfossil and molecular analyses of relevance to the investigation of early agriculture are discussed. Advances in microfossil analysis have largely been botanical, whereas molecular investigations have been applied with varying success to identify centres of plant and animal domestication, to identify genetic loci that correspond to morphological traits associated with domestication, and to ancient specimens. These methodological advances have expanded the investigation of early agriculture and food production to new regions of the globe and required reappraisals of more well-established regions. Only with the advent of microfossil studies, particularly phytolith and starch grain analyses, is the significance of a range of root crops (i.e. tuber, rhizome and corm-bearing plants) and other starch-rich staples (e.g. *Musa* bananas) to the development and spread of early agriculture being realised for several regions of the world formerly considered marginal, such as West Africa (Mbida *et al.* 2001), lowland South America (Iriarte *et al.* 2004; Perry 2005) and New Guinea (Denham *et al.* 2003, 2004b). Similarly, although the importance of seed-bearing grasses to the development of early agriculture in Africa, Southwest Asia, India, Southeast China and some parts of the Americas is unquestioned, there is a growing awareness that the relative importance of root crops requires reappraisal in these regions as well (Hather 1996).

Microfossils: parenchyma, phytoliths and starch grain analyses

Three microfossil techniques of broadest application to the investigation of early agriculture, specifically plant-based agriculture, are the microscopic examination of parenchyma, phytoliths and starch grains.

The analysis of parenchymatous tissue was developed to assist with the identification of root crops, which had been largely invisible in the archaeological record (Hather 1994a, 1996, 2000). The charred and, in rare cases, uncharred tissues of root crops can be preserved at archaeological sites and sometimes identified to genus and species levels (e.g. Hather and Kirch 1991). Although still not widely practised, largely due to limited reference collections and a lack of training, this technique holds considerable promise for those areas of the world where early agriculture is likely to have depended initially upon the exploitation of starch-rich tuberous plants, such as taro (*Colocasia esculenta*) and yams (*Dioscorea* spp.) in New Guinea (Yen 1985) and Southeast Asia (Hather 1996), yams (*Dioscorea* spp.) across Africa (Dumont and Vernier 2000), and manioc (*Manihot esculenta*) in lowland South America (Piperno and Pearsall 1998: 120–6). However, the potential of this technique has been eclipsed in the last decade by advances in other plant microfossil analyses, most notably phytoliths and starch grain analyses.

Phytoliths are mostly siliceous, although sometimes calcareous, concretions that have formed within the cells and in intracellular spaces of plants (see Piperno 2006). Phytoliths adopt distinctive shapes depending upon the part of the plant in which they have formed, i.e. different parts of the same plant can yield vastly different phytolith morphologies. It should be noted that some plants do not produce phytoliths. Phytoliths can be preserved in archaeological deposits, soils and sediments after plants have died and decayed. Siliceous and calcareous phytoliths form and preserve differentially depending upon soil geochemistry. Phytolith analysis is significant to the study of early agriculture in two ways: the reconstruction of vegetation histories, and the identification of specific crop plants.

Firstly, siliceous phytoliths preserve well in aerated neutral and acidic environments, which sometimes do not yield good pollen records. Consequently, phytoliths can be used instead of, or in combination with, pollen and charcoal frequency distributions to construct local and regional vegetation histories – a technique pioneered in the lowland neotropics (Piperno 1989 [this volume]; Pearsall 1999 [this volume]) and now being applied in other regions of the world, most notably New Guinea (Denham *et al.* 2003, 2004b). The combined use of phytolith and pollen analyses, together with macro- and microcharcoal frequency distributions, provides a complementary and more robust interpretation of vegetation history than the application of these techniques in isolation (e.g. Piperno *et al.* 1991a, 1991b; Piperno and Pearsall 1998). Such studies have greatly augmented the understanding of human impacts on the environment and have been used to infer regional-scale and local-scale vegetation changes associated with agricultural practices during the Holocene (e.g. Pearsall 2004, in press).

Secondly, phytoliths can be used to identify to the species level crop plants that do not produce abundant pollen or usually preserve well in macro-botanical assemblages. One of the earliest such studies was undertaken to identify and discriminate between *Musa* banana sections in New Guinea (Wilson 1985). Although of limited success, Wilson's pioneering studies have been developed further to enable the discrimination of Musaceae (*Musa* and *Ensete* bananas) in New Guinea (Denham *et al.* 2003) and Africa (Mbida *et al.* 2000, 2001; Lejju *et al.* 2006; Ball *et al.* 2006). However, the greatest advances have occurred in the Americas – where phytoliths have been used to document, date and trace the domestication of maize and its subsequent dispersal across north and south America (e.g. Piperno and Flannery 2001). Similar studies have been undertaken for other species in the Americas, e.g. squashes and gourds (*Cucurbita* spp.; Piperno and Stothert 2003), as well as for important cultivars in other regions of early agricultural development, e.g. rice in China (Zhao 1998).

Another relatively new technique which has made a significant impact on early agricultural studies is the identification of fossil starch grains preserved on artefacts and in the soil (see Torrence and Barton 2005). Although some of the soil geochemistry determining the preservation of starch grains is not fully understood, starch accumulations formed within the cells of some plants preserve after the plant, or plant part, has died and decayed. Starch grains with diagnostic features and shapes can be used to identify some former crop plants and starch grain frequencies have been used to augment land use histories (Therin *et al.* 1999). Starch grain analysis is revolutionising the investigation of early plant use, domestication and agriculture in several regions of the world – most notably in the Americas (e.g. Piperno and Holst 1998; Piperno *et al.* 2000; Iriarte *et al.* 2004; Perry 2004; Perry *et al.* 2006) and Australasia (e.g. Loy *et al.* 1992; Barton and White 1993; Fullagar *et al.* 2006), as well as elsewhere (e.g. Piperno *et al.* 2004; Barton 2005).

The above microfossil techniques can be applied to the investigation of soil and sediment samples from archaeological sites, as well as residues extracted from utilised artefacts and tools (e.g. Loy 1994). The extraction and analysis of artefact and tool residues, particularly when undertaken in conjunction with the analysis of comparable materials in associated soil and sediment samples, provides greater levels of understanding of plant use in the past (Perry in press; Perry *et al.* 2006). Other types of animal and plant residues can also be investigated, including blood, chemical deposits, fats and lipids, raphides and so on (see papers in Hather 1994b and Fullagar 1998).

Molecular analyses: DNA and aDNA

Although molecular techniques have been used for decades to investigate the origins and domestication of important plant and animal species (e.g.

Doebley 1990; Matthews and Terauchi 1994), over the last decade their application has been revolutionised through advances in mitochondrial deoxyribonucleic acid (mtDNA) and nuclear DNA research, and through the ability to simultaneously analyse numerous genetic loci using amplified fragment length polymorphism (AFLP) (Allaby and Brown 2003). The advent of recent DNA techniques has opened up vast new fields for the study of early agriculture and animal and plant domestication (Jones and Brown 2000, in press). These new research fields fall into three cross-cutting themes: the construction of phylogenies using modern DNA of a particular species, genus or family; the identification of genetic loci that correspond to phenotypic (morphological) changes thought to accompany domestication of a plant or animal; and the analysis of ancient DNA (aDNA) in plant and animal remains collected from archaeological, and in some cases palaeontological, contexts.

Phylogenies display the degree of genetic inter-relatedness among groups of subspecies, species, genera and families, and can provide information on the relative order in which particular species and intraspecific genetic traits came to exist. Thus phylogenies can show which species may have evolved first and how these may have changed through various processes of selection, mutation and hybridisation. If this information is associated with spatial information on the present-day distributions of species and, in some cases, with historical information (derived from macrofossil and microfossil research) on how the distributions and phenotypes of these species have changed through time, it can be possible to identify wild progenitors of domesticates, their region of origin, and their region of domestication (Sanjur *et al.* 2002). Global and regional studies have been undertaken for several commercially important domesticated animals (e.g. Loftus *et al.* 1999) and plants (e.g. Huang *et al.* 2002; Matsuoka *et al.* 2002). However, a major problem concerns the application of this technique to the investigation of varieties and subspecies of the same species which are not genetically isolated; inter-breeding between varieties and subspecies may be complex, difficult to untangle, and may undermine the assumptions underlying the construction of phylogenies (Jones and Brown in press).

Research primarily on modern populations of domesticates and their wild progenitors has enabled the identification of genetic loci that correspond to phenotypic changes considered to have resulted from domestication. For example, cereals are considered to have been selected for nonshattering varieties, thereby enabling the collection of a higher proportion of the edible seeds during harvesting. For some such species, it is now possible to isolate the genetic loci and biochemical process associated with the development of nonshattering varieties (Li *et al.* 2006). However for other species, the correspondences between phenotypic and genotypic traits are more complex and need not be direct (see Jones and Brown in press).

Major advances in ancient DNA research have been made over the last decade (Gugerli *et al.* 2005; Willerslev and Cooper 2005). The technique

involves extracting genetic information from archaeologically, or palaeonto-
logically, derived specimens for subspecies and species level identification,
thereby enabling genetic fingerprinting, genetic changes and relationships
among ancient plant and animal populations to be inferred, and comparisons with modern populations to be undertaken. Studies have been used
to fingerprint archaeobotanical (e.g. Freitas *et al.* 2003) and zooarchaeological (e.g. Matisoo-Smith and Robins 2004) samples, establish regions of
domestication for species (e.g. Larson *et al.* 2005), and to reconstruct the
domestication of species through time and across space using genotypic
and phenotypic data from archaeological specimens (e.g. Jaenicke-Després
et al. 2003).

In sum, microfossil and molecular techniques have revolutionised research
into early agriculture over the last decade. As these techniques are developed and applied further, especially in combination and with macrofossil
analysis and accurate dating (after Smith 2001b), the types of information
generated and the types of question that researchers can ask will expand.
Archaeologists investigating early agriculture will need to embrace these new
technologies and associated specialists as a matter of course; these methods
should become incorporated as 'best and standard practice'.

The diversity of early agriculture

At present, six to eight regions are generally considered to have been independent centres of domestication and early agricultural development (Table
1.2). In part, the number of regions of early and independent agricultural
development, as well as the nature and antiquity of early agriculture within
each region, is a function of perspective. Depending upon how agriculture
is delimited from other food-producing strategies, researchers use various
types of archaeological, archaeobotanical, genetic, geomorphological and
palaeoecological evidence to identify and date agriculture in the past.

In part, the contributions to this volume have been chosen to represent
widely dispersed geographical regions of early, but not necessarily independent, agricultural development. Contributors hold diverse conceptions
of early agriculture and, consequently, they draw on diverse lines of evidence
to investigate agriculture in the past and to substantiate their claims. Primarily
though, each chapter is a key conceptual or substantive contribution to the
global understanding of how agriculture came into being.

Table 1.2 Regions of early and potentially independent agricultural development (based on Smith 1998b: 13; Bellwood 2005: Figure 0.1)

Region[1]	Time period[2] (years ago)	Key references[3]	This volume
Sub-Saharan Africa	4000	Mbida et al. 2001 Marshall and Hildebrand 2002 Kahlheber and Neumann in press	Robertshaw 1993
Southwest Asia	9500	Bar-Yosef and Meadow 1995 Moore et al. 2000 Verhoeven 2004	Zohary 1989 Willcox 1999
China	8500–7800	Bellwood 1995 Zhang and Wang 1998 Lu et al. 2002	
New Guinea[4]	7000–10,000	Hope and Golson 1995 Denham et al. 2003, 2004a	Golson 1989
Eastern Woodlands (USA)	4500	Smith 1992 Scarry 1993 Gremillion 2002 Flannery 1986 MacNeish 1992 Smith 2001a, 2005	Watson 1989
Central Mexico	9000		
Northern South America	7000	Hastorf 1998 Piperno and Pearsall 1998 Pearsall 2004	Piperno 1989 Hastorf 1999 Pearsall 1999

Notes
1 Additional regions covered in this book are India (Mehra 1999, reprinted in this volume) and Japan (D'Andrea 1999, reprinted in this volume). For updated references for these regions refer to the respective updates.
2 Different authors attribute different age periods to the earliest agriculture and domestication in different regions of the world: the dates presented here are from Smith (1998b: 13) and represent the 'approximate time periods when plants and animals were first domesticated'.
3 Not all authors listed for a region necessarily consider that region to be an early and independent centre of agricultural development.
4 The inclusion and age range for New Guinea are based on Denham et al. 2003 and debates in Denham et al. 2004a.

References

Allaby, R.G. and Brown, T.A. (2003) 'AFLP data and the origins of domesticated crops', *Genome*, 46: 448–53.

Ammerman, A.J. and Cavalli-Sforza, L.L. (1984) *The Neolithic Transition and the Genetics of Populations in Europe*, Princeton, NJ: Princeton University Press.

Ball, T., Vrydaghs, L., van den Hauwe, I., Manwaring, J. and E. de Langhe (2006) 'Differentiating banana phytoliths: wild and edible *Musa acuminata and Musa balbisiana*', *Journal of Archaeological Science*, 33: 1228–36.

Barton, H. (2005) 'The case for rainforest foragers: the starch record at Niah Cave, Sarawak', *Asian Perspectives*, 44: 56–72.

Barton, H. and White, J.P. (1993) 'Use of stone tools and shell artefacts at Balof 2, New Ireland, Papua New Guinea', *Asian Perspectives*, 32: 169–81.

Bar-Yosef, O. and Meadow, R. (1995) 'The origins of agriculture in the Near East', in T. D. Price and A. B. Gebauer (eds) *Last Hunters, First Farmers*, Santa Fe, CA: School of American Research.

Bellwood, P. (1995) 'Early agriculture, language history and the archaeological record in China and southeast Asia', in C.-T. Yeung and B. Li (eds) *Conference Papers on Archaeology in Southeast Asia*, vol. I, Cambridge: Cambridge University Press.

Bellwood, P. (2001) 'Polynesian prehistory and the rest of mankind', in C. M. Stevenson, G. Lee and F. J. Morin (eds) *Pacific 2000*, Los Osos, CA: Easter Island Foundation.

Bellwood, P. (2002) 'Farmers, foragers, languages, genes: the genesis of agricultural societies', in P. Bellwood and C. Renfrew (eds) *Examining the Farming/Language Dispersal Hypothesis*, Cambridge: McDonald Institute for Archaeological Research.

Bellwood, P. (2005) *First Farmers: the origins of agricultural societies*, Oxford: Blackwell.

Bellwood, P. and Diamond, J. (2005) 'On explicit "replacement" models in Island Southeast Asia: a reply to Stephen Oppenheimer', *World Archaeology*, 37: 503–6.

Bellwood, P. and Renfrew, C. (eds) (2002a) *Examining the Farming/Language Dispersal Hypothesis*, Cambridge: McDonald Institute for Archaeological Research.

Bellwood, P. and Renfrew, C. (2002b) 'Concluding observations', in P. Bellwood and C. Renfrew (eds) *Examining the Farming/Language Dispersal Hypothesis*, Cambridge: McDonald Institute for Archaeological Research.

Bender, B. (1978) 'Gatherer-hunter to farmer: a social perspective', *World Archaeology*, 10: 204–22.

Benz, B. (2001) 'Archaeological evidence of teosinte domestication from Guilá Naquitz, Oaxaca', *Proceedings of the National Academy of Sciences USA*, 98: 2104–6.

Binford, L.R. (1981) *Bones*, New York: Academic Press.

Caballero, J. (2004) 'Patterns in human–plant interaction: an evolutionary perspective', paper presented at the International Society of Ethnobiology, Ninth International Congress, Canterbury, England.

Cauvin, J. (2000) *The Birth of the Gods and the Origins of Agriculture*, Cambridge: Cambridge University Press.

Crawford, G.W. (2005) 'East Asian plant domestication', in M. T. Stark (ed.) *Archaeology of Asia*, London: Blackwell.

D'Andrea, C. (1999) 'The dispersal of domesticated plants into north-eastern Japan', in C. Gosden and J. Hather (eds) *The Prehistory of Food: appetites for change*, London: Routledge.

David, B. and Denham, T.P. (2006) 'Unpacking Australian prehistory', in B. David, B. Barker and I. McNiven (eds) *The Social Archaeology of Indigenous Societies: essays on Aboriginal and Torres Strait Islander history in honour of Harry Lourandos*, Canberra: Aboriginal Studies Press.

Decker-Walters, D.S., Walters, T.W., Cowan, C.W. and Smith, B.D. (1993) 'Isozymic characterisation of wild populations of *Cucurbita pepo*', *Journal of Ethnobiology*, 13: 55–72.

Denham, T.P. (2004) 'The roots of agriculture and arboriculture in New Guinea: looking beyond Austronesian expansion, Neolithic packages and Indigenous origins', *World Archaeology*, 36: 610–20.

Denham, T.P. (2005) 'Envisaging early agriculture in the Highlands of New Guinea: landscapes, plants and practices', *World Archaeology*, 37: 290–306.

Denham, T.P. (2006) 'The origins of agriculture in New Guinea: evidence, interpretation and reflection', in I. Lilley (ed.) *Archaeology of Oceania: Australia and the Pacific islands*, Oxford: Blackwell.

Denham, T.P. (in press) 'Thinking about plant exploitation in New Guinea: towards a contingent interpretation of agriculture', in T. P. Denham, J. Iriarte and L. Vrydaghs (eds) *Rethinking Agriculture: archaeological and ethnoarchaeological perspectives*, Walnut Creek, CA: Left Coast Press.

Denham, T.P., Golson, J. and Hughes, P.J. (2004a) 'Reading early agriculture at Kuk (Phases 1–3), Wahgi Valley, Papua New Guinea: the wetland archaeological features', *Proceedings of the Prehistoric Society*, 70: 259–98.

Denham, T.P., Haberle, S.G., and Lentfer, C. (2004b) 'New evidence and revised interpretations of early agriculture in Highland New Guinea', *Antiquity*, 78: 839–57.

Denham, T.P., Haberle, S.G., Lentfer, C., Fullagar, R., Field, J., Therin, M., Porch, N. and Winsborough, B. (2003) 'Origins of agriculture at Kuk Swamp in the Highlands of New Guinea', *Science*, 301: 189–93.

Denham, T.P., Iriarte, J. and Vrydaghs, L. (eds) (in press) *Rethinking Agriculture: archaeological and ethnoarchaeological perspectives*, Walnut Creek, CA: Left Coast Press.

Derrida, J. (1978) 'Structure, sign, and play in the discourse of the human sciences', in J. Derrida, trans. A. Bass, *Writing and Difference*, London: Routledge.

Diamond, J. and Bellwood, P. (2003) 'Farmers and their languages: the first expansions' *Science*, 300: 597–603.

Doebley, J. (1990) 'Molecular evidence and the evolution of maize', *Economic Botany*, 44: 6–28.

Dumont, R. and Vernier, P. (2000) 'Domestication of yams (*Dioscorea cayenensis-rotundata*) within the Bariba ethnic group in Benin', *Outlook on Agriculture*, 29: 137–42.

Erickson, D.L., Smith, B.D., Clarke, A.C., Sandweiss, D.H. and Tuross, N. (2005) 'An Asian origin for a 10,000-year-old domesticated plant in the Americas', *Proceedings of the National Academy of Sciences USA*, 102: 18315–20.

Fairbairn, A. (2005) 'An archaeobotanical perspective on plant-use practices in lowland northern New Guinea', *World Archaeology*, 37: 487–502.

Flannery, K.V. (1986) *Guilá Naquitz*, Orlando, FL: Academic Press.

Ford, R.I. (1985) 'The processes of plant food production in prehistoric North

America', in R. I. Ford (ed.) *Prehistoric Food Production in North America*, Anthropological Paper No.75, Ann Arbor, MI: Museum of Anthropology, University of Michigan.

Freitas, F.O., Bendel, G., Allaby, R.G. and Brown, T.A. (2003) 'DNA from primitive maize landraces and archaeological remains: implications for the domestication of maize and its expansion into South America', *Journal of Archaeological Science*, 30: 901–8.

Fullagar, R. (ed.) (1998) *A Closer Look: recent Australian studies of stone tools*, Sydney: Archaeological Computing Laboratory, University of Sydney.

Fullagar, R., Field, J., Denham, T.P. and Lentfer, C. (2006) 'Early and mid Holocene tool-use and processing of taro (*Colocasia esculenta*), yam (*Dioscorea* sp.) and other plants at Kuk Swamp in the highlands of Papua New Guinea', *Journal of Archaeological Science*, 33: 595–614.

Glover, I.C. and Higham, C.F.W. (1996) 'New evidence for early rice cultivation in South, Southeast and East Asia', in D. R. Harris (ed.) *The Origins and Spread of Agriculture and Pastoralism in Eurasia*, London: UCL Press.

Golson, J. (1989) 'The origins and development of New Guinea agriculture', in D. R. Harris and G. C. Hillman (eds) *Foraging and Farming: the evolution of plant exploitation*, London: Unwin Hyman.

Golson, J. and Ucko, P. (1994) 'Foreword', in J. Hather (ed.) *Tropical Archaeobotany*, London: Routledge.

Gosden, C. and Hather, J. (1999) *The Prehistory of Food: appetites for change*, London: Routledge.

Gremillion, K. (2002) 'The development and dispersal of agricultural systems in the Woodland Period Southeast', in D. Anderson and R. Mainfort, Jr. (eds) *The Woodland Southeast*, Tuscaloosa, AL: University of Alabama Press.

Guddemi, P. (1992) 'When horticulturalists are like hunter-gatherers: the Sawiyano of Papua New Guinea', *Ethnology*, 31: 303–14.

Gugerli, F., Parducci, L. and Petit, R.J. (2005) 'Ancient plant DNA: review and prospects' *New Phytologist*, 166: 409–18.

Harris, D.R. (1989) 'An evolutionary continuum of people–plant interaction', in D. R. Harris and G. C. Hillman (eds) *Foraging and Farming: the evolution of plant exploitation*, London: Unwin Hyman.

Harris, D.R. (1995) 'Early agriculture in New Guinea and the Torres Strait divide', *Antiquity*, 69 (Special Number 265): 848–54.

Harris, D.R. (1996a) 'Domesticatory relationships of people, plants and animals', in R. Ellen and K. Fukui (eds) *Redefining Nature: ecology, culture and domestication*, Oxford: Berg.

Harris, D.R. (1996b) 'Introduction: themes and concepts in the study of early agriculture', in D. R. Harris (ed.) *The Origins and Spread of Agriculture and Pastoralism in Eurasia*, London: UCL Press.

Harris, D.R. (in press) 'Agriculture, cultivation and domestication: exploring the conceptual framework of early food-production' in T. P. Denham, J. Iriarte and L. Vrydaghs (eds) *Rethinking Agriculture: archaeological and ethnoarchaeological perspectives*, Walnut Creek, CA: Left Coast Press.

Harris, D.R. and Hillman, G.C. (eds) (1989) *Foraging and Farming: the evolution of plant exploitation*, London: Unwin Hyman.

Hastorf, C. (1998) 'The cultural life of early domestic plant use', *Antiquity*, 72: 773–82.

Hastorf, C. (1999) 'Cultural implications of crop introductions in Andean prehistory', in C. Gosden and J. Hather (eds) *The Prehistory of Food: appetites for change*, London: Routledge.

Hastorf, C. and Popper, V. (eds) (1988) *Current Paleoethnobotany: analytical methods and cultural interpretations of archaeological plant remains*, Chicago, IL: University of Chicago Press.

Hather, J. (1994a) 'The identification of charred root and tuber crops from archaeological sites in the Pacific' in J. Hather (ed.) *Tropical Archaeobotany*, London: Routledge.

Hather, J. (ed.) (1994b) *Tropical Archaeobotany*, London: Routledge.

Hather, J.G. (1996) 'The origins of tropical vegeculture: Zingiberaceae, Araceae and Dioscoreaceae in Southeast Asia', in D. R. Harris (ed.) *The Origins and Spread of Agriculture and Pastoralism in Eurasia*, London: UCL Press.

Hather, J.G. (2000) *Archaeological Parenchyma*, London: Archaeotype Publications.

Hather, J. and Kirch, P.V. (1991) 'Prehistoric sweet potato (*Ipomoea batatas*) from Mangaia Island, central Polynesia', *Antiquity*, 65: 887–93.

Heun, M., Schäfer-Pregl, R., Klawan, D., Castagna, R., Accerbi, M., Borghi, B. and Salamini, F. (1997) 'Site of einkorn wheat domestication identified by DNA fingerprinting', *Science*, 278: 1312–14.

Hillman, G.C. (1996) 'Late Pleistocene changes in wild plant-foods available to hunter-gatherers of the northern Fertile Crescent: possible preludes to cereal cultivation' in D. R. Harris (ed.) *The Origins and Spread of Agriculture and Pastoralism in Eurasia*, London: UCL Press.

Hodder, I. (1999) *The Archaeological Process: an introduction*, Oxford: Blackwell.

Hodder, I. (2003) *Reading the Past: current approaches to interpretation in archaeology*, 3rd edn, Cambridge: Cambridge University Press.

Hope, G.S. and Golson, J. (1995) 'Late Quaternary change in the mountains of New Guinea', *Antiquity*, 69 (Special Number 265): 818–30.

Huang, X.O., Borner, A., Roder, M.S. and Ganal, M.W. (2002) 'Assessing genetic diversity of wheat (*Triticum aestivum* L.) germplasm using microsatellite markers', *Theoretical and Applied Genetics*, 105: 699–702.

Hurles, M. (2002) 'Can the hypothesis of language/agriculture co-dispersal be *tested* with archaeogenetics?', in P. Bellwood and C. Renfrew (eds) *Examining the Farming/Language Dispersal Hypothesis*, Cambridge: McDonald Institute for Archaeological Research.

Hynes, R. and Chase, A. (1982) 'Plants, sites and domiculture: Aboriginal influence on plant communities', *Archaeology in Oceania*, 17: 138–50.

Ingold, T. (1996) 'Growing plants and raising animals: an anthropological perspective on domestication', in D. R. Harris (ed.), *The Origins and Spread of Agriculture and Pastoralism in Eurasia*, London: UCL Press.

Ingold, T. (2000) *The Perception of the Environment: essays on livelihood, dwelling and skill*, London: Routledge.

Iriarte, J., Holst, I., Marozzi, O., Listopad, C., Alonso, E., Rinderknecht, A. and Montaña, J. (2004) 'Evidence for cultivar adoption and emerging complexity during the mid-Holocene in the La Plata Basin', *Nature*, 432: 614–27.

Jaenicke-Després, V., Buckler, E.S., Smith, B.D., Gilbert, M.T.P., Cooper, A., Doebley, J. and Pääbo, S. (2003) 'Early allelic selection in maize as revealed by ancient DNA', *Science*, 302: 1206–8.

Johnson, M. (2000) *Archaeological Theory*, Oxford: Blackwell

Jones, M.K. and Brown, T.A. (2000) 'Agricultural origins: the evidence of modern and ancient DNA', *Holocene*, 10: 775–82.

Jones, M.K. and Brown, T.A. (in press) 'Selection, cultivation and reproductive isolation: a reconsideration of the morphological and molecular signals of domestication', in T. P. Denham, J. Iriarte and L. Vrydaghs (eds) *Rethinking Agriculture: archaeological and ethnoarchaeological perspectives*, Walnut Creek, CA: Left Coast Press.

Kahlheber, S. and Neumann, K. (in press) 'The development of plant cultivation in semi-arid West Africa', in T. P. Denham, J. Iriarte and L. Vrydaghs (eds) *Rethinking Agriculture: archaeological and ethnoarchaeological perspectives*, Walnut Creek, CA: Left Coast Press.

Larson, G., Dobney, K., Albarella, U., Fang, M., Matisoo-Smith, E., Robins, J., Lowden, S., Finlayson, H., Brand, T., Willerslev, E., Rowley-Conwy, P., Andersson, L. and Cooper, A. (2005) 'Worldwide phylogeography of wild boar reveals multiple centers of pig domestication', *Science*, 307: 1618–21.

Lejju, B.J., Robertshaw, P. and Taylor, D. (2006) 'Africa's earliest bananas', *Journal of Archaeological Science*, 33: 102–13.

Lévi-Strauss, C. (1969) *The Elementary Structures of Kinship*, J. H. Bell and J. R. von Sturmer (trans.) and R. Needham (ed.) Boston, MA: Beacon Press.

Li, C., Zhou, A. and Sang, T. (2006) 'Rice domestication by reducing shattering', *Science*, 311: 1936–9.

Loftus, R.T., Ertugrul, O., Harba, A.H., El-Barody, M.A., MacHugh, D.E., Park, S.D. and Bradley, D.G. (1999) 'A microsatellite survey of cattle from a centre of origin: the Near East', *Molecular Ecology*, 8: 2015–22.

Loy, T. H. (1994) 'Methods in the analysis of starch residues on prehistoric stone tools', in J. H. Hather (ed.) *Tropical Archaeobotany*, London: Routledge.

Loy, T. H., Spriggs, M. and Wickler, S. (1992) 'Direct evidence for human use of plants 28,000 years ago: starch residues on stone artefacts from northern Solomon Islands', *Antiquity*, 66: 898–912.

Lu H., Liu Z.X., Wu N.Q., Berné, S. Saito, Y., Liu, B.Z. and Wang, L. (2002) 'Rice domestication and climate change: phytolith evidence from East China', *Boreas*, 31: 378–85.

MacNeish, R. (1992) *The Origins of Agriculture and Settled Life*, Norman, OK: University of Oklahoma Press.

Marshall, F. and Hildebrand, E.A. (2002) 'Cattle before crops: the beginnings of food production in Africa', *Journal of World Prehistory*, 16: 99–143.

Matisoo-Smith, E. and Robins, J.H. (2004) 'Origins and dispersals of Pacific peoples: evidence from mtDNA phylogenies of the Pacific rat', *Proceedings of the National Academy of Sciences USA*, 101: 9167–72.

Matsuoka, Y., Vigouroux, Y., Goodman, M.M., Sanchez, J., Buckler, E. and Doebley, J. (2002) 'A single domestication for maize shown by multilocus microsatellite genotyping', *Proceedings of the National Academy of Sciences USA*, 99: 6080–4.

Matthews, P. and Terauchi, R. (1994) 'The genetics of agriculture: DNA variation in taro and yam', in J. Hather (ed.) *Tropical Archaeobotany*, London: Routledge.

Mbida, Ch., Van Neer, W., Doutrelepont H. and Vrydaghs, L. (2000) 'Evidence for banana cultivation and animal husbandry during the first millennium BC in the forest of southern Cameroon', *Journal of Archaeological Science*, 27: 151–62.

Mbida Ch., Doutrelepont, H., Vrydaghs, L., Swennen, Ro., Swennen, Ru.,

Beeckman, H., De Langhe, E. and Maret, P. de (2001) 'First archaeological evidence of banana cultivation in Central Africa during the third millennium before present', *Vegetation History and Archaeobotany*, 10: 1–6.

Mehra, K.L. (1999) 'Subsistence changes in India and Pakistan: the Neolithic and Chalcolithic from the point of view of plant use today', in C. Gosden and J. Hather (eds) *The Prehistory of Food: appetites for change*, London: Routledge.

Moore, A.M.T., Hillman, G.C. and Legge, A.J. (eds) (2000) *Village on the Euphrates*, Oxford: Oxford University Press.

Oppenheimer, S. (2004) 'The "express train" from Taiwan to Polynesia: on the congruence of proxy lines of evidence', *World Archaeology*, 36: 591–600.

Oppenheimer, S. and Richards, M. (2002) 'Polynesians: devolved Taiwanese rice farmers or Wallacean maritime traders with fishing, foraging and horticultural skills', in P. Bellwood and C. Renfrew (eds) *Examining the Farming/Language Dispersal Hypothesis*, Cambridge: McDonald Institute for Archaeological Research.

Pearsall, D.M. (1999) 'The impact of maize on subsistence systems in South America: an example from the Jama river valley, coastal Ecuador', in C. Gosden and J. Hather (eds) *The Prehistory of Food: appetites for change*, London: Routledge.

Pearsall, D.M. (2004) *Plants and People in Ancient Ecuador: the ethnobotany of the Jama River Valley*, Belmont, CA: Wadsworth/Thomson Learning.

Pearsall, D.M. (in press) 'Modeling prehistoric agriculture through the palaeo-environmental record: theoretical and methodological issues', in T. P. Denham, J. Iriarte and L. Vrydaghs (eds) *Rethinking Agriculture: archaeological and ethnoarchaeological perspectives*, Walnut Creek, CA: Left Coast Press.

Perry, L. (2004) 'Starch analyses reveal the relationship between tool type and function: an example from the Orinoco valley of Venezuela', *Journal of Archaeological Science*, 31: 1069–81.

Perry, L. (in press) 'Starch grains, preservation biases and plant histories: an example from Highland Peru', in T. P. Denham, J. Iriarte and L. Vrydaghs (eds) *Rethinking Agriculture: archaeological and ethnoarchaeological perspectives*, Walnut Creek, CA: Left Coast Press.

Perry, L. (2005) 'Reassessing the traditional interpretation of "manioc" artefacts in the Orinoco valley of Venezuela', *Latin American Antiquity*, 16: 409–26.

Perry, L., Sandweiss, D.H., Piperno, D.R., Rademaker, K., Malpass, M.A., Umire, A. and de la Vera, P. (2006) 'Early maize agriculture and interzonal interaction in southern Peru', *Nature*, 440: 76–9.

Piperno, D.R. (1989) 'Non-affluent foragers: resource availability, seasonal shortages, and the emergence of agriculture in Panamanian tropical forests', in D. R. Harris and G. C. Hillman (eds) *Foraging and Farming: the evolution of plant exploitation*, London: Unwin Hyman.

Piperno, D.R. (2006) *Phytoliths: a comprehensive guide for archaeologists and paleoecologists*, Lanham, MD: AltaMira.

Piperno, D.R., and Flannery, K.V. (2001) 'The earliest archaeological maize (*Zea mays* L.) from highland Mexico: new accelerator mass spectrometry dates and their implications', *Proceedings of the National Academy of Sciences USA*, 98: 2101–3.

Piperno, D.R. and Holst, I. (1998) 'The presence of starch grains on prehistoric stone tools from the humid neotropics: indications of early tuber use and agriculture in Panama', *Journal of Archaeological Science*, 25: 765–76.

Piperno, D.R. and Pearsall, D.M. (1998) *The Origins of Agriculture in the Lowland Neotropics*, San Diego, CA: Academic Press.

Piperno, D.R. and Stothert, K.E. (2003) 'Phytolith evidence for early Holocene *Cucurbita* domestication in Southwest Ecuador', *Science*, 299: 1054–7.

Piperno, D.R., Bush, M.B. and Colinvaux, P.A. (1991a) 'Paleoecological perspectives on human adaptation in Central Panama. I. The Pleistocene', *Geoarchaeology*, 6: 210–26.

Piperno, D.R., Bush, M.B. and Colinvaux, P.A. (1991b) 'Paleoecological perspectives on human adaptation in Central Panama. II. The Holocene', *Geoarchaeology*, 6: 227–50.

Piperno, D.R., Ranere, J.A., Holst, I. and Hansell, P. (2000) 'Starch grains reveal early root crop horticulture in the Panamanian tropical forest', *Nature*, 407: 894–97.

Piperno, D.R., Weiss, E., Holst, I. and Nadel, D. (2004) 'Processing of wild cereal grains in the Upper Palaeolithic revealed by starch grain analysis', *Nature*, 430: 670–3.

Price, T.D. (1996) 'The first farmers of southern Scandinavia' in D. R. Harris (ed.) *The Origins and Spread of Agriculture and Pastoralism in Eurasia*, London: UCL Press.

Renfrew, C. (1987) *Archaeology and Language*, London: Jonathan Cape.

Renfrew, C. (2002) '"The emerging synthesis": the archaeogenetics of farming/language dispersals and other spread zones', in P. Bellwood and C. Renfrew (eds) *Examining the Farming/Language Dispersal Hypothesis*, Cambridge: McDonald Institute for Archaeological Research.

Renfrew, C. and Bahn, P. (2004) *Archaeology: theories, methods and practice*, 4th edn, London: Thames and Hudson.

Robertshaw, P. (1993) 'The beginnings of food production in southwestern Kenya', in T. Shaw, P. Sinclair, B. Andah and A. Okpoko (eds) *The Archaeology of Africa: food, metals and towns*, London: Routledge.

Roscoe, P. (2002) 'The hunters and gatherers of New Guinea', *Current Anthropology*, 43: 153–62.

Sanjur, O., Piperno, D.R., Andres, T.C. and Wessel-Beaver, L. (2002) 'Phylogenetic relationships among domesticated and wild species of Cucurbita (Cucurbitaceae) inferred from a mitochondrial gene: implications for crop plant evolution and areas of origin', *Proceedings of the National Academy of Sciences USA*, 99: 535–40.

Scarry, M. (ed.) (1993) *Foraging and Farming in the Eastern Woodlands*, Gainesville, FL: University Press of Florida.

Shaw, T., Sinclair, P., Andah, B. and Okpoko, A. (eds) (1993) *The Archaeology of Africa: food, metals and towns*, London: Routledge.

Smith, B.D. (1992) *Rivers of Change: essays on early agriculture in the Eastern North America*, Washington, DC: Smithsonian Books.

Smith, B.D. (1997) 'The initial domestication of *Cucurbita pepo* in the Americas 10,000 years ago', *Science*, 276: 932–4.

Smith, B.D. (1998a) 'Between foraging and farming', *Science*, 279: 1651–2.

Smith, B.D. (1998b) *The Emergence of Agriculture*, New York: Scientific American Library.

Smith, B.D. (2001a) 'Low-level food production', *Journal of Archaeological Research*, 9: 1–43.

Smith, B.D. (2001b) 'Documenting plant domestication: the consilience of biological and archaeological approaches', *Proceedings of the National Academy of Sciences USA*, 98: 1324–6.

Smith, B.D. (2005) 'Reassessing Coxcatlan Cave and the early history of domesticated plants in Mesoamerica', *Proceedings of the National Academy of Sciences USA*, 102: 9438–45.

Specht, J. (2003) 'On New Guinea hunters and gatherers', *Current Anthropology*, 44: 269.

Spriggs, M. (1996) 'Early agriculture and what went before in Island Melanesia: continuity or intrusion?', in D. R. Harris (ed.) *The Origins and Spread of Agriculture and Pastoralism in Eurasia*, London: UCL Press.

Stiner, M.C. (1994) *Honor among Thieves: a zooarchaeological study of Neanderthal Ecology*, Princeton, NJ: Princeton University Press.

Tanno, K-i and Willcox, G. (2006) 'How fast was wild wheat domesticated?', *Science*, 311: 1886.

Therin, M., Fullagar, R. and Torrence, R. (1999) 'Starch in sediments: a new approach to the study of subsistence and land use in Papua New Guinea', in C. Gosden and J. Hather (eds) *The Prehistory of Food: appetites for change*, London: Routledge.

Thomas, J. (1996) 'The cultural context of the first use of domesticates in continental Central and Northwest Europe', in D. R. Harris (ed.) *The Origins and Spread of Agriculture and Pastoralism in Eurasia*, London: UCL Press.

Thomas, J. (1999) *Understanding the Neolithic*, London: Routledge.

Torrence, R. and Barton, H. (eds) (2006) *Ancient Starch Research*, Walnut Creek, CA: Left Coast Press.

Verhoeven, M. (2004) 'Beyond boundaries: nature, culture and a holistic approach to domestication in the Levant', *Journal of World Prehistory*, 18: 179–282.

Watson, P.J. (1989) 'Early plant cultivation in the Eastern Woodlands of North America', in D. R. Harris and G. C. Hillman (eds) *Foraging and Farming: the evolution of plant exploitation*, London: Unwin Hyman.

Willcox, G. (1998) 'Archaeobotanical evidence for the beginnings of agriculture in Southwest Asia', in A. B. Damania, J. Valkoun, G. Willcox and C. O. Qualset (eds) *The Origins of Agriculture and Crop Domestication*, Aleppo, Syria: ICARDA.

Willcox, G. (1999) 'Agrarian change and the beginnings of cultivation in the Near East: evidence from wild progenitors, experimental cultivation and archaeobotanical data', in C. Gosden and J. Hather (eds) *The Prehistory of Food: appetites for change*, London: Routledge.

Willerslev, E. and Cooper, A. (2005) 'Ancient DNA', *Proceedings of the Royal Society B*, 272: 3–16.

Wilson, S.M. (1985) 'Phytolith analysis at Kuk, an early agricultural site in Papua New Guinea', *Archaeology in Oceania*, 20: 90–7.

Yen, D.E. (1985) 'Wild plants and domestication in Pacific islands', in V. N. Misra and P. Bellwood (eds) *Recent Advances in Indo-Pacific Prehistory*, New Dehli: Oxford and IBH Publishing.

Yen, D.E. (1989) 'The domestication of environment', in D. R. Harris and G. C. Hillman (eds) *Foraging and Farming: the evolution of plant exploitation*, London: Unwin Hyman.

Yen, D.E. (1998) 'Subsistence to commerce in Pacific agriculture: some four thousand years of plant exchange', in H. D. V. Pendergast, N. L. Etkin, D. R. Harris and P. J. Houghton (eds) *Plants for Food and Medicine*, Kew: Royal Botanic Gardens.

Zhang, J. and Wang, X. (1998) 'Notes on the recent discovery of ancient cultivated rice at Jiahu, Henan province', *Antiquity*, 72: 897–901.

Zhao, Z. (1998) 'The Middle Yangtze region in China is one place where rice was domesticated', *Antiquity*, 72: 885–96.

Zohary, D. (1989) 'Domestication of the Southwest Asian Neolithic crop assemblage of cereals, pulses, and flax: evidence from the living plants', in D. R. Harris and G. C. Hillman (eds) *Foraging and Farming: the evolution of plant exploitation*, London: Unwin Hyman.

Zvelebil, M. (1996) 'The agricultural frontier and the transition to farming in the circum-Baltic region', in D. R. Harris (ed.) *The Origins and Spread of Agriculture and Pastoralism in Eurasia*, London: UCL Press.

2   An evolutionary continuum of people–plant interaction

David R. Harris

Introduction

Philosophical speculation about how plants and animals were domesticated and about how agriculture arose can be traced in the Western intellectual tradition at least back to Classical times – for example, in Lucretius' discussion of animal domestication (Glacken 1967: 139–40) – but substantive enquiry into the beginnings of agriculture and the history of domesticated plants and animals is little more than a century old. Indeed, field and laboratory investigations designed specifically to throw light on the emergence of agriculture, conducted by archaeologists and biologists, have been underway for little more than four decades. During that brief period an impressive array of bioarchaeological evidence has been recovered from early agrarian sites in many tropical and temperate regions of the world, and ethnographic and historical research has made a major contribution to the interpretation of that evidence. But the exciting and often controversial debates that have accompanied attempts to understand 'the origins of agriculture' have often been bedevilled by confusion over the meanings attributed to such terms as agriculture, cultivation, domestication, and food production.

To point this out is not to engage in semantic quibbling, because the meanings attributed to such general concepts can and do directly affect research design and the interpretation of evidence. The purpose of this chapter is therefore to present – against the background of a review of earlier uses of such concepts – a classificatory model which arranges them along a continuum of people–plant interaction. It is hoped that this will help to clarify our thinking about the processes involved in the emergence of agriculture, and also that it will provide a useful prelude to the other contributions to this book. The concept of a continuum of interaction, developed in this chapter, need not of course be restricted to plants and people; it could productively be extended to animal–people interaction. Its limitation here to plants is a function of the overall theme of the book, and in part also a reflection of the primacy of plants in the structure and function of agricultural systems (agroecosystems), whether or not they incorporate domesticated animals.

The intellectual assumptions that underlie the model presented here are ecological and evolutionary: ecological in that the analytical target is *interaction* between people and plants, evolutionary in that the *results* of the processes involved in domestication and the emergence of agriculture – i.e. the crops, domestic animals, and agricultural practices that we seek to trace in the archaeological record – are assumed to be the products of selection working on both biological and cultural variation. It is therefore evolutionary in a Darwinian sense (cf. Rindos 1989 [this volume]), but not in the progressive sense of the cultural-evolutionary school of mid-twentieth century American anthropology exemplified by Sahlins and Service (1960). Before discussing the model itself (in the last section of this chapter), it is therefore necessary to emphasize that it is not unidirectional, and it certainly does not imply that, given sufficient 'time', human societies would inevitably progress from one level of interaction with plants (or animals) to the next. The levels of interaction specified in the model (Figure 2.1) are not to be regarded as pre-ordained steps on a ladder of increasingly 'advanced' stages of general societal development; nor is it implied that transitions from one level to another, e.g. from cultivation to domestication, are necessarily irreversible. However, the model is progressive in one specific sense, in that the proposed continuum *is* presented as a gradient of increasing input of human energy per unit area of exploited land (Figure 2.1). This and other aspects of the model are examined more fully below, but first it needs to be set against the background of the ecological and evolutionary paradigm that has strongly influenced recent approaches to understanding the emergence of agriculture.

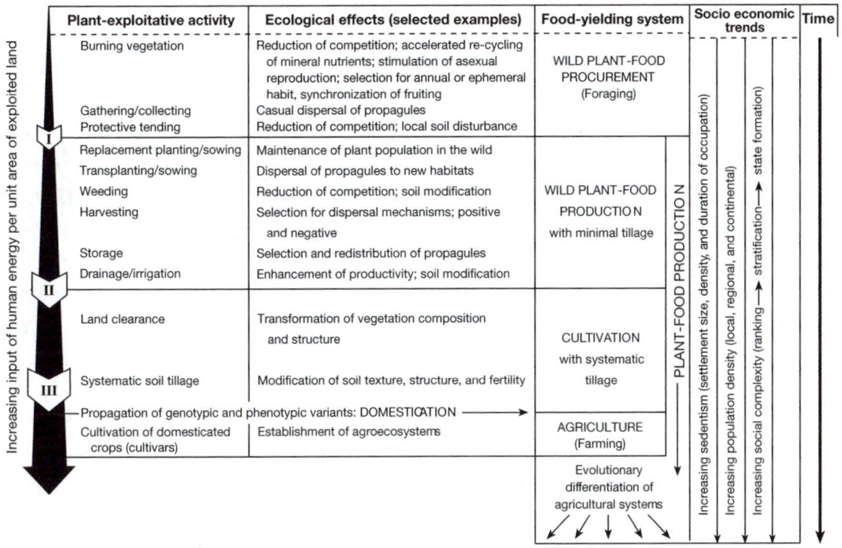

Figure 2.1 Schematic diagrams of an evolutionary continuum of people-plant interaction (the Roman numerals indicate postulated energy thresholds)

Ecological and evolutionary approaches to understanding the emergence of agriculture

It was during the 1960s that models were first proposed in explicitly ecological and evolutionary terms to attempt to explain the transition from hunting and gathering (dependence on wild foods) to agriculture (dependence on domesticated plants and animals). The gradualist view of that transition which was adopted by such ecologically minded students of the subject as Binford (1968), Flannery (1968, 1969), Harris (1969), and Higgs and Jarman (1969) can be traced at least as far back as Darwin's characteristically cogent description (1868: 309) of the first step[s] in cultivation; but it only came to be widely accepted during the last twenty years. The contributions of these authors to the ecological-evolutionary paradigm need little rehearsal here, but it is worth signalling some of the changes in terminology which they introduced.

The new, more explicitly ecological orientation of the 1960s, which stressed the continuities rather than the contrasts between hunting and gathering and agriculture, was in part a reaction to the then prevalent view, derived from Gordon Childe's seminal concept of the 'Neolithic Revolution', of the transition to agriculture as a relatively abrupt event induced by a climatic shift to greater aridity in Southwest Asia in the early Holocene. Childe contrasted the Neolithic 'food-producers' with the 'food-gatherers' of earlier times, but he did not distinguish conceptually between agriculture, cultivation, and domestication, although he used all three terms in his accounts of the Neolithic Revolution (Childe 1936, 1942).

The use of the term 'food production', as synonymous with agriculture, was further promulgated by Braidwood (e.g. 1952, 1960), and has continued to the present. In the 1960s, particularly in two highly influential papers by Binford (1968) and Flannery (1968), it came to be contrasted with the term 'food procurement' which was applied to the food-gathering and food-collecting activities of hunter-gatherers. This tended, at one level of analysis, to reinforce the long-established dichotomy between hunter-gatherers and agriculturalists, but because both Binford and Flannery were exploring the transition to agriculture in systemic terms by postulating positive and negative interactions of particular environmental and behavioural variables, their papers also had the effect of emphasizing continuities that linked hunter-gatherer 'food procurement' to agricultural 'food production'.

A diminished emphasis on the dichotomy between hunter-gatherer and agriculturalist – or forager and farmer – within a systemic framework of analysis, was also implicit in my ecological approach to the study of the beginnings of agriculture in the tropics (Harris 1969, 1972, 1973). In particular, I proposed a distinction between the 'manipulation' of biotic resources which could lead to sufficiently sustained intervention in the breeding systems of wild plants and animals that 'domestication' resulted; and the 'transformation' of natural into artificial ecosystems which accompanied the later establishment of fully developed agricultural economies. Manipulation and transformation were thus envisaged as two phases on a gradient or continuum of ecological change induced by human modification of natural ecosystems, which led, in the remote past, from hunting and gathering through domestication to agriculture. I did not at that time, however, make any finer distinctions in terms of such variables as gathering, tending, planting, sowing, tilling, etc., nor did I distinguish conceptually between cultivation and agriculture.

It was during the 1960s that Eric Higgs and his associates at the University of Cambridge also sought to broaden the study of 'agricultural origins'. They redefined the objective as the study of prehistoric economies, regardless of whether such economies were predominantly of hunter-gatherer or agricultural type. Higgs argued that the archaeological record should be interpreted in terms of biological and economic principles, and ethnographic analogies, and he selected the term 'husbandry', in preference to domestication, to denote the whole spectrum of human intervention in and control over the biology and behaviour of animals and plants – intervention which, he postulated, reached back into Palaeolithic times (Higgs 1972).

By the mid-1970s these ecological and evolutionary approaches had brought about a transformation in how the study of early agriculture was perceived: it was no longer viewed in isolation but in the broader context of prehistoric 'subsistence systems' or 'palaeoeconomies', and the formerly rigid dichotomy between hunter-gatherers and agriculturalists had become blurred. Since then, the attention of ecologically oriented students of prehistoric subsistence has begun to focus more precisely on the diversity and interconnections of the activities through which people have, in the past, exploited both 'wild' and 'domestic' plants and animals.

Theoretical contributions to this recent phase in the development of the ecological-evolutionary paradigm were made during the 1980s by Rindos (1980, 1984), Hynes and Chase (1982), Jarman *et al.* (1982), and Ford (1985). Their contributions relate directly but differently to the model proposed in this chapter, and they are, accordingly, briefly reviewed as a prelude to presentation of the model.

The third and final volume of the *Papers in Economic Prehistory*, in which Higgs and his colleagues reported the results of their research on early agriculture in Europe and Southwest Asia, appeared in 1982 after his death. In it, Jarman *et al.* looked back over the development of the Higgs' 'school' of palaeoeconomy and offered their revised formulation of its theoretical basis and methodology. They reaffirmed Higgs' distinction between domestication, in the strict sense of morphological change in plants and animals resulting from their selective breeding by humans, and the much broader concept of husbandry. They then went on to elaborate the distinction by proposing more complex classifications of both 'human-animal' and 'human-plant' relationships, as follows: for animals, six categories (random predation, controlled predation, herd following, loose herding, close herding, factory farming); and for plants, five categories (casual gathering, systematic gathering, limited cultivation, developed cultivation, intensive cultivation); stressing, however, that such classifications did not represent 'an economic ladder of progress, with one stage inevitably developing towards, and eventually into, the next' (Jarman *et al.* 1982: 51–4). As we are concerned in this chapter with plants, it is also worth pointing out that they strongly endorsed Helbaek's original distinction (1960) between plant cultivation and plant domestication – a distinction which first introduced into the study of early agriculture the concept of 'pre-domestication cultivation' that has since been used effectively by Hillman (1975) and others.

A more comprehensively biological and ecological-evolutionary approach to 'the origins of agriculture' has been developed recently by Rindos (1980, 1984). In the context of this chapter, his major contribution has been to embed the concept of domestication within that of 'co-evolution', defined as 'an evolutionary process in which the establishment of a symbiotic relationship between organisms, increasing the fitness of all involved, brings about changes in the traits of the organisms' (Rindos 1984: 99). This approach – by which domestication is regarded as but one type of biologically defined symbiotic relationship – was originally introduced into the study of prehistoric domestication (of animals) by Zeuner (1963: 36–64), and Rindos has extended and elaborated it, specifically in relation to plants and agricultural systems. In so doing, he has proposed a new three-fold classification of 'the domestication relationship' consisting of 'three conceptually distinct aspects mediated by different types of human behaviour and occurring in distinct environments', i.e. 'incidental domestication' which is 'the result of human dispersal and protection of wild plants in the general environment'; 'specialized domestication' which is 'mediated by the environmental impact of humans, especially in the local areas in which they reside'; and 'agricultural domestication' which is the 'culmination of the other two processes, involves the further evolution of plants in response to the conditions existing with the agroecology' and 'is roughly equivalent to what has simply been termed *domestication* in the literature of agricultural origins' (Rindos 1984: xiv–xv). The classification is explicitly evolutionary, but, like Jarman *et al.* in respect of their classifications, Rindos denies that his scheme represents 'stages' in the development of all agricultural systems. He emphasizes that the three types of human–plant relationship are not mutually exclusive; indeed, that the boundaries between them are inevitably artificial because the three categories are 'components of an integrated, natural process' (Rindos 1984: 53).

Rindos' full discussion of his taxonomy of plant domestication (1984: 152–66) represents the most comprehensive attempt (since Zeuner's for animal domestication) to broaden and systematize the ecological–evolutionary concepts which can be applied to the study of past (and present) people–plant interactions. In its comprehensiveness his taxonomy encompasses at a high level of generality the two other recent theoretical contributions already referred to – Hynes and Chase (1982) and Ford (1985) – although they differ from Rindos in some important respects. Hynes and Chase (1982) coined the term 'domiculture' to describe the interaction of people and biotic resources in local 'hearth-centred' environments or 'domuses'. They developed their ideas in the context of Australian Aboriginal attitudes towards, and uses of, plants, but the concept of domiculture has more general application. In ecological terms, it is equivalent to Rindos' category of incidental domestication (and in part also to that of specialized domestication), although Chase (1989) objects to that equation, arguing that to see hunter-gatherers as 'incidental' domesticators is to beg the central issue – which, in his view, is the primacy of human sociality in initiating, articulating, and maintaining the production and distribution of resources. According to Chase, domiculture is the result of intentional human action focused on culturally recognized plants (and animals), and is not, as is Rindos' incidental domestication, a more general biological phenomenon which people share with other domesticatory organisms. However, with that important qualification, Hynes' and Chase's concept of domiculture does closely resemble – and could be said to fit as a subsidiary concept, restricted to human actions, within – Rindos' categories of incidental and specialized domestication. So, too, does the concept of 'agronomy' among Australian hunter-gatherers (Yen 1989).

In the Preface to his 1985 publication on *Prehistoric Food Production in North America*, Ford remarks that inclusion of the term husbandry in the original title of the seminar, held in 1980, on which the book is based – 'The origins of plant husbandry in North America' – was rejected on two grounds: that it implied 'a skewed division of labour in favour of men', and because it 'customarily is applied to the management of animals' (which as domesticates – except for the dog and the turkey – were absent in prehistoric North America); so, 'following the lead of Braidwood in the Near East' the term food production was adopted instead (Ford 1985: xii). This anecdote neatly illustrates the conceptual difficulties that have troubled students of prehistoric subsistence, and it raises echoes not only of Braidwood, but of Childe before him and of Higgs after him. Ford himself, in his introductory contribution to the book, outlines his own classification of the 'stages and methods of plant food production' (Ford 1985: 2–7). He proposes two major successive stages: 'foraging' and 'food production', and divides the latter into two successive sub-stages: 'cultivation' and 'domestication'. Three main methods of food production are recognized as succeeding one another: 'incipient agriculture', 'gardening', and 'field agriculture', and several types of human behaviour toward plants, viewed as a continuum of types of interaction, are added to the classification, namely 'tending', 'tilling', 'transplanting', 'sowing', and 'plant breeding'. This sequence of behaviours or 'cultural activities' leads from the least biologically disruptive to complete domestication, when plants become completely dependent on humans for their continued existence; and the types of interaction are regarded as cumulative over time.

Ford's scheme is a more comprehensive and detailed categorization of plant-food production than the other classifications discussed, and it does help to clarify the complex interactions between people and plants that are involved. However, although it is viewed by Ford as a continuum, it is not explicitly based on any stated variable(s), such as energy input or population density; although it is, by implication, related to time, to the degree of human disruption of plant biology and ecology, and, more implicitly still, to increasing cultural complexity and size of human populations. It resembles in some ways the model of people–plant interaction presented in the next section – although when constructing early versions of that model some years ago I was unaware of Ford's scheme – and the two classifications certainly share the twin aims of attempting to clarify the concepts we use when investigating the prehistory of plant exploitation, and of specifying more precisely the relationships of those concepts along a continuum of people–plant interaction.

The model: an evolutionary continuum of people–plant interaction

As has been stated in the introduction to this chapter, the model summarized in Figure 2.1 is based on ecological and evolutionary assumptions, but it is not unidirectional and deterministic. It does not address the question of *why* some past human societies shifted from primary dependence on wild plant foods to primary dependence on cultivated crops. It seeks only to specify a series of plant-exploitative activities and associated ecological effects arranged sequentially along a continuum, which is, however, also conceived as a gradient of increasing input of human energy per unit area of exploited land. This correlation cannot at present be demonstrated quantitatively and must remain hypothetical. It rests, in turn, on the assumption that there has been, over time, a positive relationship between energy input into food procurement/production and energy output measured in terms of the calorific value of the harvested and processed plant foods. However, I make no attempt here to answer the underlying question of whether the suggested trend of increasing energy input and output per unit area of exploited land was a function – in any given situation in the past – of increases in human population density, in sedentary settlement, in social stratification, or in other socio-demographic factors, in varying systemic combinations. The aim is to present a descriptive not an explanatory model, except in so far as the posited correlation with energy input can be regarded as 'explanatory'.

In Figure 2.1 the human activities specified are based on ethnographic observations and historical accounts of interactions between people and the plants they exploit for food, and it is presumed that these activities had prehistoric antecedents which, to varying degrees, may be archaeologically traceable. Although the activities, from burning vegetation to the cultivation of domesticated crops, and the differentiation of agricultural systems are presented as sequential, it is not implied that they succeeded *and replaced* one another over time, except in the very general sense of comparative importance on a world scale. To put it another way, all the specified activities are still practised today in agricultural, and, to a reduced extent, in non-agricultural contexts (environments), but as agriculture progressively replaced gathering (and hunting) as the predominant food-yielding system, so the relative importance of those activities by which wild plant foods were exploited declined. Activities such as planting and sowing, harvesting and storage, irrigation and drainage, land clearance and tillage, which are assumed to pre-date agriculture (as here defined), were, of course, incorporated into evolving systems of cultivation and eventually became highly elaborated, integral components of agricultural production. Likewise, the burning of vegetation was incorporated as an essential technique into certain agricultural systems, notably shifting or swidden cultivation, and the protective tending of 'naturally' occurring useful plants anticipated the weeding of intentionally planted or sown crops. Even the gathering of edible parts of 'wild' plants has persisted as a minor, but sometimes dietarily significant, activity in developed agroecosystems.

Given the above qualifications, Figure 2.1 is intended to represent a gradient as well as a continuum of progressively closer people–plant interaction. Along it, the input of human energy per unit area of land exploited for plant foods increases, and so too does the modification of 'natural' ecosystems, and their replacement by agroecosystems, which results from that energy input. The gradient of interaction extends from the (relatively) spatially diffuse activity of burning vegetation, through the more localized gathering, collecting and protective tending of wild plant products, to the planting, sowing, weeding, harvesting and storing of (undomesticated) crops, with associated irrigation and drainage, land clearance and tillage, eventually to crop domestication: this latter condition having come about (according to the orthodox criterion of domestication accepted here) when the reproductive system of the plant population has been so altered by sustained human intervention that the domesticated forms – genetically and/or phenotypically selected – have become dependent upon human assistance for their survival. Figure 2.1 makes a distinction between cultivation, as a method of plant-food production which incorporates land clearance and systematic tillage but which can be (and in the past widely was) applied to undomesticated crops, and agriculture, which term is restricted to the cultivation of domesticated crops. I readily acknowledge that the distinction between undomesticated and domesticated crops is not absolute, if for no other reason than that the genetic/phenotypic selection processes leading to domestication are cumulative, but the distinction between cultivation and agriculture proposed here is at least clear, and it has the added merit of making redundant the vague (and by implication deterministic) category of 'incipient agriculture'.

It will be apparent that I have not introduced the term 'horticulture' into the model. It could have been equated with agriculture or regarded as a distinctive type of agricultural system in order to distinguish between small-scale garden cultivation or *gartenbau* and larger-scale field cultivation or *ackerbau*. But, although that is a valid and useful distinction to make when discussing the evolution of agricultural systems, it raises at least two definitional difficulties. The first arises from the fact that in some of the literature on agricultural systems and their evolution, particularly much of that which relates to Melanesia and the Pacific Islands, the term horticulture or 'gardening' has come to be used as a synonym for agriculture (e.g. Groube 1989; Jones and Meehan 1989) rather than as a means of distinguishing between 'field' and 'garden' cultivation.

The second difficulty is more problematic and arises from the distinctive ecology of 'house' or 'door-yard' gardens to which Anderson first (1952: 136–42) and Kimber later (1966, 1973, 1978) drew particular attention. Investigation by Kimber of present-day 'traditional' gardens in Puerto Rico and elsewhere revealed that nearly 50 per cent of the plant species present in them were adventitious wild and weedy taxa rather than domesticated crops, although almost all the taxa were perceived by the owners of the gardens as making useful contributions to the household economy. This situation contrasts strongly with the ratio of wild and weedy taxa to domesticated crops that tends to characterize field cultivation, even in situations where within-field mixed cropping rather than within-field monoculture is the norm. House gardens characteristically combine the cultivation of domes-ticated crops with a significant component of wild plant-food production, and indeed, as I have previously suggested (Harris 1973: 398–401), they probably functioned in the past as important arenas for plant domestication. Therefore, if the term horticulture is to be used to denote small-scale garden cultivation involving the exploitation of almost as many 'wild' as domes-ticated species, then it should not be equated with agriculture but instead regarded as a distinctive type of agroecosystem.

It is not necessary in this discussion to exemplify from ethnographic and historical sources all the plant-exploitative activities listed in Figure 2.1. Many of the contributions to Harris and Hillman (1989) do so in consid-erable detail, particularly the following examples: the replacement planting of yams and the incidental 'tillage' of yam grounds in Australia referred to by Hallam (1989), Jones and Meehan (1989), and Yen (1989); the transplanting of acorns in southern California mentioned by Shipek (1989); and the sowing, harvesting, and processing of wild-grass seeds in southern California, North Africa, and Australia described, respectively, by Shipek (1989), Harlan (1989), and, for Australia, by Cane (1989), Jones and Meehan (1989), Smith (1989), and Yen (1989) (see also Allen 1974). There are fewer references in Harris and Hillman (1989) to the burning of vege-tation to enhance the yields of plant foods and to make their gathering easier, but see Yen (1989) for a summary discussion of Australian Aboriginal use of fire to promote the productivity of cycads, grasses, and tuberous plants, and still fewer to non-agricultural contexts in which irrigation and drainage were applied to the exploitation of wild plants to regularize and increase harvests – probably the best-known example of which is the relatively large-scale irrigation of grasses and tuberous plants (such as *Cyperus esculentus*, cf. Hillman 1989: 226–7) which was practised in historical times (and perhaps earlier) by the Paiute Indians of Owen's Valley in eastern California (summarized in Harris 1984).

It has already been suggested that the sequence of plant-exploitative activities in Figure 2.1 represents a gradient of increasing input of human energy per unit area of exploited land. It can now be further suggested that, qualitatively at least, we can envisage thresholds along the gradient which represent stepped increases in energy input, at which points markedly more effort is invested in selected areas of exploitation, and human intervention in the ecology and reproductive biology of particular plants intensifies. Three such thresholds are postulated in Figure 2.1. The first is between the spatially diffuse and low-energy activities of burning, gathering, and protective tending, and it can be said to separate the food-yielding system of 'wild plant-food procurement' or 'foraging' from 'wild-food production'. The second is between the more spatially focused, labour demanding, and ecologically interventionist activities that range from planting and sowing to irrigation and drainage, and the still more energy-intensive, activities of land clearance and systematic tillage.

The second threshold separates 'wild plant-food production' from 'cultivation'. This is seen as a crucial threshold because, once land clearance and tillage is practised regularly on more than a very small scale, the energy-input demands of the system increase substantially. The biblical injunction (Genesis 3:17–19) is indeed true, that 'In the sweat of thy face shalt thou eat bread', or, as Rousseau (1755) ironically described the beginning of agriculture when 'vast forests were changed into smiling fields which had to be watered with the sweat of men'. Larry Gonick (1978) makes the same point (Figure 2.2) visually but equally emphatically! The separation of cultivation from wild plant-food production by the second energy threshold may appear somewhat arbitrary, in that transplanting, weeding, and drainage and irrigation all involve some degree of soil disturbance, but, in the context of wild plant-food production, such disturbance amounts to no more than minimal tillage, and does not undermine the contention that systematic clearing of the land and tilling of the soil (presumably initially by digging stick or hoe rather than by plough) require much greater investment of energy.

We can, then, define cultivation as a combination of systematic land clearance and tillage with the planting or sowing (as well, of course, as harvesting, etc.) of undomesticated crops. Its inception marks an important point on the evolutionary continuum of people–plant interaction, but it does not necessarily lead to domestication. Crop domestication (in the narrow orthodox sense), or at least the adoption from elsewhere of already domesticated

Figure 2.2 The beginning of agriculture, according to Larry Gonick (© Larry
      Gonick, all rights reserved, reproduced with his permission)

crops, is, however, a necessary component of agriculture. And, in so far as
the cultivation of domesticates, if successfully developed and maintained,
required that additional effort be devoted to such activities as soil preparation, the maintenance of soil fertility, weeding, seed selection and storage,
and the exclusion of potential predators attracted by the enlarged food-
storage organs of domesticated plants, then the division between cultivation
and agriculture can be said to constitute a third energy threshold on the
continuum.

   Although only three energy thresholds are postulated in Figure 2.1, we
could of course define further thresholds *within* the general category of
agriculture, which would separate different agricultural systems – such as
horticulture, swidden cultivation, floodwater farming, irrigation agriculture,
mixed grain livestock farming, etc. – along the gradient of increasing energy
input: an elaboration of the model which is, however, not attempted here.

In characterizing the interaction continuum as a gradient of increasing input of human energy, and postulating thresholds along it, I here disregard the question of how that input was provided, e.g. by a larger population and/or by changes in the sexual or age-related division of labour and/or by changes in the seasonal scheduling of activities. These are important but subsidiary aspects of the present model, which deliberately adopts as an organizing principle the key variable of increasing input of energy per unit of exploited land. Nor do I explore possible correlations between the energy gradient and such socio-demographic trends as increasing sedentism, increasing population density, and increasing social complexity: all aspects of what has recently come to be referred to by some authors as the process of 'intensification' (cf. Lourandos 1983; Yen 1989). It is sufficient here just to portray them in Figure 2.1 as assumptive correlations only. The variable of time is treated similarly in Figure 2.1, because any attempt to attach a scale in millennia to the continuum requires more knowledge than we presently have of the chronology of plant exploitation. Such a calibration might, however, usefully be attempted for those few regions of the world, such as parts of Southwest Asia, Europe, Middle and North America, where we are beginning to assemble a chronological overview of the evolution of plant exploitation.

The last aspect of the model which calls for comment here is the question of its utility – or lack of it. As stated at the start, my main aim is to help clarify the general terminology we use in thinking and writing about the emergence of agriculture. It is hoped that the model has at least logical validity and some theoretical value, but if it is to prove useful in investigating the actual history and prehistory of plant exploitation in particular geographical regions, more comprehensive means than we have at present will have to be devised to trace in the archaeological record the range of plant-exploitative activities that make up the continuum. At present, relatively few of those activities are open to direct archaeobotanical or palaeoenvironmental investigation.

Palynology, and the less advanced technique of the stratigraphic analysis of charcoal frequencies, can provide some information on land clearance and fire history. Phytolith analysis, too, is proving a promising technique for the investigation of vegetation change and crop history. The most important set of techniques, however, are those that are applied to the study of macroscopic plant remains preserved by charring, mineralization, waterlogging, and desiccation. Thus far they have been applied principally to the investigation of domesticated seed crops, particularly the staple cereals of modern agriculture, maize, wheat, barley, and rice; much less so to pulses (but see Butler 1989) and other non-cereal seed crops, and hardly at all to root and tuber crops. New chemical and anatomical-micromorphological techniques are now being developed which may open new avenues to the identification of the remains of roots and tubers (Hather 1988; Hill and Evans 1989) and there is also growing interest among archaeobotanists in the investigation of pre-agrarian plant exploitation (see Constantine 1989; Hillman 1989; Hillman *et al.* 1989; Pearsall 1989; Piperno 1989 [this volume]; Pyramarn 1989).

Field archaeology can sometimes provide direct evidence of irrigation (e.g. Oates and Oates 1976) and of drainage systems in swamp environments (e.g. Golson 1989 [this volume]), and it is beginning also to reveal the capacity of some prehistoric agriculturalists for large-scale landscape modification by mound and terrace construction, etc. (e.g. Bulmer 1989; Gallagher 1989). But in the absence of surviving traces of such features in the landscape, it is extremely difficult to demonstrate whether such activities as irrigation, drainage, and tillage were practised. A new experimental approach to the question of tillage is currently being developed by Unger-Hamilton (1989), who has combined harvesting experiments on a range of Southwest Asian wild grasses and other herbaceous plants with micro wear studies of flint sickle blades. It appears that striations on the blades may be attributable specifically to the harvesting of plants growing on tilled as opposed to untilled soils. If this is confirmed by more comprehensive experiments, the technique could provide us for the first time with a direct method of determining, at least in parts of Southwest Asia, how long ago soil tillage was practised and thus of tracing the beginnings of cultivation (as here defined).

There are therefore a variety of methods, some well established and others highly experimental, for investigating several of the activities that make up the continuum of people–plant interaction outlined here. In presenting it, I emphasize that it is highly schematic and tentative, but I also hope that it may help to clarify our thinking and assist future enquiry into the evolution of plant exploitation from foraging to farming.

References

Allen, H. (1974) 'The Bagundji of the Darling Basin: cereal gatherers in an uncertain environment', *World Archaeology*, 5: 309–22.

Anderson, E. (1952) *Plants, Man and Life*, Berkeley, CA: University of California Press.

Binford, L.R. (1968) 'Post-Pleistocene adaptations', in S. R. Binford and L. R. Binford (eds) *New Perspectives in Archaeology*, Chicago, IL: Aldine.

Braidwood, R.J. (1952) 'From cave to village', *Scientific American*, 187: 62–6.

Braidwood, R.J. (1960) 'The agricultural revolution', *Scientific American*, 203: 130–48.

Bulmer, S. (1989) 'Gardens in the south: diversity and change in prehistoric Maaori Agriculture', in D. R. Harris and G. C. Hillman (eds) *Foraging and Farming: the evolution of plant exploitation*, London: Unwin Hyman.

Butler, A. (1989) 'Cryptic anatomical characters as evidence of early cultivation in the grain legumes (pulses)', in D. R. Harris and G. C. Hillman (eds) *Foraging and Farming: the evolution of plant exploitation*, London: Unwin Hyman.

Cane, S. (1989) 'Australian Aboriginal seed grinding and its archaeological record: a case study from the Western Desert', in D. R. Harris and G. C. Hillman (eds)

Foraging and Farming: the evolution of plant exploitation, London: Unwin Hyman.

Chase, A.K. (1989) 'Domestication and domiculture in northern Australia: a social perspective', in D. R. Harris and G. C. Hillman (eds) *Foraging and Farming: the evolution of plant exploitation*, London: Unwin Hyman.

Childe, V.G. (1936) *Man Makes Himself*, London: Watts.

Childe, V.G. (1942) *What Happened in History*, Harmondsworth: Penguin.

Costantine, L. (1989) 'Plant exploitation at Grotta del1'Uzzo, Sicily: new evidence for the transition from Mesolithic to Neolithic subsistence in southern Europe', in D. R. Harris and G. C. Hillman (eds) *Foraging and Farming: the evolution of plant exploitation*, London: Unwin Hyman.

Darwin, C. (1868) *The Variation of Animals and Plants under Domestication*, vol. I, London: John Murray.

Flannery, K.V. (1968) 'Archaeological systems theory and early Mesoamerica', in B. J. Meggers (ed.) *Anthropological Archaeology in the Americas*, Washington, DC: Anthropological Society of Washington.

Flannery, K.V. (1969) 'Origins and ecological effects of early domestication in Iran and the Near East', in P. J. Ucko and G. W. Dimbleby (eds) *The Domestication and Exploitation of Plants and Animals*, London: Duckworth.

Ford, R.I. (1985) 'The processes of plant food production in prehistoric North America', in R. I. Ford (ed.) *Prehistoric Food Production in North America*, Anthropological Paper No.75, Ann Arbor, MI: Museum of Anthropology, University of Michigan.

Gallagher, J.P. (1989) 'Agricultural intensification and ridged-field cultivation in the prehistoric upper Midwest of North America', in D. R. Harris and G. C. Hillman (eds) *Foraging and Farming: the evolution of plant exploitation*, London: Unwin Hyman.

Glacken, C.J. (1967) *Traces on the Rhodian Shore: nature and culture in western thought from ancient times to the end of the eighteenth century*, Berkeley, CA: University of California Press.

Golson, J. (1989) 'The origins and development of New Guinea agriculture', in D. R. Harris and G. C. Hillman (eds) *Foraging and Farming: the evolution of plant exploitation*, London: Unwin Hyman.

Gonick, L. (1978) *The Cartoon History of the Universe*, San Francisco, CA: Rip Off Press.

Groube, L. (1989) 'The taming of the rain forests: a model for Late Pleistocene forest exploitation in New Guinea', in D. R. Harris and G. C. Hillman (eds) *Foraging and Farming: the evolution of plant exploitation*, London: Unwin Hyman.

Hallam, S.J. (1989) 'Plant usage and management in Southwest Australian Aboriginal societies', in D. R. Harris and G. C. Hillman (eds) *Foraging and Farming: the evolution of plant exploitation*, London: Unwin Hyman.

Harlan, J.R. (1989) 'Wild grass-seed harvesting in the Sahara and Sub-Sahara of Africa', in D. R. Harris and G. C. Hillman (eds) *Foraging and Farming: the evolution of plant exploitation*, London: Unwin Hyman.

Harris, D.R. (1969) 'Agricultural systems, ecosystems and the origins of agriculture', in P. J. Ucko and G. W. Dimbleby (eds) *The Domestication and Exploitation of Plants and Animals*, London: Duckworth.

Harris, D.R. (1972) 'The origins of agriculture in the tropics', *American Scientist*, 60: 180–93.

Harris, D.R. (1973) 'The prehistory of tropical agriculture: an ethnoecological model', in C. Renfrew (ed.) *The Explanation of Culture Change: models in prehistory*, London: Duckworth.

Harris, D.R. (1984) 'Ethnohistorical evidence for the exploitation of wild grasses and forbs: its scope and archaeological implications', in W. van Zeist and W. A. Casparie (eds) *Plants and Ancient Man: studies in palaeoethnobotany*, Rotterdam: Balkema.

Harris, D.R. and Hillman, G.C. (eds) (1989) *Foraging and Farming: the evolution of plant exploitation*, London: Unwin Hyman.

Hather, J.G. (1988) 'The morphological and anatomical interpretation and identification of charred vegetative parenchymatous plant remains', unpublished PhD dissertation, Institute of Archaeology, University College London, University of London.

Helbaek, H. (1960) 'The palaeoethnobotany of the Near East and Europe', in R. J. Braidwood and B. Howe (eds) *Prehistoric Investigations in Iraqi Kurdistan*, Studies in Ancient Oriental Civilization 31, Chicago, IL: Chicago University Press.

Higgs, E.S. (ed.) (1972) *Papers in Economic Prehistory*, Cambridge: Cambridge University Press.

Higgs, E.S. and Jarman, M.R. (1969) 'The origins of agriculture: a reconsideration', *Antiquity*, 43: 31–41.

Hill, H.E. and Evans, J. (1989) 'Crops of the Pacific: new evidence from chemical analysis of organic residues in pottery', in D. R. Harris and G. C. Hillman (eds) *Foraging and Farming: the evolution of plant exploitation*, London: Unwin Hyman.

Hillman, G.C. (1975) 'The plant remains from Tell Abu Hureyra: a preliminary report', in A. M. T. Moore 'The excavation of Tell Abu Hureyra in Syria: a preliminary report', *Proceedings of the Prehistoric Society*, 41: 70–3.

Hillman, G.C. (1989) 'Late Palaeolithic plant foods from Wadi Kubbaniya, Upper Egypt: dietary diversity, infant weaning, and seasonality in a riverine environment', in D. R. Harris and G. C. Hillman (eds) *Foraging and Farming: the evolution of plant exploitation*, London: Unwin Hyman.

Hillman, G.C., Colledge, S.M. and Harris, D.R. (1989) 'Plant-food economy during the Epipalaeolithic period at Tell Abu Hureyra, Syria: dietary diversity, seasonality, and modes of exploitation', in D. R. Harris and G. C. Hillman (eds) *Foraging and Farming: the evolution of plant exploitation*, London: Unwin Hyman.

Hynes, R.A. and Chase, A.K. (1982) 'Plants, sites and domiculture: Aboriginal influence upon plant communities in Cape York Peninsula', *Archaeology in Oceania*, 17: 38–50.

Jarman, M.R., Bailey, G.N. and Jarman, H.N. (1982) *Early European Agriculture: its foundations and development*, Cambridge: Cambridge University Press.

Jones, R. and Meehan, B. (1989) 'Plant foods of the Gidjingali: ethnographic and archaeological perspectives from northern Australia on tuber and seed exploitation', in D. R. Harris and G. C. Hillman (eds) *Foraging and Farming: the evolution of plant exploitation*, London: Unwin Hyman.

Kimber, C.T. (1966) 'Dooryard gardens of Martinique', *Yearbook of the Association of Pacific Coast Geographers*, 28: 97–118.

Kimber, C.T. (1973) 'Spatial patterning in the dooryard gardens of Puerto Rico', *Geographical Review*, 63: 6–26.

Kimber, C.T. (1978) 'A folk content for plant domestication: or the dooryard garden revisited', *Anthropological Journal of Canada*, 16: 2–11.

Lourandos, H. (1983) 'Intensification: a late Pleistocene-Holocene archaeological sequence from southwestern Victoria', *Archaeology in Oceania*, 18: 81–94.

Oates, D. and Oates, J. (1976) 'Early irrigation agriculture in Mesopotamia', in G. de G. Sieveking, I. H. Longworth and K. E. Wilson (eds) *Problems in Economic and Social Archaeology*, London: Duckworth.

Pearsall, D.M. (1989) 'Adaptation of prehistoric hunter-gatherers to the high Andes: the changing role of plant resources', in D. R. Harris and G. C. Hillman (eds) *Foraging and Farming: the evolution of plant exploitation*, London: Unwin Hyman.

Piperno, D.R. (1989) 'Non-affluent foragers: resource availability, seasonal shortages, and the emergence of agriculture in Panamanian tropical forests', in D. R. Harris and G. C. Hillman (eds) *Foraging and Farming: the evolution of plant exploitation*, London: Unwin Hyman.

Pyramarn, K. (1989) 'New evidence on plant exploitation and environment during the Hoabinhian (Late Stone Age) from Ban Kao Caves, Thailand', in D. R. Harris and G. C. Hillman (eds) *Foraging and Farming: the evolution of plant exploitation*, London: Unwin Hyman.

Rindos, D. (1980) 'Symbiosis, instability, and the origins and spread of agriculture: a new model', *Current Anthropology*, 21: 751–72.

Rindos, D. (1984) *The Origins of Agriculture: an evolutionary perspective*, New York: Academic Press.

Rousseau, J.-J. (1755) *Discours sur l'Origine et les Fondements de l'Inégalité parmi les Hommes*, Amsterdam: Michel Rey; trans. R. D. Masters and J. R. Masters (1964) in R. D. Masters (ed.) *Jean-Jacques Rousseau. The first and second discourses*, New York: St Martin's Press.

Sahlins, M.D. and Service, E.R. (eds) (1960) *Evolution and Culture*, Ann Arbor, MI: University of Michigan Press.

Shipek, F.C. (1989) 'An example of intensive plant husbandry: the Kumeyaay of southern California', in D. R. Harris and G. C. Hillman (eds) *Foraging and Farming: the evolution of plant exploitation*, London: Unwin Hyman.

Smith, M.A. (1989) 'Seed gathering in inland Australia: current evidence on the antiquity of the ethnohistorical pattern of exploitation', in D. R. Harris and G. C. Hillman (eds) *Foraging and Farming: the evolution of plant exploitation*, London: Unwin Hyman.

Unger-Hamilton, R. (1989) 'Epi-Palaeolithic Southern Levant and the origins of cultivation', *Current Anthropology*, 30: 88–103.

Yen, D.E. (1989) 'The domestication of environment', in D. R. Harris and G. C. Hillman (eds) *Foraging and Farming: the evolution of plant exploitation*, London: Unwin Hyman.

Zeuner, F.E. (1963) *A History of Domesticated Animals*, London: Hutchinson.

Update: Refining concepts and terminology

Tim Denham

Harris has continued to refine the ideas discussed in his 1989 paper. These modifications have, in part, resulted from his continued investigations into early agricultural development in several regions of the world, including Southwest Asia (Harris 2002a), the Torres Strait (Harris 1995) and Turkmenistan (Harris and Gosden 1996). They have also been stimulated by critique and substantive findings yielded by recent developments in archaeobotany (macro- and microfossil) and the application of genetic techniques to understanding animal and plant evolution and domestication. These refinements cluster around two thematic couplets: concepts and terminology, and centres and diffusion.

First, Harris expanded and fine-tuned the conceptual and terminological frameworks needed to classify, discuss and understand different types of food production (Harris 1996a, 1996b, in press). These frameworks seek to understand the transition to early agriculture from pre-existing plant and animal exploitation practices, and to account for those practices and people who fall between the traditional 'hunting and gathering' and 'agriculture' dichotomy (also see Smith 2001). Sometimes these 'in-between' lifeways of animal protection and plant management change into agriculture, whereas sometimes they do not (Harris in press). Harris' current focus on understanding the 'transitional' is not universally accepted. Some researchers interpret the archaeological and ethnographic records to be bimodal; they identify few 'in-between' groups and consider the transition of hunting and gathering to agriculture to be a very rare event (e.g. Bellwood 2005).

While the 1989 chapter focused solely on plant exploitation, subsequent papers have also included a parallel evolutionary continuum for animal exploitation. These continua are based on two entwined processes: the manipulation of biotic resources culminating in their domestication, and the transformation of natural to anthropic ecosystems. Subsequent papers have not emphasised correspondences among food-yielding systems, demography and socio-economic trends to the same degree. The most significant conceptual developments concern a partial decoupling of agriculture and domestication, and the reclassification of food-yielding systems between wild-food procurement – essentially hunter-gatherer foraging – and agriculture.

In 1989, the term agriculture was 'restricted to the cultivation of domesticated crops' (Harris 1989: 19); subsequently, agricultural systems have been 'defined as those in which (morphogenetically) domesticated crops [or animals] are the predominant source of food' (in press). The conceptual boundary demarcating agriculture is more porous in recent schemas; it allows for the cultivation and management of domesticates as minor components under wild-food production, an 'in-between' subsistence system that is neither agricultural nor wholly based on the exploitation of wild resources (in press). The revised category of wild-food production has absorbed the original independent category (in Harris 1989) of 'cultivation with systematic tillage' to yield a simplified schema for both plants and animals of 'wild-food procurement', 'wild-food production' and 'agricultural production' (Harris in press).

Second, Harris (1990, 1996b) has criticised recurrent attempts (from Vavilov to Sauer to Harlan to Hawkes) to equate geographical centres of origin of cultivated plants, where crop diversity is high and wild progenitors are assumed to have been domesticated, with primary centres of early and independent agriculture – the two need not correspond and should be decoupled. For Harris (1990, 2006), the concept of 'centres' has misdirected research and is outdated; instead, he has advocated focusing research on 'the evolutionary history of individual crops and regional crop associations' and the adoption of 'a more rigorous approach to the identification and dating of archaeologically-recovered plant remains' (Harris 1990: 15). Recent research in several regions of the globe, e.g. Africa, India, the Americas and New Guinea (see papers in Denham *et al.* in press; for India see Fuller *et al.* 2004), is beginning to illustrate greater complexity of process and more diffuse spatial and temporal patterns in the domestication of animals and plants.

Diffusion, dispersal, expansion and spread are conceptual corollaries to centres and cores. Whether a centre of origin for a species, a centre of domestication, a centre of early and independent agriculture, or the core of an early agricultural system (see Harris 2002b) is under consideration, there is subsequent movement beyond the original location. The historical processes through which utilised species, food-production practices and people, including their genes, languages and material culture, became distributed across the globe continue to be of great debate. Three models have dominated thinking on these issues: (1) independent innovation, i.e. the independent development of practices in different places; (2) cultural diffusion, i.e. selective movement of cultural traits and their adoption among interacting groups; and (3) demic diffusion, i.e. the spatial expansion of (in this case) agricultural groups that absorbed, displaced or replaced neighbouring groups, their languages and their cultures. In recent years, demic diffusionary perspectives have dominated debate on the spread of agriculture (e.g. Bellwood and Renfrew 2002). However, the local complexity emerging from new data in different regions of the world is beginning to challenge such large-scale, comparative hypotheses (see papers in Harris 1996c and Denham *et al.* in press).

References

Bellwood, P. (2005) *First Farmers: the origins of agricultural societies*, Oxford: Blackwell.

Bellwood, P. and Renfrew, C. (eds) (2002) *Examining the Farming/Language Dispersal Hypothesis*, Cambridge: McDonald Institute for Archaeological Research.

Denham, T.P., Iriarte, J. and Vrydaghs, L. (eds) (in press) *Rethinking Agriculture: archaeological and ethnoarchaeological perspectives*, Walnut Creek, CA: Left Coast Press.

Fuller, D., Korisettar, R., Venkatasubbaiah, P.C. and Jones, M.K. (2004) 'Early plant domestications in southern India: some preliminary archaeobotanical results', *Vegetation History and Archaeobotany*, 13: 115–29.

Harris, D.R. (1989) 'An evolutionary continuum of people–plant interaction', in D. R. Harris and G. C. Hillman (eds) *Foraging and Farming: the evolution of plant exploitation*, London: Unwin Hyman.

Harris, D.R. (1990) 'Vavilov's concept of centres of origin of cultivated plants: its genesis and its influence on the study of agricultural origins', *Biological Journal of the Linnean Society*, 39: 7–16.

Harris, D.R. (1995) 'Early agriculture in New Guinea and the Torres Strait divide', *Antiquity*, 69 (Special Number 265): 848–54.

Harris, D.R. (1996a) 'Domesticatory relationships of people, plants and animals', in R. Ellen and K. Fukui (eds) *Redefining Nature: ecology, culture and domestication*, Oxford: Berg.

Harris, D.R. (1996b) 'Introduction: themes and concepts in the study of early agriculture', in D. R. Harris (ed.) *The Origins and Spread of Agriculture and Pastoralism in Eurasia*, London: UCL Press.

Harris, D.R. (ed.) (1996c) *The Origins and Spread of Agriculture and Pastoralism in Eurasia*, London: UCL Press.

Harris, D.R. (2002a) 'Development of the agro-pastoral economy in the Fertile Crescent during the Pre-Pottery Neolithic period', in R. T. J. Cappers and S. Bottema, (eds) *The Dawn of Farming in the Near East*, Studies in Early Near Eastern Production, Subsistence, and Environment 6, Berlin: ex oriente.

Harris, D.R. (2002b) 'The expansion capacity of early agricultural systems: a comparative perspective on the spread of agriculture', in P. Bellwood and C. Renfrew (eds) *Examining the Farming/Language Dispersal Hypothesis*, Cambridge: McDonald Institute for Archaeological Research.

Harris, D.R. (in press) 'Agriculture, cultivation and domestication: exploring the conceptual framework of early food-production' in T. P. Denham, J. Iriarte and L. Vrydaghs, (eds) *Rethinking Agriculture: archaeological and ethno-archaeological perspectives*, Walnut Creek, CA: Left Coast Press.

Harris, D.R. and Gosden, C. (1996) 'The beginnings of agriculture in western Central Asia', in D. R. Harris (ed.) *The Origins and Spread of Agriculture and Pastoralism in Eurasia*, London: UCL Press.

Smith, B.D. (2001) 'Low-level food production', *Journal of Archaeological Research*, 9: 1–43.

3 Darwinism and its role in the explanation of domestication

David Rindos

Dedicated to the memory of Michael E. Whalen

He was a scholar, and a ripe and good one
Henry VIII

Introduction

Anthropology has long been pre-eminently a discipline unto itself. It has separated itself from its sister social sciences by acceptance of the rather sublime observation that humans are, at least in some sense, animals, mammals, and primates. Divorce from the biological sciences has been uncontested and amicable. Anthropology has been able to provide the grounds for the divorce by providing expert testimony on how humans are totally unlike the rest of creation. And, in providing itself with the justification of its own existence, it has provided the rest of biology with defences for continued belief in the fundamental difference between our own species and the rest of the animal kingdom. In a rather rare instance of interdisciplinary co-operation, anthropology has been able to provide biology with all the reasons necessary to maintain an unquestioned and unquestioning acceptance of the incommensurability of one species with all others. One might expect a critical mind to note the self-serving nature of the argument and question it on those grounds if no other.

The fundamental and underlying rationale for compartmentalizing the study of human behaviour in a separate discipline may best be understood by appreciating the role given to a specific type of 'cultural' process in the explanation of human behaviour. Humans, it is held, are cultural animals. Human culture, however, is seen as the means by which humans *consciously and intentionally* adapt to a multitude of environments. Here, intentional adaptation effectively removes humankind from the materialistic and mechanistic processes that govern other natural processes. My purpose in this chapter is to attack this central belief. In it I defend the idea that cultural processes are natural; that cultural change is best understood by means of a natural process. Darwinian evolution provides the theoretical backdrop for the approach that I advance, in place of intentional cultural adaptation and adjustment; change in subsistence patterning provides the context for the discussion.

My intent here is to shed some light on a central problem in human cultural change – the evolution of agricultural systems – by looking at human culture and cultural change in a different way. I do not criticize in this chapter earlier models for cultural evolution, whether in general or specifically in terms of agricultural origins (see Rindos 1984, 1985, 1986). Instead, I focus upon agricultural change using a specific Darwinian model – the 'cultural-selectionist' view of culture.

Cultural selectionism is based upon three interrelated postulates:

(a) The human capacity for culture (and the innate morphologies and psychological processes thereby implied) has evolved by means of natural selection. Humans are not cultural because they choose to be cultural; instead the capacity for culture may only be explained in terms of the enhanced fitness that it induced in those hominids who had a greater capacity for cultural behaviours.

(b) The same processes which originally brought about the genetic capacity for culture in humans, continued, and indeed continues, to act upon the specifics of cultural acts, beliefs, and structures. Here, natural selection is the ordering force in non-genetically transmitted cultural phenomena. It is important to note that cultural selectionism, in contradistinction to sociobiology, holds that, while human culture taken as a whole is genetically permitted, *none* of the differences existing between human cultures may be explained on the basis of genetic differences between members of those cultures. Instead, these differences arise as the result of differing selective pressures experienced by various human cultures during their history.

(c) In contrast to the 'evolutionism' of Spencer, White, and Sahlins and Service, cultural selectionism posits a strictly Darwinian model for cultural function and change. Here the most significant statement of cultural selectionism is that no inherent direction underlies cultural evolution and that, instead, all change is the result of selection acting upon the undirected variant cultural forms existing at earlier points in time.

The Darwinian perspective on plant domestication and agricultural evolution

Darwinists hold that evolutionary change results from the natural selection of heritable variation. Ernst Mayr has repeatedly pointed out (e.g. 1942, 1969, 1982: 519–20) that Darwinian evolutionary change is based upon a two-step process: (1) the production of undirected variation, and (2) its sorting by means of the differential success and failure of various forms over time. In this, Darwinism, unlike any other evolutionary theory, places major emphasis upon the *undirected nature of the processes generating variation* in heritable traits. Yet, in saying this, it is essential to stress that the Darwinian concept of undirected variation does not hold to the absurd claim that variation is generated 'randomly' in the mathematical sense of that term, i.e. that the process is totally stochastic and unbounded. Clearly, no human will exhibit variation in wing structure or photosynthetic pathways. Instead, variation at any moment in time will always be bounded in very important ways by the nature of the organism itself, i.e. by its evolved history.

An example stressing the historicity of Darwinism may be seen in the process underlying the earliest beginnings of plant domestication. As I have pointed out (1984), a simple relationship exists between humans and the plants on which they feed. Over long periods of time, human feeding behaviour will alter the local flora in such a manner as to place certain morphological traits of members of a plant species at a competitive advantage over others. This competitive advantage arises in terms of how effective a particular morphology is in attracting human consumers as dispersal agents for the plant. The further evolution of the plant species, therefore, will be altered by the feeding and dispersal behaviour of humans (cf. Chase 1989; Harris 1989 [this volume]). Yet this evolution, in any specific case, takes place in the context of two interdependent historical processes – that of the plant genome, including mutation and recombination, and that of the learned subsistence behaviour of the humans. A subsistence pattern that lacks a particular behaviour, for example the processing of tubers for starch, will place limits upon the development of specific domestication events quite as effectively as the non-appearance of an 'appropriate' genetic event within the plant. Hence, we must recognize that speaking of the general evolutionary pressures within the development of agricultural systems may only sensitize us to the types of symbioses that might have occurred; it cannot replace the careful study of the particulars that have occurred in any specific system (as exemplified by Chikwendu and Okezie 1989; Johns 1989; Ladizinsky 1989; Pearsall 1989; Zohary 1989 [this volume]).

The possible direction of evolution will also be affected by the peculiarities of the specific transmission system that codes for variation. The nature of the coding system is of major importance when we discuss any evolutionary process. For example, the effects of recombination during evolutionary change must be explained with sensitivity to the fact that different organisms may have radically different types of recombination options open to them. Prokaryotes (bacteria and their allies) may exchange variable amounts of genetic information during 'mating', while eukaryotes ('higher' organisms) are generally forced by the existence of true sexuality and meiosis to contribute equal amounts of information to individuals of the next generation. In the same manner, information that is coded and transmitted genetically will have different evolutionary potentialities and limitations than information affecting the organism's behaviour that is transmitted directly from one phenotype to another (i.e. 'culturally' in the broadest sense of that term).

Hence, we may see that while variation does not exist independently of organisms, organisms do not exist independently of their evolutionary history. This is true both in terms of the types of traits that may vary and also in terms of the inheritance systems that transmit traits, and their variant forms, between organisms over time. Yet, when we wish to explain changes in traits existing in biological entities, an understanding of the evolved peculiarities of organisms is literally the object of our inquiry. Therefore, we will expect that our understanding of evolution must be informed by the peculiarities of the specific inheritance systems of the organisms we are studying.

In this context, the properties of the cultural transmission system that governs variable human behaviours must be taken into account when we seek to understand the origin and evolution of cultural traits. Here, much useful work has already been done by Cavalli-Sforza and Feldman (1981) and Boyd and Richerson (1985). Cultural change may profitably be analogized with genetic evolution (Campbell 1965, 1976). For example, innovations appear in populations, and spread if favoured or are abandoned if not, by processes showing striking similarities to natural selection and random drift. Nevertheless, we must recognize that these sorts of general descriptions are only a heuristic model and that the explanation of specific cultural changes must take into account the specifics of the system being considered. Secondly, and of greater importance, we must stress that transmission processes should not be confused with evolutionary ones. Transmission mechanisms may indeed place biases upon the possible direction of evolution (Boyd and Richerson 1985), but the changes that *have* occurred in cultural evolution 'are hardly made intelligible by the transmission modes, but rather by examining the interaction between demography, environment, technology, and organizational variables' (Marks *et al.* 1983: 15).

Plant domestication and prehistoric agriculture in the American Bottom

For an example of this type of interactive analysis, we may consider work that has been done on domestication and the origins and further development of agricultural systems in an area of the central United States known as the American Bottom (Rindos and Johannessen 1988; cf. Watson 1989 [this volume]). Following a long period of 'incidental domestication' (Rindos 1984: 154–8) of several species of nut-bearing trees, a complex of starchy and oily seeded native plants began to grow in importance in this region during the Middle Woodland period (*c.* 150 BC–AD 300). The contribution of this complex of seed plants to the diet increased, in both absolute and relative terms, until the latest phases of the Mississippian period (AD 1000–1500). At about AD 800, maize begins to appear in the archaeobotanical record from the region, with the evidence indicating a widespread and remarkably abrupt adoption of this imported plant. Yet, the fact that

the starchy seed complex remains abundant in the record, despite the introduction of maize, indicates that this new crop was not grown *instead of*
the existing plant complex, but in *addition to* plants that had been part
of an evolved agricultural system with humans for as much as 1000 years.
Furthermore, the speed at which maize appears in the record is remarkable.
Seeds and cobs, often in very substantial quantities, have been recovered from
50 per cent to 90 per cent of the features analysed at sites of the Emergent
Mississippian period (AD 800–1000). In the sites dated to the immediately
previous phase, maize is virtually unknown, having been recovered in minute
quantities from only 2 per cent of the features analysed. The data clearly
indicate that the appearance of maize in the record marks the introduction of
a new crop rather than the appearance of agriculture itself.

The most parsimonious explanation for the rapid rise of maize in importance in the area holds that while maize had been present for a very long time
in the region, it was represented by soft-seeded varieties that were grown for
their immature cobs. The Mississippian maize horizon represents not the
introduction of the species itself into the area, but rather the appearance
of a new variety having hard seeds that were used in the mature form. In the
context of this discussion, it is important to note that the diffusion of this
new, hard-seeded variety of maize into the region could not have been
successful unless humans were already practising the necessary agricultural
behaviours. Hence, the spread of the new crop was not in any sense a
'random' event based upon any inherent qualities of the maize plant, but was
preconditioned by the existence of an already functioning indigenous
agricultural system.

As has been stressed, the Darwinian view of cultural change does not claim
that the variant forms upon which selection was to act over time had to be
generated in a totally 'random' manner. We need not claim that specific
human characteristics such as decision-making, experimentation, or cultural
bias must be excluded from consideration in understanding the genesis of
the original variant behaviours that were to form the foundations for the
evolution of new cultural traits. We need only claim that these processes *in
and of themselves* were insufficient to generate the evolved systems.

Adopting a Darwinian perspective involves a reorientation of our thought
processes. Rather than concentrating upon the *origin* of the particular
variant trait that was to form the basis for future developments, we stress
the *effect* the possession of this trait, in its incipient form, was to have upon
humans and their cultures. Here our attention is directed to the fact that
all cultural behaviours have some influence, no matter how small, upon
human survival and reproductive success. This will be true even if changes
in these behaviours are completely independent of any change in gene
frequencies in the populations under consideration. Put in other terms,
cultural behaviours may affect human demography. Hence, the concept of
'pure' or 'demographic' Darwinian fitness is wholly applicable to the effects
of cultural traits upon human populations.

Let us return to the introduction of maize into the American Bottom. We have already noted that it was introduced into a cultural and agricultural system that had been in operation for at least a millennium. Nevertheless, following its adoption, major changes may be seen in the archaeological record. These include increases in population, nucleation, social complexity, and centralization. We have argued (Rindos and Johannessen 1988) that some of these changes were precipitated by the introduction of the storable form of maize, which, by means of its higher yield potential, permitted increases in populations in the region. Of greater importance, however, is the possibility that the qualities of the varieties of maize that came into use may have had major effects upon the reliability and predictability of the agricultural system itself, and hence upon the social structuring of the region.

As population increased as a function of the higher average yield obtainable from maize, so did the need for farmland. Increased farmland could be obtained only by clearing the native forests. Our evidence indicates that this occurred, at least in part, by clearance of the incidentally domesticated 'nut groves' that had arisen over many centuries in regions of human habitation. A major change occurs in the charcoal record when maize appears as a major component of the diet. Before the introduction of maize, most firewood was from soft-wooded genera such as *Populus* (poplars) and *Salix* (willows). The burning of hard-wooded genera such as *Carya* (hickory) and *Juglans* (walnut) appears to become common only after maize becomes abundant, with charcoal from these species appearing for the first time in the archaeological record in large quantities.

We should note that, all other things being equal, the hard woods make a better source of fuel for both cooking and heating than do the soft woods. Yet despite this, soft-wooded genera were utilized preferentially throughout the pre-maize periods. We assume that the nut trees were originally valued more for their mast crops than as a superior source of firewood. We might also note that culinary change involving a new need to cook the maize as a gruel cannot be invoked to explain this change in patterns of wood utilization. Braun (1983) has tied changes in ceramic technology during pre-maize periods to the demands placed upon the vessels in response to the increasing use of cooked starchy and oily seeds in the diet. Hence, we cannot explain the change in wood utilization as a response to new cooking requirements. We might also note, in passing, that acceptance and integration of the new variety of maize into the diet might also have been facilitated by a pre-existing procedure for the preparation of the dried, starchy seeds.

It follows that the most logical explanation for the change in charcoal would be population pressure. The growing need for land on which to grow maize to support a burgeoning population probably brought about the destruction of what had previously been an important dietary resource – the mast crops harvested from nut trees. We should not lose sight of the fact that this destruction of resources probably represents the loss of a valuable oil and protein supplement in a region that lacked both domesticated animals (save the dog which was little consumed) and domesticated sources of plant and animal fats.

Much data indicates that while maize is higher yielding in the region than the native complex of starchy seed crops, this increased yield is probably accompanied by a radical increase in the variability of that yield, i.e. even though average yield obtainable from maize cultivation increases dramatically, the year-to-year variance on yield increases even more. It must be stressed that any change in absolute yield is 'progress' only at the moment of its first occurrence; over relatively short periods of time increases in yield will literally be eaten up by the increased populations they generate. Yet, as population increases, the negative effects of increased variability on yield become increasingly severe: one cannot consume during times of scarcity the no longer existing surplus that had been generated during times of abundance.

The most obvious way to deal with the interacting factors of increasing population, increasing potential yield and increased variance in that yield would be an attempt to buffer the system by increased association and trade within and between regions. Then, if a crop is bad in one locality, maize could be imported from other localities during the crisis period. This is a type of activity that requires no foresight, merely a response to a specific condition of immediate reduced food availability. Furthermore, over time such arrangements could grow and have consequences that were totally unforeseeable at the moment that the exchange systems were initially established. Thus, the increased centralization and integration characteristic of Mississippian culture may be traced to attempts to deal with the new variability in yield characteristic of a maize-based agricultural system.

The evolution of agricultural systems

There is no doubt that agriculture, and changes in agricultural systems, may have major effects upon local demography and these, in turn, may affect social systems in radical ways. However, it is significant that differential fitness, the 'currency' of evolutionary change, requires that more than one state may be observed in the population of concern. If all individuals have exactly the same set of traits, evolutionary change is, by definition, impossible, because no differential fitness associated with specific traits can exist when only one set of traits exists. Cultural processes may be of major importance in determining which traits are acceptable to members of a culture. Therefore, a Darwinian view of cultural evolution does not restrict itself solely to the demographic aspects of cultural behaviours, but must also look inside the system and consider the impact of variable, culturally defined behaviours upon the further evolution of the system. I have dealt elsewhere with this distinction between the 'demographic' and 'symbolic' aspects of cultural-transmission systems under the rubric of cultural selection of the first and second types (CS$_1$ and CS$_2$: Rindos 1985).

Redirection of our thoughts to a Darwinian perspective requires a reinterpretation of most of our preconceptions regarding cultural practices and beliefs. We have generally seen the meaning of human innovations solely in terms of their *causal* role in cultural evolution. I claim that these innovations are better viewed as events that *facilitate* evolution. The distinction is of major importance. And again, I will draw upon a genetic analogy. Provine (1983) has recently reviewed some aspects of the development of Sewall Wright's genetic theorizing, and he provides a useful account of the changing interpretations given to Wright's theory of genetic drift. He notes that when Wright first proposed genetic drift in the late 1920s and early 1930s it was widely adopted to explain what appeared to be 'adaptively neutral' differences between species. However, with the development of the 'New Synthesis' in the 1940s and 1950s, it was discovered that many of these traits, in fact, were of adaptive significance. Given this change in intellectual atmosphere, Provine notes that Wright

> could now emphasize the view his shifting balance theory had incorporated from the very beginning – that random drift served the important function of providing novel genetic interaction systems upon which natural selection could act to yield more rapid progress of adaptive evolution than could occur under mass selection alone.
>
> (Provine 1983: 65)

Hence, the significance of random genetic drift is not that it *causes* evolution, but that it *facilitates* evolution. Likewise, cultural processes such as innovation or discovery are processes that *permit*, but do not directly cause, cultural change. In the case under consideration here, the true reason for cultural change may be detected only in the social and demographic consequences of agriculturally induced changes in environment and behaviour.

As should be apparent with a little reflection, the manifold variations produced in any cultural setting can explain nothing in and of themselves. If we were to claim that a given change in subsistence patterning resulted solely from a change in a cultural pattern, we have, in fact, explained nothing. We have merely recast the problem in new terms. Instead of wondering why the subsistence pattern changed we must now query why the culture changed. We cannot use the evolved capacity of humans within a cultural setting to respond to the environment as explanation for the specific cultural changes that have occurred within a given historical setting. To explain the specific we cannot merely invoke the general; instead, we should seek insights by investigating directly the system itself that is of interest.

Consider another example from the American Bottom. As already noted, it is likely that the 'introduction' of maize around AD 800 into the region actually marked the appearance of new varieties of flinty, early maturing maize which were stored as dry grain. Previously, it is likely that maize was grown for its immature ears which were stored in a processed form. Here, culinary and storage techniques and traditions interacted to affect the growth potential of the agricultural system. If a crop is stored in a processed form, the seed needed to plant the next year's crop must be estimated and left unharvested until it is mature. In a year with a particularly good crop, much food could be preserved and this could serve as a buffer against unpredictable reductions in other resources. Of course, the same can be done if the crop is stored as a dry grain. However, the potential growth rates of these two systems would not be the same.

Consider years of abundance: the stored crop is not consumed in its totality. If the stored crop were in a processed form, some might even end up going to waste. But if the stored crop were a dry grain, an alternative exists – planting of some of the left-over grain, increasing the area under cultivation by a slight amount. In this manner, potential mean productivity could rise as the result of a succession of favourable years. Storage of a crop in its reproductive form may increase the potential rate of growth of the system. However, this same identity of 'food' and 'seed' would have negative effects during bad seasons. Under conditions of moderate stress, some of the seed grain for the next season's planting could be consumed. Here, the farmer is willing to take a gamble that next year's crop will be sufficiently good that it is worth risking consuming some portion of the seed in the face of present needs. Of course, this is a risky tactic, in that it reduces the long-term stability of the system. And it is important to note that such a reduction in stability is far less likely to occur when the crop is stored in a processed form: a cultural and culinary marker sets the processed, 'edible' food apart from the 'seed'. In the most extreme form, the edible part of the plant is totally differentiated from the reproductive part both culturally and biologically (for example, manioc and many other tropical tubers). Here the much discussed stability of tropical systems of root-crop cultivation (cf. Hawkes 1989) may be seen, in part, as a function of cultural classification systems concerning what is edible.

Fitness and relative, limited adaptation

The distinction between culture seen as explanation and culture seen as the result of natural, evolutionary processes is neither trivial nor purely definitional. Instead, adopting the Darwinian perspective completely changes the manner in which we approach the historical, ethnographic, and archaeological records. It is not an easy point of view to adopt. Much of the aversion to treating cultural processes as natural arises from a cultural bias (Rindos 1985), and is largely centred upon the issue of the potency of human intentionality in explaining cultural change (Rindos 1984). Translated into evolutionary terms, the common-sense view of cultural change holds that

> the variations are generated as specific responses to adaptive needs – i.e. that the variations arising in cultural systems are directional, and

therefore the variations themselves, not selection, order evolutionary processes in human culture.

This observation is of great importance for the understanding of cultural processes, in that it completely eliminates any need to presume an adaptive function for all cultural traits. Traits, of course, may be adaptive but this is a result of the fact that they gave a relative advantage to the individuals with these traits. Here we analyse cultural traits in exactly the same terms used for the evolution of adaptations within any species. But we must also be willing to go beyond this analysis. Cultural traits may spread not because they are adaptive to some need but because they indirectly increase the relative fertility (fitness in the pure Darwinian sense) of individuals within a cultural setting. If, for example, religious affiliation is strongly transmitted from one generation to the next, then we can expect that over time (and all other things being equal) the proportion of individuals within any group belonging to 'procreative' religions such as Islam, Roman Catholicism, Orthodox Judaism, and Mormonism will rise. It is absurd to call any such change in the proportions of individuals belonging to these sects a result of an 'adaptation' by its members to any environmental 'need' or, put in other terms, that a positive correlation between relative fitness and environmental adaptation must always exist.

In a previous discussion of the spread of agricultural systems (Rindos 1984), I maintained that fitness and 'adaptiveness' might even show a negative correlation. The relative fitness induced in a culture by means of its agricultural behaviour is seen as being simply the result of a higher realized rate of population growth – agricultural behaviours increase the carrying capacity of the local environment for humans and, hence, the proportion of individuals per unit area who will have agricultural modes of subsistence will inevitably be larger than the proportion of individuals with most other subsistence strategies. It is important to realize that this will hold true even if agricultural behaviours bring with them a decrease in robustness, a decline in life expectancy, an increase in morbidity and mortality, or a higher infant mortality rate (accompanied, of course, by an even higher fertility rate). While all of these factors may easily be judged as indicators of decreased adaptation, the higher growth rate of agriculture will nevertheless favour it over other forms of human subsistence.

A very striking example of how fitness and adaptiveness may become decoupled may be seen by considering the relative fitness of competing agricultural traditions. Begin with the assumption that agricultural behaviours bring with them a decrease in overall 'adaptiveness' of human populations (as measured by the types of parameters mentioned above). Consider two competing agricultural populations, one of which has a more adaptive agricultural tradition than the other, measured in terms of variables such as stability in average yield. It is easily demonstrated (Rindos 1984: 254–85), that, on the average, decreased stability in productivity will increase the probability that a given agricultural tradition will spread. Here, instability in agricultural production serves as a driving force in spreading a particular agricultural tradition by literally driving out individuals to colonize new regions. Occasional episodes of lowered productivity, induced not by the environment but rather by the plants and techniques of the agricultural system itself, will cause the spread of that tradition to occur at a rate greater than that of other, more adaptive and stable, agricultural traditions. Hence, not only is agriculture more fit while being less adaptive, but a positive selection for instability in production will tend to increase the maladaptiveness of agricultural systems over time.

A recent volume, edited by Cohen and Armelagos (1984), presents abundant evidence, which indicates that the archaeological record is largely in accord with predictions that may be drawn from the co-evolutionary model for the origins and spread of agriculture. Under the co-evolutionary model, it would be predicted that major population stress would originate with highly developed agricultural systems – the phase of 'agricultural domestication' (Rindos 1984: 164–72 and see his discussion of population pressure [1984: 205–17]). It would be further intensified as agricultural systems developed and spread by means of the positive selection for optimally unstable systems during diffusion episodes.

These predictions stand in stark contrast to those of the two other contemporary schools modelling the origins of agriculture. The first school represents the mainstream of anthropological and archaeological theory. Despite great differences in approach by specific authors, it is unified by an adaptationistic, cultural-ecological perspective. An equilibrium-based analysis of cultural function and change is one of the major assumptions underlying work done by members of this school. I include here such authors as Flannery (1965, 1968, 1973), Binford (1968), Harris (1969, 1972, 1977), Bray (1976, 1977), Reed (1977), and Wright (1977). As Roosevelt (1984: 569) points out, an equilibrium-centred view of cultural change has clear implications in terms of stress on humans that might be found in the archaeological record: 'the equilibrium theory predicts that physiological stress should occur only rarely and that cultural adaptation should increasingly buffer people from stress'. Under this model, the transition to sedentism would be expected to be accompanied by a 'decrease in mortality'. Cultural ecology, with its emphasis upon adaptation and homeostasis, sees cultural change as motivated by human adaptation; *increased adaptiveness* should therefore result from realized cultural changes.

The other contemporary school of thought concerning agricultural origins applies a population-pressure model. This is best exemplified in the work of Cohen (1977); although others such as Smith (1972), Spooner (1972), Grigg (1976), and Abernathy (1979) have advanced similar views. The theory (which I will not criticize here on theoretical grounds) holds that cultural change is the result of human adaptations to their own increasing numbers. Population pressures generated by the slow increase of human populations forces new adaptations to be adopted if humans are simply to 'stay in the same place'; cultural change is the result of the need to *maintain adaptiveness*. Here, the predictions for the archaeological record would be 'that physiological stress should be recurrent and persistent, with particularly severe stress possibly occurring during incipient agriculture' (Roosevelt 1984: 569).

In Roosevelt's review (1984) of the archaeological indicators of skeletal stress, she was able to make the following generalizations:

> Although there is a relative lack of evidence for the Paleolithic stage, enough skeletons have been studied that it seems clear that seasonal and periodic stress regularly affected most prehistoric hunting-gathering populations. . . . What also seems clear is that severe and chronic stress . . . is not characteristic of these populations. There is no evidence of frequent, severe malnutrition, so the diet must have been adequate . . .
>
> Stress, however, does not seem to have become common and widespread until after the development of high degrees of sedentism, population density and reliance on intensive agriculture. At this stage in all regions the incidence of physiological stress increases greatly, and average mortality rates increase appreciably. . . . Stature in many populations appears to have been considerably lower than would be expected if genetically-determined height maxima had been reached, which suggests that the growth arrests documented by pathologies were causing stunting . . .
>
> It seems that a large proportion of most sedentary populations under intensive agriculture underwent chronic and life-threatening malnutrition and disease, especially during infancy and childhood. The causes of the nutritional stress are likely to have been the poverty of the staple crops in most nutrients except calories, periodic famines caused by the instability of the agricultural system, and chronic lack of food due to both population growth and economic expropriation by elites.
>
> (Roosevelt 1984: 572–3)

As Roosevelt notes in summary, '[t]he origin of agriculture, then, cannot accurately be attributed to the existence of unusually high levels of [population] pressure at the time.' Furthermore, the increased stress occurring with the appearance of developed agricultural systems contradicts the expectations of the cultural ecologists, whereas the general pattern and the specific timing of the appearance of indicators of greatly heightened stress is completely congruent with the predictions of the co-evolutionary model.

Natural selection and cultural change

The issue of *undirected* variation is critical to the development of a scientific understanding of human cultural evolution. Viewing variation as undirected brings about a change in the way in which we set about attempting to explain cultural evolution. Here, the spread of behaviour throughout a society, or the spread of a particular type of behaviour (rather than another) throughout the species, is the result of the fitness induced by that behaviour (and, again, I am using 'fitness' in a broad sense that includes both demographic and symbolic aspects and goes beyond simple genetic contribution to future generations). Rather than seeing change as a consequence of the adoption of a particular form of behaviour, emphasis is placed upon the historical *consequences* of a particular variant form of behaviour for the humans exhibiting that behaviour.

The critical issue in this context is whether natural selection is the process responsible for the changes that have occurred over time in human subsistence patterns. The centrality of natural selection in Darwinism arises from its ability to bring about evolution. From the Darwinian perspective, undirected variation is important for its role in fuelling the engine of evolutionary change by generating new forms, which may then be subject to selection. Indeed, we may claim confidently that without a true concept of undirected variation, natural selection is not only unnecessary but is actually impossible. Natural selection, within Darwinian theory, is the only directional force in evolution. If variation is less than undirected, then natural selection cannot be seen as a *creative* force in evolution and must perforce maintain its simple, pre-Darwinian role of removing those variant forms that accidentally deviate from the true type of the species (see discussion in Rindos 1984). Only if we see variation as being produced randomly with respect to selective pressures, may we claim that the directionality that may be observed in evolution over time is the result of natural selection.

References

Abernathy, V. (1979) *Population Pressure and Cultural Adjustment*, New York: Human Science Press.

Binford, L.R. (1968) 'Post-Pleistocene adaptations', in S. R. Binford and L. R. Binford (eds) *New Perspectives in Archaeology*, Chicago, IL: Aldine.

Boyd, R. and Richerson, J. (1985) *Culture and the Evolutionary Process*, Chicago, IL: University of Chicago Press.

Braun, D. (1983) 'Pots as tools', in J. A. Moore and A. S. Keene (eds) *Archaeological Hammers and Theories*, New York: Academic Press.

Bray, W. (1976) 'From predation to production: the nature of agricultural evolution in Mexico and Peru', in G. de G. Seveking, T. H. Longworth and K. E. Wilson (eds) *Problems in Economic and Social Archaeology*, London: Duckworth.

Bray, W. (1977) 'From foraging to farming in early Mexico', in J. V. S. Megaw (ed.) *Hunters, Gatherers and First Farmers beyond Europe*, Leicester: Leicester University Press.

Campbell, D.T. (1965) 'Variation and selective retention in sociocultural evolution', in R. W. Mack, G. Blanksten and H. R. Barringer (eds) *Social Change in Underdeveloped Areas: a reinterpretation of evolutionary theory*, Cambridge: Schenkman.

Campbell, D.T. (1976) 'Comment on Richards' "natural selection model for conceptual evolution"', *Philosophy of Science*, 44: 502–7.

Cavalli-Sforza, L.L. and Feldman, M.W. (1981) *Cultural Transmission and Evolution: a quantitative approach*, Princeton, NJ: Princeton University Press.

Chase, A.K. (1989) 'Domestication and domiculture in northern Australia: a social perspective', in D. R. Harris and G. C. Hillman (eds) *Foraging and Farming: the evolution of plant exploitation*, London: Unwin Hyman.

Chikwendu, V.E. and Okezie, C.E.A (1989) 'Factors responsible for the ennoblement of the African yams: inferences from experiments in yam domestication', in D. R. Harris and G. C. Hillman (eds) *Foraging and Farming: the evolution of plant exploitation*, London: Unwin Hyman.

Cohen, M.N. (1977) *The Food Crisis in Prehistory: overpopulation and the origins of agriculture*, New Haven, CT: Yale University Press.

Cohen, M.N. and Armelagos, G.J. (eds) (1984) *Paleopathology at the Origins of Agriculture*, Orlando, FL: Academic Press.

Flannery, K.V. (1965) 'The ecology of early food production in Mesopotamia', *Science*, 147: 1247–56.

Flannery, K.V. (1968) 'Archeological systems theory and early Mesoamerica', in B. J. Meggers (ed.) *Anthropological Archeology in the Americas*, Washington, DC: Anthropological Society of Washington.

Flannery, K.V. (1973) 'The origins of agriculture', *Annual Review of Anthropology*, 2: 271–310.

Grigg, D.B. (1976) 'Population pressure and agricultural change', *Progressive Geography*, 8: 135–76.

Harris, D.R. (1969) 'Agricultural systems, ecosystems and the origins of agriculture', in P. J. Ucko and G. W. Dimbleby (eds) *The Domestication and Exploitation of Plants and Animals*, London: Duckworth.

Harris, D.R. (1972) 'The origins of agriculture in the tropics', *American Scientist*, 60: 180–93.

Harris, D.R. (1977) 'Alternative pathways toward agriculture', in C. A. Reed (ed.) *Origins of Agriculture*, The Hague: Mouton.

Harris, D.R. (1989) 'An evolutionary continuum of people–plant interaction', in D. R. Harris and G. C. Hillman (eds) *Foraging and Farming: the evolution of plant exploitation*, London: Unwin Hyman.

Hawkes, J.G. (1989) 'The domestication of roots and tubers in the American tropics', in D. R. Harris and G. C. Hillman (eds) *Foraging and Farming: the evolution of plant exploitation*, London: Unwin Hyman.

Johns, T. (1989) 'A chemical-ecological model of root and tuber domestication in the Andes', in D. R. Harris and G. C. Hillman (eds) *Foraging and Farming: the evolution of plant exploitation*, London: Unwin Hyman.

Ladizinsky, G. (1989) 'Origin and domestication of the Southwest Asian grain legumes', in D. R. Harris and G. C. Hillman (eds) *Foraging and Farming: the evolution of plant exploitation*, London: Unwin Hyman.

Marks, J., Staski, E. and Schiffer, M.B. (1983) 'Cultural evolution: a return to the basics', *Nature*, 302: 15–16.

Mayr, E. (1942) *Systematics and the Origin of Species*, New York: Columbia University Press.

Mayr, E. (1969) *Principles of Systematic Zoology*, New York: McGraw-Hill.

Mayr, E. (1982) *The Growth of Biological Thought*, Cambridge, MA: Harvard University Press.

Pearsall, D.M. (1989) 'Adaptation of prehistoric hunter-gatherers to the high Andes: the changing role of plant resources', in D. R. Harris and G. C. Hillman (eds) *Foraging and Farming: the evolution of plant exploitation*, London: Unwin Hyman.

Provine, W. (1983) 'The development of Wright's theory of evolution: systematics, adaptation and drift', in M. Grene (ed.) *Dimensions of Darwinism: themes and counter themes in twentieth-century evolutionary theory*, Cambridge: Cambridge University Press.

Reed, C.A. (1977) 'Origins of agriculture: discussion and some conclusions', in C. A. Reed (ed.) *Origins of Agriculture*, The Hague: Mouton.

Rindos, D. (1984) *The Origins of Agriculture: an evolutionary perspective*, New York: Academic Press.

Rindos, D. (1985) 'Darwinian selection, symbolic variation and the evolution of culture', *Current Anthropology*, 26: 65–88.

Rindos, D. (1986) 'The evolution of the cultural capacity: structuralism, sociobiology and cultural selectionism', *Current Anthropology*, 27: 315–32.

Rindos, D. and Johannessen, S. (1988) 'Agriculture and cultural change in the American Bottom', in T. E. Emerson and R. B. Lewis (eds) *Cahokia and its Hinterlands*, Kent, OH: Kent State University Press.

Roosevelt, A.C. (1984) 'Population, health, and the evolution of subsistence: conclusions from the conference', in M. N. Cohen and G. A. Armelagos (eds) *Paleopathology at the Origins of Agriculture*, Orlando, FL: Academic Press.

Smith, P.E.L. (1972) 'Changes in population pressure in archaeological explanation', *World Archaeology*, 4: 5–18.

Spooner, B. (ed.) (1972) *Population Growth: anthropological implications*, Cambridge, MA: MIT Press.

Watson, P.J. (1989) 'Early plant cultivation in the Eastern Woodlands of North America', in D. R. Harris and G. C. Hillman (eds) *Foraging and Farming: the evolution of plant exploitation*, London: Unwin Hyman.

Wright, H.E., Jr. (1977) 'Environmental change and the origin of agriculture in the Old and New Worlds', in C. A. Reed (ed.) *Origins of Agriculture*, The Hague: Mouton.

Zohary, D. (1989) 'Domestication of the Southwest Asian Neolithic crop assemblage of cereals, pulses, and flax: the evidence from the living plants', in D. R. Harris and G. C. Hillman (eds) *Foraging and Farming: the evolution of plant exploitation*, London: Unwin Hyman.

Update: Rindos' continuing influence

Peter White

This paper was almost the last in a series, in which Rindos had developed both the important general concept of cultural selectionism and the specific idea of a very long-term co-evolution of people and plants. An expanded account of his Darwinian approach was developed in Rindos (1989). He argues there that culture is an entity in an evolutionary sense, within which there is a 'tremendous store' of variation. This variation can arise in many

ways, including human decisions, experiments and cultural bias. All variations are selected for demographic and/or symbolic 'fitness' at the cultural
level; in Rindos' words, 'selection may be working on phenotypically transmitted traits that are coded as parts of a culturally defined inheritance
system, but it is selection nonetheless' (1989: 40). Before his death in 1996,
he was working on a Darwinian account of the settlement of Australia
(Rindos and Webb 1997).

Rindos' ideas have been significant to those outside the neo-Darwinian
stream. His work is an important historical contribution, alongside Higgs
(1972), Ford (1985), Harris (1989 [this volume], 1996) and Smith (2001),
to our understanding of domesticatory relationships and how we concep-
tualise early agriculture. Harris (1989 [this volume]) discusses Rindos' work
in historical context and with reference to alternative cultural explanations.

During the last 15 years the idea that cultural change can be explored
within a Darwinian (or neo-Darwinian) framework has continued to be
developed in various guises (e.g. Maschner 1996; Barton and Clark 1997;
Lyman and O'Brien 1998). The most wide-ranging exposition, specifically
related to large archaeological questions, is by Shennan (2002), who in
Chapter 3, entitled 'Culture as an evolutionary system', reviews many recent
approaches.

Smith (2000) divides Darwinian approaches into three 'styles':

- Evolutionary psychology, which argues that the patterning within the
  present-day human mind has been established by very long-term selective pressures which have developed a number of cognitive fields.
  Mithen (1996) is one of the rare examples which directly addresses
  archaeological evidence; most others infer prehistory.
- Classical Darwinian 'behavioural ecology' views human behaviour as
  simply that of another unique species, making 'decisions' on the basis of
  hopeful future reproductive success. Optimal foraging theory is perhaps
  the best known application in archaeology (see papers in Winterhalder
  and Smith 1981 and Kennett and Winterhalder 2006 for early and
  recent, respectively, developments).
- Dual inheritance theory, which argues that cultural transmission occurs
  through specifically cultural mechanisms analogous to genetic ones
  (Boyd and Richerson 1985). Rindos' viewpoint lies within this framework. Other important aspects are Dawkins' (1976) concept of 'memes',
  which are basically self-replicating ideas, and Cullens' related, but much
  more elaborated, cultural virus theory (2000), which allows both for
  undirected variation and heritage constraint in the cultural evolutionary
  process. Dawkins and Cullen, unlike Rindos, reject the 'whole culture'
  as the basic unit of cultural evolution.

In relation to the specific geographical area Rindos discusses, Rindos and
Johannessen (1991) expanded the discussion given here. Smith (1992) and

Watson's update in this volume point to more recent research. Additionally, Gremillion (1997) presents a series of studies concerned with both domestication processes and their ecological and cultural context. Hart (1999) brings together Rindos' co-evolutionary theory and Sewell Wright's shifting balance theory to develop a model of adoption and evolution of maize agriculture in the Eastern Woodlands.

References

Barton, C.M. and Clark, G.A. (eds) (1997) *Rediscovering Darwin: evolutionary theory and archaeological explanation*, Archaeological Papers of the American Anthropological Association No. 7, Washington, DC: American Anthropological Association.

Boyd, R. and Richerson, P.J. (1985) *Culture and the Evolutionary Process*, Chicago, IL: University of Chicago Press.

Cullen, B.S. (2000) *Contagious Ideas*, Oxford: Oxbow Books.

Dawkins, R. (1976) *The Selfish Gene*, Oxford: Oxford University Press.

Ford, R.I. (1985) 'The processes of plant food production in prehistoric North America', in R. I. Ford (ed.) *Prehistoric Food Production in North America*, Anthropological Paper No.75, Ann Arbor, MI: Museum of Anthropology, University of Michigan.

Gremillion, K.J. (ed.) (1997) *Plants, People, and Landscapes*, Tuscaloosa, AL: University of Alabama Press.

Harris, D.R. (1989) 'An evolutionary continuum of people–plant interaction', in D. R. Harris and G. C. Hillman (eds) *Foraging and Farming: the evolution of plant exploitation*, London: Unwin Hyman.

Harris, D.R. (1996) 'Domesticatory relationships of people, plants and animals', in R. Ellen and K. Fukui (eds) *Redefining Nature: ecology, culture and domestication*, Oxford: Berg.

Hart, J.P. (1999) 'Maize agriculture evolution in the Eastern Woodlands of North America: a Darwinian perspective', *Journal of Archaeological Method and Theory*, 6: 137–80.

Higgs, E.S. (ed.) (1972) *Papers in Economic Prehistory*, Cambridge: Cambridge University Press.

Kennett, D.J. and Winterhalder, B. (eds) (2006) *Behavioral Ecology and the Transition to Agriculture*, Berkeley, CA: University of California Press.

Lyman, R.L. and O'Brien, M.J. (1998) 'The goals of evolutionary archaeology: history and explanation', *Current Anthropology*, 39: 615–52.

Maschner, H.D.G. (ed.) (1996) *Darwinian Archaeologies*, New York: Plenum Press.

Mithen, S. (1996) *Prehistory of the Mind*, London: Thames and Hudson.

Rindos, D. (1989) 'Undirected variation and the Darwinian explanation of cultural change', *Archaeological Method and Theory*, 1: 1–46.

Rindos, D. and Johannessen, S. (1991) 'Human–plant interactions and cultural change in the American Bottom', in T. E. Emmerson and R. B. Lewis (eds) *Cahokia and the Hinterlands: Middle Mississippian cultures of the Midwest*, Urbana, IL: University of Illinois Press.

Rindos, D. and Webb, R.E. (1997) 'The mode and tempo of the initial human colonization of empty landmasses: Sahul and the Americas compared', in

C. M. Barton and G. A. Clark (eds) *Rediscovering Darwin: evolutionary theory and archaeological explanation*, Archaeological Papers of the American Anthropological Association No. 7, Washington, DC: American Anthropological Association.

Shennan, S. (2002) *Genes, Memes and Human History*, London: Thames and Hudson.

Smith, B.D. (ed.) (1992) *Rivers of Change: essays on early agriculture in the Eastern North America*, Washington, DC: Smithsonian Institution Press.

Smith, B.D. (2001) 'Low-level food production', *Journal of Archaeological Research*, 9: 1–43.

Smith, E.A. (2000) 'Three styles in the evolutionary analysis of human behavior', in L. Cronk, N. Chagnon and W. Irons (eds) *Adaptation and Human Behavior*, New York: Aldine de Gruyter.

Winterhalder, B. and Smith, E.A. (eds) (1981) *Hunter-Gatherer Foraging Strategies*, Chicago, IL: University of Chicago Press.

4 Non-affluent foragers

Resource availability, seasonal shortages, and the emergence of agriculture in Panamanian tropical forests

Dolores R. Piperno

Introduction

The concept that hunters and gatherers are affluent, i.e. that there exists a positive relationship between population and available resources enabling a considerable degree of cultural development, has become a dominant theme in studies of foraging societies, past and present. Ethnographic studies over the past 15 years have demonstrated that many foraging groups have fairly stable and secure resource bases, leading to a life that is not nasty, brutish, or short (Lee and DeVore 1968) to quote the original counter-argument to traditional portrayals of hunting and gathering.

Recent archaeological investigations have carried this concept even further. Economic, technological, and settlement data from Late Pleistocene and early Holocene occupations in many parts of the world have been interpreted as indicating that prehistoric hunters and gatherers were sedentary, increasing and intensifying production of resources, and developing complex social organizations (Koyama and Thomas 1981; Price and Brown 1985). The broad economic shifts immediately antecedent to the Neolithic, variously called the Archaic in the Americas or the Mesolithic in parts of Europe, are increasingly seen as parts of trends toward population growth, settlement nucleation and permanence, and social complexity. Domesticated food sources are almost viewed as by-products of the successes of early Holocene hunting and gathering (see the papers in Price and Brown 1985).

The corollary to the view that hunters and gatherers are well provisioned with high-quality, reliable resources, and spend little time in the food quest (but see Hawkes and O'Connell 1981; O'Connell and Hawkes 1981) is the argument that early farmers experienced diminishing returns to labour as they were forced to increasingly rely on lower quality, less preferred food-stuffs. Therefore, food production, though severely increasing the demands of labour, was necessitated by increasing population densities and/or declining wild resources (Binford 1968; Cohen 1977).

In reading this literature one can lose sight of the fact that hunters and gatherers are adversely affected by periodic imbalances with resources, and random, severe fluctuations in rates of mortality and fertility brought about by small group size and high mobility. Negative aspects of foraging life have been underplayed in recent evaluations of prehistoric non-food producing societies because of the view that marginal environments occupied by present-day foragers represent an inappropriate analog by which to judge the environs of archaeological hunters and gatherers. This is undoubtedly true for some, but not for all situations.

This chapter re-examines these issues with regard to data from the tropical forests of Panama. Characteristics of the natural environment as potential food sources for hunter-gatherers are described, and evidence is presented that wild resources, especially plant carbohydrates, were severely limited, unstable, and unpredictable, making life as a forager tenuous and highly mobile. It is suggested that the initial domestication of indigenous plants and acceptance of introduced cultivars represented a low-cost strategy to buffer resource variation and unpredictability. Wild resource availability in Panamanian forests is estimated by reference to plant and, to a lesser degree, animal distribution and fluctuations in mature and late secondary vegetational formations. Given the limited mammalian fauna, assessments of plant productivity and quality should lead to a reasonably accurate picture of the food supply. Archaeological settlement and botanical data are then presented for early human occupations of the forests, which were apparently numerous, stable, and, in the Darwinian sense of the word, successful, only after food producing strategies were employed 7000 years ago.

Archaic and early food producing economies in American tropical forests have seldom been considered from either an archaeological perspective or one that considers the productivity of the natural plant environment. Archaeological sequences that span long periods of the Holocene are notoriously difficult to acquire, and relevant subsistence, settlement, and demographic data are accordingly rare. Similarly, insufficient information about the highly diverse and complex tropical forest flora and fauna make estimations of food availability in natural situations difficult. In Panama, neither of these factors pose singular problems. The Proyecto Santa Maria, a large multi-disciplinary archaeological project directed by Anthony Ranere and Richard Cooke, has accumulated an impressive body of information on settlement, economy, and population over the past 9000 years in Central Pacific Panama. Phytolith, pollen, and macrobotanical data on wild and domesticated plant usage spanning this period are available.

The tropical forests of Panama are arguably among the best studied in the world. The Missouri Botanical Garden sponsored a formal effort to catalogue all the plants occurring in Panama. Published as *The Flora of Panama* (*Annals of the Missouri Botanical Garden* 1943–1981), it includes descriptions, ranges, and habitats for over 5000 species of plants. Collections by specialists continue in remote and inaccessible areas, and recent updates of the expanded floral inventory have been published (D'Arcy and Correa 1985). In addition, long-term ecological studies of semi-evergreen forests have been made, leading to new information on forest dynamics, seasonal rhythms, and multi-annual fluctuations of resources (Leigh *et al.* 1982). Some mature sections of these forests have been mapped and recorded, tree by tree (Hubbell and Foster 1983), providing sound quantitative data on resource density.

Intensive investigations have been carried out in the deciduous forests in Guanacaste Province, Costa Rica (Frankie *et al.* 1974; Opler *et al.* 1980). They probably form the nearest modern analogue to formations that once existed in much of the Proyecto Santa Maria study area, but which are now almost completely gone. Deciduous and semi-evergreen forests are focused on here because it is in these contexts that the earliest domesticated foodstuffs are found.

Wild resource availability in tropical forests

The question of carbohydrate limitation

In analysing the relationship between tropical-forest peoples and their environment, much attention has been paid to the role of protein scarcity as a major factor limiting population size and permanence (e.g. Gross 1975; Ross 1978; Beckerman 1979; Chagnon and Hames 1979, 1980). However, very little consideration has been given to the issues of caloric extraction and its predictability and reliability due to seasons and multi-annual fluctuations of wild-plant resources. Earle (1980: 3) reminds us that the 'primary objective of all procurement strategies under investigation is their caloric yield, in as much as energy is a most basic requirement of any population'. Recent ethnographic data from tropical forests suggest that the traditional emphasis on protein availability has indeed been misdirected.

Milton (1984) presents evidence showing that fisher-farmers in Amazonia exist at much higher population density than neighbouring hunter-gatherers primarily because they have an ample supply of carbohydrates, while experiencing seasonal shortages of protein. Hunter-gatherers were limited mainly by severe seasonal and annual shortages of carbohydrates from wild resources. Hart and Hart (1986) document a similar situation in the rain forests of Zaire, where Mbuti pygmies, though having ample meat resources all year round, experience severe seasonal shortages of starch-dense foods from wild plants.

Further, it is suggested that neither protein nor carbohydrates as such, but the relative proportions of calories derived from plant and animal foods, are important in determining population size. The demographic implications of a subsistence strategy that derives calories mainly from animal foods have received little attention from anthropologists, but they appear to be extremely important. Milton (1984) notes that, in general, populations oriented toward securing food from the first trophic level (plants) are numerically more abundant than populations relying primarily on animal resources.

A primary reason for this relationship is the high metabolic costs of extracting calories from protein, which becomes necessary if meat is not high in fat.

> Typically, the higher the trophic level the fewer the organisms. . . . A population meeting much of its energetic as well as protein needs from animal food will require considerably more meat each day to sustain itself than will a population meeting energy needs from plant foods and using animal foods only to meet protein requirements. Given the same amount of available protein the second population will be able to exist at a higher density, all else being equal. . . . Indeed, catabolizing protein for energy is a wasteful process because of the costs involved in degradation of the individual carbon skeletons of the amino acids.
>
> (Milton 1984: 19–20)

It is predicted that a resource base deficient in available carbohydrates, especially from plants, should support only small populations. Such a situation appears to have existed in Panama. A complete list of forest plants with edible parts would be lengthy, as would a list of wild plants incidentally eaten at one time or another by Archaic and early food-producing populations in Panama. However, the number of edible resources turns out to be an inaccurate measure of environmental productivity, as inspection of species inventoried in dry and semi-evergreen forests shows that few are heavy producers of food calories; good starch producers are scarce (Frankie *et al.* 1974; Croat 1978; Hubbell 1979; Opler *et al.* 1980; Hubbell and Foster 1983; Foster and Piperno field observations). Wild herbaceous perennials with large roots and tubers that might serve as good energy sources, such as *Dioscorea, Calathea, Ipomoea, Heliconia,* and *Xanthosoma,* are scarce in undisturbed contexts. They are, however, common in secondary growth, a point that is explored further below.

   In addition, useful plants tend to be too dispersed in mature forests to support sizeable, even semi-permanent human communities. That tropical forests have a great diversity of species and widely dispersed food sources are hardly new revelations. However, quantitative data on these patterns are now available from dry forests in Guanacaste Province, Costa Rica and semi-evergreen forest on Barro Colorado Island (BCI), Panama (Hubbell 1979; Hubbell and Foster 1983).

   In the 400–600-year-old forest on BCI (Piperno 1990) only 33 species out of 186 (with diameter at breast height of at least 20 cm) had an average density of one or more trees per hectare (Hubbell and Foster 1983). Many forest plants bear small fruits no more than 2–3 cm in diameter, which are consumed and dispersed by bats, birds, and other forest animals. Large quantities of such fruits would have to be collected and processed to provide a significant level of energy for human consumption. One must also take into account the high proportion of plants with secondary or toxic compounds

(Janzen 1969; Freeland and Janzen 1974), which either would render them inedible or lead to increased processing time to achieve edible foodstuffs.

Hubbell's and Foster's studies have shown that many trees in the forest are clumped, i.e. they show significantly greater probabilities of one or more conspecifics among their nearest neighbours than would be expected statistically. However, for a number of reasons, too much significance should not be attached to this in relation to the human exploitation of resources. Clumped dispersion patterns are exhibited at very local scales and many species show a greater tendency to be clumped simply because they are among the most common. Furthermore 'clumped' species are still widely dispersed in space when compared to, say, the dense stands of wild legumes, cactuses, and grasses that fed Mesoamerican Archaic populations (Flannery 1968, 1986). For example, Flannery (1986) estimates that *mesquite* (*Prosopis* sp.) and other wild plants known to have been heavily exploited during the Pre-Ceramic period in the Oaxaca Valley achieve densities of several hundred individuals per hectare. Compare this figure with tree density in dry forests, where the degree of clumping is greatest because of decreased species diversity, and yet no more than 12 adult conspecifics can be expected to occur within 100 m of an adult of that species (Hubbell 1979). The combination of these factors – high diversity, dispersion, and the production of predominantly small fruits – makes for resources whose utilization costs in terms of search and handling (collecting, processing) time are high.

Palms are frequently cited as providing a major source of calories and perhaps high-quality protein for tropical forest groups (e.g. Levi-Strauss 1950; Beckerman 1979; Hawkes *et al.* 1982). The extensive use of wild plants today by South American indigenous populations is heavily oriented toward palm products. It is of major significance then that palms are rare or inconspicuous components of mature and late secondary dry and semi-evergreen forests in Costa Rica and Panama. Major economic taxa such as *Acrocomia vinifera* (corozo palm), *Euterpe* sp., *Manicaria* sp., and *Bactris gasipaes* (peach palm) do not appear on the extensive species lists available from these areas, nor have they been observed in these forests (author and Robin Foster, observations) or in those of the same type from other regions in Panama (Hugh Churchill and Greg DeNevers, pers. comm.). Peach palm, an important source of calories to contemporary indigenous populations, is almost certainly an introduction, and the same may be true of the corozo palm. Janzen (1983) notes that in Costa Rica it is never found in any habitat except sites disturbed by humans: pastures, old fields, roadsides, and house sites. The situation is the same in Panama and Janzen suspects, as I do, that the palm was introduced into southern Central America.

Deciduous forests, especially, are depauperate in palms. There are virtually none in extensive stretches of Santa Rosa National Park and other areas of Guanacaste Province, Costa Rica, far removed from human influences (Frankie *et al.* 1974; Opler *et al.* 1980; author's observations). Gallery forests today contain numbers of *Scheelia zonensis* and *Bactris* spp., as they no doubt did in the past, and edaphically distinctive sites like seasonal and stream-fed swamps may have contained concentrations of such species as *Elaeis oleifera* and *Bactris* sp. But it is clear that in deciduous forest the availability of palms is low, and that they could hardly have provided much in the way of food to hunting and gathering populations.

In sum, the picture that emerges is an environment seriously deficient in available carbohydrates. There are certainly many edible species, but these are dispersed in space, supply little in the way of bulk, and are likely to yield low returns per unit of foraging time because their search and handling costs are high. These are not the only negative aspects of a foraging existence, for the seasonality of wild tropical resources may have presented other serious problems to human exploitation.

Seasonality of resources

Seasonality has long been considered an important factor influencing many aspects of hunting and gathering life. It determines changes in diet, patterns of mobility, group size, and reproductive strategy (e.g. Lee 1979; Wilmsen 1982). As Hill *et al.* (1984) have noted, the effects of seasonal variability on human behaviour are generally considered to be greater at higher latitudes and least pronounced in equatorial regions. However, recent studies of seasonal rhythms in tropical forests leave little doubt that marked seasonality of rainfall in tropical environments can have fundamental effects on biological productivity that parallel seasonal temperature changes at higher latitudes (Harris 1978; Leigh *et al.* 1982).

Many forest species show considerable seasonal variation in phenological activity. In the semi-deciduous forests of Panama there are two peaks of fruiting, occurring in September–October and March–June. The late wet and early dry seasons (November–February) are known as the 'season of scarcity', when wild plant resources, including fruits, nuts, and young leaves, are at a minimum and, in response, mammals are leaner and fewer in number (Foster 1982a). In deciduous forests there is a single peak of fruiting occurring during March–June and especially at the end of the dry season in April, so the lean season here is much longer (Frankie *et al.* 1974; Opler *et al.* 1980).

Multi-annual variation in vegetal production can also be extreme. There are years when many species do not fruit, or fruit very little, after having produced copious or moderate amounts in preceding years. Two-year lags in production have been noted for several species (Foster 1982a). These phenomena, though not widely discussed in the literature, are common to many tropical trees. After rainy dry seasons, a circumstance which happens on average about once every five years, near-famine conditions exist, with virtually no fruit production occurring. Animal populations during these years are under severe stress, exemplified by their leaner body weight and high mortality rates (Foster 1982b).

Tropical forests have often been depicted as benign, stable environments rich in wild plant resources resulting from the diversity and productivity of plant biomass. However, the Panamanian example makes it clear that neither the stability nor the quality of the edible resource base is positively correlated with the diversity and overall productivity of the ecosystem. Carbohydrates are in short supply. Seasonal and annual scarcities of high-quality fruit and leaf items occur, which, in turn, cause fluctuations in the availability of animals. Recent ethnographic evidence from Amazonia documents the implications of the resource base for human habitation. Milton (1984) found that the Maku, a group of interfluve hunter-gatherers, experienced serious seasonal shortages of carbohydrates from wild fruits and other forest products, during which time they gave meat or labour to neighbouring horticulturalists (who were experiencing seasonal shortages of protein) in exchange for manioc.

The natural environment of Panama would have presented serious constraints on environmental adaptation by foraging groups. Selective pressures favoured small group sizes, high mobility, and the enforcement of appropriate cultural reproductive measures to ensure small, highly mobile populations. This portrayal of a rather tenuous existence hardly fits the concept of affluent foragers. I suggest that in these circumstances an economic strategy predicated on some degree of food production would result in a more predictable, secure, and synchronous resource base, in addition to a substantial increase in the total recoverable yield during any single year.

I suspect that the proximal cause of the shift toward horticulture may have been a conscious, short-term goal of ensuring the society's immediate needs, i.e. getting them through the lean periods that occurred every year and avoiding the sudden and unpredictable crashes that occurred every few years. Ultimately, one of the results was a very substantial increase in population, largely made possible by the dramatically increased calorific food base from domesticated plants and also from useful wild plants whose reproductive fitness and densities were increased by the developing agroecology. Evidence for the earliest domesticated plants in Panama and their ecological correlates and consequences will now be presented.

Early plant domestication in Panama

The Proyecto Santa Maria (PSM), which is studying human adaptations in the Santa Maria watershed of Central Pacific Panama, has carried out systematic surveys from the coast to the Continental Divide and discovered over 500 archaeological sites, 250 of which are pre-Ceramic, or at least 'aceramic' (Cooke and Ranere 1984; Weiland 1984, n.d.; Ranere n.d.). Archaeobotanical analysis has been carried out on stratified deposits from eight rockshelters, one early 1st millennium bc nucleated village, and one late 1st millennium bc village. Seven of the rockshelters contain both pre-ceramic and early ceramic components which are dated by radiocarbon from

6700 bc to 1000 bc. It is possible to trace over a period of 9000 years the initial and partial conversion of foraging into horticultural economies, the elaboration of these into slash-and-burn (swidden) systems, and, after a 4000-year period of relatively small-scale cultivation, the development of fully agricultural economies that supported nucleated and sedentary villages.

The PSM has accumulated an extraordinary amount of data on subsistence, settlement, and demography, and much of this is still being analysed. In broad outline, it appears that the region was very sparsely inhabited until around 7000 years ago, when the number of sites and the density of material found in them increased dramatically. Bifacial flaking as a strategy for shaping chipped stone tools disappears from Central Panama before 5000 bc (Cooke and Ranere 1984; Ranere n.d.). Only ten sites with bifacial work have been identified, whereas pre-Ceramic occupations without bifacial work and hence dating from 5000 bc to 2500 bc number about 250 (Weiland 1984, n.d.). At several excavated rockshelters, occupations do not begin until 5000 bc or shortly after, and at others very small amounts of bifacial and associated material are overlain by substantially greater quantities of later pre-ceramic debris. The bifacial assemblages indicate that the natural environment supported very small, widely dispersed populations until 7000 years ago, when a dramatic increase in population number and density becomes apparent. This demographic upturn appears to be associated with the introduction of maize, and almost certainly other crops, by 5000 bc.

Maize

We have documented an early pattern of seed cropping in Central Panama. Maize pollen and phytoliths were recovered from the pre-Ceramic occupation of a rockshelter, Cueva de los Ladrones, the earliest levels of which are radiocarbon dated to 4910 bc (Piperno and Husum-Clary 1984; Piperno *et al.* 1985). Maize phytoliths are also present in the pre-Ceramic levels of another rockshelter radiocarbon dated to 5125 bc. This evidence confirms suspicions long held by botanists (e.g. Pickersgill and Heiser 1977; Pickersgill 1989) that early dispersals of primitive maize from Mexico to South America occurred. It indicates that cultivation practices coeval, or nearly coeval, with those in highland Mexico (MacNeish 1967) and Peru (Kaplan *et al.* 1973) were present in the humid tropical lowland forest of Panama.

Because phytolith analysis is a relatively recent development in archaeobotany, a brief digression on the technique and on the maize-identification system used is necessary. Phytoliths are the most ubiquitous type of plant material recovered from tropical archaeological sites, and they appear to be sensitive, accurate, and reliable indicators of prehistoric cropping patterns and land usage; in some cases, even more so than either pollen or macrobotanical remains. Many plants, both monocots and dicots, contribute highly diagnostic shapes that are constant within species sampled from widely different environmental regions, and phytoliths are no more prone to vertical and horizontal movement in soils after deposition than are pollen grains (Piperno 1984, 1985a, 1985b, 1985c, 1988a; Piperno and Starczak 1985).

The maize-identification procedure rests on morphological and metric attributes of 'cross-shaped' phytoliths found only in maize. These attributes are short axis length, three-dimensional structure, and percentages of cross-shaped phytoliths in leaf specimens. They have been determined for 23 races of maize, six races of teosinte, and 39 wild grasses forming the native Panicoid grass cover of Panama. To provide a measure of interpopulation variability of phytoliths, four replicate samples of different plants were studied for wild species where cross- or dumbbell-shaped phytoliths were most common. For five races of maize, husks, leaves, and tassels of four replicate samples from distinct plants were studied (Piperno 1984, 1988a; Piperno and Starczak 1985).

The results indicate that shapes and sizes of short-cell phytoliths are constant in, and characteristic of, species in which they occur, regardless of environmental conditions of growth. Moreover, there is clearly a correlation between the types of phytoliths and the taxonomic affinities of plants containing them. Therefore, short-cell phytolith morphology and size must be under a great deal of genetic control. Maize phytoliths were consistently larger than those of most wild grasses ($P < 0.05$) and displayed a predominance of 'Variant 1-type' (Piperno 1984) three-dimensional morphology, in contrast to many wild grasses. These variables of modern plants were used in a discriminant function analysis, which demonstrated that maize and wild grasses could be separated into two groups on a formal statistical basis (Piperno and Starezak 1985; Piperno 1988a). A discriminant function analysis of archaeological cross-shaped phytoliths indicated that the pre-Ceramic deposits mentioned above, dated to the late 6th and early 5th millennia bc, contained maize (Piperno 1988a), confirming identifications made on a more intuitive basis (Piperno 1984; Piperno *et al.* 1985).

It has often been assumed, for rather tenuous reasons (see Rindos 1984), that the cultivation of root and tuber crops would have been the earliest form of food production adopted in the humid tropics. However, consideration of the ecology of maize and its probable wild ancestor teosinte, and of the early evolutionary history of maize, shows why its occurrence 7000 years ago in Central Pacific Panama is not surprising. Recent protein evidence assembled by Doebley, Goodman, and others indicates that of six extant teosinte varieties, the Balsas populations, native to the seasonally dry Balsas watershed of western Mexico, are genetically closest to maize and may be its wild ancestor (Doebley 1983; Doebley *et al.* 1984; Smith *et al.* 1985; cf. Wilkes 1989). The Tehuacan Valley, where a completely domesticated maize morphologically far removed from teosinte was present 7000 years ago, and indeed all of the Central Mexican highland region, may have been marginal at best to the earliest evolutionary history of maize, if maize, as seems possible, was domesticated considerably earlier in the wetter, low- to mid-altitudinal environments of western Mexico.

A description of the general ecology of the regions where Balsas teosinte is found applies almost equally well to Central Pacific Panama – thorn scrub and tropical deciduous forest, warm, seasonally dry, receiving an annual rainfall of 1200–2000 mm. Primitive races of maize were then pre-adapted to the environments of the study region. The similarity of ecology may have promoted a rapid spread of early maize; although an average diffusion rate of only 2 km a year is required to bring the plant from western Mexico to Central Panama by 7000 years ago, assuming that maize domestication was well underway by 8000 years ago. Rates of 1 km per year have been proposed for the spread of wheat and barley from Southwest Asia into Europe, through environments that sometimes differed drastically in rainfall, temperature, length of growing season, and photoperiod (Ammerman and Cavalli-Sforza 1984). The process by which maize may have spread is not considered here, but Ammerman and Cavalli-Sforza's model for Europe of local small-scale movements of individuals may be preferable to postulating long-distance population migrations or population replacement.

Recently, maize pollen has been discovered in geological deposits from the Calima Valley, Colombia, radiocarbon dated to 5300 bc (Monsalve 1985). Maize phytoliths are also present in the pre-Ceramic late Vegas occupation of the Santa Elena Peninsula, Ecuador, dated to the late 6th millennium bc (Piperno 1988b). It seems that we may not as yet have placed the earliest date on maize in Central Panama and that the diffusion from North to South America was indeed a fairly rapid one through seasonally dry, warm environments.

Other crops

No other crop plants have as yet been evidenced during the period from 7000 to 1000 bc. It is exceedingly difficult to demonstrate the presence of root crops, especially because many, including manioc, *Xanthosoma* sp., and sweet potato, have no identifiable siliceous remains. Squash (*Cucurbita*) phytoliths do not occur until about 300 bc, in contexts associated with nucleated and sedentary villages. However, because the rinds of different squash varieties appear to be somewhat capricious in terms of their production of the distinctive spherical, scalloped phytoliths, I believe their late appearance may not indicate a late introduction of *Cucurbita* itself, but perhaps of different species moving as a complex with productive races of maize from South America. Despite the paucity of crop plants recovered thus far, it is probable that maize was only one of a large number of species taken into cultivation by 7000 years ago.

There is a significant degree of variability between the phytolith records of the excavated rockshelters. On-site cultivation of maize is not indicated for several shelters during either the Pre-Ceramic or the early Ceramic period. At two sites 80 per cent of the fine-silt phytolith record is contributed by the remains of arboreal fruits and seeds such as *Chrysobalanus icaco* and *Hirtella* spp., and there is no indication of environmental disturbance near the sites in the form of grass, sedge, or *Heliconia* phytoliths. A long-term, stable orientation toward the exploration of tree products seems to be indicated, qualified, however, by the fact that we can say little about the possible contribution of root crops.

It would surely be misleading to assume that all residential groups in Central Panama from 5000 to 1000 bc were cultivating crops, the same crops, or the same crop mixtures. Considerable variation in subsistence practices probably existed, with economic reciprocity between foragers and farmers occurring that may have further raised the carrying capacity of the region. Local groups no doubt engaged to varying degrees in each economic strategy from one year to the next. Hence, the characterization of economies as either agricultural or hunting-gathering during this period probably has little meaning.

Early land usage and the 'cost' of early food production

The nature and chronology of the archaeological settlement data from Central Panama suggest that pre-Ceramic and early Ceramic-phase maize (5100–1000 bc) was part of a shifting system carried out by small groups who exploited environments away from the major rivers. Settlements were often less than one hectare in size and situated on promontories overlooking streams, or on interfluvial spurs (Weiland n.d.). The earliest nucleated and sedentary village situated on river alluvium, La Mula-Sarigua, was not occupied until around 870 bc. Thus, for at least 4000 years, a shifting and small-scale system of cultivation appears to have been practised. At first, land was plentiful, gardens and fields small, and fallow periods optimal, and low population density prevented the competition and social conflicts created by conditions of dense settlement. Similarly, crop pests may not have been a serious problem because small, polycultural plots did not provide a dense enough host population for major outbreaks of pest infestations. Therefore, early food production may have been a relatively energetically inexpensive and reliable subsistence strategy which provided the most secure and preferred food base compared both to hunting-gathering and developed agriculture.

Pollen and phytolith data from geological sequences which would allow us to measure the environmental impact of early cultivation are not yet available from Central Panama. We can, however, look to Eastern Panama for evidence on the nature of land usage from 5000 to 1000 bc. Phytolith evidence from geological profiles here indicates that maize had expanded into the Caribbean watershed near the present-day Panama Canal by 5000 years ago (Piperno 1985c). Associated with the appearance of maize are significant increases in phytoliths from weedy plants, and in phytoliths with carbon occlusions, which are the remains of burnt plants. It appears that a slash-and-burn mode of planting involving the clearing of new spaces for fields was being carried out by 5000 years ago. It is important to emphasize that this region, although receiving an annual rainfall of 2600 mm, still has a long and marked dry season, one favourable to the niche expansions of crop plants through the cutting and burning of vegetation.

We can envisage that the drier and more burnable forests of Central Pacific Panama were also in some degree of slash-and-burn agriculture and out of a 'kitchen garden' horticultural pattern by at least 5000 years ago. The numerous small settlements that pre-date 1000 bc which have been found by the PSM survey may represent hamlet clusters of several families. Bearing in mind that the amount of land required to feed even a small family of five or six amounts to several hectares (Bort 1979), and that the number of sites identified on a 4 per cent coverage survey exceeded 500, it is reasonable to conclude that extensive areas of land would have been either in cultivation or in fallow by 1000 bc.

By 300 bc, large-scale environmental degradation is indicated. In deposits from the coastal plain rockshelter of Aguadulce, phytoliths from *Curatella americana*, a major indicator species for fire disclimax vegetation, increase markedly in strata dated to the 1st millennium bc, indicating severe deforestation and habitat destruction near the site by that time (Piperno 1985a). Scarcity of good agricultural land in the interior forests, the soil cover of which had been exhausted, may have been an important factor in the settlement shift to the alluvium of major rivers. In these locations, sedentary villages with primarily agricultural economies are numerous by shortly after the beginning of the Christian era.

The implications of wild resource availability in regenerating plots and other regrowth vegetation

In all stages of regeneration the total yield of wild useful products appears greater than under purely natural conditions. Wild tuber-producing plants are common in abandoned plots. Many other herbaceous and woody plants valued for their leaves and fruits are more common in regrowth vegetation, and they provide important dietary supplements and utilitarian items to indigenous populations. When humans cleared the forests and planted their fields they unknowingly increased the reproductive fitness of many plants most beneficial in the diet. In fact, one major effect of early domestication may have been the increased densities of important wild resources favoured by regrowth ecology.

Conclusions

In Panama, fixed or partly fixed settlements, population growth, and intensification of production post-dated the first appearance of domesticated plants. If, as seems likely, such trends among hunter-gatherers are a response to a secure subsistence base, then they did not develop in the Panamanian tropical forests because of the low ecological potential. As Gould (1985) has argued, we must guard against the assumption that nucleation and sedentism are inevitable in the evolution of hunter-gatherer societies. Panama was one place where such developments apparently did not take place.

In considering the factors limiting population size and permanence, it has been argued that calories, and severe seasonal and multi-annual fluctuations in their availability, were far more serious constraints than were protein shortages. Small-scale food production significantly increased the yield of available plant calories and, over the long term, this resulted in a significant increase in population and in the permanence of settlements. However, in considering proximal factors, the dietary importance of a resource should not be measured solely in terms of its calorific contribution. 'Reliability' of resources looms large as a major factor contributing to diet choice among present-day hunter-gatherers (Lee 1968, 1979; Hayden 1981). Maize may have been a more reliable carbohydrate source than indigenous plants in the prehistoric economy, and was thus accepted into tropical forest subsistence systems at an early date.

In searching for proximal causes of early farming in Panama, I take the view that food production represented a reliable and inexpensive alternative and buffer to the low productivity and periodic shortages of naturally available foodstuffs. I suggest that people with short-term goals consciously sought to improve their food supply; thus human decision-making, on this level, is seen as an essential part of the process. In Panama, population growth was a correlate, not a cause, of the adoption of agricultural practices.

This is not to dispute the current widely held view that mobile hunting and gathering is generally less laborious than settled, large-scale agriculture. However, in Panama these two extremes of socio-economic development were separated by at least 4000 years of small-scale, shifting agriculture, the advent of which was preceded by a low-density, highly mobile foraging existence. In such circumstances, the negative correlation often drawn between early agriculture, labour demands, and the quality and desirability of foods (e.g. Cohen 1977) is probably not applicable.

Although I take an essentially ecological view of events and causation, decisions made by people that altered their economic, demographic, and social situation were certainly made in the context of a social group. As Hawkes *et al.* (1982: 380) have noted, 'appeals to cultural preference or systems of meaning beg precisely the question with which we are concerned, namely the explanation of the preferences themselves'. It seems likely that economic and ecological factors were critical determinants of subsistence during the development of early food production in Panama.

Acknowledgements

This research was supported by a post-doctoral fellowship from the Smithsonian Tropical Research Institute, Balboa, Panama, and a Scholarly Studies grant (12345407) from the Smithsonian Institution, Washington.

References

Ammerman, A. and Cavalli-Sforza, L.L. (1984) *The Neolithic Transition and the Genetics of Populations in Europe*, Princeton, NJ: Princeton University Press.

Beckerman, S. (1979) 'The abundance of protein in Amazonia: a reply to Gross', *American Anthropologist*, 81: 533–60.

Binford, L. (1968) 'Post-Pleistocene adaptations', in S. R. Binford and L. Binford (eds) *New Perspectives in Archaeology*, Chicago, IL: Aldine.

Bort, J. (1979) 'Ecology and subsistence on opposite sides of the Talmancan Range', in O. Linares and A. Ranere (eds) *Adaptive Radiations in Prehistoric Panama*, Peabody Museum Monographs 5, Cambridge, MA: Peabody Museum.

Chagnon, N. and Hames, R. (1979) 'Protein deficiency and tribal warfare in Amazonia: new data', *Science*, 20: 910–13.

Chagnon, N. and Hames, R. (1980) 'La "Hipotesis Proteica" y la adaptacion indigena a la cuenca del Amazonas: una revision critica de los datos y la teoria', *Interciencia*, 5: 346–58.

Cohen, M. (1977) *The Food Crisis in Prehistory*, New Haven, CT: Yale University Press.

Cooke, R. and Ranere, A. (1984) 'The "Proyecto Santa Maria". A multidisciplinary analysis of prehistoric adaptations to a tropical watershed in Panama', in F. Lange (ed.) *Recent Developments in Isthmian Archaeology*, Proceedings of the 44th International Congress of Americanists, Oxford: British Archaeological Reports, International Series 212.

Croat, T. (1978) *The Flora of Barro Colorado Island*, Stanford, CA: Stanford University Press.

D' Arcy, M.D. and Correa, A. (1985) *The Botany and Natural History of Panama*, St. Louis, MO: Missouri Botanical Garden.

Doebley, J.F. (1983) 'The maize X teosinte male inflorescence: a numerical taxonomic study', *Annals of the Missouri Botanical Garden*, 70: 32–70.

Doebley, J.F., Goodman, M. and Stuber, C. (1984) 'Isoenzymatic variation in *Zea*', *Systematic Botany*, 9: 203–18.

Earle, T. (1980) 'A model of subsistence change', in T. Earle and A. Christenson (eds) *Modeling Change in Prehistoric Subsistence Economies*, New York: Academic Press.

Flannery , K. (1968) 'Archaeological systems theory and early Mesoamerica', in B. J. Meggers (ed.) *Anthropological Archaeology in the Americas*, Washington, DC: Anthropological Society of Washington.

Flannery, K. (ed.) (1986) *Guilá Naquitz: archaic foraging and early agriculture in Oaxaca, Mexico*, Orlando, FL: Academic Press.

Foster, R. (1982a) 'The seasonal rhythm of fruitfall on Barro Colorado Island', in E. Leigh, A. S. Rand and D. Windsor (eds) *The Ecology of a Tropical Forest: seasonal rhythms and long-term changes*, Washington, DC: Smithsonian Institution Press.

Foster, R. (1982b) 'Famine on Barro Colorado Island', in E. Leigh, A. S. Rand and D. Windsor (eds) *The Ecology of a Tropical Forest: seasonal rhythms and long-term changes*, Washington, DC: Smithsonian Institution Press.

Frankie, G., Baker, H. and Opler, P. (1974) 'Comparative phenological studies of trees in tropical wet and dry forests in the lowlands of Costa Rica', *Journal of Ecology*, 62: 881–919.

Freeland, W.J. and Janzen, D.H. (1974) 'Strategies in herbivory by mammals: the role of plant secondary compounds', *American Naturalist*, 108: 269–89.

Gould, R. (1985) '"Now Let's Invent Agriculture [.]": a critical review of concepts of complexity among hunter-gatherers', in T. Price and J. Brown (eds) *Prehistoric Hunter-gatherers: the emergence of cultural complexity*, New York: Academic Press.

Gross, D. (1975) 'Protein capture and cultural development in the Amazon Basin', *American Anthropologist*, 77: 526–49.

Harris, D.R. (1978) 'Adaptation to a tropical rainforest environment: Aboriginal subsistence in northeastern Queensland', in N. Blurton-Jones and V. Reynolds (eds) *Human Behaviour and Adaptation*, London: Taylor and Francis.

Hart, T. and Hart, J. (1986) 'The ecological basis of hunter-gatherer subsistence in African rain forests: the Mbuti of eastern Zaire', *Human Ecology*, 14: 29–55.

Hawkes, K. and O'Connell, J. (1981) 'Affluent hunters? Some comments in light of the Alyawara case', *American Anthropologist*, 82: 622–6.

Hawkes, K., Hill, K. and O'Connell, J. (1982) 'Why hunters gather: optimal foraging and the Ache of eastern Paraguay', *American Ethnologist*, 9: 379–91.

Hayden, B. (1981) 'Subsistence and ecological adaptations of modern hunter/gatherers', in R. S. Harding and G. Teleki (eds) *Omnivorous Primates*, New York: Columbia University Press.

Hill, K. , Hawkes, K., Murtado, M. and Kaplan, H. (1984) 'Seasonal variance in the diet of Ache hunter-gatherers in eastern Paraguay', *Human Ecology*, 12: 101–35.

Hubbell, S. (1979) 'Tree dispersion, abundance, and diversity in a tropical dry forest', *Science*, 203: 1299–309.

Hubbell, S. and Foster, R. (1983) 'Diversity of canopy trees in a Neotropical forest and implications for conservation', in S. Sutton, T. Whitmore and S. Chadwick (eds) *Tropical Rain Forest: ecology and management*, Oxford: Blackwell Scientific Publications.

Janzen, D. (1969) 'Seed-eaters versus seed size, number, toxicity and dispersal', *Evolution*, 23: 1–27.

Janzen, D. (1983) '"Species accounts"', in D. Janzen (ed.) *Costa Rican Natural History*, Chicago, IL: University of Chicago Press.

Kaplan, L., Lynch, T. and Smith, C.E. (1973) 'Early cultivated beans (*Phaseolus vulgaris*) from an intermontane Peruvian valley', *Science*, 179: 76–7.

Koyama, S. and Thomas, D.H. (eds) (1981) *Affluent Foragers, Pacific Coasts East and West*, Senri Ethnological Series 9.

Lee, R. (1968) 'What hunters do for a living or how to make out on scarce resources', in R. Lee and I. DeVore (eds) *Man the Hunter*, Chicago, IL: Aldine.

Lee, R. (1979) *The !Kung San*, New York: Cambridge University Press.

Lee, R. and Devore, I. (eds) (1968) *Man the Hunter*, Chicago, IL: Aldine.

Leigh, E., Rand, A. and Windsor, D. (eds) (1982) *The Ecology of a Tropical Forest: seasonal rhythms and long-term changes*, Washington, DC: Smithsonian Institution Press.

Levi-Strauss, C. (1950) 'The use of wild plants in tropical South America', in J. Steward (ed.) *Handbook of South American Indians*, vol. 6, Washington, DC: Bureau of American Ethnology.

MacNeish, R. (1967) 'A summary of subsistence', in D. Byers (ed.) *The Prehistory of the Tehuacan Valley*, vol. 1, Austin, TX: University of Texas Press.

Milton, K. (1984) 'Protein and carbohydrate resources of the Maku Indians of northwestern Amazonia', *American Anthropologist*, 86: 7–27.

Monsalve, J. (1985) 'A pollen core from the Hacienda Lusitania', *Pro Calima*, 4: 40–4.

O'Connell, J. and Hawkes, K. (1981) 'Alyawara plant use and optimal foraging theory', in B. Winterhalder and E. Smith (eds) *Hunter-gatherer Foraging Strategies: ethnographic and archaeological analyses*, Chicago, IL: University of Chicago Press.

Opler, P., Frankie, G. and Baker, H. (1980) 'Comparative phenological studies of treelet and shrub species in tropical wet and dry forests in the lowlands of Costa Rica', *Journal of Ecology*, 68: 167–88.

Pickersgill, B. (1989) 'Cytological and genetical evidence on the domestication and diffusion of crops within the Americas', in D. R. Harris and G. C. Hillman (eds) *Foraging and Farming: the evolution of plant exploitation*, London: Unwin Hyman.

Pickersgill, B. and Heiser, C. (1977) 'Origins and distributions of plants domesticated in the New World tropics', in C. Reed (ed.) *The Origins of Agriculture*, The Hague: Mouton.

Piperno, D. (1984) 'A comparison and differentiation of phytoliths from maize and wild grasses: use of morphological criteria', *American Antiquity*, 49: 361–83.

Piperno, D. (1985a) 'Phytolith taphonomy and distributions in archaeological sediments from Panama', *Journal of Archaeological Science*, 12: 247–67.

Piperno, D. (1985b) 'Phytolith analysis and tropical paleoecology: forms in New World plant domesticates and wild species', *Review of Paleobotany and Palynology*, 45: 185–228.

Piperno, D. (1985c) 'Phytolithic analysis of geological sediments from Panama', *Antiquity*, LIX: 13–19.

Piperno, D. (1988a) *Phytolith Analysis: an archaeological and geological perspective*, San Diego, CA: Academic Press.

Piperno, D. (1988b) 'Pimer informe sobre los fitolitos de las plantas del OGSE- 80 y la evidencia del cultivo de maíz en el Ecuador', in K. Stothert (ed.) *La prehistoria temprana de la península de Santa Elena, Ecuador: Cultura Las Vegas*, Guayaquil: Muesos del Banco Central del Ecuador.

Piperno, D. (1990) 'Fitalitos, arquealogía y cambios prehistóricos de la vegetacióen un lote de cincuenta hectareas de la Isla de Barro Colorado', in E. G. Leigh, A. S. Rand and D. M. Windsor (eds) *Ecología de un Bosque Tropical*, Balboa, Panama: Smithsonian Tropical Research Institute.

Piperno, D. and Husum-Clary, K. (1984) 'Early plant use and cultivation in the Santa Maria Basin, Panama: data from phytoliths and pollen', in F. Lange (ed.) *Recent Developments in Isthmian Archaeology*, Proceedings of the 44th International Congress of Americanists, Oxford: British Archaeological Reports, International Series 212.

Piperno, D. and Starczak, V. (1985) 'Numerical analysis of maize and wild grass phytoliths using multivariate techniques', paper presented at the 2nd Phytolith Research Workshop, Duluth, Minnesota.

Piperno, D., Husum-Clary, K., Cooke, R., Ranere, A. and Weiland, D. (1985) 'Preceramic maize from Central Panama: evidence from phytoliths and pollen', *American Anthropologist*, 87: 871–8.

Price, T. and Brown J. (eds) (1985) *Prehistoric Hunter-gatherers: the emergence of cultural complexity*, New York: Academic Press.

Ranere, A. (n.d.) 'The manufacture and use of stone tools during the preceramic in the Santa Maria Basin of Central Panama', prepared for G. Correal and R. Cooke (eds) *Cazadores y Recolectores Prehistoricas en Centro- y Suramerica*, Oxford: British Archaeological Reports, International Series.

Rindos, D. (1984) *The Origins of Agriculture*, Orlando, FL: Academic Press.

Ross, E. (1978) 'Food taboos, diet, and hunting strategy: the adaptation to animals in Amazon cultural ecology', *Current Anthropology*, 19: 1–36.

Smith, J., Goodman, M. and Stuber, C. (1985) 'Relationships between maize and teosinte of Mexico and Guatemala: numerical analysis of allozyme data', *Economic Botany*, 39: 12–24.

Weiland, D. (1984) 'Prehistoric settlement patterns in the Santa Maria Drainage of Central Pacific Panama: a preliminary analysis', in F. Lange (ed.) *Recent Developments in Isthmian Archaeology*, Proceedings of the 44th International Congress of Americanists, Oxford: British Archaeological Reports, International Series 212.

Weiland, D. (n.d.) 'Preceramic settlement patterns in the Santa Maria Basin, Central Pacific Panama', prepared for G. Correal and R. Cooke (eds) *Cazadores y Recolectores Prehistoricas en Centro- y Suramerica*, Oxford: British Archaeological Reports, International Series.

Wilkes, G. (1989) 'Maize: domestication, racial evolution, and spread', in D. R. Harris and G. C. Hillman (eds) *Foraging and Farming: the evolution of plant exploitation*, London: Unwin Hyman.

Wilmsen, E. (1982) 'Studies in diet, nutrition, and fertility among a group of Kalahari Bushman in Botswana', *Social Science Information*, 21: 5–125.

Update: A retrospective on non-affluent foragers

Dolores R. Piperno

In the last 18 years, our knowledge about early foraging and farming in Panama and throughout the Neotropics has dramatically changed. Methodological improvements have taken place that have allowed archaeobotanists to markedly increase the amount and quality of empirical data bearing on prehistoric plant exploitation. In addition, our theoretical approaches to prehistoric foraging and farming have become more rigorous and increasingly testable with archaeological and other empirical retrospective data. I highlight some points I considered to be most important in 1989, then I will summarise these newer developments.

My main thesis in the original paper was that the characterisation of hunting and gathering societies as 'affluent' (e.g. they easily met most of their subsistence needs without working very hard), despite gaining currency in the archaeological literature, probably was not applicable to tropical forest cultures. I argued then, and continue to do so, that when compared to extra-tropical habitats, tropical forests have limited natural supplies of calories that probably constrained the size and permanence of pre-agrarian societies. Moreover, these caloric issues were probably more limiting for the growth and long-term stability of human populations than the supposed and often-discussed protein shortages of the tropical forest. I argued that early tropical food production was, therefore, likely to be a more reliable and less energetically-expensive strategy of food procurement than tropical foraging.

Then-available archaeobotanical data from Panama that could be used to assess the characteristics and chronology of early food production was essentially limited to the presence of maize pollen and phytoliths in late pre-Ceramic sediments from a few sites that indicated the crop was introduced to Panama during the seventh millennium BP. Nonetheless, I noted how an early introduction of maize into the seasonally dry Panamanian tropics made good ecological sense because work by John Doebley and Hugh Iltis was beginning to suggest that maize domestication had originally taken place in the seasonally dry tropical forest of southwestern Mexico, not in arid mountain zones of Mexico as traditionally believed. Despite the often-inferred, probably important role of root crops in early foraging and farming I could not discuss this issue at all, because we did not have techniques capable of retrieving and identifying soft, starchy remains of underground plant organs in sites from the humid tropics. And I could not provide evidence on how pre-Columbian human populations may have modified the tropical landscape because we did not yet possess vegetational or climate histories from lake sediment cores.

Between 1989 and 1998, major improvements were made in our ability to recognise crop plants of various types (maize; squashes and gourds of *Cucurbita* spp.; arrowroot [*Maranta arundinacea*]; achira [*Canna edulis*]; bottle gourd [*Lagenaria siceraria*]) using archaeological phytolith data. As a result, early food producing systems dating to the early and middle Holocene periods (c. 9000 to 4000 BP) involving these and other plants were documented by a number of investigators working over a large region from southern Central America (Panama) into northern South America (Piperno and Pearsall 1998 review the evidence with references). Moreover, a number of lakes had been discovered in the humid lowlands with sediments old enough to study late-glacial and early to middle Holocene environmental history. Multiproxy analysis (pollen, phytolith, and charcoal studies) of lake sediments was shown to be an effective approach for reconstructing tropical climate, vegetation and fire history, including human land usage and slash-and-burn cultivation. The data showed: that in some areas human alteration and firing of forests started shortly after the Pleistocene ended between 11,000 and 10,000 BP; that between 7000 and 4000 BP, depending on the region, slash-and-burn cultivation using plants such as maize and manioc was initiated; that from Belize to the Ecuadorian Amazon, the tropical forest had been altered, sometimes profoundly, by millennia of intensive agriculture; and, that in some areas species-diverse forest recovered when agricultural pressure decreased after indigenous peoples tragically encountered early Europeans (e.g. Mora *et al.* 1991; Piperno *et al.* 1991; Bush *et al.* 1992; Jones 1994; Pohl *et al.* 1996).

Also during the 1990s, molecular biologists began to provide crucial data on crop plant ancestry and the geography of New World plant domestication, making it ever more clear that the tropical forest contributed a myriad of seed, root and tree crops, many of which are important staple foods today. These developments in the fields of archaeology, paleoecology, and molecular biology were reviewed and summarised in Piperno and Pearsall (1998). The volume made the case that the lowland Neotropics from Mexico to South America were early and independent centres of plant domestication and crop plant dispersals, and that the origins of tropical forest agriculture had much to do with the profound ecological transformations in the tropical forest that had been shown to accompany the end of the Pleistocene.

The final important development relating to reconstructing indigenous foraging and farming in the tropical forest is starch grain analysis. Long known to botanists and other researchers in plant science, archaeobotanists learned that these microscopic grains in which plants store their energy can be commonly found well-preserved in tiny cracks on the surfaces of stone tools used to process plants. The grains are highly diverse in morphology and it appears that they can frequently identify plants to the genus and even species level. During the past eight years, archaeobotanists have identified the remains of manioc, maize, yams, arrowroot, beans and other plants on ancient stone tools from sites located throughout Central and South America, providing confirmation and additional evidence for the early emergence and diffusion of tropical forest agriculture (e.g. Piperno *et al.* 2000; Iriarte *et al.* 2004; Perry 2005). Starch grain analysis is providing us with that long hoped for avenue for empirically documenting the history of the root crop complex of tropical America. The technique probably will considerably advance our knowledge of plants of all types from deep time periods (review in Torrence and Barton 2006).

With regard to explaining why, when and how foragers first turned to a life of farming in the tropics and elsewhere, archaeologists have recently adapted models from evolutionary (behavioural) ecology (Kennett and Winterhalder 2006). In my view and others', the models are better suited for studying cultural change than other evolutionary programmes (e.g. co-evolution, stricter forms of Darwinian theory) because they view flexible decision-making, local ecological circumstances and rapid, phenotypic-level adjustments as being fundamental to evolutionary change. They also formalise the idea that early forms of food production were less labour intensive than foraging and, importantly, they accommodate short-term intentionality as a source of the cultural traits and variability on which natural and cultural selection act.

With the advent of robust methods with which to study cultural uses of plants and new, more ecumenical and testable theories, the next 20 years of investigating prehistoric foraging and farming promises to be as exciting and interesting as the previous few decades.

References

Bush, M.B., Piperno D.R., Colinvaux, P.A., DeOliveira, P. E., Krissek, L.A., Miller, M.C. and Rowe, W.E. (1992) 'A 14,300-year paleoecological profile of a lowland tropical lake in Panama', *Ecology*, 62: 251–75.

Iriarte, J., Holst, I., Marozzi, O., Listopad, C., Alonso, E., Rinderknecht, A. and Montaña, J. (2004) 'Evidence for cultivar adoption and emerging complexity during the mid-Holocene in the La Plata Basin, Uruguay', *Nature*, 432: 614–17.

Jones, J.G. (1994) 'Pollen evidence for early settlement and agriculture in Northern Belize', *Palynology*, 18: 205–11.

Kennett, D. and Winterhalder, B. (eds) (2006) *Behavioral Ecology and the Transition to Agriculture*, Berkeley, CA: University of California Press.

Mora, S.C., Herrera, L.F., Cavelier, I. and Rodríguez, C. (1991) *Cultivars, Anthropic Soils and Stability*, University of Pittsburgh Latin American Archaeology Report No. 2, Department of Anthropology, University of Pittsburgh.

Perry, L. (2005) 'Reassessing the traditional interpretation of "manioc" artifacts in the Orinoco valley of Venezuela', *Latin American Antiquity*, 16: 409–26.

Piperno, D.R. and Pearsall, D.M. (1998) *The Origins of Agriculture in the Lowland Neotropics*, San Diego, CA: Academic Press.

Piperno, D.R., Bush, M.B. and Colinvaux, P.A. (1991) 'Paleoecological perspectives on human adaptation in Central Panama. II. The Holocene', *Geoarchaeology*, 6: 227–50.

Piperno, D.R., Ranere, A.J., Holst, I. and Hansell, P. (2000) 'Starch grains reveal early root crop horticulture in the Panamanian tropical forest', *Nature*, 407: 894–97.

Pohl, M.D., Pope, K.O., Jones J.G., Jacob, J.S., Piperno D.R., de France, S., Lentz D.L., Gifford, J.A., Valdez, F. Jr., Danforth, M.E. and Josserand, J.K. (1996) 'Early agriculture in the Maya lowlands', *Latin American Antiquity*, 7: 355–72.

Torrence, R. and Barton, H. (eds) (2006) *Ancient Starch Research*, Walnut Creek, CA: Left Coast Press.

5 The impact of maize on subsistence systems in South America

An example from the Jama River valley, coastal Ecuador

Deborah M. Pearsall

Introduction

Archaeologists are fascinated by maize. *Zea mays* L. has undoubtedly been the subject of more debate, more publications, and more archaeological research than any other New World crop; perhaps more than all the others put together. A recent compendium of this research (Johannessen and Hastorf 1994) illustrates the point.

Maize deserves all this interest; at the time of European contact it was the mainstay of diet of peoples from the Eastern Woodlands of the United States to the Andes of Peru and beyond. One issue of continuing interest throughout the New World is when, and under what sets of circumstances, maize came to occupy this role. As a recent overview of South American data relevant to this issue has shown (Pearsall 1994a), we are only beginning to understand this process, since we still lack good, regional archaeological sequences documenting when maize became incorporated into subsistence, and how its transition to a dietary staple occurred. It is especially important that the role of maize be considered in the context of the indigenous foraging and horticultural practices of the people who accepted it. In the case of the tropical lowlands, for example, maize was introduced into subsistence systems that were likely based primarily upon tuber and root resources and tree fruits, rather than on small-seeded annuals (Pearsall 1992a). Maize would be unlikely to supplant such indigenous plant staples until a number of key innovations occurred: maize productivity outstripped that of competing crops, maize was able to fill a previously unoccupied niche in the crop landscape or calendar, and food storage became critical for economic, political, or social reasons. In this chapter I discuss a case study from the lowlands of western Ecuador, the Jama Valley Archaeological-Palaeoethnobotanical Project, to illustrate one approach to understanding this complex process of innovation in subsistence.

Before turning to the Jama study, it is necessary to discuss several issues relevant to the process of subsistence change, and how change is documented through the archaeological botanical record. First, in the case of a crop introduction, one should not assume that the 'full' impact of a new crop is felt immediately upon its appearance in the archaeological record. The importance of the crop must be documented, not assumed: ecological and cultural factors such as those discussed above may slow the process of acceptance and increased dependence; other factors may hasten it. In the case of the introduction of maize into temperate eastern North America, for example, there is a gap of a thousand years or more between an early appearance of the crop (charred remains accelerator-dated to 200 BC, Middle Woodland period, reviewed in Riley *et al.* 1990, 1994) and its nearly ubiquitous occurrence in late prehistoric village sites throughout the region (Smith 1989; Johannessen 1993; Scarry 1993; Bendremer and Dewar 1994). Interestingly, the change in maize use appears to be gradual in some regions, such as southern Ontario, Canada (Katzenberg *et al.* 1995), and the northern United States (Buikstra and Milner 1991), and more abrupt in others, such as parts of the southern United States (Lynott *et al.* 1986). Crop introduction and innovation in subsistence are different processes, and may be widely separated in time and space.

From this distinction it follows that different methods may be necessary to document crop introduction and innovation in subsistence. The initial introduction may leave a very ephemeral mark in the archaeological record: a few charred remains (if the crop was cooked before being consumed); the appearance of a few phytoliths (opaline silica bodies) or pollen grains in refuse areas; and, little to no shift in the isotopic signature of human skeletal remains. If sites themselves are ephemeral (i.e. seasonal camps rather than villages), this may compound the problem of documenting the presence of a new crop. One effective way to circumvent this difficulty is to look not just at archaeological sites but at whole landscapes. Lake coring can reveal the impact of humans on vegetation on both local and regional scales (e.g. Piperno 1993, 1995); if this impact included preparing fields and growing crops, pollen, phytoliths, and even macroremains of those crop plants may be preserved in the lake core record. If the introduced crop has a major, immediate impact on subsistence, this should be clear in a regional vegetation record, even if sites are difficult to locate or have poorly preserved botanical remains. If the impact is light, studying the regional vegetation record is more likely to 'catch' the introduction than is testing at a single site in that region. Documenting the initial introduction of a crop should thus rely on multiple indicators, and include off-site data. In the case of the spread of maize from southern Mesoamerica into Central and South America, half of the early occurrences of the crop are documented in lake cores, not archaeological sites (Table 5.1; Pearsall 1995a). Without the core data, our knowledge of the spread of maize in the Neotropics would be greatly reduced. These same cores indicate when maize became important by documenting increasing abundances of maize pollen and/or phytoliths, evidence of extensive forest clearance, and appearance of weedy taxa (Pearsall 1995a).

Table 5.1 Early occurrences of corn in the New World tropics (dates are uncalibrated C-14)

	Location	Date	Comments/reference
Lake Cores			
Peten Lake	Guatemala	2300 BP	Pollen; Vaughn *et al.* 1985
Lake Yojoa	Honduras	4770 BP	Pollen; Rue 1989
Gatun Lake	Panama	4750 BP	Pollen, phytoliths; Piperno 1985
La Yequada	Panama	4200 BP	Pollen, phytoliths; Piperno *et al.* 1990, 1991a, 1991b
Lake Wodehouse	Panama	3900 BP	Phytoliths; Piperno 1994
Hacienda Lusitania	Colombia	Older than 5150 BP	Pollen; Monsalve 1985
Hacienda El Dorado	Colombia	6680 BP	Pollen; Bray *et al.* 1987
Lake Ayauchi	Ecuador	5300 BP	Pollen, phytoliths; Bush *et al.* 1989; Piperno 1990
Lake San Pablo	Ecuador	4000 BP	Pollen, charred tissue; Athens 1990, 1991
Archaeological sites			
Tehuacan	Mexico	4700 BP	Dried cobs; Long *et al.* 1989
Aguadulce	Panama	4500 BP	Phytoliths; Piperno 1985, 1988
Cueva de los Ladrones	Panama	6910 BP	Pollen, phytoliths; Piperno 1985, 1988; Piperno *et al.* 1985
Vegas type site	Ecuador	Older than 6600 BP	Phytoliths; Piperno 1988; Pearsall and Piperno 1990
Real Alto	Ecuador	5200 BP	Phytoliths; Pearsall 1979; Pearsall and Piperno 1990
Loma Alta	Ecuador	5000 BP	Charred kernels; Pearsall 1988, 1995c

Another point illustrated by Table 5.1 is how many of these earliest finds of maize in the Neotropics are either pollen grains or phytoliths. Note that phytoliths are as important for tracing maize in the archaeological record as in lake cores. Why is the macroremain record of early maize so sparse? Each taphonomic process (i.e. amount of burning activity to produce charred remains) and set of recovery techniques (i.e. flotation technique, screen size employed) is unique, but I suggest part of the answer lies in differential preservation of charred macroremains and phytoliths. I have discussed in detail elsewhere (Pearsall 1995b) some of the factors that contribute to poor preservation of macroremains in some settings in the lowland tropics. Basically, in heavy clay soils that are wetted and dried on a regular basis (seasonally, for example), charred remains can be broken up over time, while phytoliths are unaffected. Figure 5.1 illustrates this phenomenon for macroremains from site M3D2-009 (Finca Cueva) in the Jama valley. The graph represents over 3000 years of occupation of this village site, from Terminal Valdivia (Piquigua) through Muchique 3 (E. Engwall, pers. comm., 1996). Artefact densities indicate that the site was intensely occupied during Muchique 2 and 3 (surface through 120 cm in this test pit), with a much lighter occupation for Muchique 1, Tabuchila and Piquigua (120 cm through 240 cm). Although artefact densities are high through 120 cm, note the decline in wood charcoal density beginning at 40 cm. This drop-off in charred material in a part of the sequence with dense occupational debris appears to be a taphonomic phenomenon. Phytoliths extracted from the same levels are abundant and well preserved. In settings where macroremains are influenced by post-depositional destruction, they may not be a reliable indicator of plant abundance, or, in cases as extreme as that illustrated in Figure 5.1, even the absence of a target species such as maize may be illusory.

My point in raising these issues in the context of documenting the impact of maize on subsistence is a simple one: before charred macroremains data are used to demonstrate an apparent shift in abundances of food resources, the analyst must demonstrate that differential destruction of charred material

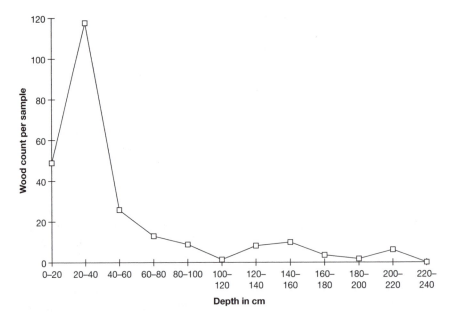

Figure 5.1 Abundance of charred wood with depth. Data from test pit 2, site M3D2-009 (Finca Cueva), Jama valley, Ecuador.

with depth (time) has not occurred. This can be done by graphing abundance of charred material per litre of soil, by depth, as illustrated in Figure 5.1. Contexts of samples to be compared should also be similar; a change in site function or intensity of occupation may cause an increase or decrease in burning activity, and hence preservation (e.g. Pearsall 1983). Comparing data from preceramic and ceramic-using sites is especially problematic; if cooking techniques changed with the appearance of pottery, so might the ways foods enter the archaeological record. If preservation of charred botanical remains is a problem in earlier ceramic phases, as it is in the Jama valley, phytoliths provide a robust alternative source of data on early crop occurrences.

Maize in coastal Ecuadorian subsistence

It is difficult not to equate the importance of maize and the importance of agriculture when looking at palaeoethnobotanical data from coastal Ecuadorian sites, since the most important lowland root crop, manioc (*Manihot esculenta*), is nearly 'invisible' in the archaeological record. Maize is present in coastal Ecuador since the late Preceramic (Late Las Vegas phase, maize phytoliths in strata older than 4600 BC) (Piperno 1988; Pearsall and Piperno 1990). It is impossible, however, to assess the importance of the 'new' crop relative to other foods at this time period because the poor preservation of macroremains at Vegas and subsequent Valdivia (Early Formative, first ceramic phase) sites limits both precision of identification and application of quantitative measures. Bone collagen in human skeletal samples from the Vegas type site, OGSE-80, is poorly preserved, but eight samples with preserved collagen from Valdivia 1–2 strata at the Loma Alta site show no dietary impact by maize (average delta 13C, –19.0‰; van der Merwe *et al.* 1993). Maize kernels are rare at Loma Alta. The single Valdivia 3 sample with preserved collagen from the large Real Alto village is similar (delta 13C, –18.8‰). Maize phytoliths occur in many contexts at that site. The isotopic data are silent on the identity of the major plant contributors to the Vegas and Valdivia diets.

Archaeobotanical data do contribute some information on this. 'Porous' tissue that could be root remains, and phytoliths from *Canna*, a taxon producing edible tubers, at Real Alto suggest that root/tuber foods, as well as maize, were in use during the Valdivia period, along with jack beans (*Canavalia*), cotton (*Gossypium*), tree fruits, and small seed resources (Pearsall 1979; Damp *et al.* 1981; Damp and Pearsall 1994). Whether the root/tuber foods and cotton were domesticated is unknown; however, *Canna* does not occur naturally in the region, and the jack beans are likely the domesticated species, *C. plagiosperma*. Thus while we know that a variety of crops was present by the Early Formative in coastal Ecuador, we do not have good answers to two interrelated questions: was subsistence based on agriculture, and how important was maize early in coastal prehistory?

The available bone isotope data for the later Formative Machalilla and Chorrera periods document that maize had some impact on diet during Machalilla (average delta 13C, −12.3‰), with an increase in maize use at one Chorrera site (Loma Alta, average delta 13C, −10.1‰) and steady levels at another (Salango, average delta 13C, −12.5‰) (van der Merwe *et al.* 1993). The absence of late Valdivia samples, and the evidence of variability of isotopic signature between Chorrera sites, makes it difficult to assess whether this change in maize use was gradual or abrupt. The transition from low levels of maize use to its role as a dietary staple is still poorly documented for coastal Ecuador, complicated by poor preservation at early sites and the availability of relatively few datasets.

One of the goals of the Jama valley project was to gather data relevant to the evolution of coastal subsistence from Terminal Valdivia through the contact period from one region (Zeidler and Pearsall 1994). Through a programme of valley-wide survey and site testing, such a database has been compiled. Although analyses are not completed for all sites, preliminary results are available which provide insight into agricultural evolution in this valley and suggest a model of change in the relative importance of maize and local foods that may be applicable more widely in the lowland tropics of the New World.

The Jama valley archaeobotanical database, as it currently exists, has limitations that must be acknowledged. Because Terminal Valdivia and Chorrera Formative deposits are often buried by metres of later occupation, the database for the earlier time periods is smaller both in numbers of sites and contexts tested, and in abundance of botanical remains recovered per flotation sample (Pearsall 1994b). Many Formative-age samples appear to be heavily affected by post-depositional destruction of remains, and cannot be compared quantitatively to later, better-preserved samples. The sequence immediately after the Formative in the Jama valley, the Muchique sequence (Jama-Coaque I and II) is less impacted by taphonomic factors in many cases.

Thus the Jama valley database does not provide a direct means, at this time, of testing whether the Late Formative marks an important transition in the use of maize in the coastal lowlands as suggested by the van der Merwe *et al.* (1993) isotope study. However, the Muchique sequence does provide some insight into the process of innovation in subsistence. If maize came to dominate subsistence during the late Formative in the Jama valley, then we should see evidence for this in the subsequent Muchique I period. In other words, maize should already be abundant at sites. If this transition occurred later in time in the Jama case, then the sequence should document changes in subsistence from Muchique 1–2 or during the Muchique 2 sequence. These issues will be discussed below. An evaluation of the overall importance of agriculture, relative to the use of wild and tended plant resources, awaits final identifications of root/tuber foods and tree fruits.

The Jama valley project

The Jama Valley Archaeological-Palaeoethnobotanical Project was initiated by James A. Zeidler and myself in the mid-1980s for the purpose of conducting an interdisciplinary archaeological investigation of long-term sociopolitical change through the successive prehispanic occupations of northern Manabi province (Zeidler and Pearsall 1994). One of the major foci of the project was to investigate the process of agricultural intensification in the lowland tropics. The ultimate goal of this focus was to test models of agricultural evolution and cropping intensification by using biological data recovered from sites in the valley.

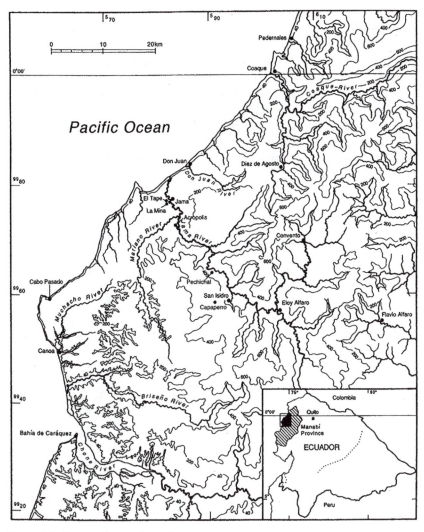

Figure 5.2 Jama valley study region

The Jama river drainage is one of the numerous river valleys flowing directly into the Pacific Ocean along the coastal strip of western Ecuador (Figure 5.2). It is situated just below the equatorial line in northern Manabi province. The Jama is the largest drainage basin of northern Manabi, and has its headwaters in the low hills of the coastal cordillera. The main channel of the river extends 75 km. The valley occupies a transitional area from dryer to wetter (coastal to inland) conditions (dry megathermic tropical to semi-humid megathermic tropical). Although the valley is largely deforested today, the natural vegetation cover is dry tropical forest along the coast and humid pre-montane tropical forest further inland (Zeidler and Kennedy 1994).

As a result of a valley-wide archaeological survey and testing programme carried out from 1989 through 1991, the cultural chronology presented in Table 5.2 (Zeidler *et al.* 1998) was established. An important feature of the chronology is the presence of three discrete tephra layers, thick deposits of wind-transported volcanic ash and pumice, throughout the valley. These tephra deposits originated from volcanic eruptions in the western Andean cordillera and were distributed onto the coastal plain by the prevailing easterly winds (Isaacson 1994). Originally blanketing the landscape, the tephras were redeposited within each coastal watershed by erosion from hill slopes into valley bottoms, where deposits up to 2 m thick were created.

Table 5.2 Cultural chronology of the Jama River valley. Model dates (cal. BC) based on an analysis of 37 radiocarbon dates (Zeidler *et al.* 1998)

Culture	Phase	Date	Period
Campace (?)	Muchique 5 Spanish conquest (AD 1532)	AD 1430–1640	Colonial
Jama-Coaque II	Muchique 4	AD 1290–1430	Integration
Jama-Coaque II	Muchique 3	AD 880–1260	Integration
Jama-Coaque II	Muchique 2 Tephra III (c. AD 400)	AD 420–790	Integration
Jama-Coaque I	Muchique 1 Tephra II (c. 750 BC)	1240 BC–AD 90	Regional Developmental
Chorrera	Tabuchila Hiatus	1300–750 BC	Late Formative
Valdivia	Late Piquigua Tephra I	1800 BC	Early Formative
	Early Piquigua	2030 BC	Early Formative

Ash deposition of this magnitude produces a wide range of environmental hazards, including damage to forests and crop destruction, and can lead to long-term disruption of agricultural systems, especially those that are based on cultivation of alluvial lands (Isaacson 1994).

In the case of the Jama valley, understanding the impact of tephra deposition is essential for understanding human adaptation in the valley. While the small Terminal Valdivia populations survived the first tephra fall, the valley was abandoned within a hundred years of the event, and remained unoccupied for some 550 years. Tephra II ended the Chorrera occupation of the valley, resulting in a major cultural discontinuity that is seen not only in the Jama valley, but widely in north-west Ecuador (Isaacson 1994). The valley was quickly reoccupied by Jama-Coaque I populations (Muchique 1 phase). The third tephra event, resulting in the deepest deposits, had by contrast less impact on cultural continuity in the valley than did Tephra II. A short abandonment, of perhaps a generation, occurred after Tephra Ill, followed by re-establishment of Jama-Coaque populations (Muchique 2 phase).

A reconstruction of prehistoric subsistence in the Jama River valley

Data recovery and analysis procedures

The primary data used in this discussion are charred botanical remains recovered by water flotation of sediments from test excavations in the Jama valley. The flotation system used, an IDOT-style manual system with 0.5 mm screen (Pearsall 1989), permitted recovery of all size classes of botanical remains. Non-buoyant remains were hand-sorted in the field lab from heavy fractions, ensuring that materials of all densities were represented. Flotation samples were sorted at the University of Missouri Paleoethnobotany Laboratory following standard procedures (Pearsall 1989). Determining final identifications is ongoing; many small seed taxa and fruit fragments remain unidentified to species. To make a preliminary assessment of the impact of maize on subsistence, four types of remains are considered here: maize or corn, bean (*Phaseolus vulgaris*), tree fruit (palm and other wild/tended tree taxa), and root/tuber (root-like storage organ fragments, not yet identified to taxon). Since the majority of small seeds appears to be from weedy plants, they are omitted from this analysis.

It is likely that final identification of remains will result in at least three types of tubers (*Maranta, Canna* and *Manihot*), and as many, or more, species of tree fruits (for example, taxa in the families Palmae and Sapotaceae) being identified. This increased level of precision will allow refinement of the patterns discussed below, and may permit use of diversity measures to examine patterning in the botanical data. What is unlikely to change are patterns of bias in the data due to differences in the 'toughness' of the various classes of botanical materials. Fruit fragments, dense meats and rinds, are durable materials that are much less likely to be destroyed by wetting and drying and soil pressure than are the fragile remains of tubers. These are the remains most likely to be dramatically over- and under-represented, respectively, throughout the sequence. In broad terms, tuber-root remains are more important in subsistence than is suggested by the quantity of remains recovered, and tree fruits less so. Beans and maize fall in between, with maize kernels being more subject to destruction, and somewhat under-represented, than are dense bean cotyledons.

The botanical data discussed below pertain to seven chronological phases, and come from five sites (Table 5.3). Features (F) and Deposits (Dep. = natural stratigraphic layer) in domestic occupation debris make up the majority of the database; arbitrary levels assignable to Muchique 1 from the Don Juan site were included to augment this early period. Data from individual samples were grouped by summing raw data counts by phase.

The Muchique 1 phase is represented by materials from the Don Juan site, located at the mouth of the river of the same name (Figure 5.2). One feature from this site, Feature 7, dating to 480 BC, is examined separately, since it falls before the main Muchique 1 occupation at 355 BC. As will be discussed further, abundance of materials is lowest for the Muchique 1 phase. Two deep storage pits provide data for the Muchique 2 phase. The El Tape pit is about 200 years younger than the pit from the Pechichal site, providing an opportunity to look at change within the Muchique 2 phase. Both pits have abundant remains. The El Tape site is in the lower Jama valley; Pechichal in the upper. Three sites provide material dated to the Muchique 3 phase; the Capaperro site in the upper valley dates to early in this phase; Don Juan and the Acropolis, both in the lower valley, are later and roughly contemporary. No samples clearly attributable to Muchique 4 (AD 1250–1430) were available for this analysis, so the upper two deposits at the Don Juan site (Deposits 1 and 2), known to post-date Muchique 3, were combined to give some indication of later subsistence patterning.

A number of ways of quantifying macroremains data could be applied to the Jama valley dataset (Hastorf and Popper 1988; Pearsall 1989). To assess the degree of preservation bias, I graphed wood count per 10 litres of floated soil for each phase; abundance fluctuates, but does not decline dramatically with depth (Figure 5.3). This suggests that taphonomic phenomena have not biased the overall plant assemblage to a great extent. Wood is especially abundant in the El Tape feature samples; food remains very common in the Pechichal pit samples. Ratios of each class of food remain per 10 litres of floated soil (corn/10 litres, tree fruit/10 litres, bean/10 litres, tuber-root/10 litres) allow abundance of individual remains to be tracked over time. A direct comparison of maize to all other foods (corn: other food ratio) contrasts the occurrence of the target species to all other foods as a group.[1]

Table 5.3 Macroremain database, in chronological order

Site number (name)	Strata	Phase	C-14 date	No. litres	Wood[1]	Corn	Other food
M3B2-001 (Don Juan)	Dep. 1, 2	Post-Much. 3		302.5	853	208	57
M3B3-012 (Acropolis)		Late Much. 3	AD 1150	94	395	265	44
M3B2-001 (Don Juan)	Dep. 3	Late Much. 3		151	592	162	24
M3D2-065 (Cappaperro)	F4	Early Much. 3	AD 755	51	138	162	48
M3B4-011 (Pechichal)	F5	Much. 2	AD 545	831.5	2702	3568	1922
M3B3-002 (El Tape)	F4	Early Much. 2	AD 340	184.5	8863	647	43
TEPHRA III (c. AD 400)							
M3B2-001 (Don Juan)	Dep. 4	Much. 1		190	331	85	11
M3B2-001 (Don Juan)	F7	Early Much. 1	480 BC	18	55	9	0

Note
1 Wood, corn, and other food data are presented in counts.

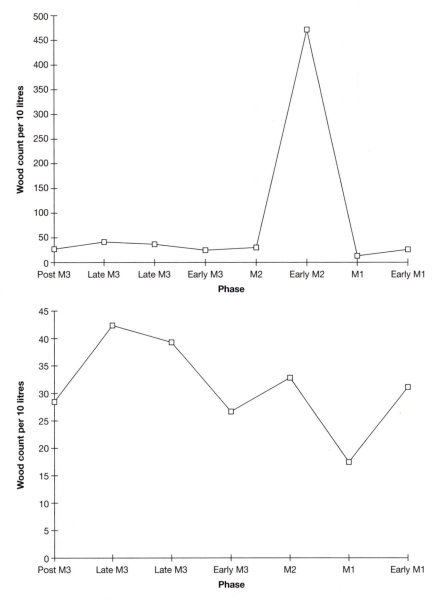

Figure 5.3 Abundance of charred wood by phase: (top) all phases; (bottom) excluding the early Muchique 2 phase in order to illustrate the pattern for the other phases more clearly

Patterning in Muchique phase macroremains data

Figure 5.4 illustrates the abundance of each class of food remains by phase. All foods increase in abundance during the later Muchique 2 phase; these are the rich Pechichal pit samples. The most significant pattern, however, is that maize is present in greater abundance than other food remains in all phases. After maize, tree fruits are most abundant. The relative abundance of beans and tuber-root fragments varies by phase, with tubers being significantly more abundant than beans in the Late Muchique 3 sample from the Acropolis. Since tuber remains are extremely fragile, this is a significant finding.

Comparing maize directly to other foods (corn : other food ratio, Figure 5.5) reveals some interesting patterns. Maize is very abundant relative to other foods during the Muchique 1 and early Muchique 2 phases, increasing in abundance between them. There is then a significant drop in the relative abundance of maize; it is still the most common food remain in the later part of the Muchique 2 phase, but other foods contribute substantially to the archaeobotanical record. The corn : other food ratio goes up again, but never to the levels observed early in the sequence.

Qualitative comparisons of Muchique to Formative period data

As discussed above, the Formative macroremains database from the Jama valley project, as it currently exists, cannot be compared quantitatively to that of the Muchique sequence because of preservation and sampling problems. The best information on plants utilized for subsistence during the Formative derives from phytoliths. It is difficult to determine the relative importance of crops from phytolith data, however, since phytolith production patterns vary widely among species (Piperno 1988; Pearsall 1989). The strength of phytolith data lies in documenting plants poorly preserved in the charred botanical record.

Phytolith data from a series of test pits in the San Isidro site (M3D2-001), the central place of the valley, document the presence of a suite of cultivated and utilized plants which remains much the same from late Valdivia through Jama-Coaque II. Maize, Marantaceae (probably *Maranta*, arrowroot tuber), and *Canna* (achira tuber) are present throughout the sequence. Palms and sedges, either cultivated or encouraged, were also consistently present, as were wild grasses, especially bamboos. Squash or gourd were identified in Formative samples (Pearsall 1992b; Pearsall and Zeidler 1994). Palm and achira phytoliths are especially abundant late in the Jama-Coaque II period; this hints at a shift in importance of these resources at San Isidro, but this requires corroboration. Chorrera phase deposits from two smaller sites, M3B4-031 and M3D2-009, essentially duplicate the plant suite documented at San Isidro.

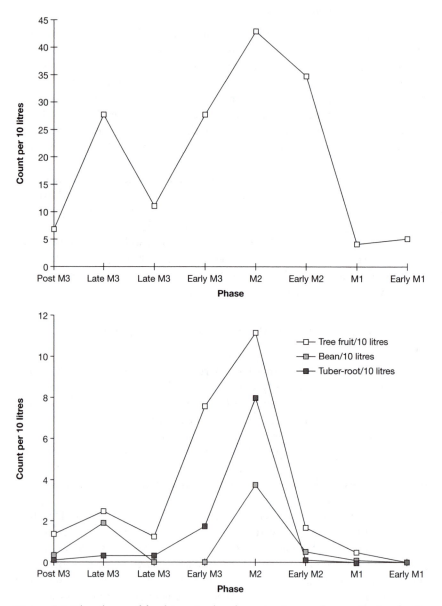

Figure 5.4 Abundance of food remains by phase: (top) corn; (bottom) other foods

What the phytolith data contribute for comparing Formative period
and later subsistence in the Jama River valley is to (1) confirm that maize
was present from the beginning of the sequence, (2) identify two of the
root crops, arrowroot and achira, and document their continued presence,
(3) suggest that an enhanced role for root crops and palms in the later part

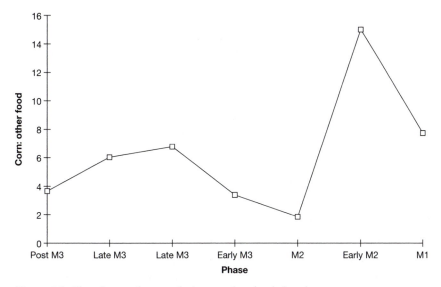

Figure 5.5 Abundance of corn relative to other foods by phase

of the sequence be investigated, and (4) document that the variety (rich-ness) of resources utilized stayed high throughout the sequence. The last point does not negate an increased reliance on maize during Muchique 1 and early Muchique 2, but indicates this occurred in the context of a broad-based subsistence system.

Discussion

Perhaps the most striking point revealed by this preliminary look at the Jama valley archaeobotanical data is that the numbers of kinds of foods used, the richness of the resource base, remained very consistent through time. This is the major contribution of the phytolith data, which show continuity of resources present from Terminal Valdivia (1700 BC) through Jama-Coaque II (AD 1532). Maintaining a broad subsistence base, a natural feature of the lowland forest environment and early subsistence systems, would be highly adaptive in a setting subjected to catastrophic events like tephra fall: the more crops/resources used, the more likely some would be to survive.

Agricultural technology would also play a role in successful human adap-tation in such a setting. Even given a subsistence system characterized by richness, Terminal Valdivia and Chorrera period peoples of the Jama were severely affected by tephra events. One likely contributing factor was con-centration of settlements and fields on the river alluvium, which was buried deeply by redeposited tephra. Archaeological survey data show no Valdivia period settlements off the alluvium, and only a few small Chorrera and Muchique 1 sites in non-alluvium; appreciable expansion of settlement into the uplands and the beginning of upland agriculture, presumably utilizing the slash and burn technique, does not occur until Muchique 2, after the Tephra III ash fall (Pearsall and Zeidler 1994). This suggests that Muchique 2 populations took advantage of 'new' agricultural lands to weather the effects of the tephra. Population growth resulted, with a rapid increase in sites and evidence for storage, such as the pit analysed from the Pechichal site.

It is during the Muchique 2 phase that changes occur in the apparent importance of maize and other food plants. As detailed above, maize increases in abundance relative to tree fruits, beans, and root/tuber foods from Muchique 1 to early Muchique 2. The relationship of this change to the Tephra III event, which occurred between Muchique 1 and 2, is suggestive: of the available crops, was maize best adapted to the altered growing conditions in the valley, namely, very deep tephra deposits on alluvial soils that necessitated use of newly cleared fields in the uplands?

Later in the Muchique phase, maize abundance declines sharply, then rises again in subsequent phases but not to the levels seen previously. Today in the Jama valley both maize and manioc are grown in the uplands; maize first, to take advantage of soil nutrients, followed by manioc. As-yet-unanalysed agronomic data will allow more precise modelling of agricultural productivity in the valley, but perhaps a mixed cropping strategy, as suggested by the lower maize:other food ratios of late Muchique 2 and after, contributed to long-term stability of subsistence in the valley.

In what sense, then, does maize cultivation represent an innovation in subsistence in this case? First, the abundance of charred maize remains relative to other foods is highest in the early part of the Muchique sequence. If, as the van der Merwe *et al.* (1993) isotope study suggests, maize was important in diet beginning in the late Formative (Chorrera) in coastal Ecuador, then it is not surprising that the crop holds this position in the immediate post-Formative period (i.e. Muchique 1 in the Jama valley). While root crops such as manioc, achira, or arrowroot must be processed into flour for storage 'above ground', maize can be readily stored in the form of dried grain. The changing economic and political conditions in the valley marking the emergence of the Jama-Coaque chiefdom may have provided an impetus for maize production in the context of a broad-based subsistence system.

The Jama data also suggest, however, that maize, in combination with the opening of new agricultural lands, may have contributed to the success of the population in quickly reoccupying the valley following the catastrophic Tephra III ash fall. In this sense, an innovation in cropping was perhaps as important as the crop itself.

Conclusion

This chapter has presented a case study focused on the role of maize in innovation in subsistence in lowland South America. To investigate this, or any topic related to subsistence in the tropical lowlands, requires not only systematic recovery of charred macroremains but also analysis of phytoliths which are preserved under conditions where charred materials may be destroyed.[2] Because understanding the quality of preservation is critical for applying quantitative methods to macroremains data (and for knowing when not to apply such methods), these issues were discussed at length, and only one part of the Jama valley sequence, the Muchique phase, was considered from a quantitative perspective.

One of the goals of the Jama Valley Archaeological-Palaeoethnobotanical Project was to test when maize became important in subsistence in western Ecuador – specifically, to test whether the late Formative, the Chorrera period, marked the beginning of maize-based subsistence systems in this region. Unfortunately, the Formative period macroremains database available at this time from the Jama is not robust enough to test this model. We have documented, however, that all the elements of the subsistence system observed at contact, including maize, were in place by the Formative. Maize was the most abundant food throughout the post-Formative, Muchique phase, but was only part of a broad-based subsistence system that contributed to long-term stability. Abundance of maize relative to other foods peaked in early Muchique 2, when it may have played an important role in the rapid recolonization of the valley following a major tephra event. Innovation in coastal Ecuadorian agricultural systems will be investigated further in upcoming research in the Jama River valley.

Acknowledgements

Pearsall and Zeidler's research in the Jama River valley has been supported by grants from the National Science Foundation of the United States.

Notes

1 The corn:other food ratio is not calculated for early Muchique I, since only corn is present among foods.
2 This chapter has not considered pollen evidence, which in some regions can provide valuable insight into subsistence, because pollen has not been well preserved in contexts studied to date in the Jama valley (Zimmerman 1994).

References

Athens, J.S. (1990) *Prehistoric Agricultural Expansion and Population Growth in Northern Highland Ecuador: interim report for 1989 fieldwork*, Honolulu, Hawaii: International Archaeological Research Institute, Inc.

Athens, J.S. (1991) 'Early agriculture in northern highland Ecuador', paper presented at the 56th Annual Meeting of the Society for American Archaeology, New Orleans.

Bendremer, J.C.M. and Dewar, R.E. (1994) 'The advent of prehistoric maize in New England', in S. Johannessen and C.A. Hastorf (eds) *Corn and Culture in the Prehistoric New World*, Boulder, CO: Westview Press.

Bray,W., Herrera, L., Schrimpff, M.C., Botero, P. and Monsalve, J.G. (1987) 'The ancient agricultural landscape of Calima, Colombia', in W. M. Denevan, K. Mathewson and G. Knapp (eds) *Pre-Hispanic Agricultural Fields in the Andean Region*, Oxford: BAR International Series 359 (ii).

Buikstra, J.E. and Milner, G.R. (1991) 'Isotopic and archaeological interpretations of diet in the central Mississippi valley', *Journal of Archaeological Science*, 18: 319–29.

Bush, M.B., Piperno, D.R. and Colinvaux, P.A. (1989) 'A 6000-year history of Amazonian maize cultivation', *Nature*, 340: 303–5.

Damp, J.E. and Pearsall, D.M. (1994) 'Early cotton from coastal Ecuador', *Economic Botany*, 48: 163–5.

Damp, J.E., Pearsall, D.M. and Kaplan, L. (1981) 'Beans for Valdivia', *Science*, 212: 811–12.

Hastorf, C. and Popper, V. (eds) (1988) *Current Paleoethnobotany*, Chicago, IL: University of Chicago Press.

Isaacson, J. (1994) 'Volcanic sediments in archaeological contexts from western Ecuador', in J. A. Zeidler and D. M. Pearsall (eds) *Regional Archaeology in Northern Manabí, Ecuador; Volume 1. Environment, Cultural Chronology, and Prehistoric Subsistence in the Jama River Valley*, Pittsburgh, PA: University of Pittsburgh Memoirs in Latin American Archaeology, No. 8.

Johannessen, S. (1993) 'Farmers of the Late Woodland', in C. M. Scarry (ed.) *Foraging and Farming in the Eastern Woodlands*, Gainesville, FL: University Press of Florida.

Johannessen, S. and Hastorf, C.A. (eds) (1994) *Corn and Culture in the Prehistoric New World*, Boulder, CO: Westview Press.

Katzenberg, M.A., Schwarcz, H.P., Knyf, M. and Melbye, F.J. (1995) 'Stable isotope evidence for maize horticulture and paleodiet in southern Ontario, Canada', *American Antiquity*, 60: 335–50.

Long, A., Benz, B.E., Donahue, D.J., Jull, A.J.T. and Toolin, L.J. (1989) 'First direct AMS dates on early maize from Tehuacan, Mexico', *Radiocarbon*, 31: 1035–40.

Lynott, M.J., Boutton, T.W., Price, J.E. and Nelson, D.E. (1986) 'Stable carbon isotopic evidence for maize agriculture in south-east Missouri and north-east Arkansas', *American Antiquity*, 51: 51–65.

Monsalve, J.G. (1985) 'A pollen core from the Hacienda Lusitania', *Pro Calima*, 4: 40–4.

Pearsall, D.M. (1979) 'The application of ethnobotanical techniques to the problem of subsistence in the Ecuadorian Formative', unpublished PhD dissertation (Anthropology), University of Illinois. University Microfilms, Ann Arbor, Michigan.

Pearsall, D.M. (1983) 'Evaluating the stability of subsistence strategies by use of paleoethnobotanical data', *Journal of Ethnobiology*, 3: 121–37.

Pearsall, D.M. (1988) 'An overview of Formative period subsistence in Ecuador: palaeoethnobotanical data and perspectives', in B. V. Kennedy and G. M.

LeMoine (eds) *Diet and Subsistence: current archaeological perspectives*, Proceedings of the Nineteenth Annual Chacmool Conference, Calgary: The Archaeological Association of the University of Calgary.

Pearsall, D.M. (1989) *Paleoethnobotany: a handbook of procedures*, San Diego, CA: Academic Press.

Pearsall, D.M. (1992a) 'The origins of plant cultivation in South America', in C. Wesley Cowan and P. J. Watson (eds) *The Origins of Agriculture: an international perspective*, Washington, DC: Smithsonian Institution Press.

Pearsall, D.M. (1992b) 'Prehistoric subsistence and agricultural evolution in the Jama river valley, Manabi province, Ecuador', *Journal of the Steward Anthropological Society*, 20: 181–207.

Pearsall, D.M. (1994a) 'Issues in the analysis and interpretation of archaeological maize in South America', in S. Johannessen and C. A. Hastorf (eds) *Corn and Culture in the Prehistoric New World*, Boulder, CO: Westview Press.

Pearsall, D.M. (1994b) 'Macrobotanical analysis', in J. A. Zeidler and D. M. Pearsall (eds) *Regional Archaeology in Northern Manabí, Ecuador; Volume 1. Environment, Cultural Chronology, and Prehistoric Subsistence in the Jama River Valley*, Pittsburgh, PA: University of Pittsburgh Memoirs in Latin American Archaeology, No. 8.

Pearsall, D.M. (1995a) 'Domestication and agriculture in the New World tropics', in T. D. Price and A. B. Gebauer (eds) *Last Hunters-First Farmers: new perspectives on the prehistoric transition to agriculture*, Santa Fe, NM: School of American Research.

Pearsall, D.M. (1995b) '"Doing" paleoethnobotany in the tropical lowlands: adaptation and innovation in methodology', in P. W. Stahl (ed.) *Archaeology in the Lowland American Tropics: current analytical methods and recent applications*, Cambridge: Cambridge University Press.

Pearsall, D.M. (1995c) 'Subsistence in the Ecuadorian Formative: overview and comparison to the central Andes', paper presented at the Dumbarton Oaks Conference on the Ecuadorian Formative, October.

Pearsall, D.M. and Piperno, D.R. (1990) 'Antiquity of maize cultivation in Ecuador: summary and reevaluation of the evidence', *American Antiquity*, 55: 324–37.

Pearsall, D.M. and Zeidler, J.A. (1994) 'Regional environment, cultural chronology, and prehistoric subsistence in northern Manabi', in J. A. Zeidler and D. M. Pearsall (eds) *Regional Archaeology in Northern Manabí, Ecuador; Volume 1. Environment, Cultural Chronology, and Prehistoric Subsistence in the Jama River Valley*, Pittsburgh, PA: University of Pittsburgh Memoirs in Latin American Archaeology, No. 8.

Piperno, D.R. (1985) 'Phytolithic analysis of geological sediments from Panama', *Antiquity*, LIX: 13–19.

Piperno, D.R. (1988) *Phytolith Analysis: an archaeological and geological perspective*, San Diego, CA: Academic Press.

Piperno, D.R. (1990) 'Aboriginal agriculture and land usage in the Amazon basin, Ecuador', *Journal of Archaeological Science*, 17: 665–77.

Piperno, D.R. (1993) 'Phytolith and charcoal records from deep lake cores in the American tropics', in D. M. Pearsall and D. R. Piperno (eds) *Current Research in Phytolith Analysis: applications in archaeology and paleoecology*, Philadelphia: MASCA, the University Museum of Archaeology and Anthropology, University of Pennsylvania.

Piperno, D.R. (1994) 'Phytolith and charcoal evidence for prehistoric slash-and-burn agriculture in the Darien rainforest of Panama', *The Holocene*, 4: 321–5.

Piperno, D.R. (1995) 'Plant microfossils and their application in the New World tropics', in P. W. Stahl (ed.) *Archaeology in the Lowland American Tropics: current analytical methods and recent applications*, Cambridge: Cambridge University Press.

Piperno, D.R., Bush, M.B. and Colinvaux, P.A. (1990) 'Paleoenvironments and human occupation in late-glacial Panama', *Quaternary Research*, 33: 108–16.

Piperno, D.R., Bush, M.B. and Colinvaux, P.A. (1991a) 'Paleoecological perspectives on human adaptation in central Panama. I. The Pleistocene', *Geoarchaeology*, 6: 201–26.

Piperno, D.R., Bush, M.B. and Colinvaux, P.A. (1991b) 'Paleoecological perspectives on human adaptation in Central Panama. II. The Holocene', *Geoarchaeology*, 6: 227–50.

Piperno, D.R., Husum-Clary, K., Cooke, R.G., Ranere, A.J. and Weiland, D. (1985) 'Preceramic maize in central Panama: phytolith and pollen evidence', *American Anthropologist*, 87: 871–8.

Riley, T.J., Edging, R. and Rossen, J. (1990) 'Cultigens in prehistoric eastern North America', *Current Anthropology*, 31: 525–41.

Riley, T.J., Walz, G.R., Bareis, C.J., Fortier, A.C. and Parker, K.E. (1994) 'Accelerator mass spectrometry (AMS) dates confirm early *Zea mays* in the Mississippi River valley', *American Antiquity*, 59: 490–8.

Rue, D.J. (1989) 'Archaic middle American agriculture and settlement: recent pollen data from Honduras', *Journal of Field Archaeology*, 16: 177–84.

Scarry, C.M. (1993) 'Variation in Mississippian crop production strategies', in C. M. Scarry (ed.) *Foraging and Farming in the Eastern Woodlands*, Gainesville, FL: University Press of Florida.

Smith, B.D. (1989) 'The origins of agriculture in eastern North America', *Science*, 246: 1566–71.

van der Merwe, N.J., Lee-Thorp, J.A. and Scott Raymond, J. (1993) 'Light, stable isotopes and the subsistence base of Formative cultures at Valdivia, Ecuador', in J. B. Lambert and G. Grupe (eds) *Prehistoric Human Bone: archaeology at the molecular level*, Berlin: Springer-Verlag.

Vaughn, H.H., Deevy, E.S., Jr. and Garrett-Jones, S.E. (1985) 'Pollen stratigraphy of two cores from the Petén Lake district, with an appendix on two deep-water cores', in M. Pohl (ed.) *Prehistoric Lowland Maya Environment and Subsistence Economy*, Cambridge, MA: Peabody Museum of Archaeology and Ethnology, Harvard University.

Zeidler, J.A. and Kennedy, R. (1994) 'Environmental setting', in J. A. Zeidler and D. M. Pearsall (eds) *Regional Archaeology in Northern Manabí, Ecuador, Volume 1. Environment, Cultural Chronology, and Prehistoric Subsistence in the Jama River Valley*, Pittsburgh, PA: University of Pittsburgh Memoirs in Latin American Archaeology, No. 8.

Zeidler, J.A. and Pearsall, D.M. (eds) (1994) *Regional Archaeology in Northern Manabí, Ecuador, Volume 1. Environment, Cultural Chronology, and Prehistoric Subsistence in the Jama River Valley*, Pittsburgh, PA: University of Pittsburgh Memoirs in Latin American Archaeology, No. 8.

Zeidler, J.A., Buck, C.E. and Litton, C.O. (1998) 'The integration of archaeological phase information and radiocarbon results from the Jama river valley, Ecuador: a Bayesian approach', *Latin American Antiquity*, 9: 160–79.

Zimmerman, L.S. (1994) 'Palynological analysis', in J. A. Zeidler and D. M. Pearsall (eds) *Regional Archaeology in Northern Manabí, Ecuador, Volume 1. Environment, Cultural Chronology, and Prehistoric Subsistence in the Jama River Valley*, Pittsburgh, PA: University of Pittsburgh Memoirs in Latin American Archaeology, No. 8.

Update: Early occurrences of maize

Deborah M. Pearsall

New data from archaeological sites and environmental cores confirm the early domestication and spread of maize. At the San Andres site in Tabasco, Mexico, cultivated *Zea* pollen dates to 5100 cal. BC, and large *Zea* pollen, typical of maize, appears about 5000 cal. BC (Pope *et al.* 2001). Dates of 4300 cal. BC have been determined on maize cobs from the Guilá Naquitz site in Mexico (Piperno and Flannery 2001). In Pacific coastal Guatemala, maize phytoliths and pollen are present in cores by 3500 cal. BC (Neff *et al.* 2006). Additionally, residue analyses of stone tools and ceramics are providing exciting new data on the antiquity and distribution of maize and other Neotropical crops, including manioc, arrowroot and lleren. Maize phytoliths and starch occur on all 17 stone tools studied from a Valdivia 3 (2800–2400 cal. BC) household at the Real Alto site, Ecuador (Pearsall *et al.* 2004). Maize starch grains and phytoliths were recovered from grinding stones and soil samples from the Waynuna site in southern Andean Peru dated to 2000–1600 cal. BC (Perry *et al.* 2006). Piperno and Pearsall (1998) and Neff *et al.* (2006) provide overviews.

Concerning the Jama project, paleoethnobotanical research has now been completed. Data include plant remains from 14 archaeological sites spanning Piquigua through Muchique 4 and six seasons of observing modern agriculture. Pearsall (2004) discusses the nature of plant–people inter-relationships in the Jama Valley through analysis of macroremains and phytoliths from Muchique 2 (early Jama-Coaque II), and models the valley's agricultural potential through a study of modern maize and manioc yields.

Well-preserved assemblages reflect the diversity of plant resources in this tropical coastal setting. Maize, beans and squash were annual seed crops and manioc, *Canna*, *Calathea allouia* (lleren) and *Maranta arundinacea* (arrowroot) perennial root/tuber crops were among the domesticated foods grown. At least two kinds of palm, *coroso* and *cadi*, were eaten, as were *Psidium*, Annonaceae, *Sideroxylon*, other Sapotaceae and Chrysobalanaceae fruits. Many other tree fruit fragments were recovered that could only be described as morphotypes.

Jama valley maize is a small-kerneled, somewhat variable 16-row variety. Phytoliths extracted from cupules exhibit some primitive characteristics. Beans are also small, but in the size range of other common beans from archaeological contexts in South America. None of the plants contributing small seeds to the assemblages appear to be significant food sources. Some, such as *Amaranthus*, *Passiflora* and *Rubus*, are edible, but there are no seed caches or other evidence that a 'small seed complex' played a significant role in subsistence. Nearly all identified taxa grow today along roadsides, in overgrown agricultural fields and similar disturbed habitats.

Some plants identified in Jama samples provided materials for construction, household implements, clothing and containers. Gourds and tree gourds are useful containers, serving utensils and net floats. Bamboo and wood are used for wall construction and household furniture such as sleeping platforms. Palm, grasses and bird-of-paradise are all useful for roof thatch. Cotton was likely spun and woven into cloth for clothing, and netted to make hammocks, carrying nets and fishing nets. *Achiote* provided a red dye for cloth, body paint or food colouring.

Table 5.4 is a summary of richness – numbers of plant taxa present – by period for all sites compiled from site reports. These data further document the emergence of an agroecology and the role of maize. In spite of taphonomic and sampling issues, there appear to be underlying behavioural patterns in the data. For example, richness in arboreal taxa, as measured by both macroremains and phytoliths, is fairly even from Tabuchila through Muchique 3. If all sites had equal macroremain preservation, numbers of tree fruits would be higher, increasing evenness. This suggests two things. First, that tree fruits played a role in subsistence throughout the sequence, and were not replaced by maize and root/tuber crops later in time. Some phytolith profiles show an increase in useful trees, such as palms, in the later phases. Second, arboreal indicators in background vegetation do not drop off evenly over time. A major decline happens early, with more gradual change thereafter. As the Rio Grande profile studied by Veintimilla (2000) suggests, cutting of primary forest for agriculture occurred during the Formative period, and secondary forests continued to make up a significant part of the vegetation until late in the sequence.

There also seems to be a 'real' trend in increased numbers of open habitat/weedy indicators in the later phases. Increased kinds of small seeds – taxa that favour open habitats, including fallow agricultural fields – contribute

Table 5.4 Number of plant taxa for each period, for all sites

Phase	Economic	Arboreal	Open habitat	Total	Number of sites
Piquigua	5	9	10	24	4
Tabuchila	6	18	13	37	7
Muchique 1	7	19	14	40	6
Muchique 2	10	34	46	90	5
Muchique 3	7	21	28	56	6
Muchique 4	4	6	11	21	1

greatly to increased richness during Muchique 2 and 3. The phytolith record indicates that open habitats were being maintained, at the expense of re-growing forest, even earlier in the sequence. For example, Asteraceae and *Heliconia* are two taxa that thrive in open areas and forest openings, respectively. At the El Tape site, Asteraceae and *Heliconia* are absent in Piquigua phase samples, appear in the Tabuchila phase, then increase slightly in frequency in Muchique 2. Increases in useful trees, such as palms, occur subsequently to increases in open area indicators.

Over the course of prehistory in the Jama Valley, we see the creation of an agroecology in which maize played a key role, useful arboreal species were maintained, weedy herbaceous and woody plants proliferated, and a complex mosaic of areas maintained as open habitats, secondary forests and remnant mature forests emerged. This process of landscape evolution began soon after the valley was settled, and intensified in Muchique 2, following the Tephra III ash fall.

References

Neff, H., Pearsall, D.M., Jones, J.G., Arroyo, B., Collins, S.K. and Friedel, D.E. (2006) 'Early Maya adaptive patterns: mid-late Holocene paleoenvironmental evidence from Pacific Guatemala', *Latin American Antiquity*, 17: 23–53.

Pearsall, D.M. (2004) *Plants and People in Ancient Ecuador: the ethnobotany of the Jama River Valley*, Belmont, CA: Wadsworth/Thomson Learning.

Pearsall, D.M., Chandler-Ezell, K. and Zeidler, J.A. (2004) 'Maize in ancient Ecuador: results of residue analysis of stone tools from the Real Alto site', *Journal of Archaeological Science*, 31: 423–42.

Perry, L., Sandweiss, D.H., Piperno, D.R., Rademaker, K., Malpass, M.A., Umire, A. and de la Vera, P. (2006) 'Early maize agriculture and interzonal interaction in southern Peru', *Nature*, 440: 76–9.

Piperno, D.R. and Flannery, K.V. (2001) 'The earliest archaeological maize (*Zea mays* L.) from highland Mexico: new accelerator mass spectrometry dates and their implications', *Proceedings of the National Academy of Sciences of USA*, 98: 2101–3.

Piperno, D.R. and Pearsall, D.M. (1998) *The Origins of Agriculture in the Lowland Neotropics*, San Diego, CA: Academic Press.

Pope, K.O., Pohl, M.E.D., Jones, J.G., Lentz, D.L., von Nagy, C., Vega, F.J. and Quitmyer, I.R. (2001) 'Origin and environmental setting of ancient agriculture in the lowlands of Mesoamerica', *Science*, 292: 1370–3.

Veintimilla, C.I. (2000) 'Reconstrucción paleo-ambiental y evolución agrícola en el Valle del Río Jama, Provincia de Manabí, Ecuador', *Revista del Museo Antropológico del Banco Central del Ecuador, Guayaquil*, 9: 135–51.

6 Cultural implications of crop introductions in Andean prehistory

Christine A. Hastorf

Introduction

Plants participate in political processes at many levels: civic, ceremonial, ritual, as well as daily practice, creating and recreating the world that people perceive and live in through the meals that are prepared and eaten, the tools that are produced and used, and the kin groups that exist across the landscape. Through plant patterns in the archaeological record, archaeologists can identify cultural activities. In this chapter, I shall look at the onset of agriculture and the entrance of crop use seen archaeologically along the west coast of Peru with a focus on the tempo of uptake of foreign crops. With that evidence, I shall explore what plant use might illustrate about the social dynamics in these early sedentary groups. I will use the example of Peruvian coastal plant data, spanning the time of the first plants up to the evidence for the political developments of the Early Horizon. The dates and traditional phase names span the Preceramic and the Initial Phases:

- Preceramic Phase III (8000–6000 BC);
- Preceramic Phase IV (6000–4200 BC);
- Preceramic Phase V (4200–2500 BC);
- Preceramic Phase VI (2500–2100 BC) – Cotton Preceramic;
- Initial Period (2100–1400 BC).[1]

The greater Andean region of South America is considered one of the centres of pre-modern civilization. This area includes modern Ecuador, Peru, Bolivia, northern Chile and north-west Argentina. It lies along the main spine of the South American continental mountain range. It is notable for its diverse environmental zones that can be very close together. The area this study focuses on is the Peruvian coast, along hundreds of kilometres of very dry coastline. Many scholars describe this long time-span there, like the Neolithic in Europe, as a unified, homogeneous cultural and economic trajectory. But, looking at this time-span from another angle, I think we can see diversity in this sequence that illustrates the growth and maintenance of cultural identities as well as the values of the plants that were farmed.

My question is not why did intensive agriculture take so long to develop on the coast of Peru, which it did, but what can the introductions of the crops and their distributions during this long time period illustrate about the political and cultural processes that were occurring? Here I shall view the creation of cultural difference through food and its preparation and investigate what meanings might have accompanied such a process. By moving on from the well-discussed models of population pressure and climatic constraints of the coast, I think we can see a dynamic of cultural difference along the coast in the Preceramic phases between 8000–1400 BC that only minimally relates to environmental differences (Lanning 1967). Many ideas have been put forward for why agriculture began and why it spread. While most models hold a grain of truth, none satisfy the archaeological community with an explanation. I think we can gain further understanding about this transition by looking at the differences in these changes more closely.

Marek Zvelebil, in his edited volume on the transition to farming in Eurasia, presents a series of models for agrarian onset with an eye towards geographical and temporal differences. In the concluding chapter he makes a case that this innovation occurs for different reasons in different settings. He lists a series of traditional causes for taking up agriculture in different geographical settings. These include filling gaps in the local resources (Lewthwaite 1986), contact with farmers (Zvelebil 1986), a decline in resources through climate change, environmental stress or population pressure and thus the need for increased calorific output (Cohen 1978, 1981), social competition (Bender 1978, 1985; Hayden 1990), and colonization (Ammerman and Cavalli-Sforza 1984). This last model for the uptake of agriculture outside of a plant (or animal) domestication core suggests that when a set of crops was adopted, it was accompanied by new technologies, paraphernalia and people. Zvelebil (1986) notes that when crops arrived as a package, people were probably moving into the region, bringing along their own cultural traits and subsistence strategies. While this should be the most easily visible model in the archaeological record, it does not have supporting evidence along the coast of Peru.

The other above-mentioned models are well known and have been suggested for the Peruvian onset of agriculture, therefore I will not elaborate on these models here. I claim that these models do not provide us with the closest explanations for the onset and spread of agriculture. I would like to re-focus our view of this transition by taking a slightly different look at the agricultural evidence to see if we cannot get closer to the changes during the Preceramic years, setting the stage for the later, rich and elaborate Andean political (pre)histories.

Some models

The traditional economic models of agricultural origins do not fit most individual examples; their scales are not correct. This challenges us to seek out new perspectives about domestication, directing us to look at the smaller events in food use. Perhaps these events are more tied to inter-community relations, settlement configuration, marriage patterns and exchange (Goody 1982), harvesting shifts (Hillman and Davies 1990; Bohrer 1991), as well as the definition of the people's ethnicities through daily practice.

What were the first domesticates and what might have been their value to the people tending them? A traditional model for Peruvian agriculture is that people were hungry so they focused on producing high carbohydrate foods to ease resource pressure and feed their growing population (Cohen 1978; Wilson 1981). Food shortage could have been brought about by many causes, including climate change, change in the resource base, or just more people in the area. I find these models particularly dubious for the Peruvian coast. The Peruvian coast is one of the richest marine food resource areas in the world (Moseley 1975; Quilter and Stocker 1983). Models for the onset of agriculture also include the impact of the periodic torrential storms (El Niño) and the need for storage along the Peruvian coast (Osborne 1977). This storm model is curious because periodic storms, which occur in many places of the world, have not been used as a model for agricultural origins in other regions.

Of the two main classes of foragers who adopt agriculture world-wide, one is mobile with small groups following clustered, patchy resources, the other is more sedentary with larger communities and steady, local resources. Zvelebil (1986) suggests that farming was more likely to be taken up by mobile foragers first, while more sedentary and complex foragers would accept it more slowly and for different reasons. Sedentary coastal foragers with good marine and littoral resources, like Peru, at some point in time would have had access to and knowledge about the use of various crops but clearly chose *not* to add their production and tending to their daily activities, or to change their cuisine and symbolic economy for some time – if ever in some cases.

The *regular* use of domestic crops in the early days of farming, especially among the more sedentary foragers, seems to be more about cultural symbols and kinship relationships than hunger. Farrington and Urry's model for domestication (1985) suggests that the first domesticated plants were herbaceous plants of a tasty, oily or spicy flavour, consumed to diversify meals rather than to bulk them up; exotic (even medicinal) foods added to special family or group meals rather than to ward off starvation. While the authors do not speculate beyond the desirability of this food type, their refreshing model prompts one to ask how and why *specific* plants may have entered into a group's daily practice? Can we suggest that the tasty plants that were taken up also had some special meaning or identity due to their links with places, events or peoples? I would think that the new foods had to have a (positive) meaning in order to be added into the cuisine.

The Farrington and Urry model is a variation of the idea proposed by Braidwood for grain domestication in the Near East (1953). He suggests that early grain cultivation was due to an interest in beer production; people took the extra time for plant tending to provide a bit of 'spice' in their daily routine with the consumption of fermented beverages and all that might have entailed culturally and socially (Braidwood 1953). The role of fermented beverages and hallucinogens in early agriculture comes and goes in the archaeological literature, but I think they probably played a larger part in initiating new activities than archaeologists give them credit for.

A more politically driven model for the use of domesticates is seen in Barbara Bender's (1978) and Brian Hayden's (1990) ideas that people adopted and cultivated crops because of an increased interest in political activities and exchange. They assume that agricultural produce would provide exchangeable goods, thus making groups regularly operate in a larger network. Gaining items for exchange can be linked to an increased desire for public display, alliance building and group construction of identity through feasts and food gifts. These political acts would probably be initiated by important families, leaders or religious persons, keen to introduce plants and encourage the cultivation of crops once they were present. Such acts, however, seem to occur after the cultural changes that are initiated with agriculture in changing daily practice. This political stage, involved in the growth of hierarchy and surplus, is a different level of interest and access than the differences being formed in early agriculture.

We see more appropriate small-scale beginnings without overt political pressures (but probably covert social pressures) in the model proposed by Watson and Kennedy (1991). They suggest that women gatherers first initiated the cultivation of plants in North America through their tending of wild taxa that were of interest to them in their daily rounds of food and medicine gathering. Women thus were the plant nurturers that instigated the morphological and genetic changes that we associate with domestication, not as an economic behaviour, but as nurturers of, and experimenters with, people and plants. This point cannot be overemphasized. Women foragers are constantly collecting and experimenting with plants for nibbling, spicing foods, and medicines. The female Barasana of Colombia, a foraging, swidden farming group, are the collectors of plants. They bring back cuttings, exchange with friends and kin, in a constantly nurturing mode of plant and family raising (Hugh-Jones, pers. comm.). Women also are involved in tending specific taxa that they inherit along their family lines; special family crops that have symbolic meanings linked to the origin myths of their ancestors. These would be carried with women when they moved, planted in each new home, and fed to their families. Their neighbours would recognize that specific variety as that family's plant, with all of its connotations.

Helping us develop a different model of agricultural onset in Peru are the activities from modern Amazonian forager-farmers. Current evidence suggests that small-scale familial inter-regional relationships have wide-ranging catchments due to exogamous marriage patterns. Through these networks of periodic visits or while on hunting and gathering journeys away from home-base villages, plants are brought back from near and far, not for gain but for curiosity, pleasure and value (Hugh-Jones and Posey, pers. comm.). These plants are planted along local paths and in encircling kitchen gardens and include exotics, medicinal, magical, industrial, mind-altering, and spicy food plants. In this way, plants enter into a people's cuisine because of experimentation, interest and curiosity. Further, in the Amazon, some plant varieties are community markers. Communities have specific taxa or varieties that are associated with their community identity (Hugh-Jones, pers. comm.). These plants are passed on through the generations to grow and eat, especially at feasts in the process of defining ethnicity. As ethnic markers their neighbours emphasize different plants in their own feasts and myths. Thus these plants move with the people as part of their rituals, renewing their social ties past and present as well as marking their territory.

Such a scenario for plant entry is likely for the Peruvian coast, as most plants were brought in from elsewhere, and thus had to be cared for as special things within the landscape from the start. In fact, the earliest coastal evidence suggests that the plants were grown in a world that was neither domesticated nor sedentary. We don't know much about the pre-agricultural sites, but probably there was movement from the coast seasonally inland with fishing and foraging in the *lomas* cloud forests on the coast and gathering and hunting inland, even up into the intermontane region and over into the jungle. We have evidence for cave use and tool processing sites, but coastal sites hint at sedentism only by around 4000 BC.

About domestication

How does domestication first become possible and then active in a group? Hodder (1991) has addressed this question for the European Neolithic by suggesting that people first had to create the concept of domestication before actions could be taken. I suggest that the physical and social development and maintenance of the kin-line and family was an active ingredient in initiating the concept of both farming and territoriality. Things and places would begin to be associated with activities that surround families. A jurisdiction over a plant, tree or place on a stream (a loose ownership) was probably developed through using the thing or place in special ritual time. This concept could have been expanded upon and other *things* could then become 'domesticated' or incorporated into a family's array of collective memories and associated things. This could include clay for pottery, springs for water, plants and where they grow, resources for building shelters and making tools, as well as whole landscapes for living in. The objects have to take on new meanings and identities. Human influence (impact, power, or a sense that humans have made a difference) is linked to meaningful interactions with a thing ('a loose form of domestication'), and this interaction creates a sense of identity.

How did people change their view of the landscape such that they began to see it as a place and a territory rather than just something they move through? Thomas (1993) has suggested that, as seasonal rounds became more regular and as locations were repeatedly visited by the same people, a series of encounters with these specific locales would become incorporated into the people's collective memories and cosmologies. Each place became invested with past memories and meanings. These special places in turn influenced the activities that occurred there, creating group identity and social relations within the group (Thomas 1993: 82). Such locations and associated remembrances would have existed where specifically charged interactions transpired. At times these would have been events that included the use of the local vegetation and animals. These marked places could have become special, expressly because they were where certain plants or animals inhabited and/or where these life-forms interacted with humans. These places or plants could have gained meaningful identity through such recurring activities. People identify with and therefore signify ('domesticate') places, as well as flora and fauna, probably well before morphologically defined domestication is evident in the archaeological record.

Social identity therefore is associated with food preferences. As individuals and families begin to identify with a place or with specific activities, they also begin to identify with the food they eat together there (Appadurai 1981; Douglas 1984). A version of this is seen in the totems of many societies, where kin groups identify with certain taxa. So too, food presentations have meanings, associated with people, events, and spatial or temporal places where they are consumed. Foods and activities can be social markers used in group affiliation, often without other material signs that archaeologists look for being visible and well before hierarchy is codified. Food can separate one sub-group from another not only in fasting and taboos (males and females, young and old), but also in foods that are feasted. This is done through identifying preferences such as one group eating maize at their feast, while their neighbours down the road feast on manioc. Further, cultural and political differences can be negotiated and accentuated through food preparation and presentation (Hastorf and Johannessen 1993; Welch and Scarry 1995).

Plants that were adopted by groups early on surely had special meanings or identities due to their links with places, events and histories. It is up to us now to search for and propose what these associations and meanings might have been in the groups we study. One goal therefore is to chart the acceptance of domestic plants and the social and political changes that must have accompanied these processes.

We see in various examples around the world that, after local plant cultivation began and the concepts of domestication and territory were initiated, groups incorporated foreign plants, but these often provided only a small portion of the diet for a long time. Why did people take up some crops and not others into their diet either as new foods or as substitutes of something previously foraged? Was it that these plants had different meanings for the farmers, that some plants were brought in with a mythology while others were connected to their neighbours' mythology? What can we learn from a sequence of plant additions into diets and cuisines about cultural developments?

The Peruvian case

Returning to the earlier models, the Peruvian coastal environmental situation fits the sedentary forager model of rich marine resources best. Yet, it is one of the driest places in the world, with habitable areas restricted to the coast and along the rivers. What we find is that hundreds and sometimes thousands of years passed before certain coastal valley residents adopted some of the crops that their neighbours were growing and consuming. We will see in the data that, while there are several different patterns of crop adoption, in general crops entered the region in a patchy manner. I do not think there is strong evidence for stress on resources during these times. The evidence reflects different selective cultural strategies and meanings at each site.

The data we have for coastal Peru are of irregular quality but of superb preservation. With more than twenty sites that have botanical remains on or near the coast, the data are in no way complete or systematic. Over the years, many different collection strategies have been implemented, making it impossible to quantitatively compare the samples. Because of this, I present the plant taxa qualitatively, as either present or absent.[2]

The first evidence for crop plants on the coast comes in the Preceramic III phase, 8000–6000 BC. However, substantial agriculture, with a regular array of fifteen to twenty crops growing up and down the coast, occurs only by the end of the Initial phase, 2100–1400 BC, some 4–5000 years later. By this time we have irrigation systems associated with civic architecture.

The plant material

Figures 6.1–6.5[3] present a selective set of twelve crop taxa in five archaeological phases spanning the earliest crop evidence through large ceremonial centres and semi-urban ways of life. Most of these crops occur regularly at coastal sites after the Initial Period, after 1400 BC. By then we have evidence for a qualitatively different form of hierarchy and stratification in the record of both difference within and between communities. Not all plant taxa found on the sites are included in this presentation. I have chosen only a range of crops to focus on the trends. The point of this subset is to look at general trends of taxa introduction through time. The plants are plotted on the maps by presence only, so that the viewer can see the general pattern through time without too many plants to comprehend at one time. My hope is that patterns and trends of plant entry will be clearer if we track fewer plants. I selected a representative array of plants from three major plant categories to give a balanced perspective of the most important plant entries. These plants include three locally 'domesticated' plants, begonia (*Begonia geraniifolia*), cotton (*Gossypium barbedense*) and bottle gourd (*Lagenaria siceraria* (Mol.) Standl.) and nine introduced, foreign plants.

These nine plants encompass several plant life-forms that are important when thinking about people actually planting and tending the crops; in other words, the types of human–plant interactions necessary for the successful growing of the plant. These plant categories include root crops: manioc (or yucca *Manihot esculenta* Crantz), achira (*Canna edulis*), potatoes (*Solanum* spp. L.) and begonia; annuals: chile peppers (*Capsicum* spp., *chinensis* and *baccatum*), common bean (*Phaseolus vulgaris*), lima bean (*Phaseolus lunatus*), bottle gourd, cotton and maize (*Zea mays* L.); and perennial trees, avocado (*Persea americana*) and guava (*Psidium guajava*). Most of these plants come from the eastern slopes of the central Andes or from the tropics in the northern part of the continent (Pickersgill 1969; Bergh 1976; Pickersgill and Heiser 1977; Pearsall 1992). In those places planting can occur all year long. It is becoming more accepted that the first South American domesticates were root crops, probably initially cultivated in the moister regions of southern Mesoamerica and northern South America (Sauer 1952; Harris 1969; Roosevelt 1980).

Along the west coast, differences in plant use cannot be attributed to different climatic or storm patterns, although there are slight differences in the moisture regimes and micro-environments. There is variation in water availability between the valleys. The southern valleys are drier, with more seasonal water flowing down the rivers from the Andes; the northern valleys are larger and have perennial water. The northern valleys have sandy beaches from which to launch boats and to net fish, while south of the Santa Valley the shoreline is rocky, which is good for rock-pool animals. The sea and especially the rocky littoral had abundant foods and there was regular *lomas* (cloud forest) plant exploitation. Given that the bulk of the plants in the archaeological record up and down the coast are non-local, the pattern of plant uptake suggests social and symbolic processes at work as much as if not more than economic and environmental.

Annual plants

Six annual crops are plotted on the maps, including the most prominent through prehistory. The earliest, chile pepper, is the *Capsicum baccatum*, domesticated in southern Peru or eastern Bolivia. The second American pepper, *C. chinense*, arrived on the coast also from the eastern slopes (Pickersgill 1969). Both peppers are hardy plants and need warmth and water. The lima bean arrived earlier in Peru than the common bean. While both beans are from the eastern slopes of the Andes, they were taken up differentially along the coast while becoming important crops (Kaplan 1980;

Gepts *et al.* 1986). Gourds, like cotton, are first found on the north coast and in the highlands but are thought to have been harvested wild on the west coast of South America from locally growing varieties that existed naturally along the lower river banks on the South American coastline. Andean cotton is a hybrid of several cotton species from the New World and Africa, considered to have been naturally dispersed (Stephens and Moseley 1974). Both gourds and cotton seem to have been harvested for a long time before visible morphological change occurred. These two plants grow well along the sunny coastline.

Maize is an interesting crop and actually seems to arrive quite late into the Andean region, given its locus of origin in the Rio Balsas region of western Mexico and early evidence in lowland Central and South America (Bush *et al.* 1989; Benz 1994; Pearsall 1994). It is an annual that must be tended by humans to survive, though it is quite flexible genetically and can adapt to many different environments. Its route into the western Andes was either down the western coast and/or over the mountains to the coast from the eastern slopes.

Vegetatively reproduced plants

Of the four tuberous plants, manioc is the earliest in the region. Several locations of origin have been suggested for manioc: north-eastern Brazil (the driest locale), southern Mexico-Guatemala, the Orinoco River Basin or Venezuela, all places with a dry and a wet season (Rogers 1963: 52; Harris 1969; Rogers and Appan 1972: 1). The South American locations are considered the most likely loci of origin. This perennial shrub can produce bitter or sweet root-tubers. It is thought that the sweet variety spread first into the Andes, requiring little processing to make it edible (Hawkes 1989: 486). Since it can be harvested year-round this is a very useful crop, except that a protein source must accompany it to make a balanced diet. It is propagated by replanting cuttings, and thus is not as easy to domesticate as other tubers. The archaeological evidence supports its domestication because of its spread to new locations from its homeland.

Achira is thought to have been domesticated in mid-elevation valleys, perhaps even in the western-slope Andean valleys of South America or in the eastern mid-elevation valleys (Ugent *et al.* 1984; Hawkes 1989: 492). It propagates by its tubers, and thus is very easy to cultivate. Like manioc, there is no clear evidence for domestication other than its geographical spread. Its regular presence suggests that it was easily and quickly adapted to the coast.

The potato's most likely wild progenitors come from the greater Titicaca Basin and its nearby valleys and could have spread across the Andes and down into the western valleys reasonably quickly (Hawkes 1989: 495). It is a stem tuber in that the storage organs grow off stems under the ground. It propagates by planting the previous year's tubers, which generate more underground storage tubers. It is easy to plant and can become feral easily.

Begonia is a west coast *lomas* plant that was intensively used and perhaps cultivated at the Chilca sites, but seemed never to spread much beyond there (Quilter 1989).

Perennial trees

I have included two trees, one a protein-rich food and the second a fruit tree. The avocado tree species found in Peru comes from northern South America (Bergh 1976). Its high protein and fat content would make it a very desirable food – especially so because this South American variety can yield all year round and produces for many years. It is a tree propagated by seed, and thus cropping such a plant would take dedication to plant and maintain with regular visits and/or local residence to harvest it. It would be some years before the first yield, and its presence suggests people had a long-term interest in a locale and planned for such a crop to produce years in the future. Guava is also a tree species, growing in warm, moist settings, requiring years to produce mature fruit. Its locus of domestication is unclear at this point. Guava first occurs archaeologically in mid-elevations in the Andes and could have been brought in from nearby, over the mountains (Harlan 1975).

The sequence of crop introductions

At the beginning of this sequence pre-8000 BC coastal people were living on a combination of *lomas* seasonal cloud forest plants and animals as well as a wide range of marine life. The northern coast stabilized to what we see today only by 4000 BC, the reason we have no early coastal sites in the north. What coastal evidence we do have from the south coast, like La Paloma in the Chilca Valley, indicates that people lived near and between the *lomas* and the coast (Quilter 1989). The inland Santa Valley Guiterrero Cave foodstuffs could have arrived from the eastern rivers originally but were probably grown locally (Lynch 1980). We are not yet able to reconstruct what type of communication networks existed between the western valleys and the eastern slopes. It is not surprising that foraging people moved easily across this space and that at least some members of the coastal groups travelled regularly up the western valleys into and over the mountains to the eastern areas.

In the first phase, the Preceramic III during the seventh millennium, the earliest crops in the north are beans and chile peppers, with potato and manioc to the south in the Chilca Valley and the Tres Ventanas Cave (Figure 6.1). Most of this plant evidence is of questionable identification. The best documented material comes from the Guiterrero Cave (Lynch 1980), although there has been a reassessment of the early beans using AMS dating which places the bean later in time (Kaplan 1994). While I am not convinced of the security of the date and stratigraphy of the tubers at Tres

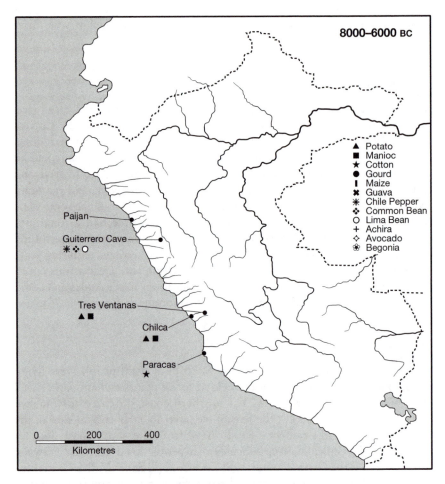

Figure 6.1 Twelve domestic plant taxa distributions of the Preceramic III: 8000–
6000 BC from the central Andean region, based primarily on Lanning
(1967) and Pearsall (1978, 1992)

Ventanas Cave in the Chilca Valley, some scholars support the early dates,
a millennium earlier than Guiterrero Cave (Engel 1973; Martins-Farias
1976). All crops are introduced from afar except perhaps the potato at Tres
Ventanas Cave.

While tubers do not become common over the next 5000 years, beans
continue to be the most common crops in the excavations, from 6000 to
4200 BC (Figure 6.2), with beans, gourd and guava entering the south coast
at La Paloma (Quilter 1989). Because of the high frequencies of begonia at
La Paloma, Quilter suggests that it was intensively harvested and perhaps
cultivated at that site. This, however, is the only site where such evidence
exists at this time.

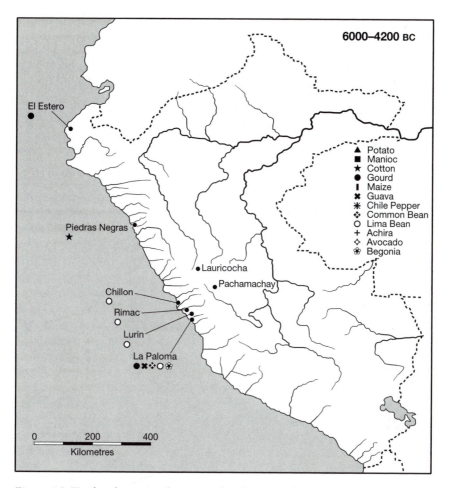

El Estero

Piedras Negras

Lauricocha

Pachamachay

Chillon

Rimac

Lurin

La Paloma

6000–4200 BC

▲ Potato
■ Manioc
★ Cotton
● Gourd
❘ Maize
✖ Guava
✳ Chile Pepper
✤ Common Bean
○ Lima Bean
+ Achira
◇ Avocado
❀ Begonia

0   200   400
Kilometres

Figure 6.2 Twelve domestic plant taxa distributions of the Preceramic IV: 6000–4200 BC from the central Andean region, based primarily on Lanning (1967) and Pearsall (1978, 1992)

When very little else was grown, beans were cultivated. Could they have been introduced as a taste treat, fitting the Farrington and Urry model? More importantly, half of the edible crops from these first two phases (chiles, beans and guava) are savoury treats. Chile peppers are still the quintessential spice in the New World; toasted beans are a common snack food today. Perhaps early starchy foods occurred in the western valley caves, but then there is a hiatus in site occupation evidence until about 2500 BC, leaving us without much solid evidence for plant use there. The annual crops are moderately hardy and could be left to grow on their own along the river banks in the same areas where riparian plants, gourds and cotton could grow, suggesting that people could have still been making seasonal rounds well through 4000 BC. This is when the climatic patterns of today probably began (periodic El Niños).

In the Preceramic V phase (4200–2500 BC), we see the continued occurrence of beans, with both bean taxa present on the south and the central coast (Figure 6.3). It is towards the end of this phase that achira and avocado enter the region. Several new crops occur at La Galgada, a ritual site in the mid-elevations of the Santa Valley (Smith, in Grieder *et al.* 1988: 125–51). This site is a ceremonial centre *en route* between the coast and the eastern slopes. Therefore, it is not surprising that it has the first evidence for achira and avocado from the east. The other achira evidence is from the Chilca Valley. Beans are most frequent at the coastal sites. The other common crops

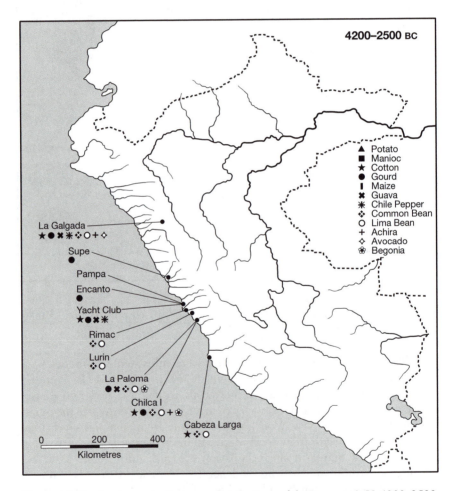

Figure 6.3 Twelve domestic plant taxa distributions of the Preceramic V: 4200–2500 BC from the central Andean region, based primarily on Lanning (1967) and Pearsall (1978, 1992)

now are the industrial cotton and gourd. Cotton occurs irregularly, with gaps of three or four valleys between. Cotton and gourd at the highland site of La Galgada diminish the thesis that these two crops were initially farmed because of their benefit to fishing (Moseley 1975).

Intriguing is the evidence that C. Earle Smith found at La Galgada that the ritual structures' central hearths contain chile peppers (Grieder *et al.* 1988). He posits that they were burned in rituals to create a potent smoke that caused irritation and therefore memorable events within these early, small, enclosed structures. Stephen Hugh-Jones relates a similar idea from groups in the modern Colombian Amazon, where, in the past, their ancestors used to throw peppers into fires to drive away demons and purify the people. La Galgada inhabitants seem to have also participated in such rituals. Chile peppers seem to be a particularly charged plant across the Americas.[4]

Looking at the distribution of the guava tree, previously it had been found only at La Paloma, and now it is also present three valleys to the north at the Yacht Club site near the Chillon Valley and at La Galgada further north and inland. It is not found to the south of the Chilca Valley. Guava's distribution gives us a sense that some groups chose to plant guava while others did not, if the data we have at present are reliable. Thousands of years after agriculture began along the coast, tasty, nutritious crops have the greatest presence. They are the only crops of the twelve that are found at every site. This phase of plant remains gives us the best explanatory view of the earliest introduced plants. The reasons for their uptake seems to be symbolic, social and flavourful.

In the Cotton Preceramic VI (2500–2100 BC), domestic plants are more common at all sites and we see new, intriguing patterns (Figure 6.4). There are now two main complexes of crops that co-occur at the sites. First, beans and peppers co-occur (with squash as well) throughout the coast, building on earlier trends. The second cluster of crops that co-occur, especially on the central coast, are gourd, cotton, achira and guava. These plants were present in the previous phase; industrial, one starchy food and one fruit. Maize, avocado, potato and manioc are present during these 400 years, but sporadically.

At this time, maize is present only every three valleys or so along the coast: in the valleys of Viru, Supe, Chancay and Chilca, as well as in the Ayacucho Caves. Maize has a large seed and is easy to identify if present in plant collections. Avocado only occurs in the north, not south of the greater Moche region. The potato is a difficult plant to identify. It has been found at Huaynuná in the Casma Valley (Ugent *et al.* 1982) and perhaps in the Ayacucho Caves (MacNeish *et al.* 1980). Manioc is found only at Guiterrero Cave in the central region, but it too is difficult to identify.

By this time, after four or five thousand years of agriculture, we can begin to assess what some of these patterns might mean socially. Manioc is especially intriguing. From the research that has been carried out on manioc and its probable early domestication in northern South America, we learn

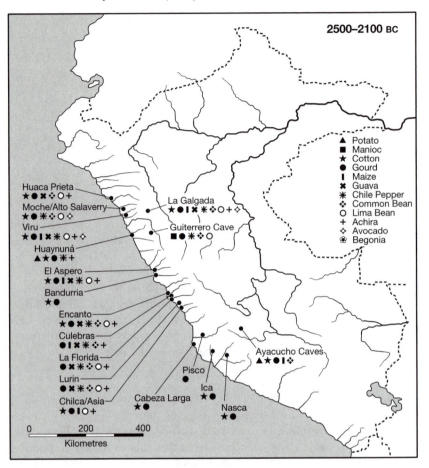

Figure 6.4 Twelve domestic plant taxa distributions of the Preceramic VI: 2500–2100 BC from the central Andean region, based primarily on Lanning (1967) and Pearsall (1978, 1992)

that it can produce more calories than other staple crops in low fertility soils, hence its great modern importance throughout the lowlands of Mesoamerica and South America (Rogers 1963; Rogers and Appan 1972). Given that it might have been present in the region by 6000 BC at Tres Ventanas Cave (Engel 1973), it is curious that it did not become as ubiquitous as achira did over the next 4000 years. If manioc was first in the region, it did not become the most common, whereas achira, also a lowland staple and equally difficult to identify, arrives in the Preceramic V and becomes ubiquitous within 500 years of its entry. Their very different patterns of distribution through space and time suggest that these two lowland, high carbohydrate root crops had different entrance routes and values associated with them. Manioc does not seem to have had the same connotations as achira. A closer look at the specific sites where manioc or achira occur should give us further clues to their meanings, and hence if these were in fact ethnicity markers as well as dietary supplements during this time period.

It is also during the Preceramic Phase VI that the first evidence for ritual space exists, with small walled enclosures and a sunken court at La Galgada (Grieder *et al.* 1988). By the end of this phase, the forerunner of the U-shaped mound and plaza at Huaynuná is also built (Pozorski and Pozorski 1993: 47). The ceramics have similar designs up and down the coast, though they still make up a simple assemblage. We assume that most inhabitants who practised farming were using simple river flood-water farming. Achira and guava became regular in this phase, with continuing sporadic finds of maize, avocado, potato and manioc. Avocado is common in the northern valleys, but not to the south. Maize is found in some central and south-central valleys only, with manioc solely at Guiterrero Cave. The potato has been so difficult to identify we only have secure evidence for it in the Casma Valley, making its distribution and that of manioc difficult to assess at this time (Ugent *et al.* 1982). These four crops have continued to have a selective use, suggesting they might have arrived as ethnicity identity markers.

The plant distributions in these last two phases (V and VI) begin to suggest that the northern valley inhabitants, down to the Santa Valley, differentiated themselves through the food they grew and ate. Did the Santa Valley form a cultural boundary between these coastal settlements? Even within that northern coastal sector there are further differences in plant use. Some northern river valley folk ate avocado along with beans and chiles but no maize (in the Moche River). To the south of the Viru Valley, sites have maize but no avocado. As these domesticates were being differentially planted and consumed by the inhabitants, overt ritual activity and associated architectural features increased in evidence. Locations where we find dense domesticates do seem to be where there is special architecture; La Galgada, Huaynuná, El Aspero and Huaca Prieta, thus supporting the idea that more intensive political-religious interests included more, yet particular, foodstuffs as key elements in their cultural constructions as well as in the daily practice of food consumption. As these plants seem to be part of the initial complex of a new intensity in political identity it would be informative to view from which contexts these plant taxa originate.

By the end of the next phase, the Initial Period (2100–1400 BC), these twelve crops occur more commonly throughout the sites that have been sampled, but by no means are they ubiquitous (Figure 6.5). While all sampled sites have evidence for agriculture during this phase, there are still regional and individual crop-use differences. The chile peppers and the beans occur everywhere, suggesting their continued highly charged value. Achira is still common, with manioc and potato hardly present on the coast. Avocado continues only in the north. Guava has a patchy pattern, present in two neighbouring valleys, then none for six valleys, then grown in two adjacent valleys, then none for three more valleys.

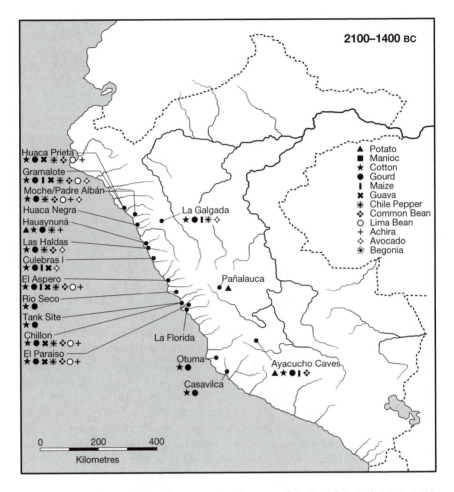

Figure 6.5 Twelve domestic plant taxa distributions of the Initial Period: 2100–1400 BC from the central Andean region, based primarily on Lanning (1967) and Pearsall (1978, 1992)

Maize continues to have a curious history during this period also. Throughout the Initial Period it is found in one valley but not the next; at Gramalote in the Moche Valley but not in the Chicama Valley just next door. Then there is a break, with no maize for six valleys to the south, until it occurs again at Culebras and El Aspero on the central coast. Like the avocado and the guava, there does seem to be something culturally noteworthy about the scattered distribution of maize. We know that maize is a highly charged crop throughout the New World by AD 1000 and that it probably was well before that. In these times we might be seeing the use of maize, and probably also avocado and guava, in defining different, neighbouring cultural identities along the coast through farming practices, cuisines and feasts.

Around 2100 BC civic architecture began to be constructed up and down the coast, although at a small, visually and audibly accessible scale up through the Initial Period (1400 BC) (Jerry Moore, pers. comm.). These structures began with segmented U-shaped compounds, that were then elaborated on through time (Williams 1985). Around 1400 BC, with the start of the Early Horizon Period, the architecture changed in scale and scope, becoming larger with a more hierarchical orientation, seen in the spatial separation of the masses from the select ritual participants. Whereas the rituals were at a small scale earlier (with everyone hearing, seeing and probably consuming at the events), after the Initial Period most people could only see from afar as the rituals changed in scale and probable strategy. By the end of the Initial Period, hierarchy became codified in several places along the coast, like El Aspero, Huaynuná, El Paraiso and La Florida. It is in the Early Horizon where the crop taxa are more regular and irrigation is more commonplace. Now there are larger-scale polities, where agricultural surplus goes hand-in-hand with political development.[5]

Discussion

One conclusion we can draw from this sequence is that the individual crops had very different life histories along the Peruvian coast. Some crops entered at 6000 BC and were planted and consumed in many places, like beans, chile peppers, cotton and gourds. Other crops entered early as well but remained irregularly present up and down the coast for many millennia, like guava, manioc and potatoes. Still other crops entered later in a second wave of crop introductions in the Preceramic V (4200–2500 BC), but then were taken up quickly, like achira. And still other crops were within this second wave of entry but were not taken up quickly, occurring more selectively for some years, like maize and avocado.

Both annuals and tree crops were planted in the first and second entries, and thus one cannot suggest differential access to technology as the reason for differential acceptance of crops. Rather there was a varying sense of territoriality and farming, interest in these specific crop-plants, as well as perhaps connections with other peoples. The different crop histories make it clear that even when crops arrived in a region they were not all adopted automatically by neighbours. Whatever maize, manioc, guava or avocado represented, they were each charged with a usefulness and a meaning that led some to propagate them while others did not. These plants should be studied more closely for their specific contextual and use patterns in these early phases.

Scholars like Cohen (1978) have suggested that the Preceramic VI saw a population increase that required agriculture to augment the food supply and ward off starvation. Alternatively, I support Quilter and Stocker (1983) who suggest that the marine food base could sustain the populations that existed at that time and even into the Initial Period. Quilter (1989: 9) rightly suggests that during the severe El Niño storms, the coastal inhabitants' menu would have altered but not disappeared.

Within this sequence, we can see that there are hints at cuisine development and the formations of group identities, even with such patchy data and only a subset of the actual plants addressed in this chapter. Early on, there are tasty beans and peppers, with a guava fruit treat. Later on we see the culturally selective use of other tasty foods, with avocado or maize occurring at different sites.

The role of food in cultural identity and politics

Social identity is closely bound to food preferences, and changes in food consumption entail an alteration in self-identification (Appadurai 1981; Goody 1982; Douglas 1984; Rao 1986). People identify themselves with the food they eat and give meaning to each item served or consumed. Further, groups separate themselves from others through different items, dishes and cuisines. Therefore, when we see that the different settlements along the coastal valleys adopted different combinations of crops, I propose that we are seeing the development of different social identities at each community through different cultural constructions. The northern valleys (e.g. the Moche and Chicama valleys) have different crops than the Santa-Casma valleys and this crop combination varies from the Ancon-Chillon area. These three areas also each have early but distinct ritual evidence. We are probably seeing ethnic differences emerging through time, each with different food traditions, highlighted by the avocado eaters and the maize eaters.

Let's return briefly to the onset of agriculture and our Peruvian example. These pre-8000 BC coastal residents were fairly sedentary, with rich coastal resources. The early coastal plant data and crop introductions reflect, in part, the Farrington and Urry model of non-local, tasty food first beginning the agricultural process, with local, industrial crops entering later. The western valley caves have local, highland plants, suggesting local plant use well before foreign incorporation. Almost none of these coastal crops present up to 4000 BC are the staples of hungry people. Nor do we see crops entering as packages. We do not see the evidence of one ethnicity or polity expanding over a wide territory. Rather, we see an irregular and diverse scattering of plants with little spatial or temporal patterning. Regional variations exist, but even neighbouring valleys have different crops. These patterns imply that local villagers decided for themselves what they would take up and when; probably plants were brought in by visitors or marriage. Pozorski and Pozorski (1993: 49) note this same localized difference in their study of ceremonial architecture and ceramic use along the north coast. They find distinct polities choosing to build different styles of monuments as well as a different acceptance rate of ceramics at different sites.

It seems likely that the motives for the acceptance of plants changed over this time-span. In the earlier phases food production was influenced by the development of social identity and place, and the concept of domestication was active at many levels. The early material indicates that agricultural and food exchanges were based on curiosity and far-away trade, with an interest in community difference and changing relations with the local landscape. Plants were adopted along different pathways, not all from east to west or north to south. In the later periods, political motives of aggrandizement and political power are more evident in the data. In the Initial Period, with increasing civic-ceremonial construction, we see more of the Bender-Hayden dynamics: crop production and use with a political edge of hierarchy and internal difference. This generation of surplus food and labour begins 4000 years after the onset of agriculture.

Summary

A likely scenario for the Preceramic periods was increasing socio-symbolic activities at certain locations, such as La Galgada, Huaynuná, the Yacht Club, El Aspero and Huaca Prieta. As ritual centres came into existence, people clearly were using and reusing certain locales symbolically as well as economically. The earliest evidence of substantial building too is ritual, not domestic. Each population's identity was emerging. This process included building structures and developing special community acts, including eating a cuisine using local and foreign foods – foods marked by the lineages that were participating. These identities were based on links with other peoples, places and meanings across the Andean region. In some ways these links (linking arguments) were arbitrary signs that the inhabitants constructed to give their lives meaning. At the same time, each region's population seemed to be differentiating themselves from their neighbours. Most likely, the inhabitants received or brought in plants from other locales as gifts or curiosity items in the early years, and began to make them special, to nurture and to raise them, to cultivate them. It is not surprising therefore to find discontinuous distributions of some species across these ecologically similar valleys.

We must now look carefully at each of these sites to see what other material forms of cultural identity can be associated with the domestic plant uptake suggested by the patterns traced here, as well as more specifically discovering the contexts of plant use at these sites (as already seen in the different architectural trajectories at north coast sites that the Pozorskis note). Clearly, plant use in special activities and in daily consumption would culturally construct meanings for each plant. We need to learn what the meanings of these plants were to the people at the individual sites, such as Huaynuná or La Galgada. We have hints, like the chile pepper at La Galgada, where people burned them in their sunken hearths, either for the smoke or as a food to be consumed in the enclosures. In this way we will get closer to the meanings of the people that participated in these cultural and political changes along the Peruvian coast before hierarchy became institutionalized.

Crop plants appear to have been brought in individually over the first 6000 years of cultivation, with regional combinations distinct by the time groups became consolidated into larger polities. Changes in ritual activities are tied to political developments. By the end of the Initial Period, such changes were not only evident in new public structures but also in the form of associated ceremonies, including feasting that accompanies public events. Political explanations for the increase in certain foodstuffs can be suggested by this phase, where the production of surplus food became important for social aggrandizement (Nassenay 1987; Hayden 1990; Hastorf and Johannessen 1994). In the earlier days, the goals of plant production may not have been for more food, but for more food of a certain kind.

More subtle is the use of certain types of dishes and cuisines, not just to gain political power but simply to unite a community through shared participation in meals and ceremonies. Some plants were highly charged, like the chile pepper that could have meaning continuities over 4000 years. This is what is suggested for the Preceramic phases along the coast. These meals of avocado, or guava or maize, became part of the memory of things and places, of ancestors and lineages, and thus helped create the social world as well as domesticate the landscape. This trajectory eventually expanded and increased the desire to plant and tend crops. In the early phases, domestication is wrapped up in identity, in influence, and in the memory of the symbolic activities that occurred across the landscape.

Acknowledgements

My trip to the New Delhi World Archaeological Congress where this paper was presented was supported by the Stahl Foundation and the Academic Senate's Committee for Research at the University of California, Berkeley. I have gained much insight about this subject from working with Sissel Johannessen. I also benefited from talking with Jerry Moore about early Andean architecture and ritual and Stephen Hugh-Jones about Amazonian beliefs. Chris Gosden helped this chapter with his thoughtful editing.

Notes

1   The phases are an updating of Lanning (1967: 25) and Rowe and Menzel (1967: ii).
2   For brevity's sake, I have worked here only with the presence or absence of these plants and tried to look at general trends rather than giving too much credit to any one find. I have not included data from two sites that are still controversial in terms of dates relating to their botanical remains and mixing of levels. These two sites are Los Gavilanes (Bonavia 1982) and the early levels of the Ayacucho Caves.
3   The data in these figures are primarily extracted from Pearsall (1978, 1992), as well as many of the references that she refers to in those two articles – especially Heiser (1965), Lanning (1967), Engel (1973), Kaplan (1980), Lynch (1980), Pozorski (1983), Pozorski and Pozorski (1987) and Smith in Grieder *et al.*

(1988). The maps were drawn on a computer by Matt Bandy and William Whitehead, in part based on plant distribution maps by Jan Greenough who kindly shared her maps with me. The choice of the taxa, sites and dates are mine, but based primarily on the Rowe-Menzel scheme.

4 This use is also reminiscent of using chile peppers in the initiations of young boys in the American Southwest by pouring peppers onto lacerated tongues, or in the Amazon Basin where male initiates pour pepper juice on their faces and up their nostrils to become stronger and purify the body (Hugh-Jones, pers. comm.). Peppers also have many sexual connotations: 'hot and spicy' even today is used in many different settings.

5 While harder to see without detailed excavations, the lineage-identity use of plants during this larger-scale political phase would also have continued. Further evidence would have to be gained only in very specific archaeological contexts.

References

Ammerman, A.J. and Cavalli-Sforza, L.L. (1984) *The Neolithic Transition and the Genetics of Population in Europe*, Princeton, NJ: Princeton University Press.

Appadurai, A. (1981) 'Gastro-politics in Hindu South Asia', *American Ethnologist*, 8: 494–511.

Bender, B. (1978) 'Gatherer-hunter to farmer: a social perspective', *World Archaeology*, 10: 204–22.

Bender, B. (1985) 'Prehistoric development in the American midcontinent and in Brittany, northwest France', in T. D. Price and J. A. Brown (eds) *Prehistoric Hunter-gatherers: the emergence of complexity*, Orlando, FL: Academic Press.

Benz, B. (1994) 'Reconstructing the racial phylogeny of Mexican maize: where do we stand?', in S. Johannessen and C. A. Hastorf (eds) *Corn and Culture in the Prehistoric New World*, Boulder, CO: Westview Press.

Bergh, B.O. (1976) 'Avocado *Persea americana* (Lauraceae)', in N. W. Simmonds (ed.) *Evolution of Crop Plants*, London: Longman.

Bohrer, V.L. (1991) 'The relation of grain and its method of harvest to plants in prehistory', *Reviews in Anthropology*, 16: 149–56.

Bonavia, D. (1982) *Preceramic Peruano: Los Gavilanes, mar, desierto y oasis en la historia del hombre*, Lima: Cooperacion Financiera de desarollo S.A. and the German Institute of Archaeology.

Braidwood, R.J. (1953) 'Query to symposium; did man once live by beer alone?', *American Anthropologist*, 55: 515–16.

Bush, M.B., Piperno, D.R. and Colinvaux, P.A. (1989) 'A 6000 year history of Amazonian cultivation', *Nature*, 340: 303–5.

Cohen, M.N. (1978) 'Archaeological plant remains from the central coast of Peru', *Nawpa Pacha*, 16: 23–50.

Cohen, M.N. (1981) 'Pacific coast foragers: affluent or overcrowded', in S. Koyama and D. H. Thomas (eds) *Affluent Foragers*, Osaka: Senri Ethnological Studies 9, National Museum of Ethnology.

Douglas, M. (1984) *Food in the Social Order: studies of food and festivities in three American communities*, New York: Russell Sage Foundation.

Engel, F. (1973) 'New facts about pre-Colombian life in the Andean lomas', *Current Anthropology*, 8: 287–97.

Engel, F. (1981) *Prehistoric Andean Ecology, Man, Settlement, and the Environment in the Andes: the deep south*, New York: Humanities Press.

Farrington, I.S. and Urry, J. (1985) 'Food and early history of cultivation', *Journal of Ethnobiology*, 5: 143–57.

Gepts, P.T., Osborn, C., Rashka, K. and Bliss, F.A. (1986) 'Phaseolin-protein variability in wild forms and landraces of the common bean (*Phaseolus vulgaris*): evidence for multiple centers of domestication', *Economic Botany*, 40: 451–68.

Goody, J. (1982) *Cooking, Cuisine and Class*, Cambridge: Cambridge University Press.

Grieder, T., Mendoza, A.B., Smith, C.E. and Malina, R.M. (1988) *La Galgada, Peru: a preceramic culture in transition*, Austin, TX: University of Texas Press.

Harlan, J. (1975) *Crops and Man*, Madison, WI: American Society of Agronomy.

Harris, D.R. (1969) 'Agricultural systems, ecosystems and the origins of agriculture', in P. J. Ucko and G. W. Dimbleby (eds) *The Domestication and Exploitation of Plants and Animals*, London: Duckworth.

Hastorf, C.A. and Johannessen, S. (1993) 'Pre-Hispanic political change and the role of maize in the central Andes of Peru', *American Anthropologist*, 95: 115–38.

Hastorf, C.A. and Johannessen, S. (1994) 'Becoming corn-eaters in prehistoric America', in S. Johannessen and C. A. Hastorf (eds) *Corn and Culture in the Prehistoric New World*, Boulder, CO: Westview Press.

Hawkes, J.G. (1989) 'The domestication of roots and tubers in the American tropics', in D. R. Harris and G. C. Hillman (eds) *Foraging and Farming: the evolution of plant exploitation*, London: Unwin Hyman.

Hayden, B. (1990) 'Nimrods, piscators, pluckers, and planters: the emergence of food production', *Journal of Anthropological Archaeology*, 9: 31–69.

Heiser, C.B. (1965) 'Cultivated plants and cultural diffusions in nuclear America', *American Anthropologist*, 67: 930–49.

Hillman, G.C. and Davies, M.S. (1990) 'Domestication rates in wild wheats and barley under primitive cultivation and their archaeological implications', *Journal of World Prehistory*, 4: 157–222.

Hodder, I. (1991) *The Domestication of Europe*, Oxford: Basil Blackwell.

Kaplan, L. (1980) 'Variation in the cultivated beans', in T. Lynch (ed.) *Guiterrero Cave*, New York: Academic Press.

Kaplan, L. (1994) 'Accelerator mass spectrometry dates and the antiquity of *Phaseolus* cultivation', *Annual Report of the Bean Improvement Cooperative*, 37: 131–2.

Lanning, E. (1967) *Peru Before the Incas*, Englewood Cliffs, NJ: Prentice Hall.

Lewthwaite, J. (1986) 'The transition of food production: a Mediterranean perspective', in M. Zvelebil (ed.) *Hunters in Transition*, Cambridge: Cambridge University Press.

Lynch, T.E. (ed.) (1980) *Guiterrero Cave*, New York: Academic Press.

Lynch, T.E, Gillespie, R., Gowlett, J.A.J. and Hedges, R.E.M. (1985) 'Chronology of Guiterrero Cave, Peru', *Science*, 229: 864–7.

MacNeish, R.S., Vierra, R.K., Nelken-Terner, A. and Phagen, C.J. (1980) *Prehistory of the Ayacucho Basin, Peru. Volume 3: Nonceramic Artifacts*, Ann Arbor, MI: University of Michigan Press.

Martins-Farias, R. (1976) 'New archaeological techniques for the study of ancient root crops in Peru', unpublished PhD thesis, University of Birmingham.

Moseley, M.E. (1975) *The Maritime Foundations of Andean Civilization*, Menlo Park, CA: Cummings Press.

Nassenay, M.S. (1987) 'On the causes and consequences of subsistence intensification in the Mississippi alluvial valley', in W. E. Keegan (ed.) *Emergent Horticultural Economies of the Eastern Woodlands*, Carbondale, IL: Southern Illinois University, Occasional Paper, No. 7, Center for Archaeological Investigations.

Osborne, A.J. (1977) 'Strandloopers, mermaids, and other fairy tales: ecological determinants of marine resources utilization – the Peruvian case', in L. Binford (ed.) *For Theory Building in Archaeology*, New York: Academic Press.

Pearsall, D. (1978) 'Paleoethnobotany in western South America: progress and problems', in R. I. Ford, M. F. Brown, M. Hodge and W. L. Merrill (eds) *The Nature and Status of Ethnobotany*, Ann Arbor, MI: University of Michigan, Anthropological Papers, No. 67, Museum of Anthropology.

Pearsall, D. (1992) 'The origins of plant cultivation in South America', in C. W. Cowan and P. J. Watson (eds) *Origins of Agriculture: an international perspective*, Washington, DC: Smithsonian Institution Press.

Pearsall, D. (1994) 'Issues in the analysis and interpretation of archaeological maize in South America', in S. Johannessen and C. A. Hastorf (eds) *Corn and Culture in the Prehistoric New World*, Boulder, CO: Westview Press.

Pickersgill, B. (1969) 'The archaeological record of chili peppers (*Capsicum* spp.) and the sequence of plant domestication in Peru', *American Antiquity*, 34: 54–61.

Pickersgill, B. and Heiser Jr., C.B. (1977) 'Origins and distribution of plants domesticated in the New World tropics', in C. A. Reed (ed.) *Origins of Agriculture*, The Hague: Mouton.

Pozorski, S. (1983) 'Changing subsistence priorities and early settlement patterns on the north coast of Peru', *Journal of Ethnobiology*, 3: 15–38.

Pozorski, S. and Pozorski, T. (1987) *Early Settlement and Subsistence in the Casma Valley, Peru*, Iowa City, IA: University of Iowa Press.

Pozorski, T. and Pozorski, S. (1993) 'Early complex society and ceremonialism on the Peruvian coast', in L. Millones and Y. Onuki (eds) *El Mundo Ceremonial*, Osaka: Senri Ethnological Studies 37: 45–68.

Quilter, J. (1989) *Life and Death at Paloma*, Iowa City, IA: University of Iowa Press.

Quilter, J. and Stocker, T. (1983) 'Subsistence economies and the origins of Andean complex societies', *American Anthropologist*, 85: 545–62.

Rao, M.S.A. (1986) 'Conservatism and change in food habits among the migrants in India: a study of gastrodynamics', in R. S. Khare and M. S. A. Rao (eds) *Food, Society and Culture*, Durham, NC: Carolina Academic Press.

Rogers, D.J. (1963) 'Studies of *Manihot esculenta* Crantz and related species', *Bulletin of the Torrey Botanical Club*, 90: 43–54.

Rogers, D.J. and Appan, S.G. (1972) 'Cassava (*Manihot esculenta* Crantz), the plant, world production and its importance in world food supply', in C. H. Hendershoot (ed.) *A Literature Review and Research Recommendations on Cassava* (Manihot esculenta Crantz), AID Contract No. csd/2492. Athens, CA: University of Georgia.

Roosevelt, A.C. (1980) *Parmana: prehistoric maize and manioc subsistence along the Amazon and Orinoco*, New York: Academic Press.

Rowe, J.H. and Menzel, D. (1967) 'Introduction', in J. H. Rowe and D. Menzel (eds) *Peruvian Archaeology, Selected Readings*, v–x, Palo Alto, CA: Peek Publications.

Sauer, C.O. (1952) *Agricultural Origins and Dispersals*, New York: American Geographical Society.

Stephens, S.G. and Moseley, M.E. (1974) 'Early domesticated cottons from archaeological sites in central coastal Peru', *American Antiquity*, 39: 109–22.

Thomas, J. (1993) 'The hermeneutics of megalithic space', in C. Tilley (ed.) *Interpretative Archaeologies*, Oxford: Berg.

Ugent, D., Pozorski, S. and Pozorski, T. (1982) 'Archaeological potato tuber remains from the Casma valley of Peru', *Economic Botany*, 36: 401–15.

Ugent, D., Pozorski, S. and Pozorski, T. (1984) 'New evidence for ancient cultivation of *Canna edulis* in Peru', *Economic Botany*, 38: 417–32.

Watson, P.J. and Kennedy, M. (1991) 'The development of horticulture in the Eastern Woodlands of North America: a woman's role', in J. Gero and M. Conkey (eds) *Engendering Archaeology*, Oxford: Basil Blackwell.

Welch, P. and Scarry, C.M. (1995) 'Status-related variation in foodways in the Moundville chiefdom', *American Antiquity*, 60: 397–419.

Williams, C. (1985) 'A scheme for the early monumental architecture of the central coast of Peru', in C. Donnan (ed.) *Early Ceremonial Architecture in the Andes*, Washington, DC: Dumbarton Oaks.

Wilson, D. (1981) 'Of maize and men: a critique of the maritime hypothesis of state origins on the coast of Peru', *American Anthropologist*, 38: 93–120.

Zvelebil, M. (1986) 'Mesolithic prelude and Neolithic revolution', in M. Zvelebil (ed.) *Hunters in Transition*, Cambridge: Cambridge University Press.

Update: Revisiting the Andean coast

Christine A. Hastorf

To investigate plant movements from the moist tropical forests and their eventual adoption into the dry coastal environment, social and cultural concepts such as enculturation and two-way domestication are important. People influence and enculturate (naturalise) the plants and animals with which they live and which they rely upon. This approach to domestication focuses on the intimate role of plant–human relationships within the formation of societies across the continent. There are many ethnographic examples of this anthropomorphising relationship (e.g. Descola 1992; Balée 1994; Hugh-Jones 1996). This perspective allows us to examine the influences that plants and animals have had on human existence and social formation, beyond their basic role in subsistence as a food supply. Plant domestication and planting domesticated plants are associated with the concept of the cultivating society or social domestication (Hodder 1991; Cauvin 2000). My thesis is ultimately anthrocentric in that it places humans as active agents in plant domestication, movement and adoption. I assume that humans have always had an impact on their environment, just as the environment has continuously crafted humans (Crumley 1994; Zimmerer 1994; Lentz 2001).

The results of interaction reflect the type and approach people have had in these environments. We know that most plant domesticates along the west coast came from the greater Amazon Basin, such as achira, beans, chile peppers, manioc and guava, to name a few. Others, such as potatoes, came from the highlands. People carried, traded and/or received gifts of these plants across the highlands and along the coast from their places of domestication. This process, occurring over thousands of years, was due to exchange more than migration or what is traditionally called 'diffusion' in the literature. I prefer not to use the term diffusion, as it has a passive connotation and I am confident that people knew they were carrying and/or trading crop plants when they traveled and traded them. Why did many of the over 100 different plants move out of their diverse home ranges and into new territories, given that they, as fragile domesticates, required human help to move and to reproduce (Clement 1999)? What led people to carry, trade, gift or steal these plants? Part of the answer lies in why these plants received more attention than other plants in the first place.

Creating identity with plants, and especially trees, simultaneously creates territoriality through their 'rootedness' and immobility in space while they are alive (Rival 1998). During plant domestication, movement and adoption, people focused on selected plants and animals. Foragers began to repeatedly associate themselves with certain plants. Groups differentiated themselves through their perceptions of their environments and what they used in them. Boundaries were created based on consumption, cultural knowledge and plant distribution across the landscape.

Both Balée (1989) and Ingold (1993) have pointed out that people have always 'played their part' in the ongoing transformation of the natural world. People have lived *with* their fellow plants and animals, not just among them. The world has always been a garden in the sense that humans (and other animals) have interacted with all parts of the ecosystem, albeit at different intensities. Having become omnivores, combined with a strong sense of curiosity, people have shown a propensity to consume new things (Milton 1987). Through experimentation, humans have learned what was edible and what was not. This exploration and improvisation has developed the construction of nature both physically and mentally (Latour 1999). Wagner suggests that social groups 'create their universe . . . by constantly trying to change, readjust, and impinge upon it, in an effort to knock the conventional off-balance, and so make themselves powerful and unique in relation to it' (1975: 88–9). Thus, in some ways, our evolution and our curiosity have opened up a series of adaptive paths that includes anthropomorphising the world around us.

Balée (1994) and colleagues have recorded this systematic tinkering in the Amazon by farmers and foragers. Economic species distributions in forests today are largely due to human intentionality and manipulation over the millennia. Current plant distributions are the result of many years of people carrying clippings, root stocks and seeds as they hunt, visit relatives, go on trading or war trips, journey to new territories, or simply place plants where they are more useful when they move to a new place (Posey and Balée 1989). There are many examples of foragers who nurture and actively manipulate encountered ecological zones to increase access to plants and other resources, creating different levels of intensity and types of plant interaction

(Balée 1994). Some interaction leads to the creation of new micro-environments and new combinations of taxa, other results are shifts in taxa frequencies.

There are two gift-giving forms linked to plants. The first type is giving the plants themselves as a gift; seeds, flowers, fruit or cuttings. If the plant survives, this is an offering that keeps on giving. This form of organic gift is usually at the individual level. This live-gift giving will result in plants moving across the landscape. The second type of gift is less long-lived, and that is food exchange. While most food gifts are consumed on the spot, some foods are taken away after a feast.

While the Peruvian coast is not unique in having a long sequence of plant introductions, the excellent preservation and paucity of locally domesticated food plants make it an important example of plant movement and adoption. The earliest coastal cultivated plants were not carbohydrate-rich, staple crops. Rather they were industrial and flavourful plants; beans, gourds, squash and guava fruit trees; and, eaten as greens, seeds and fruit. It is several millennia later that starchy plants regularly enter the midden records.

In a rich marine environment like the Peruvian coast, farming began not because people were hungry, but for cultural reasons. Cultural selection is evident as neighbouring settlements adopted crops differentially. Some valley's settlements have maize while others have chile peppers, differences that may reflect separate cultural identities expressed in crop cultivation and consumption. Differences are also suggested by the varied forms of cultivation such as fields versus kitchen gardens and orchards versus annual crops. Starchy plants were added late in the sequence, occurring earlier at the larger settlements.

The distributions suggest a cultural rather than a geographical pattern of plant adoption. Notable in the plant movements is the lack of a single route of entry and origin. Plants entered the coast from the north, east and southeast. The *Phaseolus* beans demonstrate several important routes of introduction most clearly onto the coast of Peru; *P. lunatus* entered from the north and *P. vulgaris* entered from the southeast.

References

Balée, W. (1989) 'The culture of Amazonian forests', *Advances in Economic Botany*, 7: 1–21.

Balée, W. (1994) *Footprints in the Forest*, New York: Columbia University Press.

Cauvin, J. (2000) *The Birth of the Gods and the Origins of Agriculture*, Cambridge: Cambridge University Press.

Clement, C. (1999) '1492 and the loss of Amazonian crop genetic resources, I: relations between domestication and human population decline', *Economic Botany*, 53: 188–202.

Crumley, C. (ed.) (1994) *Historical Ecology*, Santa Fe, NM: School of American Research.

Descola, P. (1992) 'Societies of nature and the nature of society', in A. Kuper (ed.) *Conceptualizing Society*, London: Routledge.

Hodder, I. (1991) *The Domestication of Europe*, Oxford: Basil Blackwell.

Hugh-Jones, S. (1996) 'Bonnes raisons ou mauvaise conscience? De l'ambivalence de certains Amazoniens envers la consommation de viande [Good reasons or bad conscience? On the ambivalence of some Amazonian Indians about eating meat]', *Terrain*, 26: 123–48.

Ingold, T. (1993) 'The temporality of the landscape', *World Archaeology*, 25: 152–74.

Latour, B. (1999) *Pandora's Hope*, Cambridge, MA: Harvard University Press.

Lentz, D.L. (ed.) (2001) *Imperfect Balance*, New York: Columbia University Press.

Milton, K. (1987) 'Primate diets and gut morphology: implications for hominid evolution', in M. Harris and E. B. Ross (eds) *Food and Evolution: toward a theory of human food habits*, Philadelphia, PA: Temple University Press.

Posey, D.A. and Balée, W. (eds) (1989) *Resource Management in Amazonia: indigenous and folk strategies*, Bronx, NY: New York Botanical Garden.

Rival, L. (1998) 'Domestication as a historical and symbolic process: wild gardens and cultivated forests in the Ecuadorian Amazon', in W. Balée (ed.) *Advances in Historical Ecology*, New York: Columbia University Press.

Wagner, R. (1975) *The Invention of Culture*, New York: Prentice Hall.

Zimmerer, K.S. (1994) 'Human geography and the new ecology: the prospects and promise of integration', *Annals of the Association of American Geographers*, 84: 108–25.

7 Early plant cultivation in the Eastern Woodlands of North America

Patty Jo Watson

Introduction

Twenty-five years ago Joseph Caldwell prepared a summary of Eastern Woodlands prehistory, with emphasis on the origins of food production and subsequent developments, for a volume of comparative cultural-historical studies entitled *Courses toward urban life* (Caldwell, in Braidwood and Willey 1962). In some ways, Caldwell's chapter in that volume served as a foil or counterpoise for the other chapters because in the 1950s the Eastern Woodlands seemed to have been one of the backwaters of world prehistory where no cultural climaxes worthy of international attention were known until very late in the sequence, where in fact pre-Columbian urban life may not have been present at all, or if so only under strong stimulus from centres of civilization in Mexico. Thus, this region was cast as a kind of control situation, where nothing much happened in prehistory, at any rate no dramatic transformation from hunting-gathering to agriculture to literate, state-based and urbanized civilization. The issue of food production, in particular, seemed to be a relatively trivial affair involving transfer of cultigens – maize, squash, pumpkins, gourds, and beans – from the Southwest whence they had, in turn, diffused from Mexico.

Although there were those (Linton 1924; Gilmore 1931; Jones 1936; Quimby 1946) who wrote of indigenous Eastern Woodlands horticulture, no one thought it was of much general significance, even if it had been present here and there. Then, approximately 20 years ago, empirical evidence about plant use, sought systematically by a few archaeologists and archaeobotanists (Struever 1962, 1968; Watson 1969, 1974; Yarnell 1969, 1972, 1974; Munson *et al.* 1972; Struever and Vickery 1973), began to reveal unexpected and complex patterns. Over the past ten years, the tempo of research focused on the beginnings of plant cultivation in eastern North America has quickened to the point that it is difficult just to keep abreast of the basic data, and nearly impossible to maintain up-to-date syntheses of the data.

Eastern Woodlands prehistory: a brief summary

Detailed accounts of the culture history of the eastern United States are to be found in several sources (e.g. Willey 1966; Jennings 1974; Stoltman 1978; Griffin 1983; Muller 1983; Stoltman and Baerreis 1983; Meltzer and Smith 1986; Smith 1986).

Although the time of human entry into the Americas is a topic that inspires more or less perennial controversy (for an excellent review, see Dincauze 1985), there is no question about the presence of human groups by 12,000–15,000 bp. These hunter-gatherers of the Paleoindian period are best known for their success in killing various species of now extinct animals, many of which were considerably larger than their modern descendants, hence the phrase 'Pleistocene megafauna' that is often applied to them. However, it is unlikely that such megafauna were the focus of subsistence among most Paleoindian groups, or even a particularly significant part of it (Meltzer and Smith 1986).

By approximately 10,000 bp, a closed-canopy, deciduous forest containing oak, hickory, and chestnut as dominant species covered most of the mid-latitude United States from the Mississippi River to the east coast (Delcourt and Delcourt 1981, 1983; Wright 1981; Watts 1983). Except for the very important interval known as the Hypsithermal (Wright 1976; King and Allen 1977; McMillan and Klippel 1981) – a warm, dry period between 8000 and 5000 bp when the prairie and the more xeric vegetation zones between it and the Mississippi River expanded to the east – this deciduous forest cover is the most distinctive and characteristic feature of the North American environment between the Mississippi and the Atlantic up to the present time.

The human inhabitants of this forest were hunters, gatherers, and fishers throughout the pre-Columbian millennia. Beginning approximately 4000 bp, some of them were also part-time horticulturalists, and by about 1000 bp many groups along the central Mississippi valley, the Ohio River, and their major tributaries were heavily committed to maize agriculture. Archaeologists use a complex series of local chronological frameworks to order the material remains left by these early Eastern Woodland peoples, and these have replaced the vaguer, older terminology in many places. That older terminology is ubiquitous in all but the very latest literature, however, and is still useful as a general chronological guide; hence it is summarized in narrative fashion below.

Broadly speaking, post-Paleoindian Eastern Woodlands prehistory is divided into three phases labelled, from early to late, Archaic, Woodland, and Mississippian/Fort Ancient (Fort Ancient comprises the Mississippian period societies of the Ohio River, primarily in southern Ohio and Indiana, and in West Virginia and northern Kentucky). As traditionally conceived, Archaic groups were thought to be pre-ceramic hunter-gatherer-fishers, exploiters *par excellence* of the plant and animal foods afforded by the Holocene deciduous forest. Woodland groups were pottery-makers and part-time horticulturalists, some of whom participated in elaborate mortuary ritual systems, and in trade networks by which spectacular and exotic items (e.g. obsidian, copper, mica sheets carefully worked into human and animal forms, pearl-inlaid grizzly-bear teeth) were distributed far and wide from their sources. Mississippian peoples were maize farmers, hunters, gatherers, fishers, priests, and chieftains, most of whom lived in ranked societies in densely populated villages and towns in or near the floodplains of the Mississippi and the Ohio rivers and their major tributaries.

Older syntheses often emphasize the distinctiveness and discontinuity of these categories, but current literature stresses the remarkable degree of continuity now evident throughout the whole of Eastern Woodlands prehistory. Some aspects of this continuity are stressed in this chapter, my focus being upon the late Archaic and succeeding Woodland groups, with some attention also paid to the development of maize agriculture by later Woodland and Mississippian peoples.

Early plant cultivation in the Eastern Woodlands

The nature of the evidence

Primary evidence of plant use in general and of cultigens in particular derives from a variety of sources: pollen; macrobotanical remains in open sites, rockshelters, and caves; and trace-element analyses of human bone. Macrobotanical remains may be charred or uncharred (the latter comprising those preserved in a desiccated but perfect state in dry caves and rockshelters), and they furnish the most abundant data, although the information provided by the other sources is always illuminating and often crucial (e.g. Bender *et al.* 1981; Lynott *et al.* 1986). Charred macrobotanical material is usually recovered by flotation and other water-separation processes (Struever 1968; Watson 1976; Wagner 1989), whereas uncharred plant material is obtained simply by systematic collection, sometimes supplemented by dry-screening. A category of uncharred remains that deserves special mention is that of desiccated human faecal material. Human palaeofaeces, sometimes present in considerable quantities in dry rockshelters and caves, are excellent sources of dietary and palaeoenvironmental information (they usually contain pollen, as well as macrobotanical and animal remains), and they can also be individually dated by the radiocarbon technique (e.g. Yarnell 1969, 1974; Bryant 1974; Marquardt 1974; Stewart 1974).

There are, of course, numerous problems that have not been solved, or – in some cases – even widely recognized, with respect to the analysis and interpretation of archaeological remains relevant to early plant use and cultivation (Hastorf and Popper 1988). These range from uncertainties of identification to issues of meaningful quantification.

The earliest cultigens

Asch and Asch (1985a; Conard *et al.* 1984) have identified 7000-year-old, charred cucurbit-rind fragments from the Koster and Napoleon Hollow sites in Illinois as *Cucurbita pepo*, a warm-temperate to tropical domestic species usually thought to have first been taken into cultivation somewhere south of the Mexican border, perhaps as early as the end of the 9th millennium bc (Whitaker and Cutler 1986). The species identification for the early Illinois cucurbit is resisted by some scholars (Heiser 1985; King 1985; Smith 1987), who make two kinds of counter-claims. The first is that the rind fragments, although surely of the *Cucurbita* genus, may be from the fruits of native wild species, either *C. foetidissima*, the buffalo gourd, which is now distributed from Mexico across the Southwest and Texas to southwestern Missouri, Nebraska, and Kansas, or a variety of *C. texana*, now found only in southern Texas. The *Cucurbita* remains may then simply derive from a weedy indigenous plant tolerated, occasionally used, or even completely ignored when it sprang up near a habitation site.

The second counter-claim is that the Illinois cucurbit may indeed be an early cultigen, but one derived from *C. foetidissima* or *C. texana* rather than from *C. pepo* (introduced in a domesticated form from Mexico), although this interpretation may now be modified in view of Heiser's latest hypothesis (1989) that *C. pepo* could have been domesticated in eastern North America (as well as separately in Mexico) from *C. texana* (see also Decker and Wilson 1987) when the latter was more widely distributed during the Hypsithermal interval.

The evidence does not yet allow a decisive choice to be made among these competing interpretations, but there are an increasing number of third millennium bc *C. pepo* occurrences reported for various parts of the midwestern and midsouthern regions of the Eastern Woodlands. It has been identified in third millennium bc deposits at Phillips Spring in western Missouri (Kay *et al.* 1980; King 1985; Kay 1986), at the Napoleon Hollow, Lagoon, and Kuhlman sites in Illinois (Asch and Asch 1985a: 153), at Cloudsplitter Shelter in eastern Kentucky (Cowan 1985; Watson 1985: 130–1), at the Carlston Annis shellmound in west-central Kentucky (Crawford 1982, 2005; Watson 1985: 112, 133), and at Bacon Bend in Tennessee (Chapman and Shea 1981). In addition, it has recently been reported from a fourth millennium bc context at the Hayes site in Tennessee (Crites 1987).

Bottle gourd (*Lagenaria siceraria*) is also present at Phillips Spring, and appears at other sites in the succeeding two millennia: Jernigan II and Rose Island in Tennessee (Crites 1978; Chapman and Shea 1981); Riverton, Illinois (Yarnell 1972); Salts Cave, Kentucky (Gardener 1987). Smith (1987: 21) refers to the identification (by Newsom and Decker) of bottle gourd dating to 7300 bp at the Windover site in Florida, but this material has not yet been published.

Although there is considerable debate about the age and precise identity of the earliest *Cucurbita* species – cf. Heiser (1989) and the results of the recent allozyme analyses by Decker (1986) and Decker and Wilson (1987) – there is general agreement that, if it were used by human groups at all, it was not primarily as food but rather – together with the bottle gourd somewhat later – as a container. Even if the remains recovered archaeologically are from *C. pepo*, which is the squash and pumpkin taxon, it was a thick-walled (averaging 2 mm or thicker if domestic), thin-fleshed, gourd-like variety of the modern *C. pepo* var. *ovifera* (ornamental gourd) type; i.e. the earliest *Cucurbita* grown in the Eastern Woodlands, whatever its derivation (*foetidissima*, *texana*, or *pepo*), had a gourd-like fruit, and is best referred to as a *Cucurbita* gourd.

The earliest evidence for a cultivated food plant is of *Iva annua* (sumpweed or marshelder, an inconspicuous weedy plant that produces small, oily seeds) from Napoleon Hollow, Illinois, radiocarbon dated by the accelerator mass spectrometric method to c. 2000 bc (Conard *et al.* 1984; Asch and Asch 1985a: 161; Yarnell 1987). The seeds average 4.4 mm long and are significantly larger than those from wild populations. A mean length of 4 mm or greater is usually regarded as evidence for domestication (Asch and Asch 1978, 1985a; Yarnell 1981) because seeds from wild *Iva* stands have means ranging from 2.5 to 3.2 mm.

The next oldest cultigen on the present evidence is a subspecies of grain-bearing *Chenopodium berlandieri*, a thin-testa early domesticated form (Smith 1985a, 1985b) being present in eastern Kentucky well before 1000 bc (Smith and Cowan 1987). Although it has been suggested that domesticated thin-testa *Chenopodium* was imported into the eastern United States from Mexico (where it is known as *chia* and is still grown, Wilson 1981), it is equally possible that native wild *Chenopodium berlandieri/bushianum* (cf. Pickersgill 1989) was domesticated in the Eastern Woodlands to produce a cultivar, thin-testa form there (Asch and Asch 1985a: 181–3; Smith 1987; Watson 1988).

The third of the early trio of domesticates is sunflower (*Helianthus annuus*), seeds of which had reached cultigen size (7 mm or longer) by about 1000 bc, as indicated by finds at the Higgs site in Tennessee (Brewer 1973), and at the Marble Bluff shelter in Arkansas (Fritz 1986).

Later prehistoric cultigens

The time–space pattern of cultigen emergence alters significantly after 1000 bc. Between 800 and 700 bc, several cultigens and quasi-cultigens appear in Arkansas, Kentucky, and Tennessee. By 500 bc a full-fledged horticultural complex is evident at several sites: Marble Bluff, Arkansas (Fritz 1986); Salts and Mammoth Caves in west-central Kentucky (Watson 1969, 1974; Yarnell 1969, 1974); Cloudsplitter and Cold Oak shelters in eastern Kentucky (Cowan 1985; Gremillion and Yarnell, pers. comm.); Higgs (Brewer 1973; McCollough 1973), and several other sites in Tennessee (Chapman and Shea 1981; Crites 1987). This Early Woodland garden complex includes the two container species (*Cucurbita* gourd and bottle gourd), two oily-seeded species (sumpweed and sunflower), and at least two starchy-seeded species (*Chenopodium* and maygrass). Although the maygrass (*Phalaris caroliniana*) found archaeologically does not differ from the wild plant, its depositional context and the frequency of its occurrence in archaeological sites with the other domesticates is strong evidence that it was cultivated (Asch and Asch 1985a; Fritz 1986).

In the succeeding centuries other starchy-seeded plants are added as cultigens or, in some places, as propagens – knotweed (*Polygonum erectum*), little barley (*Hordeum pusillum*), and giant ragweed (*Ambrosia trifida*) (Yarnell 1987) – and coalesce into a variegated Middle Woodland complex. An additional species distinguishing some Middle Woodland gardens from their Late Archaic and Early Woodland predecessors is tobacco (*Nicotiana* sp., perhaps *N. rustica*: Asch and Asch 1985a: 195–6), which has recently been identified in west-central Illinois (Asch and Asch 1985b), and – rarely and in small quantities – maize (*Zea mays*, presumably of the Chapalote/ Tropical Flint/Midwestern 12-row variety), which appears between ad 200 and 600 in a few sites in Tennessee, Ohio, and Illinois (Crites 1978; Yarnell 1983, 1987; Johannessen 1984; Asch and Asch 1985a: 169–99; Lopinot *et al.* 1986; Chapman and Crites 1987). Present evidence, although quite scanty, can be read as suggesting the subsequent development of historic Northern Flint corn (also called Eastern 8-row) somewhere in the more northerly regions of the Eastern Woodlands by about ad 800 (Stothers 1976; Blake 1986; Doebley *et al.* 1986; Watson 1988; and, for an alternative view, Lathrap 1987). Eastern 8-row/Northern Flint is the maize variety central to the economic foundation of the eastern Mississippian cultural climax known as Fort Ancient, but the Mississippian societies farther west, along the Mississippi River itself, simply added maize (primarily varieties of Midwestern 12-row) to the older starchy-seed complex of Woodland times. At least by these late prehistoric times, a panoply of tolerated, encouraged, or quasi-cultivated plants was also present. Yarnell (1987) refers to some 20 species altogether, including – besides those already referred to – amaranth (*Amaranthus* sp.), maypops (*Passiflora incarnata*), wild beans (*Strophostyles helvola* and *Phaseolus polystachios*), purslane (*Portulaca oleracea*), pokeweed (*Phytolocca americana*), Jerusalem artichoke (*Helianthus tuberosus*), spurge (*Euphorbia maculata*), carpetweed (*Mollugo verticillata*), black nightshade (*Solanum americanum*), and ground nut (*Apios americana*). In addition, there are ethnohistorical accounts describing the semi-cultivation of *Ilex vomitoria* (*yapon* or *yaupon*, source of the Black Drink, which was of great ceremonial importance in the Southeast) and of a salt plant (perhaps a species of *Atriplex*), as well as fibre-yielding plants (Swanton 1948: 176, 270). These historically recorded plants were probably also in use by late prehistoric times, if not before.

Aboriginal subsistence in the eastern forests

The role of wild food resources

Wild food resources – plant and animal, terrestrial and aquatic – were extremely important everywhere at all time periods from at least 8000 bp, a generalization that is confirmed by both archaeological and ethnographic documentation (already referred to and, for the ethnographic information, Swanton 1948; Yarnell 1964; Parker 1968; Hudson 1976).

Although domestic dogs were eaten occasionally, the bulk of animal food comprised deer, turkey, raccoon, possum, squirrel, rabbit, and other small mammals, as well as a wide variety of aquatic fauna. These animals were taken by various means: spears, atlatl-and-dart (in the Archaic to Early Woodland), bow-and-arrow (later prehistoric periods), snares, traps, harpoons, hooks, gorges, and nets. Many species of wild herbaceous plants, trees, and bushes were resorted to for food, medicine, dyes, cordage, and textiles, or were employed in constructing houses, boats, containers and other domestic equipment, tools, and weapons, as well as ceremonial objects and structures.

On the average and through the millennia, the role played by plant domesticates seems to have been relatively modest. Only in the very latest prehistoric periods, and then only in those few locales where Fort Ancient and Middle Mississippian societies reached high population densities and high levels of socio-political elaboration, do domesticated plants (Northern Flint/Eastern 8-row maize and Midwestern 12-row maize, *Cucurbita pepo*, and – after ad 1000 – beans, *Phaseolus vulgaris*) become critically important. From Middle Archaic to Late Woodland times, nuts (especially hickory and acorn, but also walnut, hazel, chestnut, and beechnut) and nut products (flour and oil) are the most important staple plant foods rather than any of the cultigens discussed earlier in this chapter.

A series of related points follows from this basic one, in combination with the new archaeological evidence about early cultigens. First, semi-sedentary societies following well-established seasonal rounds and based on a diverse subsistence economy persisted in the Eastern Woodlands for very long periods of time (several millennia) in the absence of cultigens of any sort, but making considerable use of storage and preservation techniques for a variety of wild plant and animal foods (e.g. drying and smoking fish and other meat, perhaps including the flesh of freshwater or marine shellfish; drying soft fruits such as persimmons; accumulating large quantities of nuts in pits or above-ground cribs and containers, as well as processing them, and other plant seeds, to produce oil and flour).

Secondly, this same forest-food pattern, with only a modest augmentation of garden plants yielding starchy or oily seeds (sumpweed, sunflower, *Chenopodium*, knotweed, maygrass), provided the economic basis for year-around settlement (Smith 1986: 41) and, somewhat later, for the first widely recognized cultural climax in the Eastern Woodlands, that called Adena (known to us primarily as a mortuary complex). For all practical purposes this same subsistence system was also the basis for the subsequent Hopewellian florescence and related developments in the Midwest, Midsouth, and Southeast. This last statement is debatable until much more is known about the archaeobotany and human-bone chemistry of the large, classic Hopewell sites, but I do not think it likely that maize will be found to have played a critical role. Certainly the present evidence does not indicate significant levels of maize consumption prior to Fort Ancient/Mississippian times (Vogel and van der Merwe 1977; van der Merwe and Vogel 1978; Bender *et al.* 1981; Broida 1983; Lynott *et al.* 1986; Wagner 1986, 1987). In other words, it appears that a case can be made for the indigenous development of a middle-range society (i.e. one with marked high- and low-status positions), certainly of the Big Man type (Sahlins 1963) if not some form of chiefdom (i.e. a society in which status is inherited: Service 1962), based upon essentially non-maize horticulture. (For differing opinions about Hopewellian social organization, see Braun 1979; Seeman 1979; Smith 1986.)

Possible Mesoamerican influence on the origins of food production

There has long been a spectrum of informed opinion about Mesoamerican influences upon cultural developments in the Eastern Woodlands in general, and upon the origins of food production there in particular. With respect to horticultural origins, the evidence is still inconclusive, as indicated above, because the identification of the oldest (7000–5000 bp) finds of *Cucurbita* is not unequivocal. Nevertheless, one can argue convincingly that even if these ancient remains of *Cucurbita* turn out to be of *C. pepo* derived from Mexico, the unfolding of early horticulture in the Eastern Woodlands is an independent and autonomous development because the earliest food plants are native to the United States (Smith 1987). Certainly the archaeological and botanical evidence is now sufficiently abundant to show that, regardless of the question of the possible priority of some limited Mesoamerican influence, the evolution of horticulture and of social complexity in the aboriginal eastern United States are intricate indigenous phenomena with trajectories that can be traced over very long periods (at least from Middle Archaic through Woodland to the beginning of Mississippian and Fort Ancient times) without significant perturbation from outside.

Late Archaic/Early Woodland horticulture vs. Mississippian/Fort Ancient agriculture

As already made clear, at least in a summary manner, the earliest food-producing economy in the Eastern Woodlands comprised hoe and/or digging-stick cultivation of garden plots often – probably rather casual – in which some six or fewer plant species were raised. The produce of these gardens was supplementary to a considerable diversity of wild plant and animal foods, the most important of which (generally more important than the cultivated seeds) were nuts, especially hickory, acorn, and walnut. Although a moderate amount of horticultural intensification is apparent in the Little Tennessee River sequence for this time period (Chapman and Shea 1981; Delcourt *et al.* 1986), whole-hearted commitment to plant cultivation and thoroughgoing agriculture is not evidenced before Fort Ancient/ Mississippian times (c. 1000 bp) when Eastern 8-row (Northern Flint) and Midwestern 12-row maize were intensively grown along the Ohio River, the central Mississippi River, and the valleys of various tributaries. Inference based on ethnographic, ethnohistorical, and archaeological evidence leads to a number of tentative conclusions about late prehistoric agriculture that contrast it with the earlier (Late Archaic to Middle Woodland) horticulture.

The Mississippian and Fort Ancient peoples are thought to have grown maize, squash, gourds, and beans in fields rather than, or as well as, in gardens, and to have reaped harvests sufficiently abundant to last until the succeeding autumn, at least when supplemented by wild plant and animal food (especially nuts, deer, turkey, and aquatic fauna and flora). The centre of gravity with respect to subsistence as a whole had by then shifted from dependence on wild species with supplementary use of the cultigens to dependence on the cultigens with supplementary use of wild foods. Yet the Mississippians (but apparently not the Fort Ancient branch, Wagner 1987) continued to grow the older Woodland crops (sumpweed, sunflower, *Chenopodium*, maygrass, knotweed, little barley, tobacco), perhaps in household gardens rather than fields (for recent summaries of Mississippian plant use, see Watson 1988 and Yarnell 1987). Mississippian field systems are believed to have been extensive as well as rather formally planned, laid out, and maintained, although still, of course, worked by hand with hoes and digging sticks (Fowler 1969: 374; Riley *et al.* 1980–81; Sears 1982; Riley 1986; Watson 1988). By early historic times at least, intercropping and multiple cropping were commonly practised in the Southeast, whereas farther north maize planting was staggered to produce a series of small harvests two to three weeks apart, thus spreading the risk of crop failure (Hudson 1976: 298).

Interpretations of the evidence and the processes

Regarding the antecedents and origins of plant cultivation and domestication, there seems now to be a consensus that some version of the 'dump-heap theory' is most plausible in seeking to explain the initial appearance of cultigens (Anderson 1952; Fowler 1957; Harlan *et al.* 1973; de Wet and Harlan 1975; Smith 1987). The hypothesis is that the Archaic foragers who lived in the Eastern Woodlands from the earliest establishment of the deciduous forest created fertile disturbed patches in and around their settlements where many of the weedy early domesticates would have thrived after colonizing such openings on their own, or being accidentally or deliberately introduced by humans. In one of the most recent formulations of this type of explanatory model, Smith (1987) refers to climatic change (the Hypsithermal) as resulting in a greater degree of sedentism, with more regular and more prolonged use of optimal floodplain locales. This is seen as a co-evolutionary trajectory between human settlements and various plant species, especially those that were the first domesticates (pre-3000 bp *Cucurbita* gourd [which he believes to be a native species not derived from Mexican C. *pepo*], sumpweed, and *Chenopodium*). This construction is persuasive in many respects, although alternative variants are available (see Neusius 1986) emphasizing some form of social imperative (Braun 1977; Bender 1985; Brown 1985), or even the older favourite of demographic pressure, which was adopted by many anthropologists and archaeologists from Boserup (1965) during the 1960s and 1970s. This is not to say that such interpretations are mutually exclusive, far from it as all these factors (climatic fluctuations, trends in social organization and sedentism, demographic variation) are related. However, the interpretations most favoured at present seem to be those that de-emphasize stress while focusing upon long-term congruence between the behaviour of skilfully foraging human populations and the ecology of certain plant communities cohabiting with them along the streams and in the uplands of the Eastern Woodlands.

As to the consequences of early horticulture in the Eastern Woodlands, there are several relevant points to be made. First, it is very difficult to decide where to draw the line and to say that certain groups are significantly horticultural and others are not. All human communities whose economies have been investigated archaeologically appear to have been very skilful at exploiting their environments, expertly deploying a wide array of forest resources, season-by-season and generation-by-generation. Even after cultigens are undeniably in evidence, the situation is not one of presence or absence, but rather a kaleidoscopic mosaic where a small array of fully morphologically domestic plants are used in varying combinations with a much larger variety of quasi-cultigens, encouraged, and tolerated species, and a wider variety still of wild herbaceous plants, shrubs, and trees. The total combination varied seasonally, geographically, and doubtless according to local cultural preferences as well. There must also have been occasional major shifts in subsistence pattern in response to short-term climatic fluctuations (extraordinarily dry, wet, or cold years, for example, or an extraordinarily long winter with a correspondingly more severe famine period in late winter/early spring). The function of plant-food species at the time of their initial cultivation was surely most often as a buffer, an additional resource for those periods when wild foods were scarce or temporarily inaccessible.

Secondly, the span of 'early horticulture' is very long, extending minimally from 3500 bp to 2000 bp, and maximally (pending more details on Hopewellian subsistence) to 1000 bp.

Thirdly, a great many pre-Columbian groups never made the change in emphasis from harvesting of wild plants and foraging among the other resources of the forests and streams to primary dependence upon cultivated species, but relied upon some combination of the two universes or – especially in floodplains of large rivers – subsisted wholly off wild foods.

These characteristics of plant use in the Eastern Woodlands are probably widely generalizable. One thinks immediately of close parallels in several parts of Europe (Dennell 1992), also in Southwest Asia (Hillman *et al.* 1989; Miller 1992) and in Middle and South America (Flannery 1986; McClung de Tapia 1992; Pearsall 1992). In this respect the counterpoise role played by the Eastern Woodlands in comparative studies in the past, as in the Braidwood and Willey (1962) symposium referred to at the start of this chapter, is no longer appropriate. The Eastern Woodlands cannot now be regarded as a region important only in a negative sense as one where nothing much happened, or where the course of cultural history was essentially idiosyncratic and thus irrelevant to comparative studies of long-term cultural-ecological processes.

Acknowledgements

I am grateful to David Harris and Gordon Hillman for inviting me to contribute to this book. I am also indebted to Richard A. Yarnell and to Gayle Fritz for providing copies of their unpublished works and for alerting me to references I would otherwise have missed.

References

Anderson, E. (1952) *Plants, Man and Life*, Berkeley, CA: University of California Press.

Asch, D.L. and Asch, N.B. (1978) 'The economic potential of *Iva annua* and its prehistoric importance in the lower Illinois valley', in R. Ford (ed.) *The Nature and Status of Ethnobotany*, Anthropological Papers 67, Ann Arbor, MI: University of Michigan, Museum of Anthropology.

Asch, D.L. and Asch, N.B. (1985a) 'Prehistoric plant cultivation in west-central Illinois', in R. Ford (ed.) *Prehistoric Food Production in North America*, Anthropological Papers 75, Ann Arbor, MI: University of Michigan, Museum of Anthropology.

Asch, D.L. and Asch, N.B. (1985b) 'Archeobotany', in B. Stafford and M. Sant (eds) *Smiling Dan: structure and function at a Middle Woodland settlement in the Lower Illinois River Valley*, Research Series 2, Kampsville, IL: Center for American Archaeology.

Bender, B. (1985) 'Emergent tribal formations in the American midcontinent', *American Antiquity*, 50: 52–62.

Bender, M., Baerreis, D. and Steventon, R. (1981) 'Further light on carbon isotopes and Hopewell agriculture', *American Antiquity*, 46: 346–53.

Blake, L. (1986) 'Corn and other plants from prehistory into history in the eastern United States', in D. Dye and R. Brister (eds) *The Protohistoric Period in the Mid-*

South: 1500–1700, Archaeological Report 18, Mississippi Department of Archives and History.

Boserup, E. (1965) *The Conditions of Agricultural Growth*, Chicago, IL: Aldine.

Braidwood, R.J. and Willey, G.R. (eds) (1962) *Courses toward Urban Life: archaeological considerations of some cultural alternates*, Viking Fund Publications in Anthropology 32, Chicago, IL: Aldine.

Braun, D.P. (1977) 'Middle woodland – (Early) Late Woodland social change in the prehistoric central Midwestern US', unpublished PhD dissertation, University of Michigan, Ann Arbor: University Microfilms 77–26, 210.

Braun, D.P. (1979) 'Illinois Hopewell burial practices and social organization: a re-examination of the Klunk-Gibson round group', in D. Braun and N. Greber (eds) *Hopewell Archaeology*, Kent, OH: Kent State University Press.

Brewer, A.J. (1973) 'Analysis of floral remains from the Higgs site (40Lo45)', in M. McCollough and C. Faulkner (eds) *Excavation of the Higgs and Doughty sites: I-75 salvage archaeology*, Tennessee Archaeological Society Miscellaneous Papers 12, Knoxville, TN: Tennessee Archaeological Society.

Broida, M. (1983) 'Maize in Kentucky Fort Ancient diets: an analysis of carbon isotope ratios in human bone', unpublished MA thesis, Department of Anthropology, University of Kentucky, Lexington.

Brown, J.A. (1985) 'Long term trends to sedentism and the emergence of complexity in the American Midwest', in T. D. Price and J. A. Brown (eds) *Prehistoric Hunter-gatherers: the emergence of cultural complexity*, Orlando, FL: Academic Press.

Bryant, V. (1974) 'Pollen analysis of prehistoric human feces from Mammoth Cave', in P. J. Watson (ed.) *Archaeology of the Mammoth Cave Area*, New York: Academic Press.

Caldwell, J.R. (1962) 'Eastern North America', in R. J. Braidwood and G. R. Willey (eds) *Courses toward Urban Life*, Chicago, IL: Aldine.

Chapman, J. and Crites, G. (1987) 'Evidence for early maize (*Zea mays*) from the Icehouse Bottom site, Tennessee', *American Antiquity*, 52: 352–4.

Chapman, J. and Shea, A.B. (1981) 'The archaeobotanical record: Early Archaic to Contact in the lower Little Tennessee River valley', *Tennessee Anthropologist*, 6: 64–84.

Conard, N., Asch, D., Asch, N., Elmore, D., Gove, H., Rubin, M., Brown, J., Wiant, M., Farnsworth, K. and Cook, T. (1984) 'Accelerator radiocarbon dating of evidence of prehistoric horticulture in Illinois', *Nature*, 308: 443–6.

Cowan, C.W. (1985) 'Understanding the evolution of plant husbandry in eastern North America: lessons from botany, ethnography, and archaeology', in R. Ford (ed.) *Prehistoric Food Production in North America*, Anthropological Papers 75, Ann Arbor, MI: University of Michigan, Museum of Anthropology.

Crawford, G. (1982) 'Late Archaic plant remains from west-central Kentucky: a summary', *Midcontinental Journal of Archaeology*, 7: 205–24.

Crawford, G. (2005) 'Plant remains from Carlston Annis (1972, 1974), Bowles, and Peter Cave', for W. H. Marquardt and P. J. Watson (eds) *Archaeology of the Middle Green River Region, Kentucky*, Institute for Archaeology and Paleo-environmental Studies Monograph 5, Gainesville: Florida Museum of Natural History, University of Florida.

Crites, G. (1978) 'Paleoethnobotany of the Normandy Reservoir in the upper Duck River valley, Tennessee', unpublished MA Thesis, Department of Anthropology, University of Tennessee, Knoxville.

Crites, G. (1987) 'Middle and Late Holocene ethnobotany of the Hayes site (40ML139): evidence from unit 99ON918E', *Midcontinental Journal of Archaeology*, 12: 3–32.

de Wet, J.M.J. and Harlan, J.R. (1975) 'Weeds and domesticates: evolution in the man-made habitat', *Economic Botany*, 29: 99–107.

Decker, D.S. (1986) 'A biosystematic study of *Cucurbita pepo*', unpublished PhD dissertation, Department of Biology, Texas A and M University, College Station, Texas.

Decker, D.S. and Wilson, H.D. (1987) 'Allozyme variation in the *Cucurbita pepo* complex: *C. pepo* var. *ovifera* vs. *C. texana*', *Systematic Botany*, 12: 263–73.

Delcourt, P.A. and Delcourt, H.R. (1981) 'Vegetation maps for eastern North America', in R. Romans (ed.) *Geobotany II*, New York: Plenum.

Delcourt, P.A. and Delcourt, H.R. (1983) 'Late Quaternary vegetational dynamics and community stability reconsidered', *Quaternary Research*, 19: 265–71.

Delcourt, P.A., Delcourt, H.R., Cridlebaugh, P. and Chapman, J. (1986) 'Holocene ethnobotanical and paleoecological record of human impact on vegetation in the Little Tennessee River valley, Tennessee', *Quaternary Research*, 25: 330–49.

Dennell, R. (1992) 'The origins of crop agriculture in Europe', in C. W. Cowan and P. J. Watson (eds) *The Origins of Agriculture: an international perspective*, Washington, DC: Smithsonian Institution Press.

Dincauze, D.F. (1985) 'An archaeological evaluation of the case for pre-Clovis occupations', *Advances in World Archaeology*, 3: 275–323.

Doebley, J., Goodman, M. and Stuber, C.W. (1986) 'Exceptional genetic divergence of Northern Flint corn', *American Journal of Botany*, 73: 64–9.

Flannery, K.V. (1986) *Guilá Naquitz: archaic foraging and early agriculture in Oaxaca, Mexico*, Orlando, FL: Academic Press.

Fowler, M. (1957) 'The origin of plant cultivation in the central Mississippi Valley: a hypothesis', paper presented at the annual meeting of the American Anthropological Association.

Fowler, M. (1969) 'Middle Mississippian agricultural fields', *American Antiquity*, 34: 365–75.

Fritz, G. (1986) 'Prehistoric Ozark agriculture: the University of Arkansas rockshelter collections', unpublished PhD dissertation, Department of Anthropology, University of North Carolina at Chapel Hill.

Gardner, P.S. (1987) 'New evidence concerning the chronology and paleo-ethnobotany of Salts Cave, Kentucky', *American Antiquity*, 52: 358–67.

Gilmore, M. (1931) 'Vegetal remains of the Ozark Bluff-Dweller culture', *Papers of the Michigan Academy of Sciences, Arts and Letters*, 14: 83–106.

Griffin, J.B. (1983) 'The Midlands', in J. Jennings (ed.) *Ancient North Americans*, San Francisco, CA: W.H. Freeman.

Harlan, J.R., de Wet, J.M.J. and Price, E.G. (1973) 'Comparative evolution of cereals', *Evolution*, 27: 311–25.

Hastorf, C. and Popper, V. (eds) (1988) *Current Paleoethnobotany: analytical methods and cultural interpretations of archaeological plant remains*, Chicago, IL: University of Chicago Press.

Heiser, C.B. (1985) 'Some botanical considerations of the early domesticated plants north of Mexico', in R. Ford (ed.) *Prehistoric Food Production in North America*, Anthropological Papers 75, Ann Arbor, MI: University of Michigan, Museum of Anthropology.

Heiser, C.B. (1989) 'Domestication of Cucurbitaceae: *Cucurbita* and *Lagenaria*', in D. R. Harris and G. C. Hillman (eds) *Foraging and Farming: the evolution of plant exploitation*, London: Unwin Hyman.

Hillman, G.C., Colledge, S.M. and Harris, D.R. (1989) 'Plant-food economy during the Epipalaeolithic at Tell Abu Hureyra, Syria: dietary diversity, seasonality, and modes of exploitation', in D. R. Harris and G. C. Hillman (eds) *Foraging and Farming: the evolution of plant exploitation*, London: Unwin Hyman.

Hudson, C. (1976) *The Southeastern Indians*, Knoxville, TN: University of Tennessee Press.

Jennings, J. (1974) *Prehistory of North America*, New York: McGraw-Hill.

Johannessen, S. (1984) 'Paleoethnobotany', in C. Bareis and J. Porter (eds) *American Bottom Archaeology*, Urbana and Chicago, IL: University of Illinois Press.

Jones, V. (1936) 'The vegetal remains of Newt Kash Hollow Shelter', in W. Webb and W. Funkhouser (eds) *Rock Shelters in Menifee County, Kentucky*, Reports in Archaeology and Anthropology 3, Lexington, KY: University of Kentucky.

Kay, M. (1986) 'Phillips Spring: a synopsis of Sedalia Phase settlement and subsistence', in S. Neusius (ed.) *Foraging, Collecting, and Harvesting: Archaic Period subsistence and settlement in the Eastern Woodlands*, Occasional Paper No. 6, Carbondale, IL: Southern Illinois University, Center for Archaeological Investigations.

Kay, M., King, F. and Robinson, C. (1980) 'Cucurbits from Phillips Spring: new evidence and interpretations', *American Antiquity*, 45: 806–22.

King, F. (1985) 'Early cultivated cucurbits in eastern North America', in R. Ford (ed.) *Prehistoric Food Production in North America*, Anthropological Papers 75, Ann Arbor, MI: University of Michigan, Museum of Anthropology.

King, J. and Allen, W.H. (1977) 'A Holocene vegetation record from the Mississippi River valley, southeastern Missouri', *Quaternary Research*, 8: 307–23.

Lathrap, D.W. (1987) 'The introduction of maize in prehistoric eastern North America: the view from Amazonia and the Santa Elena peninsula', in W. Keegan (ed.) *Emergent Horticultural Economies in the Eastern Woodlands*, Occasional Paper No. 7, Carbondale, IL: Southern Illinois University, Center for Archaeological Investigations.

Linton, R. (1924) 'The significance of certain traits in North American maize culture', *American Anthropologist*, 26: 345–9.

Lopinot, N., Harl, J., Wright, P. and Nixon, J. (1986) *Cultural Resource Testing and Assessments: the 1985 season at Lake Shelbyville, Shelby and Moultrie Counties, Illinois*, US Army Corps of Engineers, St. Louis District, Cultural Resource Management Report 30.

Lynott, M.J., Boutton, T., Price, J. and Nelson, D. (1986) 'Stable carbon isotopic evidence for maize agriculture in southeastern Missouri and northeastern Arkansas', *American Antiquity*, 51: 15–65.

McClung de Tapia, E.M. (1992) 'Mesoamerica and Central America', in C. W. Cowan and P. J. Watson (eds) *The Origins of Agriculture: an international perspective*, Washington, DC: Smithsonian Institution Press.

McCollough, M.C.R. (1973) 'Supplemental chronology for the Higgs Site (40Lo45), with an assessment of Terminal Archaic living and structure floors', *Tennessee Archaeologist*, 29: 63–8.

McMillan, B. and Klippel, W. (1981) 'Post-glacial environmental change and hunting-gathering societies of the southern Prairie Peninsula', *Journal of Archaeological Science*, 8: 215–45.

Marquardt, W.H. (1974) 'A statistical analysis of constituents in paleofecal specimens from Mammoth Cave', in P. J. Watson (ed.) *Archaeology of the Mammoth Cave Area*, New York: Academic Press.

Meltzer, D. and Smith, B. (1986) 'Paleoindian and Early Archaic subsistence strategies in eastern North America', in S. Neusius (ed.) *Foraging, Collecting, and Harvesting: Archaic Period subsistence and settlement in the Eastern Woodlands*, Occasional Paper No. 6, Carbondale, IL: Southern Illinois University, Center for Archaeological Investigations.

Miller, N. (1992) 'The origins of plant cultivation in the Near East', in C. W. Cowan and P. J. Watson (eds) *The Origins of Agriculture: an international perspective*, Washington, DC: Smithsonian Institution Press.

Muller, J. (1983) 'The Southeast', in J. Jennings (ed.) *Ancient North Americans*, San Francisco, CA: W.H. Freeman.

Munson, P.J., Parmalee, P. and Yarnell, R. (1972) 'Subsistence ecology of Scovill, a Terminal Middle Woodland village', *American Antiquity*, 36: 410–31.

Neusius, S.W. (1986) 'Generalized and specialized resource utilization during the Archaic Period: implications of the Koster site faunal record', in S. Neusius (ed.) *Foraging, Collecting, and Harvesting: Archaic Period subsistence and settlement in the Eastern Woodlands*, Occasional Paper No. 6, Carbondale, IL: Southern Illinois University, Center for Archaeological Investigations.

Parker, A.C. (1968) 'Iroquois uses of maize and other plant foods', in W. Fenton (ed.) *Parker on the Iroquois*, Syracuse, NY: Syracuse University Press.

Pearsall, D. (1992) 'The origins of plant cultivation in South America', in C. W. Cowan and P. J. Watson (eds) *The Origins of Agriculture: an international perspective*, Washington, DC: Smithsonian Institution Press.

Pickersgill, E. (1989) 'Cytological and genetical evidence on the domestication and diffusion of crops within the Americas', in D. R. Harris and G. C. Hillman (eds) *Foraging and Farming: the evolution of plant exploitation*, London: Unwin Hyman.

Quimby, G. (1946) 'The possibility of an independent agricultural complex in the southeastern United States', *Human Origins: an introductory course in anthropology; selected readings*, 31: 206–10.

Riley, T. (1986) 'Ridged fields and the Mississippian economic pattern', paper presented at the Conference on Emergent Horticultural Economies of the Eastern Woodlands, Southern Illinois University, Carbondale, March 28–29.

Riley, T., Moffat, C. and Freimuth, G. (1980–81) 'Prehistoric raised fields in the upper midwestern United States: an innovation in response to marginal growing conditions', *North American Archaeologist*, 2: 101–16.

Sahlins, M. (1963) 'Poor man, rich man, big-man, chief: political types in Melanesia and Polynesia', *Comparative Studies in Society and History*, 5: 285–303.

Sears, W.H. (1982) *Fort Centre: an archaeological site in the Lake Okeechobee basin*, Gainesville, FL: University Presses of Florida.

Seeman, M. (1979) 'Feasting with the dead: Ohio Hopewell charnel house ritual as a context for redistribution', in D. Erase and N. Greber (eds) *Hopewell Archaeology*, Kent, OH: Kent State University Press.

Service, E. (1962) *Primitive Social Organization*, New York: Random House.

Smith, B. (1985a) 'The role of *Chenopodium* as a domesticate in pre-maize garden systems of the eastern United States', *Southeastern Archaeology*, 4: 51–72.

Smith, B. (1985b) '*Chenopodium berlandieri* ssp. *jonesianum*: evidence for a Hopewellian domesticate from Ash Cave, Ohio', *Southeastern Archaeology*, 4: 107–33.

Smith, B. (1986) 'The archaeology of the southeastern United States: from Dalton to de Soto, 10,500 B.P.-500 B.P.', *Advances in World Archaeology*, 5: 1–92.

Smith, B. (1987) 'The independent domestication of indigenous seed-bearing plants in eastern North America', in W. Keegan (ed.) *Emergent Horticultural Economies of the Eastern Woodlands*, Occasional Paper No. 7, Carbondale, IL: Southern Illinois University, Center for Archaeological Investigations.

Smith, B. and Cowan, C.W. (1987) 'The age of domesticated *Chenopodium* in prehistoric North America: new accelerator dates from eastern Kentucky', *American Antiquity*, 52: 355–7.

Stewart, R.B. (1974) 'Identification and quantification of components in Salts Cave paleofeces, 1970–72', in P. J. Watson (ed.) *Archaeology of the Mammoth Cave Area*, New York: Academic Press.

Stoltman, J. (1978) 'Temporal models in prehistory: an example from eastern North America', *Current Anthropology*, 19: 703–28.

Stoltman, J. and Baerreis, D. (1983) 'The evolution of human ecosystems in the eastern United States', in H. E. Wright, Jr. (ed.) *Late-Quaternary Environments of the United States*. vol. 2: *The Holocene*, Minneapolis, MN: University of Minnesota Press.

Stothers, D.M. (1976) 'The Princess Point complex: a regional representative of the Early Late Woodland horizon in the Great Lakes area', in D. Brose (ed.) *The Late Prehistory of the Lake Erie Drainage Basin*, Cleveland, OH: Cleveland Museum of Natural History.

Struever, S. (1962) 'Implications of vegetal remains from an Illinois Hopewell site', *American Antiquity*, 27: 564–87.

Struever, S. (1968) 'Flotation techniques for the recovery of small-scale archaeological remains', *American Antiquity*, 33: 353–62.

Struever, S. and Vickery, K. (1973) 'The beginnings of cultivation in the Midwest-riverine area of the United States', *American Anthropologist*, 75: 1197–220.

Swanton, J.R. (1948) *The Indians of the Southeastern United States*, Bureau of American Ethnology Bulletin 137; reprinted 1979 by the Smithsonian Institution Press.

van der Merwe, N.J. and Vogel, J.C. (1978) '13C content of human collagen as a measure of prehistoric diet in Woodland North America', *Nature*, 276: 815–16.

Vogel, J.C. and van der Merwe, N. (1977) 'Isotopic evidence for early maize cultivation in New York State', *American Antiquity*, 42: 238–42.

Wagner, G.E. (1986) 'The corn and cultivated beans of the Fort Ancient Indians', *Missouri Archaeologist*, 47: 107–36.

Wagner, G.E. (1987) 'Uses of plants by the Fort Ancient Indians', unpublished PhD dissertation, Department of Anthropology, Washington University, St. Louis.

Wagner, G.E. (1989) 'Comparability among recovery techniques', in C. Hastorf and V. Popper (eds) *Current Paleoethnobotany: analytical methods and cultural interpretations of archaeological plant remains*, Chicago, IL: University of Chicago Press.

Watson, P.J. (ed.) (1969) *The Prehistory of Salts Cave, Kentucky*, Reports of Investigations No. 16, Springfield, IL: Illinois State Museum.

Watson, P.J. (ed.) (1974) *Archaeology of the Mammoth Cave Area*, New York: Academic Press.

Watson, P.J. (1976) 'In pursuit of prehistoric subsistence: a comparative analysis of some contemporary flotation techniques', *Midcontinental Journal of Archaeology*, 1: 77–100.

Watson, P.J. (1985) 'The impact of early horticulture in the upland drainages of the Midwest and Midsouth', in R. Ford (ed.) *Prehistoric Food Production in North America*, Anthropological Papers 75, Ann Arbor, MI: University of Michigan, Museum of Anthropology.

Watson, P.J. (1988) 'Prehistoric gardening and agriculture in the Midwest and Midsouth', in R. Yerkes (ed.) *Interpretations of Culture Change in the Eastern Woodlands during the Late Woodland Period*, Occasional Papers in Anthropology No. 3, Columbus, OH: Department of Anthropology, Ohio State University.

Watts, W.A. (1983) 'Vegetational history of the eastern United States 25,000 to 10,000 years ago', in H. Wright and S. Porter (eds) *Late-Quaternary Environments of the United States. vol. 1: the Late Pleistocene*, Minneapolis, MN: University of Minnesota Press.

Whitaker, T. and Cutler, H. (1986) 'Cucurbits from preceramic levels at Guilá Naquitz', in K. Flannery (ed.) *Guilá Naquitz*, Orlando, FL: Academic Press.

Willey, G.R. (1966) *An Introduction to American Archaeology. vol. 1: North and Middle America*, Englewood Cliffs, NJ: Prentice-Hall.

Wilson, H. (1981) 'Domesticated *Chenopodium* of the Ozark Bluff Dwellers', *Economic Botany*, 35: 233–9.

Wright, H.E., Jr. (1976) 'The dynamic nature of Holocene vegetation: a problem in paleoclimatology, biogeography, and stratigraphic nomenclature', *Quaternary Research*, 6: 581–96.

Wright, H.E., Jr. (1981) 'Vegetation east of the Rocky Mountains 18,000 years ago', *Quaternary Research*, 15: 113–25.

Yarnell, R.A. (1964) *Aboriginal Relationships between Culture and Plant Life in the Upper Great Lakes Region*, Anthropological Papers No. 23, Ann Arbor, MI: University of Michigan, Museum of Anthropology.

Yarnell, R.A. (1969) 'Contents of human paleofeces', in P. J. Watson (ed.) *The Prehistory of Salts Cave, Kentucky*, Reports of Investigations No. 16, Springfield: Illinois State Museum.

Yarnell, R.A. (1972) '*Iva annua* var. *macrocarpa*: extinct American cultigen?', *American Anthropologist*, 74: 335–41.

Yarnell, R.A. (1974) 'Plant food and cultivation of the Salts Cavern', in P. J. Watson (ed.) *Archaeology of the Mammoth Cave Area*, New York: Academic Press.

Yarnell, R.A. (1981) 'Inferred dating of the Ozark Bluff Dweller occupations based on the achene size of sunflower and sumpweed', *Journal of Ethnobiology*, 1: 55–60.

Yarnell, R.A. (1983) 'Prehistory of plant foods and husbandry in North America', paper presented at the 48th Annual Meeting of the Society for American Archaeology, Pittsburgh.

Yarnell, R.A. (1987) 'A survey of prehistoric crop plants in eastern North America', *Missouri Archaeologist*, 47: 47–60.

Update: Eastern North America revisited

Patty Jo Watson

The original chapter was written at a time when relevant data were accumulating rapidly and their resultant patterning shifting frequently. The patterns have now stabilised considerably, although big surprises are still possible, especially when DNA analyses and AMS dating are applied (e.g. Erickson *et al.* 2005). Nonetheless, the general state of affairs summarised in the original paper still stands, but some issues can be usefully updated.

With respect to 'later prehistoric cultigens' and 'Aboriginal subsistence in the eastern forests', I now regret not providing explicit definitions for the terms 'horticulture', 'agriculture' and 'garden complex'. The meanings of these words often vary from scholar to scholar, and may carry connotations outside the Americas (for example, where draft animals were present fairly early in the development of some food-producing economies) quite different from those appropriate in the Western hemisphere. In my earlier account I was probably too diffident concerning the potential and actual yields of pre-maize and non-maize food producing economies in Eastern North America (e.g. Smith 1992; Gremillion 2002: 484ff.). The evidence available 25 years ago would probably have supported the suggestion that by 2500 uncal. BP robust agricultural systems were present at several locales in the mid-continent. The labour that sustained them was human, the implements were hand tools such as hoes and digging sticks, and the crops (sunflower [*Helianthus annua*], sumpweed [*Iva annua*] and chenopodium [*Chenopodium berlandieri*], as well as two gourd species [*Cucurbita pepo ovifera, Lagenaria siceraria*]) were combined with yields from nut-bearing forest trees, especially hickory and oak, that were quite possibly managed to a greater or lesser degree.

My 1989 use of the words 'horticulture' and 'garden complex' downplays the achievements of pre-maize and non-maize food producers in Eastern North America because at that time I thought of *horticulture* as differing rather significantly from *agriculture*. Agriculture I took to imply full-time farmers in large fields, which they prepared and worked by means of draft animals attached to ards or plows, whereas Eastern Woodlands horticulture was envisioned as practices in small plots in the forest. These garden-like plots were prepared and tilled by part-time cultivators using digging sticks and/or hoes. Therefore, in 1989 'garden complex' and 'horticultural complex' meant the diverse produce – domestic (the plants listed above), semi-domestic (maygrass, knotweed) and encouraged (wild forms of chenopodium or amaranth) – of gardens or little fields in forest openings near communities of early cultivators, who were also skilled hunter-gatherers of wild forest foods. My background in Southwest Asian prehistory had supplied a definition for agriculture that slanted my view of early Eastern North American food production, unjustifiably minimising the potential and actual achievements of its creators.

A related matter is the status of pre-maize Eastern North American agri-culture as an indigenous development independent of that in Mesoamerica. Although there are still occasional disagreements (for a recent summary, see Smith 1992: Preface), the development of agriculture in the Eastern Woodlands of North America is now much more clearly established than it was in 1989. The Eastern Woodlands is one of at least three independent trajectories to agriculture in the Western Hemisphere (America north of Mexico, Mesoamerica and South America), and hence one of approximately seven in the whole of the human past.

On a more specific level, early domestication processes and chronologies for the earliest domesticated plants in the Americas (two different genera of gourd-bearing plants, *Curcubita pepo* and *Lagenaria siceraria*) have been much clarified since 1989 (Smith *et al.* 1992; Fritz 1999; Asch and Hart 2004; Erickson *et al.* 2005). Furthermore, significant regional variation within the Eastern Woodlands in the use of domesticated, semi-domesticated, encouraged and wild plant species both before and after the incorporation of maize agriculture is increasingly well documented (e.g. Fritz 1990; Fritz and Kidder 1993; Scarry 1993; Gremillion 2002). The earliest morpho-logical evidence for domestic plants comes from upland locales (rockshelters and cave deposits dating to the Late Archaic period, c. 3000 uncal. BP) in the Midsouth, primarily the Arkansas Ozarks, eastern Kentucky and Tennessee. This evidence is contemporary with, for example, that from several large open sites (shell mounds and midden mounds) created by seasonally sedentary, non-agricultural fisher-hunter-gatherers along a big upland stream (the Green River, tributary of the Ohio) in western Kentucky (Marquardt and Watson 2005) and predates by several centuries the first evidence for domestic crops in a major riverine region of the Midwest – the lower valley of the Illinois River, a large tributary of the Mississippi. Meanwhile, contemporaneous Archaic and later hunter-gatherer groups farther south in the Mississippi River drainage created impressive earth-works (beginning as early as c. 5500 uncal. BP and continuing to c. 1300 uncal. BP) demonstrating significant sociopolitical complexity in the absence of any form of agriculture.

Similarly, with respect to the Mesoamerican domesticate, maize, which came into Eastern North America from the Southwest, the first charred fragments show up sparsely about 2000 years ago at a few sites in the mid-continent (Illinois, Ohio, Tennessee) as an addition to the earlier Eastern Agricultural Complex. However, maize did not become a dominant crop anywhere in the East until several hundred years later. Even then, some communities (including the polity that developed at Cahokia, the largest prehistoric site north of Mexico) continued to grow substantial quantities of indigenous small-seeded crops as well as maize; many other groups living in the uplands east of the Mississippi were not agriculturalists at all.

Prominent among investigators presenting relatively detailed formulations to explain when, where, how and why early agriculture arose in Eastern

North America are Smith (1997) and Gremillion (1996, 2002). As more precise information accumulates from continuing, basic palaeoethnobotanical research in combination with the recovery and analysis of ancient DNA from AMS-dated specimens of the relevant species, substantive explanatory accounts for each of the major regions within the Eastern Woodlands (Northeast, Midwest, Midsouth and Southeast) are possible and will surely be forthcoming within the next decade.

References

Asch, D. and Hart, J. (2004) 'Crop domestication in prehistoric Eastern North America', in R. M. Goodman (ed.) *Encyclopedia of Plant and Crop Sciences*, New York: Marcel Dekker.

Erickson, D., Smith, B., Clarke, A., Sandweiss, D. and Tuross, N. (2005) 'An Asian origin for a 10,000-year-old domesticated plant in the Americas', *Proceedings of the National Academy of Sciences USA*, 102: 18,315–20.

Fritz, G. (1990) 'Multiple pathways to farming in precontact eastern North America', *Journal of World Prehistory*, 4: 387–435.

Fritz, G. (1999) 'Gender and the early cultivation of gourds in North America', *American Antiquity*, 64: 417–29.

Fritz, G. and Kidder, T. (1993) 'Recent investigations into agriculture in the lower Mississippi valley', *Southeastern Archaeology*, 12: 1–14.

Gremillion, K. (1996) 'Diffusion and adoption of crops in evolutionary perspective', *Journal of Anthropological Archaeology*, 15: 183–204.

Gremillion, K. (2002) 'The development and dispersal of agricultural systems in the Woodland Period Southeast', in D. Anderson and R. Mainfort, Jr (eds) *The Woodland Southeast*, Tuscaloosa, AL: University of Alabama Press.

Marquardt, W. and Watson, P. (2005) *Archaeology of the Middle Green River Region, Kentucky*, Institute for Archaeology and Paleoenvironmental Studies Monograph 5, Gainesville, FL: Florida Museum of Natural History, University of Florida.

Scarry, M. (1993) 'Variability in Mississippian crop production strategies', in M. Scarry (ed.) *Foraging and Farming in the Eastern Woodlands*, Gainesville, FL: University Press of Florida.

Smith, B.D. (ed.) (1992) *Rivers of Change: essays on early agriculture in Eastern North America*, Washington, DC: Smithsonian Institution Press.

Smith, B.D. (1997) *The Emergence of Agriculture*, New York: Scientific Library and W.H. Freeman.

Smith, B.D., Cowan, C. and Hoffman, M. (1992), 'Is it an indigene or a foreigner?', in B. D. Smith (ed.) *Rivers of Change: essays on early agriculture in Eastern North America*, Washington, DC: Smithsonian Institution Press.

8 The dispersal of domesticated plants into north-eastern Japan

Catherine D'Andrea

Introduction

The origin and dispersal of domesticated plants has long been a focus of archaeological research, and has become an important aspect of palaeoethnobotanical studies. Large compendia of articles dealing with this research problem have been available since the late 1960s (Ucko and Dimbleby 1969; Struever 1971; Reed 1977; Harris and Hillman 1989; Cowan and Watson 1992; Gebauer and Price 1992). Studies of *in situ* agricultural origins have developed considerably over the past twenty years, progressing from deterministic, causal models (e.g. Cohen 1977; Wright 1977) to discussions on evolutionary factors in human–plant interaction (Rindos 1984), and domestication rates in plants (Hillman and Davies 1990; Blumler and Byrne 1991). Modelling the subsequent spread of agriculture has progressed beyond ideas of simple dispersal (e.g. Ammerman and Cavalli-Sforza 1973, 1984). Recent work in agricultural dispersals has emphasized the complexity of forager–farmer interactions tempered by cultural, technological, and ecological factors (e.g. Zvelebil 1986; Gregg 1988).

In Japan, there has been considerable theorizing about the origins of agriculture. The focus of research has been on dispersals, specifically of wet-rice agriculture, although there is some discussion of the possibility of *in situ* plant domestication. Wet-rice agriculture is thought to have originated in a broad region including South Asia, southern China, and Southeast Asia, and spread into south-western Japan, eventually reaching the north-east (Chang 1976; Kanaseki and Sahara 1978; Akazawa 1981, 1986a, 1986b). Comparisons have been drawn with agricultural dispersals into north-western Europe (Rowley-Conwy 1984), and north-eastern North America, where tropical cultigens (maize, beans, and squash) were adopted by groups inhabiting temperate regions (Aikens 1981; Crawford 1983). Explanations for the spread of agriculture have been largely in the form of models emphasizing environmental (Kanaseki and Sahara 1978; Akazawa 1986a) and socio-economic factors (Aikens 1981; Hayden 1990). In addition to these ideas, some researchers have proposed the existence of temperate swidden horticulture based on millets, barley, buckwheat, and other crops that predates wet-rice cultivation (e.g. Fujimori 1963, 1970; Nakao 1966; Ueyama 1969; Sasaki 1971). Kotani (1981) refers to these models collectively as the 'Jomon Farming Hypothesis', which holds that wet-rice agriculture was introduced to populations that had prior knowledge of farming techniques. More recently, the shift to agriculture in Japan has been described as a series of four transitions, beginning with indigenous gardening during the Jomon, the introduction of wet-rice paddy farming during the Yayoi, followed by two transitions associated with the northeastward dispersal of cultigens (Crawford 1992b). Data are accumulating that demonstrate the presence of Jomon domesticates (e.g. Crawford 1983, 1992a; Tsukada *et al.* 1986; Kudo and D'Andrea 1991; D'Andrea 1995a, 1995b; D'Andrea *et al.* 1995; Okada 1995). More extensive research is required, however, to determine the nature of any associated husbandry practices.

This chapter provides a brief review of the evidence for Jomon cultigens, emphasizing the Tohoku region of north-eastern Japan (Figure 8.1). It has been argued that some form of horticulture was practiced by Jomon groups, based on archaeobotanical (Crawford 1983, 1997; D'Andrea *et al.* 1995), palynological (Tsukada *et al.* 1986), and ecological/historical data on agricultural practices in adjacent regions (D'Andrea 1995b; D'Andrea *et al.* 1995). While the available archaeobotanical database is not extensive, it does indicate a steady dispersal of domesticated plants to Japan from the mainland beginning early in the Jomon period. It is possible that once introduced, these crops, which eventually included rice, may not have disrupted Jomon cultural or subsistence systems, at least on the same scale as is evident during the later infiltration of wet-rice paddy and other Yayoi cultural elements. The Jomon lifestyle of sedentary village occupation, in fact, may have facilitated the spread of these early cultigens propagated in small gardens or swidden fields. Moreover, sedentism and familiarity with horticulture on the part of Jomon cultures also may explain what is now viewed as a relatively rapid dispersal northwards of later Yayoi wet-rice paddy technology.

Evidence for Jomon domesticates

Jomon culture is commonly portrayed as comprising several temporally and regionally diverse groups of affluent foragers, occupying more or less sedentary villages, and producing large quantities of cord-marked pottery (Figure 8.2). Subsistence is thought to have been similarly heterogeneous, dominated by fishing, terrestrial and marine mammal hunting, and plant gathering (Ikawa-Smith 1980; Aikens and Higuchi 1982). The question of Jomon horticulture has been debated for many years, and although most archaeologists now agree that some form of cultivation was practiced, it is considered to have been of minor economic significance (Akazawa 1982; Kasahara 1984; Higuchi 1986; Crawford 1992b; Barnes 1993a: 91). As will be demonstrated, evidence does indeed point to the existence of cultivation

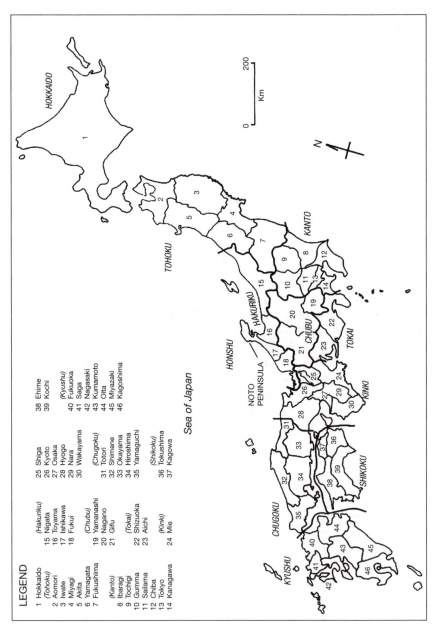

Figure 8.1 Japan: prefectures and districts

LEGEND

1 Hokkaido
(Tohoku)
2 Aomori
3 Iwate
4 Miyagi
5 Akita
6 Yamagata
7 Fukushima

(Kanto)
8 Ibaragi
9 Tochigi
10 Gumma
11 Saitama
12 Chiba
13 Tokyo
14 Kanagawa

(Hakuriku)
15 Nigata
16 Toyama
17 Ishikawa
18 Fukui

(Chubu)
19 Yamanashi
20 Nagano
21 Gifu

(Tokai)
22 Shizuoka
23 Aichi

(Kinki)
24 Mie

25 Shiga
26 Kyoto
27 Osaka
28 Hyogo
29 Nara
30 Wakayama

(Chugoku)
31 Totori
32 Shimane
33 Okayama
34 Hiroshima
35 Yamaguchi

(Shikoku)
36 Tokushima
37 Kagawa

38 Ehime
39 Kochi

(Kyushu)
40 Fukuoka
41 Saga
42 Nagasaki
43 Kumamoto
44 Oita
45 Miyazaki
46 Kagoshima

Date BP	South-western Japan	North-eastern Japan	Southern Hokkaido
765	Nara-Heian		Ezo
1240	Kofun		
1650			
1850	Yayoi	Tohoku (Northern) Yayoi	Zoku-Jomon
2100			
2150			
2300			
		Final Jomon	
3000		Late Jomon	
4500		Middle Jomon	
5600		Early Jomon	
7500		Initial Jomon	
9500		Incipient Jomon	
13,000		Late Palaeolithic	

Figure 8.2 Generalised cultural chronology for Japan (after Ikawa-Smith 1980; Aikens and Higuchi 1982; Suzuki 1986; Barnes 1988)

at certain times during the Jomon, but it is argued that at present these data are insufficient to suggest the nature and economic importance of plant husbandry activities.

Although the main focus of this chapter is on the Tohoku region (Figure 8.1), it is instructive to summarize briefly the evidence for Jomon domesticates throughout Japan, and ideas concerning the possibility of associated plant husbandry practices. This review is by no means exhaustive, but it will serve to indicate the extent to which existing archaeobotanical evidence bears on the question of Jomon cultivation. Most cultigens appearing during the Jomon originated on the East Asian mainland, or at least have their primary centres of diversity in that region (Zeven and de Wet 1982). Given other general indications of continental influences on Jomon culture (e.g. Groot 1951; Chard 1974; Sample 1978), the presence of these domesticates throughout much of the Japanese archipelago may constitute additional evidence of contact with the mainland.

The earliest domesticated plants date to the Initial Jomon (Figure 8.2), and consist of one seed each of bottle gourd (*Lagenaria siceraria*) and *shiso* (*Perilla frutescens* var. *crispa*) at the waterlogged Torihama Shell Mound, Fukui. However, it is during the following Early Jomon that evidence for several domesticates is present throughout much of Japan. In addition, this period is characterized by the development of increased sedentism and substantial village settlements (Ikawa-Smith 1980; Nishida 1983). A growing number of plant remains recovered from Early Jomon sites suggests that forms of subsistence in addition to hunting, fishing, and plant collecting were practiced at that time. Deposits at Torihama have produced remains of bottle gourd, adzuki (*Vigna angularis* var. *angularis*), *shiso*, *egoma* (*P. frutescens* var. *japonica*), paper mulberry (*Broussonetia papyrifera*), great burdock (*Arctium lappa*), and hemp (*Cannabis sativa*) (Okamoto 1979, 1983). The identifications of adzuki and bottle gourd, however, have been questioned (Akazawa 1982; Crawford 1992a). Minamiki *et al.* (1986, in Crawford 1992a) report the finding of peach stones (*Prunus persica*) at the Ikiriki site, Nagasaki, dating from 5660 ± 90 BP to 5950 ± 30 BP. At the Otsubo site, Chiba, seeds and rind fragments of bottle gourd are known from Early Jomon levels (Kokawa 1978).

The Hamanasuno site in Minamikayabe, south-western Hokkaido, has produced one buckwheat achene (Crawford *et al.* 1976). The presence of this Early Jomon domesticate is further indicated by the recovery of buckwheat pollen dating to 6600 ± 75 BP at Ubuka Bog, Yamaguchi (Tsukada *et al.* 1986). This cultigen is not native to Japan, and Tsukada (1986: 44) contends that it was imported from the Yunnan Plateau of China, which he suggests is a center of buckwheat domestication. Other sources note that buckwheat originated in temperate Asia, and its probable wild ancestor, *Fagopyrum cymosum*, is native to northern India and China (Campbell 1976). In addition, Tsukada *et al.* (1986) suggest that swidden horticulture is evidenced by the nature of charcoal fragments recovered in the Ubuka Bog pollen cores. Although these fragments could equally suggest clearance for other purposes (Barnes 1986), the existence of swidden is not unreasonable given the occurrence of cultigens during this and subsequent periods. Recently, Okada (1995) has announced the recovery of several domesticates from Early-Middle Jomon (5500–4000 BP) levels at the Sannai Maruyama site in Aomori City, Aomori. Preliminary reports indicate the presence of a planned village with ceremonial platforms supporting as many as 500 people. Crop plants recovered include barnyard millet (*Echinochloa utilis*), great burdock, gourd, *egoma*, and beans. Okada (1995) suggests the site was occupied by sedentary, horticultural populations.

The existence of agriculture in the Middle Jomon has generated considerable discussion, but, unfortunately, little in the way of archaeobotanical material is available to support the models that have been proposed. Several hypotheses are based on archaeological evidence from the Chubu district of central Honshu which indicates a marked phase of cultural fluorescence during the Middle Jomon. Populations inhabiting large villages in this region are postulated to have developed agricultural systems based on nuts (e.g. Esaka 1959; Sakazume 1959, 1961; Ueyama 1969; Ueyama *et al.* 1976; Fujimori 1970; Nishida 1983), yam, taro, and other crops (e.g. Esaka 1959; Nakao 1966, 1967; Kamikawana 1968; Sasaki 1971; Turner 1979). Several of these models have been discussed elsewhere (D'Andrea 1992).

Unequivocal evidence for domesticated plants in the Middle Jomon is known from central and north-eastern Japan. The charred Idojiri 'cakes' recovered from sites in Nagano, Gifu, and Fukushima initially were thought to have been made from starchy plant sources, including millet, barnyard millet, taro, rice, oats, and nuts (Kidder 1968: 25; Ikawa-Smith 1980). Matsutani (1983) identifies *shiso* as a major component of the cakes. In addition, Crawford (1983) suggests the possibility of Early and Middle Jomon gardening based on evidence from the Hamanasuno and Usujiri B sites in south-western Hokkaido. At these localities, the grain size of barnyard grass (*Echinochloa crus-gali*) is shown to increase steadily over a 4000-year period. It is suggested that this species was cultivated by Middle Jomon occupants of Hamanasuno. Barnyard grass is the wild ancestor of Japanese barnyard millet (Yabuno 1966: 320–1), and is the only species postulated to have been a prehistoric indigenous Japanese domesticate (Crawford 1983, 1992b). Additional evidence for Middle Jomon cultigens comes from Usujiri B, where foxtail (*Setaria italica* ssp. *italica*) and Japanese barnyard millet have been identified (Crawford 1992b). The importance of anthropogenic environments to these populations is outlined by Crawford, who suggests that disturbed habitats may be the result of activities associated with forest clearance (Crawford 1992b, 1997).

It is during the Late and Final Jomon periods that rice (*Oryza sativa* var. *japonica*) and barley (*Hordeum vulgare*) are added to the list of cultigens present throughout Japan. At the Kuwagaishimo site in Fukui, remains of charred rice, barley, and adzuki were recovered from Late Jomon deposits

(Tsunoda and Watanabe 1976). Rice has been reported from Late to Final Jomon sites in Kyushu, such as Nabatake (Kasahara 1982, 1984), Uenoharu (Kotani 1972), and several other localities (for reviews, see Hudson 1990; Crawford 1992b). The Uenoharu remains consist of rice grains and phytoliths and one barley caryopsis. Rice phytoliths are known from other Late Jomon sites in north-western Kyushu, and the earliest known rice pollen dates to 3200 BP at Itatsuke (Tsukada 1986). In the north-east, the evidence for Late Jomon cultigens comes from the Kyunenbashi site, Iwate, where Yamada (1980) reports the presence of buckwheat pollen. In addition, rice, barnyard and foxtail millet have been recovered from the Kazahari site in south-eastern Aomori. Two rice grains were dated by AMS (Accelerator Mass Spectrometry) to 2540 ± 240 BP and 2810 ± 270 BP (Kudo and D'Andrea 1991; D'Andrea *et al.* 1995). The presence of rice in northern Tohoku during this period has fostered a re-consideration of models dealing with processes of rice dispersals into north-eastern Japan. In particular, the Kazahari data indicate that the arrival of rice as a domesticate and Yayoi wet-rice paddy technology represent two separate events (D'Andrea 1992, 1995b; D'Andrea *et al.* 1995).

Wet-rice cultivation was established in Tohoku by Final Jomon times, contemporary with the Early Yayoi of south-western Japan (Figure 8.2). At Kamegaoka and other sites in Aomori, rice remains are associated with Final Jomon Obora A ceramics (Sato 1984). It has been suggested that a precocious variety of rice was introduced directly to Tohoku from Kyushu *via* the Japan Sea (Hoshikawa 1984). At the Sunazawa site, Aomori, extensive rice paddy fields contemporary with the Early Yayoi have been recovered. In addition, Ongagawa type pottery and other Yayoi artefacts, such as glass beads, are known from Sunazawa and other Sunazawa phase sites in Aomori (Murakoshi 1988). Although Tohoku Final Jomon rice was often interpreted as a trade item obtained from south-western Yayoi populations (Ikawa-Smith 1988), the discovery of the Sunazawa rice paddies (Suzuki 1986; Murakoshi 1988) demonstrates that rice was being cultivated in Aomori during the Early Yayoi.

In addition to rice, other Final Jomon cultigens include barley from Uenoharu and bottle gourd from Itatsuke and Shimpukuji in Kyushu. Buckwheat pollen has been recovered from the Kasori site and other localities along Tokyo Bay, dating to c. 2800 BP, and by 1500 BP the quantities increase markedly (Tsukada 1986). At Kamegaoka, palynological data also indicate the presence of Final Jomon buckwheat (Yamanoi and Sato 1984). Several cultigens have been identified at Nabatake: one foxtail millet grain (2680 ± 80 BP), 22 *shiso* seeds (3330–2500 BP), and two rice grains (2620 ± 60 BP and 3230 ± 100 BP) (Kasahara 1982, 1984). In addition, mung beans (*Vigna radiatus* var. *radiatus*) have been reported in Final Jomon levels at Nabatake (Watanabe and Kokawa 1982).

A north–south dichotomy in Tohoku ceramic chronology is evident at the end of the Final Jomon, and this continued into the subsequent Tohoku

Yayoi. The southern Tohoku sequence seems to have been more heavily influenced by south-western Yayoi cultures, while northern groups maintained local Jomon ceramic styles (Itoh 1966; Crawford and Takamiya 1990). It was initially believed that Yayoi populations did not penetrate northern Tohoku, and cultures represented there were referred to as Zoku-Jomon (or continuing Jomon) (Katoh and Suto 1986). However, in 1984, Itoh suggested the presence of a Yayoi period in Tohoku based on his observation that pottery from the Inakadate site, Aomori, was more similar to south-western Yayoi ceramics than to local Obora forms. Most archaeologists did not believe in the existence of late prehistoric wet-rice farming in Tohoku until rice paddy fields at Tareyanagi were dated to the first century AD, contemporary with Middle Yayoi of south-western Japan (Itoh 1984; Kuraku 1984; Katoh and Suto 1986). Rice paddies also are known in southern Tohoku, such as those recovered at the Tomizawa site in Miyagi (Crawford and Takamiya 1990). There is evidence that crops in addition to rice were grown by Final Jomon-Tohoku Yayoi populations. Phytoliths of a *Panicum* species, possibly broomcorn millet, have been identified at the Babano II site in Iwate (Itoh 1984). Also, pit-house contexts at Kazahari have produced substantial quantities of rice, in addition to hemp (*Cannabis sativa*), broomcorn and foxtail millet (D'Andrea 1992, 1995b).

Although outside the time frame of the Jomon, the Ezo period farming system of south-western Hokkaido is worthy of mention in the context of north-eastern Japanese agricultural development (Figure 8.2). Many of the traditional views of agricultural dispersals to the north-east were thrown into question with the discovery of a ninth century AD millet-based dryland agricultural complex in south-western Hokkaido at the Sakushu-Kotoni River site (Crawford 1986). The Sakushu-Kotoni archaeobotanical evidence points to the presence of intensive dry field agriculture in this region, practiced by Ezo populations who are considered the immediate ancestors of the ethnohistorically known Ainu (Crawford and Yoshizaki 1987; Crawford and Takamiya 1990). At present, the origin and development of this millet-based farming system have not been established; however, routes of introduction directly to Hokkaido from the north Asian mainland (e.g. Katoh 1986; Kuzmin *et al.* 1994) and from Tohoku (Hayashi 1969; Crawford and Yoshizaki 1987) have been proposed. Recent discussions of this problem have emphasized the likelihood of several introductions of domesticated plants to Hokkaido, from both Asian and Tohoku area sources (cf. Yamada and Tsubakisaka 1995).

New directions in the study of Jomon subsistence

As evidence mounts in support of Jomon cultivation, several workers have developed models to explain the origin and development of these plant husbandry activities. Previous explanations, such as those given by Ueyama *et al.* (1976) and others, suggest that the development of horticulture was a conscious response by Jomon populations to the resource-poor broad-leaved forest regions of south-western Japan. More innovative models emphasizing socio-economic factors have been proposed (e.g. Aikens 1981; Hayden 1990), but their applicability is hampered because of difficulties in establishing correlations between social complexity and the appearance of the earliest domesticates. As is pointed out by Crawford (1992b), the earliest cultigens in Japan predate evidence for social complexity. Others have emphasized the role of ecology and anthropogenesis in the development of Jomon plant husbandry. They view Jomon populations as active agents in the generation of disturbed environments upon which they became increasingly dependent (Crawford 1983, 1992b, 1997; Nishida 1983). In this regard, the study of archaeobotanical weed seed assemblages from several sites in north-eastern Japan has indicated that compared to earlier periods, anthropogenic environments from the Early to Late Jomon were more widespread. Furthermore, these weed assemblages comprise species that differ from later periods when wet-rice paddy cultivation was practiced. These anthropogenic communities are thought to be the result of ecological disruption associated with sedentary village life and related activities, which may have included gardening (Crawford 1997).

Perhaps the key to explaining the development of Jomon plant husbandry lies in first obtaining a clearer understanding of the nature of these practices, and then viewing their evolution within the context of Far Eastern agricultural history. A first step toward this goal would involve undertaking more archaeobotanical sampling in the north-east, in addition to re-examining other categories of archaeological evidence, such as settlement and seasonality/scheduling patterns. The relationship between increased sedentism and the appearance of several domesticates during the Early Jomon should be further investigated. This kind of work may serve to demonstrate how plant husbandry could be successfully integrated into established Jomon foraging subsistence patterns. The question of whether Kazahari Late Jomon and other contemporary northern groups were cultivating crops or acquiring them through exchange remains open (D'Andrea 1992, 1995b). Although irrigation works were present in contemporary China (Ho 1977; Chang 1983) this technology is not evident in north-eastern Japan until the Sunazawa phase, contemporary with the Early Yayoi (Murakoshi 1988). Based on ecological and historical data, it has been argued that some form of cultivation was possible, based on non-irrigated swamp cultivation or swidden (D'Andrea 1995b; D'Andrea *et al.* 1995). Several methods of rice growing have been described in the ethnographic literature, many of which do not require irrigation (e.g. Lambert 1985). In addition, Fujiwara (1993) has reported sizable yields of rice produced on experimental non-irrigated swidden plots in the mountains of Kyushu. His research on phytoliths indicates that swidden cultivation of rice in Miyazaki was practiced until 1945 (Fujiwara *et al.* 1985). This approach, in addition to palynology, holds much promise for the identification of ancient swidden fields.

The East Asian evidence points to the existence of two distinct prehistoric agricultural complexes, dryland millet farming in the north (6500–5000 cal. BC) that predates wet-rice agriculture in the south (5000 cal. BC) (Chang 1986, 1989; Crawford 1992a). Based on recent AMS dates from Primorye, in the Russian Far East, it has been proposed that following its origin in northern China, millet agriculture diffused to Korea, Primorye, and Japan sometime during the fourth and third millennia BC (Kuzmin *et al.* 1994; Kuzmin, pers. comm.). Although the earliest unequivocal evidence for a millet-based agricultural complex in Japan dates to the ninth century AD Ezo period (Crawford and Yoshizaki 1987), the origin of this system may be related to a temperate north-east Asian farming adaptation based on the cultivation of small seeded cereals, such as millets, and other dry field crops (D'Andrea 1992, 1995b). The Early to Middle Jomon suite of domesticates, including buckwheat, barnyard millet, and other crops, seems to mirror this continental pattern, but more evidence is needed to establish links between northern Asian mainland and Japanese farming traditions.

The spread of cultigens into Japan prior to the Yayoi perhaps should be viewed as a fluid process, with species arriving at various times beginning by the Early Jomon, and incorporated into small-scale gardens or horticultural fields. These dispersals also included rice by Late Jomon times. The new resources may not have caused major socio-economic disruption of Jomon foraging patterns, but may have inspired the cultivation of local herbaceous plants, such as barnyard grass (Crawford 1992b). Whether the route was overland from Kyushu or directly from the mainland *via* sea traffic (e.g. Im 1995), however, remains to be established. Assuming the dispersals were overland, their progression does not seem to have been significantly slowed by cultural or ecological factors.

The Jomon case may have some general similarity to that observed in the prehistoric American Southwest. Minnis (1992) has argued that the introduction of Mesoamerican domesticates to Late Archaic populations of the south-western United States did not result in major changes in economy or sociocultural frameworks. Instead he suggests that plant cultivation was integrated into the pre-existing seasonal scheduling of subsistence activities, and eventually it led to substantial increases in resource productivity. When first adopted, maize was probably grown in small garden plots, and it was not until at least 1000 years following the Late Archaic introduction of domesticates that irrigated field agriculture grew to dominate subsistence systems. Several introduced crops, such as maize, gourds, squashes, and beans, do not require constant attention, and as such, Minnis argues that the 'casual cultivation' of these plants can produce adequate yields. In support of this position, he cites eighteenth- and nineteenth-century accounts of Apache populations who planted maize fields in the late spring, and leaving them for the most part untended, returned to harvest in the autumn (Minnis 1992).

Several of the earliest Jomon domesticates, particularly millets, do not require intensive tending to produce respectable yields. Foxtail, broomcorn and Japanese barnyard millet can tolerate extreme ranges in environmental conditions, and the latter two may have the lowest water requirements of any cultivated cereal. These species are well adapted to both semi-arid and high altitude conditions with low precipitation and poor soils. Foxtail millet is not as tolerant to drought, but it can survive a wide range of soil conditions (Purseglove 1972; Simmonds 1976; Chang 1983). Purseglove (1972: 199) also points out that broomcorn millet was often cultivated by 'nomads' because of its ability to mature very quickly, sometimes within six weeks. Other millets also mature in a short period of time, and in general these species require less tending than many cereals (Chang 1983). Although there is not universal agreement on the view of agricultural origins in the American Southwest presented by Minnis (cf. Wills 1990), and the culture and ecology of the south-western United States is not directly comparable to that obtaining in prehistoric Japan, the American example may be of heuristic value in the development of new models of Jomon subsistence.

The introduction of wet-rice paddy farming dominates the literature dealing with the Final Jomon and the Jomon-Yayoi transition, and the significance of other cultigens, such as barley and millets, is often ignored (for exceptions, see Hudson 1990; Crawford 1992a). Yayoi culture represents an incursion of populations from the Asian mainland, who introduced wet-paddy farming as well as several other technological innovations (e.g. Brace *et al.* 1989; Hanihara 1990, 1991). The spread of wet-rice farming was thought to have taken place in two stages (e.g. Kanaseki and Sahara 1978; Akazawa 1981, 1982; Aikens and Higuchi 1982). The first dispersal was apparently rapid, going from northern Kyushu to western Tokai in the space of a few hundred years. It was believed that rice farming cultures did not penetrate northern Tohoku until a second phase of expansion, contemporary with the Middle Yayoi of south-western Japan (Minato 1977; Kanaseki and Sahara 1978). It was further proposed that rice cultivation in the south-west diffused along coastal areas, but in the north-east, it moved inland because marine-oriented coastal foragers, with their stable fishing and hunting way of life, resisted the shift to farming (Kanaseki and Sahara 1978; Akazawa 1981, 1982). Rice agriculture supposedly did not arrive in Hokkaido until the nineteenth century when the Japanese state encouraged the Ainu to undertake farming (Watanabe 1972).

The two-stage model explaining the spread of Yayoi cultural elements (e.g. Kanaseki and Sahara 1978; Akazawa 1981, 1982) has been reconsidered in light of recent evidence. New perspectives on the Jomon-Yayoi transition emphasize that the transformation in Kyushu took somewhat longer than was previously thought. Furthermore, it is now believed that the subsequent spread of rice agriculture to the north-east occurred more quickly than was proposed in the two-stage model (Murakoshi 1988; Crawford 1992b; Barnes 1993b; D'Andrea 1995b). In the south-west, at least 1000 years separate the initial appearance of rice and the initiation of intensive farming practices (Hudson 1990). Although rice is present in Kyushu by Late Jomon times, paddy fields appear during the following Final Jomon, at sites such as Itatsuke. These early paddies are located in low-lying areas, and consist of mud ridges and ditches designed for drainage control (Higuchi 1986). Fully developed irrigation was not in evidence until the Middle Yayoi, when it may have been introduced from northern China, together with Chinese mirrors and iron weapons (Kanaseki 1986). The period between the first introduction of rice farming and the beginning of the Early Yayoi (300 cal. BC) has been referred to as the Initial Yayoi (Hudson 1990).

Several workers have proposed viable alternatives to the two-stage model, which has been characterized by Hudson (1990) as a 'wave of advance' model. He suggests that concepts of forager–farmer interaction (cf. Crawford and Takamiya 1990) have more relevance in understanding the Jomon–Yayoi transition (Hudson 1990). Following on this theme, Barnes (1993b) finds Dennell's (1985) 'imitation' model useful in explaining the introduction of rice farming to south-western Japan. This process involved imitation and adoption of new technologies by Kyushu Jomon populations from a variety of sources, where the relationship between recipients and donors was rather distant. Evidence in support of this view includes the intensification of food production on the part of local groups, a long-distance exchange of technology where agriculture is one of the earliest transmissions, and the lack of a clear demarcation between Final Jomon and Initial Yayoi cultures (Barnes 1993b: 184). Barnes has further suggested that the spread of Yayoi cultural elements, including wet-rice farming, out of northern Kyushu was a complex process involving both migrations and diffusion (1993b: 184–5). This is attested to by the high degree of variability in archaeological assemblages of south-western Japan, especially in the Osaka Bay area, where there is evidence for the coexistence of Jomon and Yayoi cultures.

The apparent cultural dichotomy between south-western/central Japan and northern Tohoku suggests that the spread of Yayoi culture and technology to the north-east was more a function of acculturation than colonization, as was the case in south-western Japan. This is evidenced by the persistence of Jomon cultural elements well into the Tohoku Yayoi period (Crawford and Takamiya 1990). Although the processes by which rice-paddy farming was adopted by north-eastern Jomon groups remain to be understood, evidence indicates that the technology arrived relatively quickly (e.g. Murakoshi 1988). This suggests that the dispersal of wet-paddy techniques was facilitated by Jomon sedentary lifestyles, which may have included the swidden cultivation of rice, millets, and other crops. As such, these conditions could have produced a cultural milieu that was receptive to the adoption of new agricultural technologies.

Conclusion

The Jomon period presents several intriguing problems concerning the origins of East Asian plant husbandry. Over the past several years, archaeobotanical research in north-eastern Japan has demonstrated the presence of buckwheat, millets, rice, and several other domesticates in Jomon contexts. It has been shown that buckwheat and millets occur by the Early Jomon, while rice, barley, and other millets appear by the Late Jomon. Subsistence interpretations based on archaeobotanical studies in all areas have been plagued by small sample sizes from too few sites. Although it is now generally accepted that plant cultivation was a component of Jomon subsistence prior to the arrival of Yayoi wet-paddy technology, the nature of these plant husbandry practices remains to be elucidated. It is precisely this kind of basic issue that needs to be addressed before examining questions relating to the economic importance of these activities. It does appear, however, that dispersals of rice and other cultigens during the Jomon were not substantially delayed by cultural or ecological factors, and once introduced, the cultivation of these plants may not have instigated substantial cultural change. Moreover, various aspects of Jomon lifeways, such as sedentism and horticulture, could have acted to facilitate the later introduction of Yayoi wet-rice paddy farming.

Acknowledgements

I would like to thank the participants of a graduate seminar on the 'Origins of Agriculture' held at the Department of Archaeology, Simon Fraser University in 1994, during which some of the issues discussed in this paper were raised: Bob Muir, Mike Clark, Dave Schaepe, and John Wolf. Many thanks to Gary Crawford and Larry Pavlish (both of the University of Toronto) who provided useful criticisms of various drafts of this chapter.

References

Aikens, C.M. (1981) 'The last 10,000 years in Japan and Eastern North America: parallels in environment, economic adaptation, growth of societal complexity, and the adoption of agriculture', in S. Koyama and D. H. Thomas (eds) *Affluent Foragers*, Senri Ethnological Studies No. 9, Osaka: National Museum of Ethnology.

Aikens, C.M. and Higuchi, T. (1982) *Prehistory of Japan*, New York: Academic Press.

Akazawa, T. (1981) 'Maritime adaptation of prehistoric hunter-gatherers and their transition to agriculture in Japan', in S. Koyama and D. H. Thomas (eds) *Affluent Foragers*, Senri Ethnological Studies No. 9, Osaka: National Museum of Ethnology.

Akazawa, T. (1982) 'Cultural change in prehistoric Japan: receptivity to rice agriculture in the Japanese Archipelago', *Advances in World Archaeology*, 1: 151–211.

Akazawa, T. (1986a) 'Hunter-gatherer adaptations and the transition to food production in Japan', in M. Zvelebil (ed.) *Hunters in Transition*, Cambridge: Cambridge University Press.

Akazawa, T. (1986b) 'Regional variation in seasonal procurement systems of Jomon hunter-gatherers', in T. Akazawa and C. M. Aikens (eds) *Prehistoric Hunter-gatherers in Japan: new research methods*, University Museum Bulletin No. 27, Tokyo: University of Tokyo.

Ammerman, A.J. and Cavalli-Sforza, L.L. (1973) 'A population model for the diffusion of early farming in Europe', in A. C. Renfrew (ed.) *The Explanation of Culture Change*, London: Duckworth.

Ammerman, A.J. and Cavalli-Sforza, L.L. (1984) *The Neolithic Transition and the Genetics of Population in Europe*, Princeton, NJ: Princeton University Press.

Barnes, G.L. (1986) 'Japanese agricultural beginnings', *Nature*, 322: 595–6.

Barnes, G.L. (1993a) *China, Korea and Japan*, London: Thames and Hudson.

Barnes, G.L. (1993b) 'Miwa occupation in wider perspective', in G. L. Barnes and M. Okita (eds) *The Miwa Project*, Oxford: BAR International Series 582.

Blumler, M.A. and Byrne, R. (1991) 'The ecological genetics of domestication and the origins of agriculture', *Current Anthropology*, 32: 23–61.

Brace, C.L., Brace, M.L. and Leonard, W.R. (1989) 'Reflections on the face of Japan: a multivariate craniofacial and odontometric perspective', *American Journal of Physical Anthropology*, 78: 93–113.

Campbell, C.G. (1976) 'Buckwheat', in N. W. Simmonds (ed.) *Evolution of Crop Plants*, London: Longman.

Chang, K.C. (1986) *The Archaeology of Ancient China*, New Haven, CT: Yale University Press.

Chang, T.-T. (1976) 'The origin, evolution, cultivation, dissemination, and diversification of Asian and African rices', *Euphytica*, 25: 425–41.

Chang, T.-T. (1983) 'The origins and early cultures of the cereal grains and food legumes', in D. N. Keightley (ed.) *The Origins of Chinese Civilization*, Berkeley, CA: University of California Press.

Chang, T.-T. (1989) 'Domestication and the spread of cultivated rices', in D. R. Harris and G. C. Hillman (eds) *Foraging and Farming: the evolution of plant exploitation*, London: Unwin Hyman.

Chard, C.S. (1974) *Northeast Asia in Prehistory*, Madison, WI: University of Wisconsin Press.

Cohen, M.N. (1977) *The Food Crisis in Prehistory*, New Haven, CT: Yale University Press.

Cowan, C.W. and Watson, P.J. (eds) (1992) *The Origins of Agriculture: an international perspective*, Washington, DC: Smithsonian Institution Press.

Crawford, G.W. (1983) *Paleoethnobotany of the Kameda Peninsula Jomon*, Anthropological Papers No. 73, Ann Arbor, MI: University of Michigan, Museum of Anthropology.

Crawford, G.W. (1986) 'The Sakushu-Kotoni river site: the Ezo-Haji component plant remains', in Hokkaido Daigaku (ed.) *Sakushu-Kotoni Gawa* Iseki [The Sakushu-Kotoni River Site], Sapporo: Hokkaido Daigaku Bungakubu.

Crawford, G.W. (1992a) 'Prehistoric plant domestication in East Asia: the Japanese perspective', in P. J. Watson and C. W. Cowan (eds) *Agricultural Origins in World Perspective*, Washington, DC: Smithsonian Institution Publications in Anthropology.

Crawford, G.W. (1992b) 'The transitions to agriculture in Japan', in A. B. Gebauer and T. D. Price (eds) *Transitions to Agriculture in Prehistory*, Madison, WI: Prehistory Press.

Crawford, G.W. (1997) 'Anthropogenesis in prehistoric Northeastern Japan', in K. J. Gremillion (ed.) *People, Plants and Landscapes: studies in palaeoethnobotany*, Tuscaloosa, AL: University of Alabama Press.

Crawford, G.W. and Takamiya, H. (1990) 'The origins and implications of late prehistoric plant husbandry in northern Japan', *Antiquity*, 64: 889–911.

Crawford, G.W. and Yoshizaki, M. (1987) 'Ainu ancestors and early Asian agriculture', *Journal of Archaeological Science*, 14: 201–13.

Crawford, G.W., Hurley, W.M. and Yoshizaki, M. (1976) 'Implications of plant remains from the Early Jomon Hamanasuno site', *Asian Perspectives*, 19: 145–53.

D'Andrea, A.C. (1992) *Palaeoethnobotany of Later Jomon and Yayoi Cultures of Northeastern Japan: northeastern Aomori and southwestern Hokkaido*, Ann Arbor, MI: University Microfilms International.

D'Andrea, A.C. (1995a) 'Archaeobotanical evidence for Zoku-Jomon subsistence at the Mochiyazawa site, Hokkaido, Japan', *Journal of Archaeological Science*, 22: 583–95.

D'Andrea, A.C. (1995b). 'Later Jomon subsistence in northeastern Japan: new evidence from palaeoethnobotanical studies', *Asian Perspectives*, 34: 195–227.

D'Andrea, A.C., Crawford, G.W., Yoshizaki, M. and Kudo, T. (1995) 'Late Jomon cultigens in northeastern Japan', *Antiquity*, 69: 146–52.

Dennell, R.W. (1985) 'The hunter-gatherer/agricultural frontier in prehistoric temperate Europe', in S. W. Green and S. M. Perlman (eds) *The Archaeology of Frontiers and Boundaries*, London: Academic Press.

Esaka, T. (1959) 'Jomon bunka no jidai ni okeru shokubutsu saibai kigen no mondai ni kansuru ichikosatsu [On the problems of the origin of plant cultivation in the Jomon period culture]', *Kokogaku Zasshi*, 44(3): 10–16.

Fujimori, E. (1963) 'Theory of Jomon agriculture and its development', *Kokogaku Kenkyu*, 10(2): 21–33.

Fujimori, E. (1970) *Jomon Agriculture*, Tokyo: Gakuseisha.

Fujiwara, H. (1993) 'Research into the history of rice cultivation using plant opal analysis', in D. M. Pearsall and D. R. Piperno (eds) *Current Research in Phytolith Analysis: applications in archaeology and palaeoecology*, Philadelphia, PA: MASCA, University Museum of Archaeology and Anthropology, University of Pennsylvania.

Fujiwara, H., Sasaki, A. and Sugiyama, S. (1985) 'Fundamental studies of plant opal analysis (6)', *Archaeology and Natural Science*, 18: 111.

Gebauer, A.B. and Price, T.D. (eds) (1992) *Transitions to Agriculture in Prehistory*, Madison, WI: Prehistory Press.

Gregg, S.A. (1988) *Foragers and Farmers*, Chicago, IL: Chicago University Press.

Groot, G.J. (1951) *The Prehistory of Japan*, New York: Columbia University Press.

Hanihara, K. (1990) '*Emishi*, Ezo and Ainu: an anthropological perspective', *Japan Review*, 1: 35–48.

Hanihara, K. (1991) 'Dual structure model for the population history of the Japanese', *Japan Review*, 2: 1–33.

Harris, D.R. and Hillman, G.C. (eds) (1989) *Foraging and Farming: the evolution of plant exploitation*, London: Unwin Hyman.

Hayashi, Y. (1969) *Ainu no Noko Bunka [Ainu Agriculture]*, Tokyo: Keiyusha.

Hayden, B. (1990) 'Nimrods, piscators, pluckers, and planters: the emergence of food production', *Journal of Anthropological Archaeology*, 9: 31–69.

Higuchi, T. (1986) 'Relationships between Japan and Asia in ancient times', in R. J. Pearson (ed.) *Windows on the Japanese Past*, Ann Arbor, MI: Center for Japanese Studies, University of Michigan.

Hillman, G.C. and Davies, M.S. (1990) 'Measured domestication rates in wild wheats and barley under primitive cultivation and their archaeological implications', *Journal of World Prehistory*, 4: 157–222.

Ho, P.-T. (1977) 'The indigenous origins of Chinese agriculture', in C. A. Reed (ed.) *Origins of Agriculture*, Paris: Mouton.

Hoshikawa, K. (1984) 'Wagakuni no kodai inasaku ni tsuite no sakumotsu gaku teki na kansatsu to ni, san no jikken [A few experiments and observations on our ancient rice agriculture]', in Kobunkazai Henshu-Iinkai (ed.) *Kobunkazai no Shizen Kagakuteki Kenkyu [National Scientific Research of Antiquities]*, Tokyo: Dotosha.

Hudson, M. (1990) 'From Toro to Yoshinogari: changing perspectives on Yayoi archaeology', in G. L. Barnes (ed.) *Hoabinhian, Jomon, Yayoi, Early Korean States*, Oxford: Oxbow Books.

Ikawa-Smith, F. (1980) 'Current issues in Japanese archaeology', *American Scientist*, 68: 134–45.

Ikawa-Smith, F. (1988) 'The Kamegaoka social networks', paper presented to the Symposium on Approaches to Japanese Archaeology at the Fifty-Third Annual Meeting of the Society for American Archaeology, Phoenix, Arizona, April.

Im, H.-J. (1995) *Korea News Review*, 10 September–8 October.

Itoh, G. (1966) 'Tohoku', in S. Wajima (ed.) *Yayoi Jidai [The Yayoi Period]*, Tokyo: Kawaide Shobo.

Itoh, N. (1984) 'Aomori-ken ni okeru inasaku noko-bunka no keisei [The development of rice agriculture in Aomori prefecture]', in T. Katoh (ed.) *Hoppo Nihon Bunka no Kenkyu [Study of Northern Cultures of Japan]*, Sendai: Tohokugakuin Daigaku Tohoku Bunka Kenkyusha.

Kamikawana, A. (1968) 'Sites in middle Yamanashi-ken and Middle Jomon agriculture', *Asian Perspectives*, 11: 53–68.

Kanaseki, H. (1986) 'The evidence for social change between the Early and Middle Yayoi', in R. J. Pearson (ed.) *Windows on the Japanese Past*, Ann Arbor, MI: Center for Japanese Studies, University of Michigan.

Kanaseki, H. and Sahara, M. (1978) 'The Yayoi period', *Asian Perspectives*, 19: 15–26.

Kasahara, Y. (1982) 'Nabatake iseki no maizo shushi no bunseki dotei kenkyu [Analysis and identification of ancient seeds from the Nabatake site]', in Tosu-shi Kyoiku Iinkai (ed.) *Nabatake*, Tosu-shi: Tosu-shi Kyoiku Iinkai.

Kasahara, Y. (1984) 'Maizo shushi bunseki ni yoru kodai noko no kensho (2) – Nabatake iseki no sakumotsu to zasso no shurui o yobi to rai keiro [Examination of ancient agriculture from the perspective of archaeological seed analysis (2) – species and routes of introduction of crops and weeds at the Nabatake site]', in Kobunkazai-Henshu Iinkai (ed.) *Kobunkazai no Shizen-Kagakuteki Kenkyu*, Tokyo: Dotosha.

Katoh, M. and Suto, T. (1986) 'Tohoku', in Y. Kondo (ed.) *Iwanami Koza Nihon Kokogaku*, Tokyo: Iwanami Shoten.

Katoh, S. (1986) 'Siberia no senshi noko to Nihon eno eikyo [Prehistoric agriculture in Siberia and its influence on Japan]', in K. Sasaki and T. Matsuyama (eds)

Hatasaku-bunka no tanjo [The Origin of Dry Field Farming], Tokyo: Nihon Hoso Kyokai.

Kidder, J.E. (1968) 'Agriculture and ritual in the Middle Jomon', *Asian Perspectives*, 11: 19–41.

Kokawa, S. (1978) 'Study of ancient life and environment based on plant remains', *Annual Report of Scientific Research on Antiquities for 1977*, 149–58.

Kotani, Y. (1972) *Economic Bases During the Latter Jomon Periods in Kyushu, Japan: a reconsideration*, Ann Arbor, MI: University Microfilms International.

Kudo, T. and D'Andrea, A.C. (1991) 'Recent archaeobotanical finds from Aomori Prefecture, Japan', *Project Seeds News*, 3: 5.

Kuraku, Y. (1984) 'Tohoku chiho ni okeru kodai inasaku o saguru [The search for ancient rice agriculture in the Tohoku region]', in Kobunkazai Henshu Iinkai (ed.) *Kobunkazai no Shizen Kagakuteki Kenkyu [Natural Scientific Research of Antiquities]*, Tokyo: Dotosha.

Kuzmin, Y.V., Orlova, L.A., Sulerzhitsky, L.D. and Jull, A.J.T. (1994) 'Radiocarbon dating of Stone and Bronze Age sites in Primorye (Russian Far East)', *Radiocarbon*, 36: 359–66.

Lambert, D.H. (1985) *Swamp Rice Farming*, Boulder, CO: Westview Press.

Matsutani, A. (1983) 'Egoma-Shiso', in S. Katoh, T. Kobayashi and T. Fujimoto (eds) *Jomon Bunka no* Kenkyu [Research on the Jomon Culture], Tokyo: Yuzankaku.

Minamiki, M., Nohjo, S., Kokawa, S., Kosugi, S. and Suzuki, M. (1986) 'Shokubutsu itai to kokankyo [Plant remains and ancient environment]', in Tarami-cho Kyoiku Iinkai (ed.) *Ikiriki Iseki [The Ikiriki Site]*, Tarami-cho: Tarami-cho Kyoiku Iinkai.

Minato, M. (1977) *Japan and its Nature*, Tokyo: Heibonsha Ltd.

Minnis, P.E. (1992) 'Earliest plant cultivation in the Desert Borderlands of North America', in P. J. Watson and C. W. Cowan (eds) *Agricultural Origins in World Perspective*, Washington, DC: Smithsonian Institution Publications in Anthropology.

Murakoshi, K. (1988) 'Sunazawa iseki [The Sunazawa site]', in H. Kanaseki and M. Sahara (eds) *Yayoi Bunka no Kenkyu [Research on the Yayoi Culture]*, Tokyo: Yuzankaku.

Nakao, S. (1966) *Saibai Shokubutsu to Noko no Kigen [Cultigens and the Origin of Agriculture]*, Tokyo: Iwanami Shinsho.

Nakao, S. (1967) 'Origins of agriculture', in M. Morishita and T. Kira (eds) *Natural History Ecological Studies: contributions in honour of Dr Kinji Imanishi on the occasion of his sixtieth birthday*, Tokyo: Chukoronsha.

Nishida, M. (1983) 'The emergence of food production in Neolithic Japan', *Journal of Anthropological Archaeology*, 2: 305–22.

Okada, Y. (1995) 'Ento doki bunka no kyodai shuraku [A large village of the Ento pottery culture]', *Kikan Kokogaku*, 50: 25–30.

Okamoto, I. (1979) *Torihama Kaizuka [The Torihama Shell Mound]*, Fukui: Fukui Kyoiku Iinkai.

Okamoto, I. (1983) *Torihama Kaizuka [The Torihama Shell Mound]*, Fukui: Fukui Kyoiku Iinkai.

Purseglove, J.W. (1972) *Tropical Crops: Monocotyledons*, London: Longman.

Reed, C.A. (ed.) (1977) *Origins of Agriculture*, Paris: Mouton.

Rindos, D. (1984) *The Origins of Agriculture: an evolutionary perspective*, New York: Academic Press.

Rowley-Conwy, P. (1984) 'Postglacial foraging and early farming economies in Japan and Korea: a west European perspective', *World Archaeology*, 16: 28–42.

Sakazume, N. (1959) 'A tentative theory on primitive agriculture in Japan', *Journal of the Archaeological Society of Nippon*, 42: 1–12.

Sakazume, N. (1961) *Nihon Jomon Sekki Jidai Shokuryo Sosetsu [Complete Description of Food in Neolithic Jomon Japan]*, Kyoto: Doyokai.

Sample, L.L. (1978) 'Prehistoric cultural relations between western Japan and southeastern Korea', *Asian Perspectives*, 19: 172–5.

Sasaki, K. (1971) *Pre-rice Cultivation*, Tokyo: N.H.K. Books No. 147.

Sato, T. (1984) 'Kamegaoka iseki Sawane chiku B-ku shutsudo no ine eika narabe ni tanka mairyu [Rice caryopses and carbonized rice from the Kamegaoka site, Sawane Locality B]', in Aomori Kenritsu Kyodokan (eds) *Kamegaoka Iseki [The Kamegaoka Site]*, Archaeology Report 16, Aomori: Aomori Kenritsu Kyodokan.

Simmonds, N.W. (1976) 'Hemp', in N. W. Simmonds (ed.) *Evolution of Crop Plants*, London: Longman.

Struever, S. (1971) *Prehistoric Agriculture*, New York: Natural History Press.

Suzuki, K. (1986) *Nihon no Kodai Iseki 29: Aomori [Ancient Sites in Japan 29: Aomori]*, Tokyo: Hoikusha.

Tsukada, M. (1986) 'Vegetation in prehistoric Japan', in R. J. Pearson (ed.) *Windows on the Japanese Past*, Ann Arbor, MI: Center for Japanese Studies, University of Michigan.

Tsukada, M., Tsukada, Y. and Sugita, S. (1986) 'Oldest primitive agriculture and vegetational environments in Japan', *Nature*, 322: 632–4.

Tsunoda, B. and Watanabe, M. (1976) *Kuwagaishimo Iseki [The Kuwagaishimo Site]*, Kyoto: Heian Hakubutsukan.

Turner, C.G., III (1979) 'Dental anthropological indications of agriculture among the Jomon people of central Japan', *American Journal of Physical Anthropology*, 51: 619–36.

Ucko, P.J. and Dimbleby, G.W. (eds) (1969) *Domestication and Exploitation of Plants and Animals*, London: Duckworth.

Ueyama, S. (ed.) (1969) *Laurel Forest Culture*, vol. 1, Tokyo: Chuokoronsha.

Ueyama, S., Sasaki, K. and Nakao, S. (1976) *Laurel Forest Culture*, vol. 2, Tokyo: Chuokoronsha.

Watanabe, H. (1972) *The Ainu Ecosystem*, Tokyo: University of Tokyo Press.

Watanabe, M. and Kokawa, S. (1982) 'Nabatake Jomon Banki (Yamanotera-so) kara shutsudono tanka gobo, adzuki, egonoki to mitanka meron shushi no dotei [Identification of carbonized gobo, adzuki, egonoki, and uncarbonized melon seeds from the Final Jomon (Yamanotera) level at Nabatake]', in Tosu-shi Kyoiku Iinkai (ed.) *Nabatake*, Tosu-shi: Tosu-shi Kyoiku Iinkai.

Wills, W.H. (1990) 'Cultivating ideas: the changing intellectual history of the introduction of agriculture in the American southwest', in P. Minnis and C. Redman (eds) *Perspectives on Southwestern Prehistory*, Boulder, CO: Westview Press.

Wright, H.E. (1977) 'Environmental change and the origins of agriculture in the Old and New Worlds', in C. A. Reed (ed.) *Origins of Agriculture*, Paris: Mouton.

Yabuno, T. (1966) 'Biosystematic study of the genus *Echinochloa*', *Japanese Journal of Botany*, 19(2): 277–323.

Yamada, G. (1980) 'Iwate-ken Kitakami-shi Kyunenbashi iseki no kafun bunseki ni tsuite [Analysis of pollen from the Kyunenbashi site, Kitakami City, Iwate

Prefecture]', in Kitakami Board of Education (ed.) *Kyunenbashi Iseki [The Kyunenbashi Site]*, Kitakami: Kitakami Bunkazai Chosa Hokoku.

Yamada, G. and Tsubakisaka, Y. (1995) 'Propagation of cultivated plants from the continent', in *Final Report on Research Project of the Historical and Cultural Exchange of the North*, 107–34, Sapporo: Historical Museum of Hokkaido.

Yamanoi, T. and Sato, M. (1984) 'Kamegaoka iseki no kafun bunseki [Palynological research at the Kamegaoka site]', in K. Suzuki (ed.) *Kamegaoka Iseki [The Kamegaoka Site]*, Aomori City: Aomori Kenritsu Kyodoken.

Zeven, A.C. and de Wet., J.M.J. (1982) *Dictionary of Cultivated Plants and Their Regions of Diversity*, Wageningen: Centre for Agricultural Publishing and Documentation.

Zvelebil, M. (ed.) (1986) *Hunters in Transition*, Cambridge: Cambridge University Press.

Update: Early agriculture in Japan – research since 1999

Catherine D'Andrea

The prospect of revisiting the subject of Japanese agricultural origins and dispersals after a hiatus of several years was appealing and the result has been illuminating. While some innovative ideas have been proposed on early Japanese agriculture since 1999 (Crawford 2005), less progress has been achieved in the development of relevant archaeobotanical databases. Despite the fact that sampling for plant macroremains has been taking place at Jomon and Yayoi sites since the late 1990s, little of this work has been problem-oriented (Habu 2004: 59–60), with a few notable exceptions (e.g. Crawford 1997; Yoshizaki 1998; Takamiya 2002). Moreover only a few of these studies are available in the English language-dominated literature on early agricultural origins and dispersals published since 1999. This is unfortunate; a country with such fascinating archaeology merits a much wider appreciation.

Recent findings relating to Japanese early agriculture include a report of rice phytoliths indicating the presence of rice (*Oryza sativa*) in southwestern Japan by approximately 6000 years ago; dry field cultivation was practised at this time and these activities did not result in significant cultural impacts (references cited in Takamiya 2002: 209). These remains are noteworthy because they indicate a longer presence of rice in southwestern Japan and suggest that the spread of rice to the northeast was not as rapid as previously thought (Keally 2004). In northeastern Japan, archaeobotanical data are now available from the Sannai Maruyama Site in Aomori Prefecture. Early Jomon remains are dominated by chestnut (*Castanea crenata*), and domestication has been suggested based on pollen and DNA evidence (Sato *et al.* 2003; Habu 2004: 116–18). Small quantities of other domesticated plants recovered include bottle gourd (*Lagenaria*), burdock (*Arctium*) and unspecified beans (Fabaceae) (references cited in Okada 2003: 181; Sato *et al.*

2003; Habu 2004: 116–18). Given that the Sannai Maruyama Early Jomon remains were excavated primarily from waterlogged contexts, it would be appropriate to AMS date the macrobotanical remains to confirm a Jomon association.

In an insightful re-evaluation of the evidence bearing on the Southern Route of the introduction of rice to Japan, or the Ocean Road Hypothesis, Takamiya (2002: 216–17) observes that while there is some circumstantial evidence for the introduction of rice from the Ryukyu Islands to Honshu on the basis of geographical, botanical and ethnographical evidence, there is no supporting direct archaeobotanical evidence in the form of rice remains. Archaeobotanical studies in Okinawa demonstrate that rice farming began there sometime between the eighth/ninth–tenth centuries AD, indicating that prehistoric inhabitants did not initially adopt rice agriculture despite the fact that it was available in nearby regions. Takamiya concludes that the Ocean Road Hypothesis is not supported by new data (2002: 216–17, 221–2). More hypothesis-testing along these lines is needed to direct Japanese archaeobotanical research.

The idea of Jomon peoples as 'hunter-gatherers' (Habu 2004) has persisted despite increasing evidence for domesticated plants and cultivation practices resulting in anthropogenic impacts (Crawford 1997, 2005: 86–7). Although the majority of archaeologists now agree that domesticated plants have been present since the Early Jomon (Habu 2004: 59), inadequate sample sizes have precluded our understanding of the economic role of domesticates in Jomon societies. Related circumstantial evidence, however, suggests that cultivation remains a distinct possibility (D'Andrea 1995: 218–21). It is surprising that more palaeoethnobotanical sampling has not taken place to address this issue. Using the concept of low-level food production (Smith 2001), Crawford (2005: 86–7) suggests that neither 'foraging' nor 'farming' sufficiently characterise Jomon subsistence. Instead, subsistence during this long period may be best characterised by 'food production with domesticates' (Smith 2001: 4–5, 15). Archaeobotanical evidence accumulated by Crawford, Yoshizaki and others since the 1980s (Crawford 2005: 86–7) suggests that 'low-level food production' has characterised Jomon subsistence for millennia.

Several new contributions have recently been completed by graduate students. Of note, Hosoya (2002) has examined the social impacts of the introduction of rice agriculture to Japan and its central role in subsequent cultural developments. In addition, Kaufmann (2004) has demonstrated the complexity of subsistence systems of Ainu ancestral populations in Hokkaido, characterised by both foraging and farming activities. Both studies have taken novel approaches to the analysis and interpretation of archaeobotanical data bearing on early Japanese agriculture.

References

Crawford, G.W. (1997) 'Anthropogenesis in prehistoric northeastern Japan', in K. Gremillion (ed.) *People, Plants, and Landscapes: studies in palaeoethnobotany*, Tuscaloosa, AL: University of Alabama Press.

Crawford, G.W. (2005) 'East Asian plant domestication', in M. T. Stark (ed.) *Archaeology of Asia*, London: Blackwell.

D'Andrea, A.C. (1995) 'Later Jomon subsistence in northeastern Japan: new evidence from palaeoethnobotanical studies', *Asian Perspectives*, 34: 195–227.

Habu, J. (2004) *Ancient Jomon of Japan*, Cambridge: Cambridge University Press.

Hosoya, A. (2002) 'Sacred commonness: an archaeobotanical view to the social complexity in prehistoric Japan', unpublished PhD dissertation, Department of Archaeology, University of Cambridge.

Kaufmann, D.R. (2004) 'Archaeobotanical investigations of the Middle Jomon and Ezo-Haji at Minami-Shimamatsu, Hokkaido, Japan', unpublished MA thesis, Department of Anthropology, Washington University, St. Louis, Missouri.

Keally, C.T. (2004) 'Bad science and the distortion of history: radiocarbon dating in Japanese archaeology', *Sophia International Review*, 26: 1–16.

Okada, Y. (2003) 'Jomon culture of northeastern Japan and the Sannai Maruyama Site', in J. Habu, J.M. Savelle, S. Koyama and H. Hongo (eds) *Hunter-gatherers of the North Pacific Rim*, Senri Ethnological Series 63, Osaka: National Museum of Ethnology.

Sato, Y.I., Yamanaka, S. and Takahashi, M. (2003) 'Evidence for Jomon plant cultivation based on DNA analysis of chestnut remains', in J. Habu, J. M. Savelle, S. Koyama and H. Hongo (eds) *Hunter-gatherers of the North Pacific Rim*, Senri Ethnological Series 63, Osaka: National Museum of Ethnology.

Smith, B.D. (2001) 'Low-level food production', *Journal of Archaeological Research*, 9: 1–43.

Takamiya, H. (2002) 'Introductory routes of rice to Japan: an examination of the Southern Route Hypothesis', *Asian Perspectives*, 40: 209–26.

Yoshizaki, M. (1998) 'Kokumotsu: kotonaru kokumotsu wo tazusaeta samazama na hitobito ga Nippon retto ni yattekita [Crops: a variety of crops was introduced to the Japanese Archipelago by different populations]', in Y. S. Mook (ed.) *Gyakuten no Nihonshi Nihonjin no Rutsu Kokomade Wakatta*, Tokyo: Yosensha.

9 The origins and development of New Guinea agriculture

Jack Golson

Discussions of agricultural origins and relationships in the South Pacific have traditionally been carried out within a framework of assumptions to which many eminent botanists and geographers over the years have more-or-less explicitly subscribed (cf. Yen 1980: 140–2; Golson 1985: 307–8 and references cited). The basic notion was that the tuberous plants, and fruit and nut trees, which, together with their often vegetative reproduction, are characteristic of New Guinea and the Pacific Islands, formed the basis of an original agriculture in Southeast Asia, which was subsequently replaced by systems based on the cereal rice. It was only a short step from this to suggest that the agriculture found in New Guinea and the Pacific Islands was actually derived from Southeast Asia, the people who carried it eastward doing so before rice became dominant in the homeland. This chapter is concerned with the processes by which thinking about Pacific agricultural origins has slowly freed itself from these inherited concepts.

Agricultural origins

In 1976 I gave a paper at the Nice Congress of the UISPP (Golson and Hughes 1980) proposing an antiquity for plant and animal husbandry on the island of New Guinea greater than 9000 years. This proposition was based on the results of multi-disciplinary research being carried on in the Western Highlands of Papua New Guinea and focused on swampland at Kuk Agricultural Research Station near Mount Hagen in the upper Wahgi Valley, at an altitude of 1550 m.

The Kuk swamp proved to have a long history as an agricultural site, up to 100 or so years ago, which was characterized by episodes of large-scale drainage for cultivation separated by often substantial periods of abandonment. The evidence for agriculture consisted of a stratified sequence of features cut into the swamp deposits and representing, on the one hand, the drainage channels by which water was removed from the site and, on the other, the ditches, basins, and other diggings belonging to the associated agricultural systems then established there. These structures – channels, ditches, basins – formed virtually the totality of the archaeological evidence with which we had to work: there was no evidence of habitation until the very end of the sequence, no recognizable evidence for cultivated plants until the same period, and then always in association with houses, and no evidence for agricultural tools (almost exclusively of wood) before about 500 years ago, older ones presumably having rotted because of fluctuating water levels in the swamp caused by its periodic drainage (Golson and Steensberg 1985: 348–9). We interpreted the restricted range of archaeological evidence available in the close light of concurrent studies of the geomorphology of the swamp and its margins and palynological investigations into local and regional vegetation history, with attention to the literature on New Guinea cultivated plants and agricultural systems and the very sketchy archaeological record for the region.

In the light of this wider array of evidence, claims for agriculture in the Kuk swamp back to about 6000 years ago were fully acceptable. Pig, an animal not native to New Guinea, was well attested in the archaeological record about this date or slightly later, and throughout the Pacific, in general, pigs and agriculture go hand in hand. In addition, the pollen record showed that substantial inroads had been made into Highlands forests, a circumstance interpreted as the result of clearance for agriculture. Beyond 6000 years, however, the general archaeological record became exiguous indeed, and that for vegetation history in the zone of agricultural settlement was missing altogether until well back into the Late Pleistocene (cf. Groube 1989). Much of the Nice paper was therefore devoted to arguing from geomorphological evidence that features in the Kuk swamp 9000 years ago were best interpreted as an early form of the agricultural management manifest in later times.

I cannot claim that the past ten years have added much to the record on this score: the evidence I must use to argue a 9000-year antiquity for agriculture at Kuk is essentially the same now as then, though there is more of it. What there is to report for that ten-year period on the matter of agricultural origins concerns new thinking and new data relevant to the question of the independence or otherwise of those origins. In large part, this question has been formulated in terms of the plants that might have been cultivated in New Guinea 9000 years ago.

The 1976 paper was also exercised on this matter. Given the absence of botanical remains, the approach was perforce to inspect the range of traditional crops cultivated in New Guinea gardens and make some sort of intelligent choice. The American sweet potato (*Ipomoea batatas*), which is today dominant in Highlands agriculture, could be dismissed as an introduction of the late prehistoric period, less than 500 years ago. As regards other important plants, taro (*Colocasia esculenta*) and certain species of yam (*Dioscorea alata, D. esculenta*) and of banana (*Musa* of the Eumusa section) appeared to be of Southeast Asian origin. Indeed, the Nice paper was written in the light of the accepted view that New Guinea agriculture, and that of the Pacific as a whole, was basically derived from Southeast Asia.

The discussion nonetheless paid attention to Yen's early indication (1971, 1973) and Powell's later detailed documentation (1976) of the richness of New Guinea in plants of economic importance, including minor species of yam and banana. Some of these, including a number of apparent endemics, were accepted as having been domesticated in New Guinea, and early enough for plants such as Australimusa bananas and sugar cane to be included in the cultural equipment of the people who colonized the islands of the Pacific from perhaps 4000 years ago. All this, as Yen (1971: 6–7, 1973: 73–5, cf. 1980: 144) and Powell (1976: 175–6) pointed out, suggested the potential for independent origins of plant domestication in New Guinea. A possible solution to the problem seemed to be offered by the pig, an exotic item in the New Guinea fauna for whose presence the most satisfactory explanation was seen to be its introduction by human agency from Southeast Asia as a husbanded animal. There were, and still are, claims for the presence of pig in two Highlands rockshelters around 10,000 years ago (Bulmer 1975: 18, 1982: 188). If a Southeast Asian animal had indeed been introduced into New Guinea around the end of the Pleistocene, it was possible to think that Southeast Asian plants might be incorporated in, indeed responsible for, the agriculture claimed for Kuk at 9000 years ago.

A few years later, in a paper revised for the proceedings of a conference in Poona held in 1978 (Golson 1985), I attempted to address this question in the only way I felt was possible, given the dearth of information about early agriculture in island Southeast Asia and the failure of archaeological research on the Southeast Asian mainland to throw light on the antiquity, indeed the presence, of root-crop, tree-fruit agriculture. This was to inspect the records of vegetation history becoming available for the region as a result of pollen-analytical research, in order to see whether the impact of human interference by way of agriculture was visible in them and, if so, from what date. The exercise was prompted by the clear evidence for such interference in the pollen diagrams for the Papua New Guinea Highlands, which have been described (Flenley 1979: 122) as providing the most striking pollen evidence of recent years for early clearance, speaking on a pan-tropical or even world scale. The pollen diagrams from Southeast Asia provided no such clear evidence until far too late a date to support the hypothesis of New Guinea agricultural origins there – around 4000 bp and probably associated with rice – though the absence of evidence was not *decisive* in rejecting the hypothesis, since it might be due to the failure of less ecologically harmful forms of forest clearance under shifting cultivation to be registered (Flenley 1985: 304). The result in any case was to emphasize the need to look for explanations in evidence from New Guinea itself.

Over the past few years there have been two practical exercises of this kind, one in the laboratory, the other in the field.

The laboratory project, undertaken by S. M. Wilson while a student at the Australian National University, concerned phytoliths (Wilson 1985). Of the cultivated plants in terms of which discussions about early agriculture at

Kuk had taken place, taro and yam do not produce phytoliths, but bananas do. Fortunately, banana is an important plant from the point of view of the independent or derivative nature of New Guinea agricultural origins, as already indicated. While the Eumusa section of the genus is considered to be of Southeast Asian origin, the Australimusa section is thought to belong to the New Guinea region and to have been domesticated there. Wilson (1985: 94) found 'consistent, although not dramatic, differences in phytolith size and morphology' between the two sections of the genus, but phytoliths from *Musa ingens*, the wild New Guinea banana which is the only member of the third, Ingentimusa, section of the genus as recognized by Argent (1975), are indistinguishable from those of Eumusa. Twenty-three banana phytoliths were found in a core through the Kuk deposits, only two of which were of the probable Australimusa type, neither of them in informative chrono-logical position from the present point of view (Wilson 1985: Fig. 4). The others were found in levels contemporary with agricultural activity, back to 9000 years ago, and not in earlier deposits. In view of the impossibility of discriminating between phytoliths of the Eumusa and Ingentimusa sections, however, the conclusions remain equivocal as to whether we are dealing with bananas of early Indo-Malayan origin in the early agricultural phases at Kuk (Wilson 1985: 97) or a wild New Guinea plant able to colonize areas disturbed in the course of agricultural activities (Wilson 1985: 93). Work on phytolith discrimination between different New Guinea banana species, both wild and cultivated, is proceeding in the laboratory of H. Fujiwara, Miyazaki University, Japan.

The field investigation to which reference was made earlier was part of a larger project initiated by P. P. Gorecki of the Australian National University in the archaeologically unknown (and ethnographically little better served) region of the lower Jimi and upper Yuat valleys in the mid-montane zone (c. 500 m altitude) north of Mount Hagen. The attention devoted to agri-cultural history was prompted by a conclusion and a challenge of the 1976 Nice paper (Golson and Hughes 1980: 301). The conclusion was that the agriculture seen at Kuk at 9000 years ago did not originate at that altitude, which today is towards the upper limit for the cultivation of virtually all the relevant cultigens, and at the time must only just have been achieving the present temperature regime during the climatic amelioration which ended the Pleistocene. The challenge was to extend the search into lowland areas. In the event Gorecki's exploratory work has not established the presence of agriculture earlier than 5000 years ago (Gillieson *et al.* 1985 and subsequent unpublished revisions, Gorecki, pers. comm.), though the type of activity revealed bears a satisfactory resemblance to gardening systems at Kuk of a broadly similar date.

The new thinking that has been mentioned has been the insistence by Yen (1982 in particular) that serious consideration of the hypothesis of an independent evolution of agriculture in New Guinea is warranted by an assessment of the origins of the plants incorporated in traditional Melanesian systems overall, not simply in the Highlands, and an appreciation of the Kuk drainage record as revealing an evolutionary sequence of intensification in the sphere of production (1982: 292). As regards the plants, two points emerge (1982: 288): the central role of New Guinea in the plant-domestication process, independent of ultimate origins; and the fact that these domesticates as a whole cover virtually the range of environmental conditions in Melanesia, swamp, coral island, coast, interior, and mountain. As regards the agricultural systems, Yen (1982: 292) considers a logical sequence of events to be plant domestication earlier than environmental management through drainage, and suggests that such domestication might have begun in the 'variable ecologies of mid-altitude regions', with the development of 'simpler regimes of swidden modes of agriculture' following 'the long hunter-gatherer "phase"'. It is, of course, precisely to one such region that Gorecki's attention has been directed, as described.

The hypothesis which Yen (1982: 291) puts forward is one of the independent origins and development of agriculture in New Guinea, based on the domestication of a suite of plants that included basic staples, vegetables, and fruits able to sustain populations in various environments. At a later stage these indigenous developments were interrupted by the arrival of colonists out of Asia, who introduced domesticated plants 'which were to dominate, in many cases, the earlier evolved cultivation of indigenous domesticates'.

In these discussions Yen (1982: 254, 292–3) is exercised by the question of taro, invoked in a number of my own publications as an appropriate crop for the drained swamp systems of Kuk. Taro is a plant for which an Indian origin has been proposed, and whose carriage into New Guinea and the Pacific by human agency is taken for granted. Yen (1982: 284) refers, however, to the 'uncertain status of the origin of feral types found in New Guinea, and more recently by R. Jones and B. Meehan (pers. comm.) in inland Arnhem Land, Australia' (see Jones and Meehan 1989, and cf. Lawrence 1968: 205 for eastern Cape York, under *Colocasia antiquorum*), commenting that they may not be garden escapees, which explanation in the Arnhem Land case would require a very complex hypothesis indeed.

Yen has taken up this matter in the context of a wider project on Australia as bystander in Pacific agricultural development, in which one focus of interest is the occurrence amongst Australian Aboriginal food plants of genera familiar as cultivated foods in Asia and Oceania (Yen 1985a: 317–18, 1985b: 494; cf. Golson 1971). Yam, as well as taro, is relevant in this connection. As early as the Nice Congress of 1976, Yen (1980: 45) made reference to the parallelism in the distributions of the genus *Dioscorea* (yams) and the genus *Oryza* (rices), for which latter one hypothesis exists for its origin in Gondwanaland (see Chang 1989). At the time, Yen could only comment on the impossibility of applying the evidence of plate tectonics for the origins of *Dioscorea*, particularly in view of the lack of basic study of the genus in New Guinea and Australia, a deficiency which one aspect of his current project begins to address (see Yen 1989). The concept of a Gondwanaland inheritance as basic to the question of agricultural origins in New Guinea now arises, however, in a different and more concrete form. This results from the continued discovery in remote areas of tropical Australia of taro traditionally used by Aborigines as food (Jones and Meehan 1989 for Arnhem Land, Crawford 1984: 40–1 for the Kimberleys, as *Colocasia antiquorum*). Detailed genetic work relevant to this matter is currently under way by P. Matthews, one of Yen's students at the Australian National University, who is investigating the relationship between wild and cultivated taro from Papua New Guinea, and between wild taro from Papua New Guinea and Australia, by means of electrophoretic analysis. The aim is to clarify phylogenetic issues raised in recent research by the more 'traditional' approach of cytology and perhaps produce biological definitions for domestication in the species.

Agricultural development

If the discussion of agricultural origins in New Guinea just concluded has addressed itself to narrower questions than those of ultimate causes, it is because the data, biological, environmental, and archaeological, necessary for framing the relevant hypotheses are insufficient. Perhaps issues raised by research on the subsequent history of New Guinea Highlands agriculture make a more immediate contribution at a general level. The issues involved are relevant to the concept of agricultural intensification which has been much discussed in the literature of a number of disciplines since the publication of Boserup's *The conditions of agricultural growth* in 1965.

This is a vast subject, which I shall address here from a highly particular standpoint. Contemporary New Guinea Highlands agriculture, based on the sweet potato, which is grown in large, orderly plantations in an environment characterized by large areas of grassland and shrubby regrowth, is described (Brookfield with Hart 1971: 111) as exhibiting 'a fairly high modal level of intensity', defining intensity as 'the degree to which technology is applied to land so as to economize in its use, while gaining roughly equal or greater output per hectare' (Brookfield with Hart 1971: 92). The technology applied in the Highlands (e.g. Brookfield with Hart 1971: 111–13) consists of a distinctive set of procedures designed to allow frequent or continuous agricultural use of grassland soils.

Now it is clear from pollen-analytical research that the open landscapes which form the agricultural setting are the product of millennia of history and it is generally agreed that the major agency in their creation out of an originally forested environment was sustained clearance for cultivation (e.g. Powell 1982: 28–30). In so far, therefore, as the technical features of traditional Highlands agriculture were designed to ensure the productivity of agriculture in conditions of grassland and degraded regrowth, they were responses to circumstances of increasing and irreversible deforestation brought about by the practice of agriculture itself. It is in the light of this proposition that the long prehistoric sequence of ever more complex drainage and gardening has been interpreted at Kuk (e.g. Golson 1982).

The details need not detain us here, but there is a general point to make. If the interpretation of developments at Kuk is correct, that they were geared to an ecological transformation, from forest to grassland, which was common to the Highlands as a whole, there ought to be evidence in other areas for corresponding responses in the realm of agricultural technology (cf. Golson 1982: 135–6). Up until very recently, however, Kuk and the swamplands of the upper Wahgi stood alone.

The discovery which has supplied the confirmatory evidence has come in an unexpected way, through the reinterpretation as agricultural terracing of an extensive set of landscape features in a tolerably well-known part of the country, which, when mentioned in the literature at all, have been interpreted as purely natural phenomena (Sullivan *et al.* 1986). Only preliminary investigations have been carried out so far, but as the area is shortly to be impacted by the second stage of a major hydroelectricity scheme, it is likely that further information will become available from salvage work ahead of development. There are some general observations that can already be made, however, relevant to the issue of developments in agricultural technology in the face of environmental change.

The terraced landscapes in question occupy in discontinuous fashion some 16 km^2 of the 40 km^2 of the Arona Basin on the upper Ramu River about 1300 m above sea-level in the Eastern Highlands of Papua New Guinea. They are situated on hill slopes developed in a sedimentary formation comprising poorly consolidated gravelly sands and clays and rich in reworked volcanic ash. Other occurrences of this formation in the region appear, from aerial photographs and some ground reconnaissance, to be terraced also. The region in question is characterized by a comparatively low rainfall for the New Guinea Highlands (less than 2000 mm per year), with not only pronounced seasonality of precipitation but its occurrence as heavy downpours separated by long dry periods. In response to this character of the rainfall, the staple sweet potato is grown in beds of rectangular shape running up and down the slopes and often provided with bordering drains. The landscape in which this gardening takes place is one of extensive, short, stabilized grassland devoid of natural woodland over large areas, this extreme degree of ecological transformation being the result of the proneness of the region to drought exacerbated by firing (Brookfield 1964: 32–3).

There is no vegetation history for the Eastern Highlands of Papua New Guinea, so that we do not know over what period deforestation took place. It can be argued, however, that the hill slope terracing was an appropriate response to it in an area of low, seasonal, and heavy episodic rain, since it would have served to counter rapid runoff on steep grassed slopes and to retain moisture in the soil on top of terrace platforms. It can be further argued that such a role would have been appropriate for the cultivation of taro, which has been regularly proposed as a staple of Highlands agriculture before the arrival of the sweet potato within the last few hundred years. Certainly, it appears that the terraces are earlier than the sweet potato, because not only do local inhabitants not recognize them as other than natural features of the landscape but their sweet potato gardens are aligned quite differently and pay no regard to the presence of the terraces where they are superimposed on them.

Concluding remarks

It is, I think, obvious from the above that the study of agricultural origins and developments in New Guinea is still at an early stage, where the basic parameters for discussion are still in flux as new and often-unexpected data are gathered. Enough is known, however, to suggest that the ancient continent of which, with its larger neighbour, Australia, New Guinea forms a part holds promise of producing evidence in the long run for an independent and distinctive history in that field of socio-economic development with which this book is concerned.

Acknowledgements

My debt to co-workers in fieldwork and to present and past colleagues at the Australian National University is abundantly clear from citations in the text above and in the reference list, which follows. The prominence of the name D. E. Yen in both is a measure of his influence on my own thinking and his contribution to the field in general.

References

Argent, H. (1975) 'The wild bananas of Papua New Guinea', *Bulletin of the Royal Botanical Gardens, Edinburgh*, 30: 77–114.

Boserup, E. (1965) *The Conditions of Agricultural Growth: the economics of agrarian change under population pressure*, London: Allen and Unwin.

Brookfield, H.C. (1964) 'The ecology of highland settlement: some suggestions', in J. B. Watson (ed.) *New Guinea: the Central Highlands, American Anthropologist*, 66, Special Publication.

Brookfield, H.C., with Hart, D. (1971) *Melanesia: a geographical interpretation of an island world*, London: Methuen.

Bulmer, S. (1975) 'Settlement and economy in prehistoric Papua New Guinea: a review of the archaeological evidence', *Journal de la Société des Océanistes*, 31: 7–75.

Bulmer, S. (1982) 'Human ecology and cultural variation in prehistoric Papua New Guinea', *Monographicae Biologicae*, 42: 169–206.

Chang, T.T. (1989) 'Domestication and spread of the cultivated rices', in D. R. Harris and G. C. Hillman (eds) *Foraging and Farming: the evolution of plant exploitation*, London: Unwin Hyman.

Crawford, I.M. (1984) *Traditional Aboriginal Plant Resources in the Kalumburu Area: aspects in ethno-economics*, Perth: Records of the Western Australian Museum, Supplement No. 15.

Flenley, J.R. (1979) *The Equatorial Rainforest: a geological history*, London: Butterworth.

Flenley, J.R. (1985) 'Man's impact on the vegetation of Southeast Asia: the pollen evidence', in V. N. Misra and P. Bellwood (eds) *Recent Advances in Indo-Pacific Prehistory*, New Delhi: Oxford and IBH.

Gillieson, D., Gorecki, P. and Hope, G. (1985) 'Prehistoric agricultural systems in a lowland swamp, Papua New Guinea', *Archaeology in Oceania*, 20: 32–7.

Golson, J. (1971) 'Australian Aboriginal food plants: some ecological and culture-historical implications', in D. J. Mulvaney and J. Golson (eds) *Aboriginal Man and Environment in Australia*, Canberra: Australian National University Press.

Golson, J. (1982) 'The Ipomoean revolution revisited: society and the sweet potato in the Upper Wahgi Valley', in A. Strathem (ed.) *Inequality in New Guinea Highlands Societies*, Cambridge: Cambridge University Press.

Golson, J. (1985) 'Agricultural origins in Southeast Asia: a view from the east', in V. N. Misra and P. Bellwood (eds) *Recent Advances in Indo-Pacific Prehistory*, New Delhi: Oxford and IBH.

Golson, J. and Hughes, P.J. (1980) 'The appearance of plant and animal domestication in New Guinea', *Journal de la Société des Océanistes*, 36: 294–303.

Golson, J. and Steensberg, A. (1985) 'The tools of agricultural intensification in the New Guinea Highlands', in I. S. Farrington (ed.) *Prehistoric Intensive Agriculture in the Tropics*, part 1, Oxford: British Archaeological Reports International Series 232.

Groube, L. (1989) 'The taming of the rain forests: a model for Late Pleistocene forest exploitation in New Guinea', in D. R. Harris and G. C. Hillman (eds) *Foraging and Farming: the evolution of plant exploitation*, London: Unwin Hyman.

Jones, R. and Meehan, B. (1989) 'Plant foods of the Gidjingali: ethnographic and archaeological perspectives from northern Australia on tuber and seed exploitation', in D. R. Harris and G. C. Hillman (eds) *Foraging and Farming: the evolution of plant exploitation*, London: Unwin Hyman.

Lawrence, R. (1968) *Aboriginal Habitat and Economy*, Occasional Papers No. 6, Canberra: Department of Geography, School of General Studies, Australian National University.

Powell, J.M. (1976) 'Ethnobotany', in K. Paijmans (ed.) *New Guinea Vegetation*, Canberra: Australian National University Press.

Powell, J.M. (1982) 'Plant resources and palaeobotanical evidence for plant use in the Papua New Guinea Highlands', *Archaeology in Oceania*, 17: 28–37.

Sullivan, M.E., Hughes, P.J. and Golson, J. (1986) 'Prehistoric engineers of the Arona valley', *Science in New Guinea*, 12: 27–41.

Wilson, S.M. (1985) 'Phytolith evidence from Kuk, an early agricultural site in Papua New Guinea', *Archaeology in Oceania*, 20: 90–7.

Yen, D.E. (1971) 'The development of agriculture in Oceania', in R. C. Green and M. Kelly (eds) *Studies in Oceanic Culture History*, vol. 2, Pacific Anthropological Records No. 12, Honolulu, Hawaii: Bernice P. Bishop Museum, Department of Anthropology.

Yen, D.E. (1973) 'The origins of Oceanic agriculture', *Archaeology and Physical Anthropology in Oceania*, 8: 68–85.

Yen, D.E. (1980) 'The Southeast Asian foundations of Oceanic agriculture: a reassessment', *Journal de la Société des Oceanistes*, 36: 140–7.

Yen, D.E. (1982) 'The history of cultivated plants', in R. J. May and H. Nelson (eds) *Melanesia: beyond diversity*, vol. 1, Canberra: Australian National University, Research School of Pacific Studies.

Yen, D.E. (1985a) 'Wild plants and domestication in Pacific islands' in V. N. Misra and P. Bellwood (eds) *Recent Advances in Indo-Pacific Prehistory*, New Delhi: Oxford and IBH.

Yen, D.E. (1985b) 'The genetic effects of agricultural intensification', in I. S. Farrington (ed.) *Prehistoric Intensive Agriculture in the Tropics*, part 2, Oxford: British Archaeological Reports International Series 232.

Yen, D.E. (1989) 'The domestication of environment', in D. R. Harris and G. C. Hillman (eds) *Foraging and Farming: the evolution of plant exploitation*, London: Unwin Hyman.

Update: New research in New Guinea

Tim Denham

Since Golson's paper was published, debate has continued over the veracity of claims for the early and independent origins of agriculture on the island of New Guinea (e.g. Spriggs 1996: 528–9). However, taken in conjunction with the geomorphology that underpinned Golson's original argument, new archaeological, archaeobotanical and palaeoecological evidence reinforces claims that New Guinea was a place of early agricultural development (Denham *et al.* 2003, 2004a, 2004b).

Renewed archaeological excavations at Kuk Swamp, focusing on the early-to-mid Holocene evidence of plant exploitation and agriculture, have clarified that mound cultivation was practised by 6950–6440 cal. BP and ditched field systems were established by 4350–3980 cal. BP (Denham *et al.* 2003). Comparable finds of similar antiquity have been found at other sites in the Highlands (Denham 2003, 2005; Muke and Mandui 2003). Features dating to 10,200–9910 cal. BP at Kuk can be interpreted to represent plant exploitation or agriculture (see arguments in Denham *et al.* 2004a: 277–8, 293–4). Other evidence used by Golson to bolster claims for early agriculture in New Guinea, notably putatively early-to-mid-Holocene pig remains, is no longer accepted by him and many other archaeologists (see Golson in press). Speculations about the implications of putative dryland terracing for agriculture in the Arona Basin near Kainantu in Eastern Highlands Province were quickly and substantially modified (Golson and Gardner 1990: 410).

Significant advances to the understanding of early agriculture, cultivation and plant domestication in New Guinea have emerged through recent archaeobotanical findings at Kuk (Denham *et al.* 2003, 2004b; Fullagar *et al.* 2006). Microfossils from early Holocene contexts include starch residues on stone tools suggestive of the processing of taro (*Colocasia esculenta*) and a yam (*Dioscorea* sp.), and phytoliths in sediments indicating the presence of Eumusa section (*Musa* sp.) bananas. Similar evidence was associated with the earliest mound cultivation at 6950–6440 cal. BP, with stronger evidence of cultivation in the form of high Musaceae phytolith frequencies. These archaeobotanical findings complement ecological, genetic and phytogeographic interpretations that some varieties of these major starch staples, and potentially other crop plants, are indigenous to, and were domesticated in, the Melanesian region (Matthews 1995; De Langhe and de Maret 1999; Lebot 1999). These developments support and extend Yen's earlier hypotheses – adopted and discussed by Golson – for the independent development of agriculture in New Guinea based on the domestication of a range of plants, including starch-rich staples.

Based on recent palaeoecological records for New Guinea, particularly from the Highlands, climatic, human and tectonic contributions to landscape change can be differentiated. Of most relevance here are signals of continued disturbance by fire of rainforests, leading to the establishment and maintenance of grasslands. These signals are interpreted to represent the formation of agricultural landscapes, the earliest being in the Baliem valley from 7800 cal. BP (Haberle 2003) and Upper Wahgi valley from c. 7000 cal. BP (Denham *et al.* 2003). Other intermontane valleys show variability in the timing, duration and intensity of human disturbance before c. 4000 cal. BP, after which disturbance becomes longer lasting, more widespread and more intense.

Thus recent findings follow, develop and support Golson's original lines of argument for the early and independent development of agriculture in New Guinea. Greater understanding of the social contexts within which these events occurred is still required, but few contemporary occupation sites have been excavated and published in detail. Additionally, the locus and timing of the earliest agricultural practices in New Guinea are unknown, a situation unlikely to be remedied until there is greater understanding of plant exploitation in lowland New Guinea during the Pleistocene and early Holocene (see Fairbairn 2005). However, progress is finally being made in addressing the questions and problems posed by an earlier generation of researchers concerning the development of agriculture in New Guinea.

References

De Langhe, E. and de Maret, P. (1999) 'Tracking the banana: its significance in early agriculture', in C. Gosden and J. Hather (eds) *The Prehistory of Food: appetites for change*, London and New York: Routledge.

Denham, T.P. (2003) 'Archaeological evidence for mid-Holocene agriculture in the interior of Papua New Guinea: a critical review', *Archaeology in Oceania*, 38: 159–76.

Denham, T.P. (2005) 'Agricultural origins and the emergence of rectilinear ditch networks in the highlands of New Guinea', in A. Pawley, R. Attenborough, J. Golson and R. Hide (eds) *Papuan Pasts: cultural, linguistic and biological histories of Papuan-speaking peoples*, Pacific Linguistics 572, Canberra: Research School of Pacific and Asian Studies, Australian National University.

Denham, T.P., Golson, J. and Hughes, P.J. (2004a) 'Reading early agriculture at Kuk (Phases 1–3), Wahgi Valley, Papua New Guinea: the wetland archaeological features', *Proceedings of the Prehistoric Society*, 70: 259–98.

Denham, T.P., Haberle, S.G., and Lentfer, C. (2004b) 'New evidence and revised interpretations of early agriculture in Highland New Guinea', *Antiquity*, 78: 839–57.

Denham, T.P., Haberle, S.G., Lentfer, C., Fullagar, R., Field, J., Therin, M., Porch, N. and Winsborough, B. (2003) 'Origins of agriculture at Kuk Swamp in the Highlands of New Guinea', *Science*, 301: 189–93.

Fairbairn, A. (2005) 'An archaeobotanical perspective on plant-use practices in lowland northern New Guinea', *World Archaeology*, 37: 487–502.

Fullagar, R., Field, J., Denham, T.P. and Lentfer, C. (2006) 'Early and mid Holocene tool-use and processing of taro (*Colocasia esculenta*), yam (*Dioscorea* sp.) and other plants at Kuk Swamp in the highlands of Papua New Guinea', *Journal of Archaeological Science*, 33: 595–614.

Golson, J. (in press) 'Unravelling the story of early plant exploitation in Highland Papua New Guinea', in T. P. Denham, J. Iriarte and L. Vrydaghs (eds) *Rethinking Agriculture: archaeological and ethnoarchaeological perspectives*, Walnut Creek, CA: Left Coast Press.

Golson, J. and Gardner, D.S. (1990) 'Agricultural and sociopolitical organization in New Guinea Highlands prehistory', *Annual Review of Anthropology*, 19: 395–417.

Haberle, S.G. (2003) 'The emergence of an agricultural landscape in the highlands of New Guinea', *Archaeology in Oceania*, 38: 149–58.

Lebot, V. (1999) 'Biomolecular evidence for plant domestication in Sahul', *Genetic Resources and Crop Evolution*, 46: 619–28.

Matthews, P.J. (1995) 'Aroids and Austronesians', *Tropics*, 4: 105–26.

Muke, J. and Mandui, H. (2003) 'In the shadows of Kuk: evidence for prehistoric agriculture at Kana, Wahgi Valley, Papua New Guinea', *Archaeology in Oceania*, 38: 177–85.

Spriggs, M. (1996) 'Early agriculture and what went before in Island Melanesia: continuity or intrusion?' in D. R. Harris (ed.) *The Origins and Spread of Agriculture and Pastoralism in Eurasia*, London: UCL Press.

10 Subsistence changes in India and Pakistan

The Neolithic and Chalcolithic from the point of view of plant use today

K. L. Mehra

Introduction

Most summaries of the prehistoric evidence for subsistence from India and Pakistan emphasize the introduction of crops from Southwest Asia (wheat, barley, peas, lentils and flax) or from Asia and Africa (rice and the millets) (Glover and Higham 1996; Meadow 1996). This initial emphasis on introduction has been in many ways warranted, as new crops have transformed subsistence systems in the subcontinent over the last 5000 years. However, much less effort has been expended on attempting to understand the interaction of introduced crops and indigenous ones. In looking at local food plants there are two main sources of evidence: the distribution of such plants in the present and their use in agricultural or hunter-gatherer systems in the present and recent past. This chapter concentrates on the former set of evidence, making only brief comments on how such plants are presently used and how far these uses provide some window on the longer-term past. It should be stressed at the outset that what follows does not represent a full survey of the evidence, as this is too massive a task for such a large region for which the evidence is patchy at best. Rather, I indicate the potential of studies of present-day food plants and provide some sketch as to how these might be combined with the evidence from prehistory.

Inferences about possible means of subsistence in pre-Neolithic times can be drawn from the present-day uses of biodiversity, especially by peoples living in tribal belts of India where agricultural practices are only part of people's subsistence practices, and people continue to depend on forest products. Reviews of plant and animal species identified from different archaeological sites have mostly provided information on the presence of certain plant and animal species at specific sites, rather than broader sequences of change (Vishnu-Mittre 1977; Randhawa 1980; Kajale 1991; Saraswat 1992).

Recent crop use

Surveys of the use of wild plants have revealed that of over 20,000 plant species found in India, only 778 species, belonging to 96 families, possess edible plant parts (Singh and Arora 1978; Jain 1981; Vishnu-Mittre 1981). Of these, 648 species provide edible plant parts, which are easily separable from the whole and thus are especially useful. These include tuberous starchy roots and rhizomes (95 species), leaves and shoots (250 species), flower and flower buds (46 species), fruits (383 species), seeds including nuts and kernels (110 species), and other plant parts (14 species); while 130 species provide more than one edible plant part. Despite such a great number of potential domesticates, only about 80 plant species (only 33 prior to the Iron Age) have been found in archaeological contexts, partly because of preservation conditions in India, coupled with the different recovery techniques used on various excavations and Indian archaeobotanical studies in general (Kajale 1991).

Based on the list of wild, edible plant species presently used in different regions of India (Singh and Arora 1978), Mehra and Arora (1985) provided a list of plant species (*Vigna capensis, Moghania vistata, Erisoema chinense*), which were perhaps used as tubers and rhizomes which could be eaten raw, followed by those (*Amorphophallus, Dioscorea, Colocasia, Alocasia*) containing calcium oxalate crystals and other chemicals which had to be subjected to boiling and cooking to make them edible. Taro and yams supported the initial tuber-based cultures of the humid tropical and subtropical regions, and their domestication could only have occurred after fire was discovered and boiling which would have needed suitable containers. More sophisticated processing would be required for those plant species (*Codonopsis ovata, Dioscorea hispida, Cyperus bulbosus, Curcuma angustifolia, Tacca leontopetaloides*) which yielded edible starch, especially tubers which could be dried and made into flour. Dried tubers would have increased storage for lean periods. No archaeobotanical records of such species are available from India. Similarly, the earliest edible leaves and tender shoots came from species which could be eaten raw, and more sophisticated use as salad and condiments probably followed at a later date (for a list, see Mehra and Arora 1985). The use of raw fruits for pulps may have preceded the practice of pickling and preserving. Similarly, the use of edible grains and seeds which could be eaten raw might have preceded those needing boiling. Thus, the development of culinary techniques and preferences played a significant role in which plants were used and for what purposes.

Crop domestication

A wide range of cereals, millets and legumes was gathered and used for subsistence long before some of them were domesticated (Vishnu-Mittre 1985). The heritage of 'unconventional' staple millets/cereals still cultivated by groups in various parts of India may be very meaningful in this context. Such plants are as follows: *Coix lachryma jobi*, *Dactyloctenium aegyptium*, *Digitaria cruciata*, *D. cruciata* var. *esculenta* and *D. sanguinalis* ssp. *aegyptiaca* var. *frumentacea*, *Echinochloa colona* (sawa millet), *E. crus galli*, *E. frumentacea*, *Panicum miliaceum*, *P. sumatrense* (syn. *P. milliare*), *Paspalum scorbiculatum* (kodo millet), *Pennisetum orientale*, *Setaria glauca*, *S. italica* and *Urochloa panicoides*. *Digitaria cruciata* was domesticated in India (Harlan 1975). Kodo millet, *Paspalum scorbiculatum*, was domesticated across its range of present-day cultivation in India (de Wet *et al.* 1983). Wild, weed and cultivated, non-shattering kinds of *P. scorbiculatum* hybridize with each other, and weedy types are harvested along with the crop. Sawa millet, *Echinochloa colona*, is a tropical species domesticated in India, and differs from *E. crus galli*, a temperate species, in having smaller spikelets with membranous rather than chartaceous glumes. Sawa millet matures in less than two months and is often planted on poor soils. *Echinochloa colona* is often planted mixed with *Setaria italica* (Italian millet) or *Eleusine corocana* (finger millet). Since the growing periods of these three millets differ, present-day farmers usually harvest them in sequence to have a regular supply of staple food. This practice was also perhaps followed in the past. *Panicum sumatrense* (syn. *P. milliare*) is a native of India. Wild, weed and cultivated, non-shattering kinds occur in India. *Setaria viridis* is the ancestor of Italian millet, *Setaria italica*, grown in tropical and temperate regions of the world. Italian millet perhaps originated in eastern Asia, probably China, but it diffused into India prior to the diffusion of Southwest Asian cereals. In *Coix lachryma jobi*, another Indian domesticate, cultivated and wild types form a euploid series (Koul 1974). Many of these minor millets were identified from several archaeological sites of India. Green gram (*Vigna radiata*) and black gram (*Vigna mungo*) are related morphologically and cytologically to their ancestral wild types, V. *radiata* var. *sublobata* and V. *mungo* var. *sylvestris*. Both species were domesticated in India (Jain and Mehra 1980).

Phytogeographic distribution patterns of cultivated and closely related wild plants suggest that there are specific regions that have high diversities of economic plants and their closely related wild species (Mehra and Arora 1985). For cereals, there is a concentration of rice, *Coix* and *Digitaria* in the northeastern region and of *Paspalum* sp. and *Panicum milliare* in the southern and eastern peninsular regions. The entire peninsular region has both green and black grams, although the wild progenitor form of *Vigna radiata* (*Vigna sublobata*) is concentrated more in the Western Ghats, particularly in the Maharashtra region. *Dolichos uniflorus*, related to the horse gram (*D. biflorus*), is localized in the eastern and southern peninsular regions, while *Lablab niger*, related to *L. purpureus*, occurs on the eastern coast of India (Arora and Nayar 1984).

The archaeological evidence

There is the possibility that agriculture started in the Belan and Ganga Valley, Uttar Pradesh with the domestication and cultivation of rice in the mid-sixth millennium BC (Savithri 1976; Sharma 1980, 1985), although these early dates have been strongly disputed (Meadow 1996). However, we can be sure that rice culture had spread to different regions of India by the mid-second millennium BC.

Leaving rice aside, the indigenous peoples of India domesticated the minor millets, grain legumes, oilseeds and other crops (see Smartt and Simmonds 1995 for a complete list). They developed several culinary preparations, and experimented with many different ways of utilizing the plant biodiversity.

Several species of winter cereals, legumes and other crops were domesticated in Southwest Asia (Smartt and Simmonds 1995), and several of these are found at Mehrgarh, Pakistan (seventh millennium BC) (Meadow 1984; Costantini and Costantini-Biasini 1985). Similarly, sorghum, finger millet and pearl millet were domesticated in Africa (Harlan 1975; Mehra 1991; Smartt and Simmonds 1995), and these crops diffused into India around 2000 BC (Mehra 1991). Southwest Asian crops are adapted to winter cultivation, while those from Africa are suited for cultivation in the summer rainy season (July to September) in north India. African crops can also be grown from September–November in certain parts of India. These African crops are dual purpose (grains for humans and fodder for animals). In north India, indigenous Chalcolithic farmers practised agriculture in only one season (July–September), and they had no crop to cultivate in winter. The introduced winter season crops provided an opportunity to practise crop rotation, resulting in high surplus food production to feed people who were not food producers. Legume cultivation, in both seasons, sustained soil fertility to a large extent. Crop cultivation in winter is comparatively easier than that of rice during the summer rainy season. Domesticated non-shattering minor millets, rice and grain legumes of Indian origins were identified, along with Southwest Asian crops from the same occupational levels of several sites of north and central India. Therefore, it is likely that agriculture had a strong indigenous component, a fact which has been ignored as a result of continuously focusing on 'introductions'.

Not only were indigenous crops important in the early stages of agriculture but they were also important in the diversified agricultural systems from 2000 BC onwards. The identification of seventeen different crops cultivated at seven pre-Harappan and Harappan sites, has revealed that farmers cultivated only Southwest Asian crops at Kalibagangan, but at other sites exotic crops were sown after harvesting the indigenous crops sown in the summer season (July–September). At all sites there is evidence of diversity in the combination of local and exotic crops that were grown and in this people were responding to local environmental conditions and food preferences. The exotic crops did not all diffuse together, but may have moved in sequence so that naked barley arrived after hulled barley, bread wheat after dwarf and club wheats, several legume species after one another, and finger millet after sorghum.

Changes in subsistence patterns were brought about by (i) gradually replacing emmer, dwarf and club wheats by high yielding bread wheat; (ii) incorporating several species of grain legumes, oats and fenugreek for cultivation in winter; (iii) cultivating additional species of Indian legumes and other economic plants especially rice; (iv) replacing Italian millet with jowar and finger millet; and (v) using more species of wild economic shrubs and trees, many of which were indigenous. Increasing economic prosperity was ensured when farmers began to raise twenty-three crops and five fruits/ vegetables suited to different agro-climatic situations under dryland and wetland farming systems during summer, rainy and winter seasons. Extensive land use, crop rotation, crop diversification, animal husbandry, herding, hunting and fishing practices enhanced surplus food and animal production.

A limited number of plant species were identified from plant remains recovered from several sites. This may be either due to the cultivation of only a few species at several sites, or efforts and techniques of collection and examination of samples may not have been adequate. The processing and identification of meticulously recovered samples from Hulas, Narhan and Senuwar have provided evidence of cultivation of several crops at these sites. The same is true of plant materials collected at Surkotada (Savithri 1976) and Rojdi (Weber 1991).

Crop diversification (seventeen crops at Hulas, thirty at Narhan and fourteen at Senuwas) was an obvious subsistence strategy of the Chalcolithic period. Crops suited to drylands and wetlands were available for cultivation in both seasons, leading to better land use. There were also choices between cereals (barley being more drought-resistant than wheat), oilseeds (sesame, rape and mustard, safflower serving different culinary purposes), millets and legumes. All legume species (exotic and indigenous) can be grown under rainfed conditions, but they differ in drought resistance. They are especially useful for different purposes; that is, as dried grains (lentil, green gram, black gram), dried and immature seeds (field-pea, pigeon-pea, chick-pea), dried grain and immature seeds/pods (hyacinth-bean, cow-pea, horse-gram, *moth* bean). Early cultivars of all legume species were of indeterminate type, with pods maturing at periodic intervals. Thus, farmers could harvest green pods/immature seeds for daily use and finally harvest different crops based on their specific maturity periods. All legume species provided green/dry fodder (although to varying extents) for use as animal food, and some of them like cow-pea, hyacinth-bean and horse-gram were amenable for regrowth after cutting (for fodder) to provide grain harvest. Such subsistence strategies ensured food security in both seasons, and farmers could then decide their cropping patterns based on their culinary preferences and land use. This traditional system is still practised today in India by subsistence farmers.

A major subsistence change almost equal to the use of Southwest Asian crops for winter cultivation and crop rotation was that brought about through the use of African crops. The subsistence economies of Rajasthan, Madhya Pradesh and Maharashtra were based on minor millets and agro-pastoral systems, using species of *Panicum, Setaria, Echinochloa* and *Paspalum*. Farmers probably cultivated two or more minor millet species of different maturity periods, since mixtures of species were recovered from several archaeological sites. Farmers harvested different millets at periodic intervals from the same field. Multi-crop mixtures acted as food security for humans (seeds as staple food) and animals (vegetative parts used as fodder) because the vagaries of weather promote a differential response by different species, so that one or more species could be harvested for subsistence, This subsistence pattern is likely to have been practised by the Chalcolithic farmers of India and it is still practised by 'tribal' peoples in several parts of India. This situation began to change with the diffusion of pearl millet, sorghum and finger millet due to their specific plant character-istics and adaptability to different agro-climatic situations. Pearl millet can be grown in low rainfall (250–800 mm) areas, on poor sandy/very light/light/heavy, even red, soils; can tolerate drought; and can be stored well. Its range of adaptation is high under different day-lengths, temperatures and moisture stress. Sorghum yields are very high compared to other millets; it can be grown in medium to heavy soils, in 400–1000 mm rainfall, and can tolerate temperature fluctuations. Finger millet has good grain storage capacity, even for ten years; can be grown in areas with rainfall ranging from 50 to 100 cm and in irrigated soils, in red loams, black and sandy soils. Thus, each millet has a special ecological niche and can also yield some grains in adverse soil and climatic conditions. All of these African crops also provided fodder for animals and they rapidly started replacing minor millet cultivation (Mehra 1991).

African sorghum and millet culture thus played an important role in the agricultural history of India following the opening up of opportunities for rainfed agriculture and mixed (crop cultivation and animal husbandry) farming systems (Mehra 1991). This led to a change in settlement patterns. Instead of urban centres with neighbouring food-producing villages, several small villages began to emerge over large stretches of land. The new system progressed rapidly because the centrally controlled production and distri-bution system, so characteristic of the Indus Valley civilization, could not operate (Mehra 1991). Similarly, the incorporation of pearl millet in the dryland agriculture of Gujarat seems responsible for the sudden increase in the number of settlements during Rangpur phases B and C.

In conclusion, it can be seen that the introduction of winter cereals and legumes led to a system of crop rotation, African crops replaced or supple-mented minor millet cultivation, and appropriate land-use systems gradually developed with increasing crop diversification. All these strategies continued to produce surplus food and other products. Domesticated animals provided animal products, hunting of wild animals and fishing supplemented animal products, and increased exploitation of forest biodiversity served several useful purposes.

Conclusions

There is no doubt of the importance of introduced crops in increasing yields and in extending the range of crops that can be grown in different seasons. However, indigenous plants also played an important role and this has been consistently underestimated. The minor millets and the grams may have been important in the origins of domestication and were sets of species with which people were more familiar than the introduced species. Also, in many periods from the Chalcolithic to the present, people have cultivated a large range of crops, suitable to varying soil and climatic conditions and producing food at different seasons of the year. Although there has been an overall trend towards intensification in food production this has rarely led to the sorts of monocultures found in many other parts of the world. In looking at both origins and the long-term histories of agricultural systems in India the indigenous plants have had an important and underestimated role to play.

References

Arora, R.K. and Nayar, R. (1984) *Wild Relatives of Crop Plants in India*, New Delhi: National Bureau of Plant Genetic Resources.

Costantini, L. and Costantini-Biasini, L. (1985) 'Agriculture in Baluchistan between the seventh and the third millennium B.C.', *Newsletter of Baluchistan Studies*, 2: 16–30.

de Wet, J.M.J., Prasada Rao, K.E., Mangesha, M.H. and Brink, D.E. (1983) 'Diversity in Kodo millet', *Economic Botany*, 37: 159–63.

Glover, I.C. and Higham, C.F.W. (1996) 'New evidence for early rice cultivation in south, southeast and east Asia', in D. R. Harris (ed.) *The Origins and Spread of Agriculture and Pastoralism in Eurasia*, London: UCL Press.

Harlan, J.R. (1975) *Crops and Man*, Madison, WI: American Society of Agronomy.

Jain, H.K. and Mehra, K.L. (1980) 'Evolution, adaptation, relationships and uses of the species of *Vigna* cultivated in India', in R. J. Summerfield and R. Bunting (eds) *Advances in Legume Science*, vol. I, Kew: Royal Botanic Gardens.

Jain, S.K. (ed.) (1981) *Glimpses of Indian Ethnobotany*, New Delhi: Oxford and IBH.

Kajale, M.D. (1991) 'Current status of Indian palaeoethnobotany: introduced and indigenous food plants with a discussion of the historical and evolutionary development of Indian agriculture and agricultural systems in general', in J. Renfrew (ed.) *Recent Developments in Palaeoethnobotany*, Edinburgh: Edinburgh University Press.

Koul, A.K. (1974) 'Job's tears', in Sir Joseph Hutchinson (ed.) *Evolutionary Studies in World Crops: diversity and change in the Indian subcontinent*, Cambridge: Cambridge University Press.

Meadow, R.H. (1984) 'Notes on faunal remains from Mehrgarh, with a focus on cattle (*Bos*)', in B. Allchin (ed.) *South Asian Archaeology*, Cambridge: Cambridge University Press.

Meadow, R.H. (1996) 'The origins and spread of agriculture and pastoralism in northwestern South Asia', in D. R. Harris (ed.) *The Origins and Spread of Agriculture and Pastoralism in Eurasia*, London: UCL Press.

Mehra, K.L. (1991) 'Pre-historic Ethiopia and India: contacts through sorghum and millet genetic resources', in J. M. M. Engels, J. G. Hawkes and M. Worde (eds) *Plant Genetic Resources of Ethiopia*, Cambridge: Cambridge University Press.

Mehra, K.L. and Arora, R.K. (1985) 'Some considerations on the domestication of plants in India', in V. N. Misra and P. Bellwood (eds) *Recent Advances in Indo-Pacific Prehistory*, New Delhi: Oxford and IBH.

Randhawa, M.S. (1980) *A History of Agriculture in India*, New Delhi: Indian Council of Agricultural Research.

Saraswat, K.S. (1992) 'Archaeobotanical remains in ancient cultural and socio-economical dynamics of the Indian subcontinent', *Palaeobotanist*, 40: 514–45.

Savithri, R. (1976) 'Studies in archaeobotany together with its bearing upon socio-economy and environment of Indian Proto-Historic cultures', unpublished PhD thesis, University of Lucknow.

Sharma, G.R. (1980) *History to Prehistory: archaeology of Ganga Valley and Vindhyas*, Allahabad: Allahabad University Publications.

Sharma, G.R. (1985) 'From hunting and food gathering to domestication of plants and animals in the Belan and Ganga Valleys', in V. N. Misra and P. Bellwood (eds) *Recent Advances in Indo-Pacific Prehistory*, New Delhi: Oxford and IBH.

Singh, H.B. and Arora, R.K. (1978) *Wild Edible Plants of India*, New Delhi: Indian Council of Agricultural Research.

Smartt, J. and Simmonds, N.W. (1995) *Evolution of Crop Plants*, Harlow: Longman.

Vishnu-Mittre (1977) 'Changing economy in ancient India', in C. A. Reed (ed.) *The Origin of Agriculture*, The Hague: Mouton.

Vishnu-Mittre (1981) 'Wild plants in Indian folk life – a historical perspective', in S. K. Jain (ed.) *Glimpses of Indian Ethnobotany*, New Delhi: Oxford and IBH.

Vishnu-Mittre (1985) 'The uses of wild plants and the processes of domestication in the Indian sub-continent', in V. N. Misra and P. Bellwood (eds) *Recent Advances in Indo-Pacific Prehistory*, New Delhi: Oxford and IBH.

Weber, S.A. (1991) *Plants and Harappan Subsistence: an example of stability and change from Rojdi*, New Delhi: Oxford and IBH.

Update: The developing South Asian record

Peter White

No radical revisions to the history of subsistence in South Asia have been proposed since Mehra's paper was published. But there are some important new studies.

Mehra (2002) has published a review of the agricultural foundations of the Indus-Saraswati civilization, which stresses the diversity of plants involved and the continuing importance of non-domesticates in subsistence.

Also in 2002, Fuller published a very extensive review of archaeobotanical studies in India. This covered the history of the discipline, as well as methodology, including formation processes, taphonomy and quantification of botanical material. It rigorously reviewed current taxonomic identification of archaeological material, about which there are different views, and proposed revision of some earlier identifications. The review suggested, in line with earlier interpretations, that *Triticum, Hordeum* and pulses (pea, lentil, chickpea) were of Southwest Asian origin and that they arrived as 'a package' as early as the sixth millennium BC in the northwest of the continent. But it also admitted that the earliest identified pulses in archaeological contexts are several millennia younger. In contrast, the millets and pulses of African origin came originally from various sources in both East and West Africa, dated not earlier than the second millennium BC, and did not arrive as a package (see also Weber 1998, Mehra 2003). After arrival they seem to have been cultivated alongside native Indian millets.

There is considerable disagreement concerning the history of rice in South Asia. Recent claims of direct dating of domestic rice to c. 5000–6000 BC at the site of Lahuradeva are perhaps the best documented (PJAC:AGP 2004). Fuller (2002) notes long-standing problems with differentiating wild and domestic rice in archaeobotanical assemblages. Fuller's review, like Mehra's paper, concentrates on seed data, since seeds are macroscopic, are often well-preserved in archaeological contexts, particularly when charred, and are identifiable using comparative reference collections. Other potential subsistence data are less well explored. For example, in a study of early plant domestication in south India, Fuller *et al.* (2004) note that charred parenchyma is common in early levels of Ash-mound culture sites (c. 3000–2500 BC), with seeds being relatively much less common than they later became. This suggests that tubers or rhizomes may have been an important part of subsistence, but to date there has been little research on this material anywhere in the region. Korisettar *et al.* (2002: 197–9) note that yams (*Dioscorea* spp.) and ginger, turmeric and their relatives (Zingiberaceae) are native to the region. They also draw attention to the various fruits and nuts, such as *Ziziphus* sp., the pits of which are commonly found in excavation, and *Areca* sp. (betel nut). It is noticeable in this context that there are very few sites well dated to between the end of the Pleistocene and about 3000 BC that contain properly collected archaeobotanical remains. Thus current understanding of changing human–plant relationships over the long term is limited.

Several other research avenues remain little explored. Harvey and Fuller (2005) used phytoliths from two north Indian sites (c. 4500 BC) to show that rice was harvested and processed there while wheat and barley were probably not. Ancient starch analysis has not been applied in the region. Likewise, molecular genetic studies, which can provide additional data about species relationships, sometimes yield contradictory taxonomic interpretations to studies based on morphology.

References

Fuller, D.Q. (2002) 'Fifty years of archaeobotanical studies in India: laying a solid foundation', in S. Settar and R. Korisettar (eds) *Indian Archaeology in Retrospect*, vol. 3, New Delhi: Manohar.

Fuller, D.Q., Korisettar, R., Venkatasubbaiah, P.C. and Jones, M.K. (2004) 'Early plant domestications in southern India: some preliminary archaeobotanical results', *Vegetation History and Archaeobotany*, 13: 115–29.

Harvey, E.L. and Fuller, D.Q. (2005) 'Investigating crop processing using phytolith analysis: the example of rice and millets', *Journal of Archaeological Science*, 32: 739–52.

Korisettar, R., Venkatasubbaiah, P.C. and Fuller, D.Q. (2002) 'Brahmagiri and beyond: the archaeology of the southern Neolithic', in S. Settar and R. Korisettar (eds) *Indian Archaeology in Retrospect*, vol. 1, New Delhi: Manohar.

Mehra, K.L. (2002) 'Agricultural foundations of Indus-Saraswati civilization' in Y. L. Nene and S. L. Choudary (eds) *Agricultural Heritage of India*, Udaipur: Rajasthan College of Agriculture.

Mehra, K.L. (2003) 'The dispersal of plant cultivars between India and Africa', in V. N. Misra and M. D. Kajale (eds) *Introduction of African crops into south Asia*, Pune: Deccan College Post-graduate and Research Institute.

PJAC:AGP (2004) 'Proceedings of the Joint Annual Conference of IAS, ISPQS and IHCS: Archaeology of the Ganga Plain', Lucknow: Uttar Pradesh State Archaeology Department.

Weber, S.A. (1998) 'Out of Africa: the initial impact of millets in South Asia', *Current Anthropology*, 39: 267–74.

11 Domestication of the Southwest Asian Neolithic crop assemblage of cereals, pulses, and flax

The evidence from the living plants

Daniel Zohary

Introduction

Expertly identified and radiocarbon-dated plant remains are now available from hundreds of Neolithic and Bronze Age sites in Southwest Asia and Europe. The volume of this archaeobotanical documentation and its recent rapid growth becomes apparent when one examines the proceedings of the workshops of European palaeoethnobotanists which took place in 1971, 1975, 1978, 1981, and 1984 (e.g. van Zeist and Casparie 1984), the annual reviews by Schultze-Motel (1968–1985), Maria Hopf's *Festschrift* (Körber-Grohne 1979), and such recent reviews as van Zeist (1980) and Zohary and Hopf (1988).

This rich documentation demonstrates the following facts.

(a)   Three cereal crops: emmer wheat *Triticum turgidum* ssp. *dicoccum*, barley *Hordeum vulgare*, and einkorn wheat *Triticum monococcum* (in this order of importance) were the principal founder crops of Neolithic agriculture in this part of the world. Definite signs of their cultivation first appear in Southwest Asia (the Near East) in the 8th and 7th millennia bc.

(b)   The domestication of these cereals went hand in hand with the introduction into cultivation of five companion plants: pea *Pisum sativum*, lentil *Lens culinaris*, chickpea *Cicer arietinum*, bitter vetch *Vicia ervilia*, and flax *Linum usitatissimum*, all of which were very probably domesticated simultaneously with wheat and barley, or taken into cultivation just a short time later.

(c)   The subsequent expansion of Neolithic agriculture to Europe, central Asia, and the Nile Valley was based on this same crop assemblage. The same crops that started food production in the Near Eastern nuclear area also initiated agriculture in these vast territories.

(d)   The evidence for the early domestication of additional crops is much less convincing, although a recent find (Kislev 1985) hints that the broad bean, *Vicia faba*, might also belong to the early Neolithic Near Eastern crop assemblage.

This chapter does not aim to review the archaeological finds. Instead, it evaluates a complementary source of evidence, namely the living plants. More specifically, it focuses on the wild progenitors of the Neolithic crop assemblage in order to help answer the following questions:

(a) Where and how were these plants domesticated?
(b) Under which ecological conditions could early cultivation succeed?
(c) How does the information obtained from the living plants correlate with the evidence retrieved from the archaeological excavations?

Identification of the wild progenitors

A prerequisite for a sound assessment is the knowledge that the crops and their wild relatives are botanically satisfactorily explored and the wild progenitors reliably identified, preferably with the aid of genetic tests. With the exception of the problematic broad bean (for which the wild progenitor is still undetermined, see Zohary 1977), all members of the Neolithic crop assemblage now satisfy that prerequisite. In recent years their wild relatives were subjected to intensive studies. For most of them, genetic tests have clarified the affinities within each crop complex, and convincingly identified the wild plants from which the cultivars could have evolved. For these founder crops, therefore, the search for ancestry is more-or-less completed. It is highly unlikely that new wild types involved in the origin of these cultivated plants will be discovered in the future. The information assembled on the wild progenitors of the eight founder crops can be summarized as follows.

Barley and einkorn wheat

In these two crops the identification of the wild progenitors is straight-forward. In each cereal a wild stock occurs which is fully interfertile with the cultivars and shows chromosomal identity with them. The geographical distribution and the ecological ranges of the wild types are also well delineated. In fact, only a few basic additions or corrections have to be made to Harlan and Zohary's (1966) and Zohary's (1969) surveys of these progenitors. The most important ones are: (a) the recent discovery of wild barley, *Hordeum spontaneum*, in the western Himalayan Mountains (Witcombe 1978) and Tibet (Shao 1981), and (b) the realization that wild einkorn, *Triticum boeoticum*, thrives in primary habitats not only in western and south-eastern Turkey but also in central Anatolia. A characteristic feature of both crops is the build-up of 'wild-weed-cultivated' complexes: in addition to wild forms growing in primary niches, one encounters weedy forms which infest cultivation and colonize the margins of tilled ground, roadsides, and similar secondary habitats. Compared to the genuinely wild plants, which are centred in the Near East (Figures 11.1 and 11.2), the weeds occupy wider territories.

Emmer wheat

The situation in this cereal is more complex. Here we are faced with two wild 'sibling species', which are morphologically indistinguishable but genetically well isolated from one another. One wild type, *Triticum dicoccoides*, is chromosomally identical and fully interfertile with all the tetraploid cultivated wheats, which are today grouped under *T. turgidum* (genome constitution: AABB). It is therefore identified as the wild progenitor of cultivated emmer, *T. turgidum* ssp. *dicoccum*, and also of the more advanced free-threshing *durum*-type derivatives. The second wild type, *T. araraticum* (genome constitution: AAGG), is totally intersterile with *T. turgidum* cultivars, and played no part in their origin. It is linked to *T. timopheevi* (genome constitution: AAGG), a rare cereal crop endemic to Georgia, and very likely a local and recent episode in wheat domestication.

It is practically impossible to distinguish between *dicoccoides* and *araraticum* wheats morphologically, either in herbarium collections or during field excursions. For these reasons, taxonomists (e.g. Bor 1968) lumped them together and Harlan and Zohary (1966) had to survey them collectively. Since then, numerous seed samples of tetraploid wild wheats have been collected in the Near East and cytogenetically tested to establish their genomic constitution. The results have already clarified the distribution areas of the two sibling species. These two wild wheats overlap considerably in their distribution, and occasionally they even grow side by side. Yet *dicoccoides* (AABB) is confined to the Near Eastern 'arc' (Figure 11.3), while *araraticum* (AAGG) has a more north-easterly distribution. It is spread over eastern Turkey, northern Iraq, western Iran, and Transcaspia (Figure 11.4).

In summary, the available cytogenetic evidence makes it possible to delimit the present-day distribution area of the wild ancestor of cultivated tetraploid AABB wheats. One can also compare it with the areas of wild einkorn and wild barley. While the latter have only their centre of distribution in the Near East and extend (mainly as weeds) far beyond this region, wild emmer is a strict endemic. It is confined to the Near Eastern arc. As previously stressed (Harlan and Zohary 1966; Zohary 1969), *T. diccoccoides* also differs from the two other progenitors in its habitat preferences. Weedy races did not develop in this wild grass; it grows almost entirely in primary niches.

Pea

The cultivated pea, *Pisum sativum*, is closely related to a variable aggregate of wild and weedy peas which roughly fall into two morphological – and

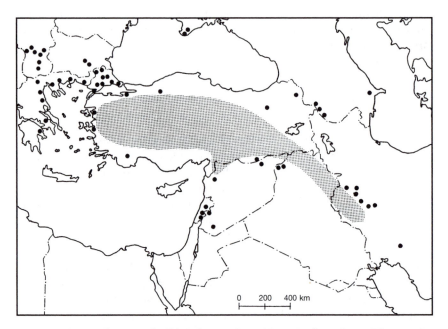

Figure 11.1 Distribution of wild einkorn wheat, *Triticum boeoticum*. The area in which this wild wheat is massively spread is shaded. Dots outside this distribution centre represent more isolated stands, mostly of weedy forms (based on Harlan and Zohary 1966)

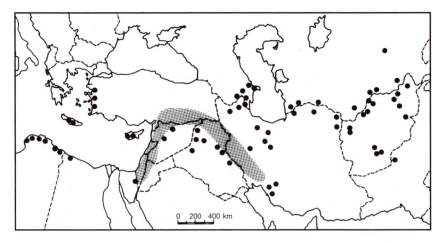

Figure 11.2 Distribution of wild barley, *Hordeum spontaneum*. The area in which wild barley is massively spread is shaded. Dots outside this distribution centre represent more isolated populations, usually of weedy forms. Towards the east, these populations extend beyond the boundaries of this map into Ladakh and Tibet (based on Harlan and Zohary 1966)

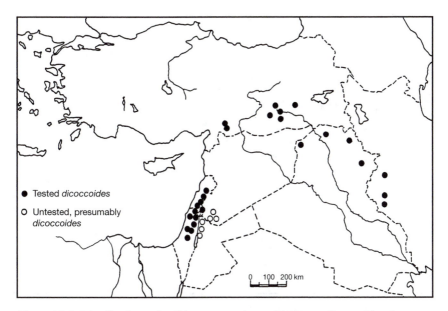

Figure 11.3 Distribution of wild emmer wheat, *Triticum dicoccoides* (genome constitution AABB): sites of plants tested cytogenetically (compiled from Rao and Smith 1968; Dagan and Zohary 1970; Tanaka and Ishii 1973; unpublished data of D. Zohary)

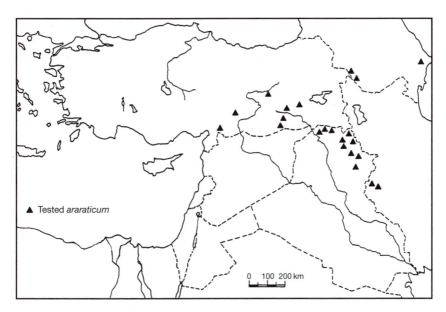

Figure 11.4 Distribution of wild Timopheev's wheat, *Triticum araraticum* (genome constitution AAGG): sites of plants tested cytogenetically (compiled from Rao and Smith 1968; Dagan and Zohary 1970; Tanaka and Ishii 1973; unpublished data of D. Zohary)

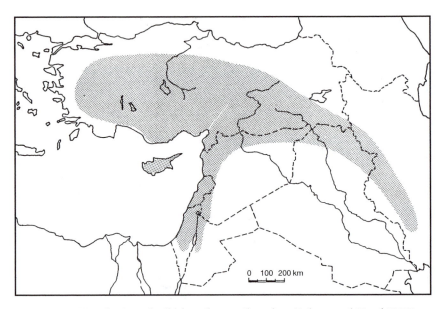

Figure 11.5 Distribution of wild *humile* peas (based on Zohary and Hopf 1973)

ecological – groups: (a) a tall '*maquis* type' traditionally named *P. elatius*, and (b) a shorter 'steppe type' traditionally called *P. humile* (= *P. syriacum*). The distribution and ecological preferences of these wild peas were surveyed by Zohary and Hopf (1973). No major additions have been made since then. *Elatius* peas are pan-Mediterranean in their distribution and grow as annual climbers in *maquis* formations. *Humile* peas are restricted to the Near East (Figure 11.5). They thrive in steppe-like habitats and also invade cultivated fields. Of the two wild types, *P. humile* resembles more closely the cultivated crop. It is also a characteristic annual constituent of the oak-dominated park-forest formation in the Near Eastern arc, i.e. the same zone that also harbours the wild progenitors of emmer wheat, einkorn wheat, and barley.

Cytogenetic tests (Ben Ze'ev and Zohary 1973) have revealed that both *humile* and *elatius* peas are closely related to the cultivated pea and are fully, or almost fully, interfertile with it. The tests also showed that the wild peas contain two chromosome arrangements. *Elatius* forms tested so far differed from the *sativum* cultivars by a single reciprocal translocation. The same interchange is present in *humile* peas in southern and central Israel. In contrast, wild *humile* peas collected on the Golan Heights and in Turkey were found to contain chromosomes identical to those present in the *sativum* cultivars. The cytogenetic tests therefore indicate that both *elatius* and *humile* peas represent the *general* wild stock from which the cultivated crop developed, while those *humile* forms with chromosomes identical to those of *sativum* cultivars constitute the *direct* source for pea domestication.

Lentil

The wild stock from which cultivated lentil, *Lens culinaris*, could have been derived is well identified (Zohary and Hopf 1973). The cultivated forms show close affinities with *L. orientalis*, an annual wild lentil distributed over the Near East and reaching into central Asia (Figure 11.6). Cytogenic tests recently performed in the genus *Lens* (Ladizinsky *et al.* 1984) confirmed the close affinities between *L. culinaris* and *L. orientalis*. They also revealed that while *culinaris* cultivars were uniform as to their chromosome structure, *orientalis* collections were not. The latter showed several structural races, which differed from one another by one or two reciprocal translocations. Significantly, one of the chromosome arrangements found in the chromo-somally polymorphic *L. orientalis* turned out to be identical with the 'standard' karyotype of the cultivated pulse. Therefore, this *orientalis* chromosome race should be regarded as the direct source from which cultivated lentil originated. The samples tested so far do not permit an exact delimitation of the geographical distribution of the various chromosome races in *L. orientalis*. However, the 'standard' chromosome arrangement is relatively widely distributed. It was detected in Turkey, Cyprus, Iran, and central Asia (Figure 11.6).

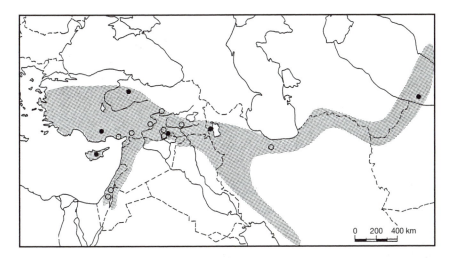

Figure 11.6 Distribution area of wild lentil, *Lens orientalis* (shaded). Black dots represent the locations of accessions known to contain the 'standard' chromosome complement; while open circles represent accessions with other chromosome types (based on Barulina 1930; Zohary and Hopf 1973; Ladizinsky *et al.* 1984)

Chickpea

The wild ancestry of the cultivated chickpea, *Cicer arietinum*, was clarified only 12 years ago (Ladizinsky and Adler 1976a, 1976b). The wild progenitor of this crop turned out to be a new species, *Cicer reticulatum*, discovered in southeastern Turkey. This wild chickpea was found to be interfertile with the cultivated pulse and it also showed full chromosomal homology with it. Other wild *Cicer* species turned out to be reproductively isolated from the crop and had to be excluded from the candidacy for its wild ancestry.

Although *C. reticulatum* was discovered only a few years ago, its distribution and ecological specificities seem to be well established. It is an element of the oak-dominated park-forest vegetation zone of the Near Eastern arc. It is today endemic to the middle segment of the crescent (Figure 11.7). Future finds may extend the known distribution area of this wild progenitor, but probably not by very much (see Postscript).

Bitter vetch

Cultivated bitter vetch, *Vicia ervilia*, is closely related to an aggregate of wild and weedy forms which closely resemble the crop morphologically (Zohary and Hopf 1973). Weedy forms and feral types are quite common in the Near East. They infest grain cultivation and also occur at the margins of cultivated ground. Truly wild forms – growing in primary habitats – are somewhat smaller than the cultivated and weedy forms and more restricted in their distribution (Figure 11.8). They are definitely known from southern Anatolia, northern Iraq, and Mt. Hermon (Zohary and Hopf 1973; Townsend 1974; Ladizinsky and van Oss 1984) where they usually grow on gravelly slopes, at 1000–1800 m altitude, sometimes together with wild lentil, *L. orientalis*. Very probably, wild bitter vetch is also native to the Anti-Lebanon mountain range.

Flax

Wild *Linum bienne* (= *L. augustifolium*) is the recognized wild progenitor of cultivated flax *L. usitatissimum*. These two flaxes show close morphological resemblance, they also intercross readily and are fully interfertile (Gill and Yermanos 1967). Among the wild progenitors of the Neolithic crop plants, wild flax shows the widest distribution. It is spread over the Atlantic coast of Europe, the Mediterranean basin, the Near East, northern Iran, and Caucasia (Figure 11.9). *Linum bienne* grows mainly in wet places, such as springs, seepage areas, marshy lands, and moist clay soils. In such habitats wild flax thrives also in the Near Eastern arc.

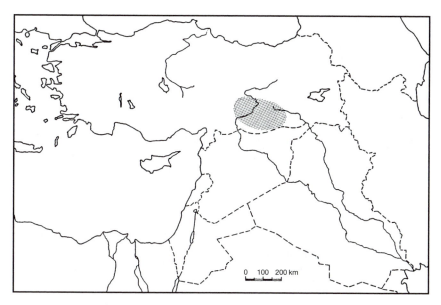

Figure 11.7 Distribution area of wild chickpea, *Cicer reticulatum* (based on Ladizinsky and Adler 1976b)

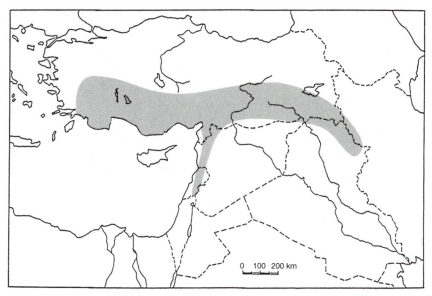

Figure 11.8 Distribution area of wild bitter vetch, *Vicia ervilia* (based on Zohary and Hopf 1973; Townsend 1974; Ladizinsky and van Oss 1984)

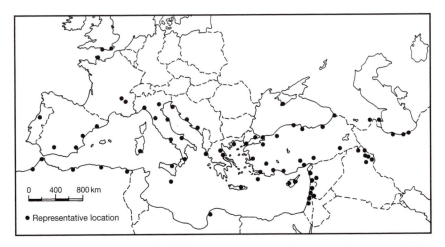

Figure 11.9 Distribution of wild flax, *Linum bienne* (based on data recorded in floras covering various European and Near Eastern countries, and a survey of the herbarium specimens at the Royal Botanic Gardens, Kew, England)

Distribution areas and the place of domestication

Palynological data (van Zeist and Bottema 1982) suggest that by 10,000–9000 bc the vegetation formations in which the wild progenitors thrive today (open oak forests, forest steppes, and steppes with scattered stands of trees) already occupied the western part of the Near Eastern arc and may possibly have started to establish themselves also in the Zagros Mountains. By 6000 bc the vegetation belts that characterize the Near East had already achieved their present-day gross distribution. Because domestication is a relatively recent development, it can be assumed that the distribution of the wild progenitors (weeds excluded) has not undergone drastic changes since the beginning of agriculture, at least in the western half of the arc. Delineation of the present-day distribution of the progenitor thus marks (more or less) the territory in which the crop could potentially have been domesticated: the narrower the distribution, the more precise the placement.

In the 1950s and 1960s archaeologists were recommended to take account of the distribution of wild progenitors (Helbaek 1959; Harlan and Zohary 1966) as a potent means of predicting where the earliest agricultural sites could be expected to occur. Now that substantial archaeological documentation is available from Europe and Southwest Asia, it is worthwhile to check again how the evidence from the two disciplines fits. Wild emmer, *T. dicoccoides* (genome constitution AABB), is an ideal indicator for such an assessment. Present-day wild emmer grows only in the Near East, where it occupies a narrow belt some 100–200 km wide and 1600 km long (Figure 11.3). Furthermore, it did not evolve secondary weedy forms that could have complicated its distribution picture. Therefore, the distribution of wild emmer indicates fairly accurately that emmer wheat could have been domesticated only in the Near Eastern arc. The archaeological finds fully corroborate this supposition. The earliest remains of cultivated emmer were discovered in the string of farming villages that first appears in this very belt (for review, see van Zeist 1976, 1980; Zohary and Hopf 1988: 35–41). Because cultivated emmer was a key crop in the expansion of Neolithic agriculture to Europe, central Asia, and the Nile Valley, the distribution of *T. dicoccoides* delimits not only the place of origin of this cereal, it also marks the area where the type of agriculture which spread to Europe and central Asia could have originated.

The same line of reasoning applies to two other members of the Neolithic crop assemblage, namely chickpea and bitter vetch. The wild progenitor of the first crop is a strict endemic confined to southeastern Turkey (Figure 11.7). This pins down the domestication of chickpea to a small territory indeed. Wild forms of bitter vetch are restricted to the Near Eastern arc and the Anatolian plateau (Figure 11.8). Thus this crop, too, has to have been taken into cultivation in the Near East. For both pulses, the available archaeological evidence (van Zeist 1980; Zohary and Hopf 1988: 101, 104) fully supports these suppositions.

The distribution areas of the wild ancestors of the other five crops are much wider, and were probably of similar breadth also by a short time after the start of the Holocene. They therefore carry much less weight. Yet it is encouraging to find that the information on the present-day distribution of these wild plants fully accords with the archaeological documentation. The wild progenitors of barley, einkorn wheat, pea, lentil, and flax all abound in the same geographical belt in which the earliest archaeological evidence of their cultivation has been retrieved. With the possible exception of wild flax, the Near East is also the centre of their distribution. Here they attain maximum density and occupy the widest ecological range.

Finally, chromosome polymorphism in pea and lentil also helps to delimit the areas of origin of these crops. At present, only preliminary information is available on the exact distribution of the various translocation races in the two wild pulses. But in each, working out the detailed geographical distribution of the 'standard' chromosome type, i.e. the karyotype that also characterizes the cultivated varieties, could indicate more precisely where domestication may have taken place. Yet it is noteworthy that the available tests already show that, in both pulses, wild types with the 'standard' chromosome arrangement grow in the Near East. Thus, this chromosomal evidence is also in full agreement with the available archaeological finds.

Preadaptation for cultivation

Various projects aimed at the screening of disease resistance in local *Triticum dicoccoides* and *Hordeum spontaneum* populations were carried out in

Israel in the past ten years. They involved growing large numbers of plants under field conditions, both in the Mediterranean belt (rain-fed cultivation) and in the drier areas (with supporting irrigation). In addition to the detection of useful genes, these experiments showed that wild emmer and wild barley can easily be taken into cultivation. The large seeds tolerate coverage by variable amounts of soil, and germinate quickly to produce vigorous seedlings. Stands and yields of both wild cereals approach quite closely to those produced by the local land races of wheat and barley grown under the same conditions. This demonstrates that it would have been easy to start wild emmer or wild barley cultivation both in the rain-fed belt or – with the help of irrigation – in the drier and warmer places below or beyond the oak-dominated park-forest belt. In the latter, an initial irrigation (in September–October) and one or two subsequent ones produce remarkable stands.

Patterns of domestication: solitary versus multiple events

A problem yet to be solved is how the Near Eastern Neolithic founder crops were domesticated. In other words, was each of these plants taken into cultivation many times and in several locations (the multiple events model) or, alternatively, did domestication consist of solitary or very rare events. The cytogenetic information available from several wild progenitors seems to support the latter proposition.

The first indication comes from wild tetraploid wheats. As already noted, two genetically distinct but morphologically inseparable sibling species occupy sympatrically the northern and eastern segments of the Near Eastern arc (compare Figure 11.3 with Figure 11.4). Both are rather common plants in these areas, yet only the *dicoccoides* AABB genomes are present in the thousands of hulled and naked tetraploid land races of the Old World. AAGG *araraticum* derivatives are absent. The only exception is local *T. timopheevi* in Georgia, which is most likely not an old relic but a more recent, secondary domesticate.

Wild pea and wild lentil provide additional indications. As already stressed, two translocation races occur in wild *Pisum humile* in the Near East, while almost all cultivated varieties of pea are chromosomally uniform and conform with only one of the wild chromosome arrangements. The situation in wild lentil, *Lens orientalis*, is even more clear-cut. The wild stock of this legume contains several translocation races (Ladizinsky *et al.* 1984). In contrast; the cultivated lentil is chromosomally uniform and again conforms to only one of the *orientalis* chromosomal races.

All these cytological observations are compatible with a model of solitary domestication events. They are hard to explain on the basis of multiple, repetitive domestications.

Additional support for this conclusion is provided by those mutations that would have been strongly advantaged (selected for) soon after the wild progenitors were brought into cultivation. The best studied are those causing the breakdown of the wild mode of seed dispersal. In most of the Neolithic founder crops (except barley) this change (from brittle ears or dehiscent pods in the wild progenitors to non-brittle ears or non-dehiscent pods in the cultivated derivatives) was brought about by mutation in a single major gene. Furthermore, as far as we know, the same gene locus determines the change in the various cultivars (only in barley are two genes, bt_1 and bt_2, involved). The evidence for the last statement comes from intervarietal crosses. Breeders have already performed crosses between numerous cultivars in each crop. Except for barley, none of these has been reported to result in brittle or dehiscent first degeneration (F_1) hybrids. Such results (for geneticists they constitute tests for allelism) indicate that within each crop the *same* gene determines the change, at least in all tested cultivars.

Mutations at single loci are compatible both with the model of solitary domestication and with the proposition of multiple events. After all, mutation in any given locus is bound to occur repeatedly, thus setting the stage for either a single domestication event or for repetitive, independent trials. But what is missing in the crops that founded Neolithic agriculture are frequent cases of parallel evolution. In other words, within each of these crops we lack mutations in several independent major genes which (a) each cause more or less the same change, and (b) are each restricted to a limited group of the full spectrum of cultivars. Patterns of parallel evolution are common when similar selection pressures operate in separate populations of the same species. In these Near Eastern crops, the almost total absence of such examples of parallel evolution in key traits, such as the loss of the wild mode of seed dispersal, again favours the proposition of single or very few domestication events in each crop.

Finally, one should note that Pinkas *et al.* (1985) recently reported on allozyme variation in *Lens culinaris* and *L. orientalis*. They interpreted the results they obtained as indicating multiple domestications in lentil. However, it is difficult to accept this interpretation, for the following reasons:

(a) The *L. orientalis* samples tested frequently exhibited considerable intra-population allozyme polymorphism, this in spite of the fact that populations of this wild lentil are usually small and scattered. Therefore, even if lentil domestication happened in a single geographical location, the initial material taken into cultivation could have been variable.

(b) Nine polymorphic gene loci were detected in *L. orientalis*, only six in *L. culinaris*. In other words, three out of the nine polymorphic loci found in the wild progenitor are monomorphic in the cultivars. At these three loci, eight alleles were detected in *L. orientalis*, but only three in *L. culinaris*. This is a substantial drop; the more so because, in these analyses, *L. culinaris* was sampled more extensively than *L. orientalis*.

To conclude, in terms of monophyletic vs. polyphyletic origin, the allozyme data obtained by Pinkas *et al.* (1985) can be argued both ways, and they do not prove or disprove either model. In contrast, chromosome poly-morphism or parallel evolution patterns seem to be much more critical indicators, and these seem to favour a monophyletic origin for each of the crops concerned.

Postscript

Dr C. R. Sperling, US Department of Agriculture, Beltsville, MD, informs me that in 1987 he collected *Cicer reticulatum* west of Hakkâri, in the southeastern corner of Turkey. This find extends (eastward) the known distribution of wild chickpea (Figure 11.7) by some 200 km.

Appendix: note on botanical names of crop plants

According to the rule of botanical nomenclature, once the wild progenitor of a cultivated plant is soundly identified it should not be considered as an independent species but ranked as the *wild race* (subspecies) of the crop. The reason for this is that the wild type and the cultivated derivatives are usually interconnected genetically. As the progenitors of the eight Near Eastern founder crops are now satisfactorily identified (both by morphological com-parisons and by genetic tests), this rule should now be applied. Indeed, crop-plant evolutionists and taxonomists have already placed each wild plant, together with its cultivated derivatives, in a single biological species. Such a collective species is sometimes also referred to as the 'crop complex'. But traditions die hard. Most, archaeobotanists and crop-plant evolutionists

Table 11.1 Southwest Asian crop-plant nomenclature

Common name	Modern taxonomic ranking	Traditional botanical name
Wild emmer	*Triticum turgidum* ssp. *dicoccoides*	*Triticum dicoccoides*
Wild einkorn	*Triticum monococcum* ssp. *boeoticum*	*Triticum boeoticum*
Wild barley	*Hordeum vulgare* ssp. *spontaneum*	*Hordeum spontaneum*
Wild lentil	*Lens culinaris* ssp. *orientalis*	*Lens orientalis*
Wild pea	*Pisum sativum* ssp. *humile* (= *P. sativum* var. *pumilio*)	*Pisum humile*
Wild chickpea	*Cicer arietinum* ssp. *reticulatum*	*Cicer reticulatum*
Wild bitter vetch	*Vicia ervilia* – wild type	Never named as an independent species
Wild flax	*Linum usitatissimum* ssp. *bienne*	*Linum bienne*

still refer to the wild progenitors by their traditional binomials. Thus, to avoid confusion, the traditional names are used in this chapter. With an eye to the future, however, the revised names of the wild progenitors are listed in Table 11.1.

References

Barulina, H.I. (1930) 'Lentils in the USSR and other countries', *Bulletin of Applied Botany, Genetics and Plant Breeding* (Leningrad) Supplement, 40: 1–319.

Ben Ze'ev, N. and Zohary, D. (1973) 'Species relationships in the genus *Pisum* L.', *Israel Journal of Botany*, 22: 73–91.

Bor, N.L. (1968) '*Triticum*', in C. C. Townsend, E. Guest and A. Al-Rawi (eds) *Flora of Iraq*, vol. 9, Baghdad: Ministry of Agriculture.

Dagan, J. and Zohary, D. (1970) 'Wild tetraploid wheat from West Iran cytogenetically identical with Israeli *T. dicoccoides*', *Wheat Information Service* (Kyoto), 31: 15–17.

Gill, K.S. and Yermanos, D.M. (1967) 'Cytogenetic studies on the genus *Linum*. I. Hybrids among taxa with 15 as the haploid chromosome number', *Crop Science*, 7: 627–31.

Harlan, J.R. and Zohary, D. (1966) 'Distribution of wild wheats and barley', *Science*, 153: 1074–80.

Helbaek, H. (1959) 'Domestication of food plants in the Old World', *Science*, 130: 365–72.

Kislev, M.E. (1985) 'Early Neolithic horsebean from Yiftah'el, Israel', *Science*, 228: 319–20.

Körber-Grohne, U. (ed.) (1979) *Festschrift Maria Hopf*, Bonn: Rheinland-Verlag.

Ladizinsky, G. and Adler, A. (1976a) 'The origin of chickpea *Cicer arietinum* L.', *Euphytica*, 25: 211–17.

Ladizinsky, G. and Adler, A. (1976b) 'Genetic relationships among the annual species of *Cicer* L.', *Theoretical and Applied Genetics*, 48: 196–203.

Ladizinsky, G. and van Oss, H. (1984) 'Genetic relationships between wild and cultivated *Vicia ervilia*', *Botanical Journal of the Linnean Society*, 89: 97–100.

Ladizinsky, G., Braun, D., Goshen, D. and Muehlbauer, F.J. (1984) 'The biological species of the genus *Lens* L.', *Botanical Gazette*, 145: 253–61.

Pinkas, R., Zamir, D. and Ladizinsky, G. (1985) 'Allozyme divergence and evolution in the genus *Lens*', *Plant Systematics and Evolution*, 151: 131–40.

Rao, P.S. and Smith, E.L. (1968) 'Studies with Israeli and Turkish accessions of *Triticum turgidum* L. emend. var. *dicoccoides* Korn. Bowden', *Wheat Information Service* (Kyoto), 26: 6–7.

Schultze-Motel, J. (1968–85) Literatur über archäologische Kulturpflanzenreste. For 1965–67: *Kulturpflanze*, 16: 215–30 (1968). For 1968: *Jahresschrift für mitteldeutsche Vorgeschichte*, 55: 55–63 (1971). For 1969: *Kulturpflanze*, 19: 265–82 (1972). For 1970–71: *Kulturpflanze*, 20: 191–207 (1972). For 1971–72: *Kulturpflanze*, 21: 61–76 (1973). For 1972–73: *Kulturpflanze*, 22: 61–76 (1974). For 1973–74: *Kulturpflanze*, 23: 189–205 (1975). For 1974–75: *Kulturpflanze*, 24: 159–78 (1976). For 1975–76: *Kulturpflanze*, 25: 71–88 (1977). For 1976–77: *Kulturpflanze*, 26: 349–62 (1978). For 1977–78: *Kulturpflanze*, 27: 229–45 (1979). For 1978–79: *Kulturpflanze*, 28: 361–78 (1980). For 1979–80: *Kulturpflanze*, 29: 447–63 (1981). For 1980–81: *Kulturpflanze*, 30: 255–72

(1982). For 1981–82: *Kulturpflanze*, 31: 281–97 (1983). For 1982–83: *Kulturpflanze*, 32: 229–43 (1984). For 1983–84: *Kulturpflanze*, 33: 287–305 (1985).

Shao, Q. (1981) 'The evolution of cultivated barley', Proceedings of the 4th Barley Genetics Symposium, Edinburgh, *Barley Genetics*, IV: 22–5.

Tanaka, M. and Ishii, H. (1973) 'Cytogenetic evidence on the speciation of wild tetraploid wheats collected in Iraq, Turkey and Iran', in *Proceedings of the 4th Wheat Genetics Symposium*, Columbia, MO: University of Missouri.

Townsend, C.C. (1974) '*Vicia ervilia*', in C. C. Townsend and E. Guest (eds) *Flora of Iraq*, vol. 3, Baghdad: Ministry of Agriculture.

van Zeist, W. (1976) 'On macroscopic traces of food plants in southwestern Asia (with some references to pollen data)', *Philosophical Transactions of the Royal Society London: Biological Sciences*, 275: 27–41.

van Zeist, W. (1980) 'Aperçu sur la diffusion des végétaux cultivés dans la région Mediterranéen', in L. Emberger (ed.) *Colloque sur la Mise en Place, l'Évolution et la Caractérisation de la Flore et la Végétation Circumméditerranéen*, Montpellier: Special volume of *Naturalia Monspeliensia*.

van Zeist, W. and Bottema, S. (1982) 'Vegetational history of the eastern Mediterranean and the Near East during the last 20,000 years', in J. L. Bintliff and W. van Zeist (eds) *Palaeoenvironments and Human Communities in the Eastern Mediterranean Regions in later Prehistory*, British Archaeological Reports, International Series 133.

van Zeist, W. and Casparie, W.A. (eds) (1984) *Plants and Ancient Man: studies in palaeoethnobotany*, Rotterdam: Balkema.

Witcombe, J.R. (1978) 'Two rowed and six rowed wild barley from the western Himalaya', *Euphytica*, 24: 431–4.

Zohary, D. (1969) 'The progenitors of wheat and barley in relation to domestication and agricultural dispersal in the Old World', in P. J. Ucko and G. W. Dimbleby (eds) *The Domestication and Exploitation of Plants and Animals*, London: Duckworth.

Zohary, D. (1977) 'Comments on the origin of cultivated broad bean, *Vicia faba* L.', *Israel Journal of Botany*, 26: 39–40.

Zohary, D. and Hopf, M. (1973) 'Domestication of pulses in the Old World', *Science*, 182: 887–94.

Zohary, D. and Hopf, M. (1988) *Domestication of Plants in the Old World*, Oxford: Oxford University Press.

Update: The domestication process

Daniel Zohary and Peter White

Part 1

Daniel Zohary

Since the publication of this paper (in 1989), Southwest Asia has been the focus of numerous research projects concerning when, where and how the Neolithic founder crops were domesticated and grain agriculture was initiated in the Near East. The various and complex ways that domestication of these crops could have happened have been intensively explored and evaluated. Verhoeven (2004) provides a comprehensive recent summary of the literature about domestication and the rise of farming in Southwest Asia. Much of what is described in Part 2 of this update derives from his review. Cappers and Bottema (2002) edited a book which provides a wide-ranging set of multi-disciplinary papers and is also highly recommended reading.

In his 1989 paper, Zohary tried to stress the fact that the evidence extracted *from the living plants* (both the crops and the wild progenitors) could be of considerable help to archaeologists in their attempts to reconstruct the rise of farming in Southwest Asia. This update follows these lines. It is concerned mainly with the additional evidence obtained from the living plants.

Wild progenitors and their role

In the 17 years that elapsed since the publication of this paper, the hunt for wild progenitors and study of their reproductive biology and ecological specialisations continued. The wild ancestors of most of the c. 50 main food crops (grains, fruit trees, vegetables, oil plants) indigenous to Southwest Asia and the Mediterranean Basin are now soundly identified. The genetic affinities between the crops and their wild counterparts have been established by crossing experiments, by cytogenetic analysis, and (increasingly) by DNA tests. Consequently, the morphological changes ('domestication traits') that evolved in these wild plants, as a result of their introduction into cultivation, are now much better understood. The role of conscious and unconscious selections in shaping the emerging crops is better appreciated. Also knowledge about the ecology and distribution of the wild progenitors improved considerably. Among the most intensively studied plants were the Neolithic founder crops. For a crop-wise review of the origin of the main Southwest Asian and Mediterranean domesticates and their wild relatives, consult Zohary and Hopf (2000).

The contribution of domestication traits

In plant remains retrieved from archaeological excavations most such indicators do not survive, or alternatively they frequently suffer deformations. Fortunately, in the Neolithic cereals (emmer, einkorn, barley) the shift from shattering ears to non-shattering ones can easily be detected by examination of the disarticulation scars. Hundreds of spikelet forks and thousands of glume bases (extracted by flotation) were retrieved; all show rough, breakage-induced scars (van Zeist and de Roller 2003). This constitutes a most convincing proof (Nesbitt 2002) that in Cayönü, southwest Turkey, wheats had already entered agriculture in early Pre-Pottery Neolithic B (PPNB) (second half of the eleventh millennium cal. BP). As argued by

Nesbitt (2002), these are the oldest *fully convincing* signs of human-dependent domesticated wheats.

The impact of self-pollination

All eight founder crops are predominately self-pollinated; so are their wild progenitors. Compared with cross-pollination, the mating system of self-pollination introduces reproductive isolation between lines, and facilitates speedy domestication.

Monophyletic or polyphyletic origin

Zohary (1996, 1999) suggested that several comparisons of the amount of genetic polymorphism present in crops with that found in the wild progenitors provide effective tools for answering the question: How did the crops originate? Were the wild progenitors taken into cultivation only once and in a single locality (monophyletic origin) or, alternatively, were they introduced into cultivation several times and in different places. The available evidence for emmer wheat, einkorn wheat, lentil, pea and chickpea seems to support a single event. However, recent studies of the domestication process using AFLP data suggest that in wheats and barley this mode of origin is not so certain (Allaby and Brown 2003).

Part 2

Peter White

Writing ten years after this paper, Zohary (1996) points out that the wild progenitors of the eight major founder crops in the Levant (actually western Fertile Crescent) have been genetically identified. Notably, all are self-pollinated annuals, which allows for the rapid development of isolating speciation characters. He suggests that domestication was in each case a single or very small number of events, based on: (a) the fact that genetic polymorphism in cultivars is very low compared to their wild relatives; and (b) domesticates *Pisum*, *Lens* and *Cicer*, as well as tetraploid and diploid wheats, have several closely related wild relatives which could have been domesticated but were not. He suggests domestication of different species occurred in somewhat different areas within the Levant. However, recent simulation studies of the genetics of the domestication process suggest that a monophyletic origin of wheats and barley is not so certain (Allaby and Brown 2003).

Since 1989, southwest Asia has been the focus of many research projects concerned with the various ways in which the 'domestication' package may have been assembled. Note that most of the discussion about domestication is focused on seed crops, which preserve well and are amenable to macroscopic examination.

The period between 14,500 and 9000 cal. BP, at the end of the last glacial cycle, was one of increasing warmth and wetness interrupted by a harsh cold, dry spell (Younger Dryas) around 12,000–11,500 cal. BP. This lengthy period saw the human use of plants which, by its end, became visibly domesticated in terms of morphological criteria. Verhoeven (2004: Table II) lists 16 domestication 'models', divided into environmental, social or anthropological, and cognitive approaches, each giving different emphases to the questions when, where, how and why domestication occurred. Major differences between these models include the supposed importance of climate change, changing seasonality, population growth/pressure, 'cultural readiness', socioeconomic competition, intentionality, and a revolution in human use of symbols. Different models also imply difference in the speeds with which changes in human–plant relationships and the morphology of crops occurred, but not all of these would have become immediately visible in the archaeological record. Verhoeven's position on the domestication process is holistic, in that he believes it was a long-term, multi-dimensional and multi-relational phenomenon. Researchers during the last decade have increasingly embraced this viewpoint, which implies, for instance, that climatic shifts such as the Younger Dryas may have been important in changing the scale and pace of the process but were not wholly responsible for it.

The actual archaeological record is now briefly summarised, since this is important to understanding Zohary's paper. In the late glacial period (23,000–14,800 cal. BP), the waterlogged site of Ohalo II (Sea of Galilee) has yielded many wild plant remains, including barley, emmer wheat and medicinal plants. Starch granules on a large slab show grinding of barley occurred (Piperno *et al.* 2004). The Natufian culture (15,000–11,700 cal. BP), which is found over the entire Levant, commonly produced pounding and grinding tools, storage pits and bins at large sites, use of a broad spectrum of wild plants and, at a few sites such as Abu Hureyra (Moore *et al.* 2000), probable cultivation of grains and lentils. There is no evidence for domestic plants. In some areas the Late Natufian, roughly contemporaneous with the Younger Dryas, returned to more mobile lifeways. In the subsequent period, covering the next 1000 years, domesticated grains may have been present, but this is much disputed, since the claims are based on small numbers of specimens some of which have problematic stratigraphy. However, plants were almost certainly being cultivated, as evidenced by weeds typical of domestic grains, sickle blades, site locations with good soil near good water sources, and many storage units. Some researchers suggest that other indications such as the large tower and accompanying wall at Jericho could not have been built without the resources of cultivated and domestic crops, but these are not clearly identifiable there. Much more certain evidence, in the form of large quantities of charred grains and chaff of plants with clearly 'domestic' morphological characteristics such as tough rachis, are found in the subsequent Pre-Pottery Neolithic B period, from 10,700 cal. BP. Sites with such evidence are found from the southern Levant to southeast Anatolia and northern Iraq, i.e. a large part of the traditional 'Fertile Crescent'.

It is important to note that the implication of these sites, from at least Ohalo II (c. 22,000 cal. BP), is that people were at least semi-sedentary. This implies that the changes we see in subsistence practices have a long lead time. Thus, however rapid the morphological changes in crops, these were built on long-term understandings of plant behaviour, along with experience, and experiments with processing and storage.

References

Allaby, R.G. and Brown T.A. (2003) 'AFLP data and the origins of domesticated crops', *Genome*, 46: 448–53.

Cappers, R.T.J. and Bottema, S. (eds) (2002) *The Dawn of Farming in the Near East*, Berlin: ex oriente.

Moore, A.M.T., Hillman, G.C. and Legge, A.J. (eds) (2000) *Village on the Euphrates*, Oxford: Oxford University Press.

Nesbitt, M. (2002) 'When and where did domesticated cereals first occur in southwest Asia?' in R. T. J. Cappers and S. Bottema (eds) *The Dawn of Farming in the Near East*, Berlin: ex oriente.

Piperno, D.R., Weiss, E., Holst, I. and Nadel, D. (2004) 'Processing of wild cereal grains in the Upper Palaeolithic revealed by starch grain analysis', *Nature*, 430: 670–3.

van Zeist, W. and de Roller G.J. (2003) 'The Çayönü archaeobotanical record', in W. van Zeist (ed.) *Reports on Archaeobotanical Studies in the Old World*, Groningen, The Netherlands: Biologisch-Archaeologisch Instituut, University of Groningen.

Verhoeven, M. (2004) 'Beyond boundaries: nature, culture and a holistic approach to domestication in the Levant', *Journal of World Prehistory*, 18: 179–282.

Zohary, D. (1996) 'The mode of domestication of the founder crops of Southwest Asian agriculture', in D. R. Harris (ed.) *The Origins and Spread of Agriculture and Pastoralism in Eurasia*, London: UCL Press.

Zohary, D. (1999) 'Monophyletic vs. polyphyletic origin of the crops on which agriculture was founded in the Near East', *Genetic Resources and Crop Evolution*, 4: 133–42.

Zohary, D. and Hopf, M. (2000) *Domestication of Plants in the Old World*, 3rd edn, Oxford: Oxford University Press.

12 Agrarian change and the beginnings of cultivation in the Near East

Evidence from wild progenitors, experimental cultivation and archaeobotanical data

George Willcox

Introduction

This chapter examines the change in the subsistence system in the Near East from a gathering economy to one of production (the beginnings of cereal and pulse cultivation), in the light of observations made during the experimental cultivation of primitive cereals at Jalès (France), together with field observations of wild cereals in their natural habitat at a number of stations in Syria. These observations are compared to recent archaeobotanical data.

Since the publications by Kislev on the difficulties of distinguishing wild and domestic emmer wheats (1989: 148, 1992), Hillman and Davies's (1990) publication on rates of domestication and Baruch and Bottema's (1991) work on climatic change, which Moore and Hillman (1992) suggest might be a contributing factor in the emergence of cereal cultivation, a number of new sites have been published and others are in the process of being analysed. Sites with well-preserved plant remains from the crucial period between 10,500 and 9000 BP are rare and frequently this period is represented only at the base of tells where extensive sampling has not been possible (Cayönü, Aswad and Cafer Höyük). Sites (see Figure 12.1) such as Cafer Höyük (de Moulins 1997) and Cayönü (van Zeist and de Roller 1994) have recently been published, and others such as Jerf el Ahmar, Dja'de (Willcox 1996), Nevali Cori (Pasternak 1995), Qermez Dere, M'lefaat, Hallan Cemi, and Nemrik (Nesbitt 1995) are now being analysed. In addition new evidence is coming to light on the distributions of wild cereals in Syria.

Experimental results from the cultivation of wild einkorn indicate that selective pressures in favour of domestic traits, such as the solid rachis, can be variable depending on harvesting techniques, and may be low (Hillman and Davies 1990; Willcox 1995). This is in contrast to the more conventional view that domestic traits were promptly selected for (Zohary 1992, 1996) once the progenitor was brought into cultivation. Low selective pressures could explain recent archaeobotanical finds which indicate that

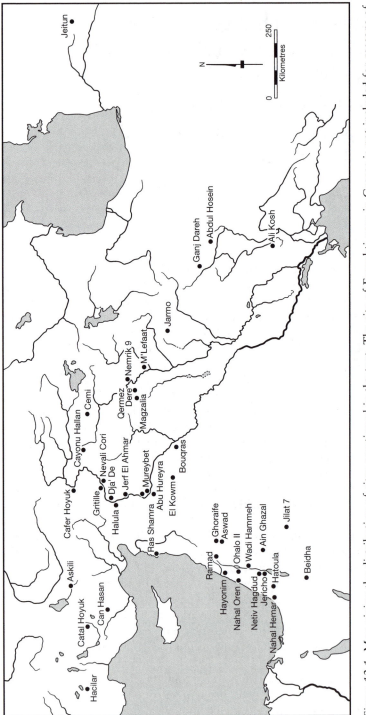

Figure 12.1 Map giving the distribution of sites mentioned in the text. The site of Franchti cave in Greece is not included for reasons of scale.

domestic and wild cereals occurred as mixtures on several early Neolithic sites over a period of at least a millennium. Archaeobotanical finds and field studies confirm that late Epipalaeolithic and early Neolithic distributions of wild cereals were more extensive (Hillman 1996) and environmental differences (soil types and humidity) between sites are reflected in the cereal assemblages at, and perhaps just after, the gathering stage (barley on poor dry soils for example). But once cultivation began, favourable soils would be chosen as would preferred crops. For example, emmer becomes more widespread at the expense of einkorn.

It is argued here that subsistence change in the Near East was a gradual process, proceeding over millennia rather than centuries, and that the adoption of cultivation required little innovation because, on the one hand, the 'tool kit' already existed and, on the other, the natural life cycle of the plants concerned had been exploited for some considerable time. After a period of small-scale cultivation an organized production economy was established, crops would have evolved more rapidly, and village size could increase and societies develop in new ways.

Present-day wild cereals

The evolutionary paths which led to present-day wild and domestic cereals are not fully understood. For example, we do not know when sterility barriers developed between *Triticum urartu* and *T. boeoticum*. Both species are present in the Levant today but we cannot tell how these compare genetically to the wild einkorn identified at sites such as Mureybet (van Zeist and Bakker-Heeres 1984a) and Abu Hureyra (Hillman *et al.* 1989). Even the BB genome donor is disputed (Konarev and Konarev 1993). Cytogenetic studies of modern populations are still providing new evidence for the early evolution of domesticates. A major limiting factor in the study of early crop evolution is the fact that we cannot know the cytogenetic relationships of ancient populations, particularly given the possibility of rapid evolution under domestication which may have led to a large number of extinctions of ancient domestic varieties. In addition, genetic exchange between different wild populations will have occurred over the last 10,000 years.

The distribution of wild cereals is well known in Turkey and Iraq (Bor 1968; Davies 1985), but has been somewhat neglected for Syria where primary stands of all four wild wheats are more widespread than has been previously suspected (Valkoun 1992; pers. comm., author's field studies in 1995). These populations, which are being studied by members of ICARDA (International Centre for Agricultural Research in Dry Areas, Aleppo), show high diversity and it is probable that genetic exchange between these closely related taxa occurs, despite the fact that they are predominantly inbreeders. *T. urartu* (AA donor for the tetraploid wheats) and *T. boeoticum* appear to be relatively common in areas with 300 mm of rain per annum but can occur occasionally in areas with as little as 250 mm. A number of recent discoveries have been made by Valkoun (1992) of ICARDA, and his results will be published in detail at a later date.

In northern Syria the present author collected *T. urartu* and *T. boeoticum* in the north-western part of the Jeseri at several stations near Ain al Arab. Mouterde (1966: 143) reports that he found wild einkorn on the Jebel Aziz (*Triticum thaoudar* Reut.). West of Aleppo several populations, which include *T. urartu*, *T. dicoccoides*, *T. boeoticum* and *T. araraticum*, have been found. A population of *T. urartu* was located north of Homs by Valkoun (pers. comms.). In the south, on the Jebel Druze, which is a basaltic massif rising to 1800 m, one can find vast stands of *T. urartu*, *T. dicoccoides* and *T. boeoticum* in their primary habitat. Finally, Valkoun (pers. comms.) reports that he has found a population of *T. urartu* as far south as Beida in southern Jordan. All these populations appear to be restricted to deep, rich, decalcified soils, such as *terra rossa* formed on limestone, or soils derived from basalt. But in higher rainfall areas they may occur on poorer soils. Wild wheats in Syria occur in open habitats, beyond the eastern margins of the Mediterranean vegetation zone, where they colonize open habitats with a continental climate. The four wild wheats found in Syria appear to occur in similar ecological zones; at certain locations they may occur as mixed populations, or in other cases will form pure stands. In either case they frequently grow with *Aegilops* spp. such as *A. speltoides*, *A. searsi*, *A. crassa* and *A. tauschii*, and form what might be described as a rich prairie habitat. In Syria wild einkorn penetrates the steppe habitat, whereas further north in Turkey it occupies the open deciduous oak parkland, described by Zohary (Zohary and Hopf 1988: 32) as the typical habitat for wild einkorn. This latter habitat does not exist in Syria today, but it is possible that this association was more widespread in the past and recent studies have indicated that deciduous oak charcoal is present on sites in Syria – not just from the Neolithic but also from the Bronze Age and later periods (Willcox 1991a, 1995, 1996). In southern Syria deciduous oak forests have been progressively replaced by evergreen oak forests (Willcox 1999) since the Bronze Age.

How far do the present-day distribution and ecology relate to the early Neolithic period? It is clear that today the wild wheats are restricted to favourable soil types. In addition, wild wheat populations appear to be very susceptible to grazing and occur only in areas where grazing is restricted. Thus what is seen today is likely to be a much-reduced distribution; with less human pressure and perhaps a more favourable climate, wild wheats may have covered a much wider zone during the Epipalaeolithic and Neolithic periods. This is indeed confirmed by the archaeobotanical finds from what is today arid steppe in that part of northern Syria which flanks the Euphrates (see also Hillman 1996 for a reinterpretation of post-glacial forest-steppe colonization).

The fact that these closely related species of wild wheat are found together has led to high genetic variability, although this may not be identifiable archaeobotanically. However, regional differences between populations of wild cereals, where different species (barley, einkorn, emmer and rye) are dominant, should show up archaeobotanically at the collecting stage during the Epipalaeolithic; but once cultivation and domestication began one might expect specialization and selection at the species level and ultimately the development of a weed flora. This would result in more uniform assemblages on a regional scale.

Experimental cultivation results and selective tendencies

In 1985, following discussions between G. Hillman, P. Anderson, J. Cauvin and the present author, it was decided to set up experiments using primitive wheats, and in particular wild einkorn, in order to test their behaviour under cultivation. An important aspect was the recording of spikelet loss under different harvesting techniques in order to estimate selection pressures and the rapidity of the domestication process. Hillman and Davies in their article (1990) discuss a wide range of possibilities for pre-domestic agriculture using a mathematical model. It emerges that spikelet loss during harvesting is one of the crucial elements which influence selective pressures and affect rates of domestication. Thus in 1989 a large-scale experiment was set up to test this aspect of the model. The reader is referred to the original article by Hillman and Davies, which discusses in detail the different variables concerned, a wide range of scenarios and the mathematical model used to calculate the experimental results given here.

The principal population of *Triticum boeoticum* was collected in 1986 in eastern Anatolia near Karaçadag, between Diyarbakir and Siverek, at an altitude of approximately 800 m above sea level, in a region where there is an annual rainfall of approximately 600 mm. This wild population prospers under the climatic and edaphic conditions at Jalès, which is situated at the extreme southern limit of the Ardèche in southern France. The difference in altitude (Jalès 130 m above sea level) appears to be compensated for by the difference in latitude (5.5°) between the two locations.

The wild population that was collected in its natural habitat showed a high diversity in, for example, gliadin analyses, and in morphological features such as glume colouring and hairiness. This original population contained low frequencies of wild emmer and *Aegilops speltoides*; the latter remained in the population for several years while the former died out after two generations.

In addition a number of other populations of both wild and domestic cereals were cultivated. The populations which were obtained from plant breeders were single-line, true-breeding populations, and are therefore less representative of early farming practices.

Before discussing the principal experiment, set up in 1989 to examine selection rates, it is necessary to present the techniques used and some relevant results obtained during the first years (between 1986 and 1989). Additional results can be found elsewhere (Willcox 1991b, 1992).

Sowing

In their natural habitat wild cereals sow themselves immediately after ripening. Thus the time of sowing is dependent on the altitude and latitude of any particular ecotype in question. The timing of natural dispersion will therefore vary from May to August, depending on the relative ripening times in different geographical areas. The advantage of early sowing for the farmer is that there is less chance of loss from vermin during storage (our samples were attacked by weevils), and the young plants get a better start and give good tillering.

Vernalization is the major factor controlling whether barley and wheat are spring or autumn sown. All wheats and barleys can be planted in the winter, but only those which lack the need for vernalization may be planted in the spring. Wild cereals exhibit varying degrees of vernalization requirement (Mathon 1985). In 1987/8 we planted *T. boeoticum aegilopoides* in both winter and spring. The spring-sown crop exhibited poor tillering. The emmer crop when spring-planted gives a highly diminished yield. We conclude that in a Mediterranean climate primitive cereals would have been predominantly winter-sown. Thus it would appear that by following the natural life-cycle the best results are obtained, though of course this could result in diminishing selective pressure.

Seed was broadcast by hand at high density in its hulled condition, that is to say the equivalent of about 140 kilos per hectare once the weight of the chaff is removed. We do not know how the earliest farmers sowed, although we do know that by the beginning of the third millennium in Mesopotamia, cereals were sown in carefully spaced rows using a seed-drill (Postgate 1984: 102).

Dormancy/inhibition of germination

Germination tests were carried out by the local agricultural college at Aubenas on samples of our seed grain under laboratory conditions. Observations on 100 grains were made at seven and fourteen days; the grains were kept humid at a temperature of 18 °C. Table 12.1 gives the results of germination tests from 7–21 October 1987.

The results from the germination tests indicate that:

1   In the case of wild einkorn, a crop harvested before maturity, still green, gives viable seed for planting the following autumn;
2   The glumes in the twinned-grained einkorns tend to inhibit the germination of the 'second grain' over a fourteen-day period and there was no twinned germination in sample number 122;
3   Wild emmer and wild barley gave poor results, perhaps because of strong germination inhibitors;
4   Sample number 77 appears to lack the dormancy factor when harvested ripe. This sample, which appears to be a single-line (true-breeding) population, also tends to have a more solid rachis.

Table 12.1 Results of germination tests carried out over a fourteen-day period. Tests were made at varying degrees of ripeness to test the viability of harvests carried out before maturity. It is clear that naked caryops gave good germination rates, while in the hulled state the glumes inhibited germination and in all but one sample only one grain germinated.

Species	Ref no.	Naked grain %	Hulled %	Double %	Comment
T. monococcum	12	92	80	0	
T. dicoccoides	18	56	17.5	0	Only 40 spikelets
T. b. thaoudar	122	82	80	0	Green
"	62	42	0	0	Half green (mouldy)
"	92	90	0	0	Ripe
"	77	94	94	0	Green
"	98	96	18	0	Half green
"	92	84	46	0	Ripe
"	38	92	98	16	Green
"	100	95	10	0	Half green
"	100	100	20	0	Ripe
T. urartu	59	82	94	6	Ripe
T. compactum	13	90	–	–	Free threshing
H. spontaneum	33	97.5	58	–	Ripe
"	52	54	–	–	Green

Dormancy was shown to exist in the laboratory experiments but these tests were only carried out over a fourteen-day period. Thus it was necessary to test whether dormant grains could germinate in the field and provide a harvest the following year. In 1989/90 we harvested a plot of wild einkorn before the grains were formed to eliminate self-seeding. The following two years saw no new germination. Thus the dormancy period under the conditions at Jalès was less than a year. However, under drier conditions germination may be inhibited for longer periods.

Uneven ripening and the brittle rachis

Wild cereals exhibit uneven ripening between different plants. In the case of wild einkorn grown at Jalès, at least a month may elapse between the earliest and the latest maturation in the same field. Uneven ripening also occurs between spikelets on the same ear, which mature progressively, with the uppermost spikelets ripening first. Primitive domestic cereals such as spelt, emmer and einkorn retained this trait, which indicates that it was not selected against during the early stages of domestication.

If the fallen grain survives to be harvested with part of the crop kept back for sowing the fragile rachis continues to be selected for in the population. The germination tests given above show that a premature harvest before ripening produces viable grain, but because of uneven ripening a small proportion of ripe grain will in fact fall (see Table 12.2). If this self-sown seed

Table 12.2 Results obtained from experimental cultivation of wild einkorn as part of a CNRS project. The experiments were devised to test rates of spikelet loss under different harvesting conditions. Initially, rates were put forward in predominantly model form by Hillman and Davies (1990), but see also Willcox (1991a, 1992). Spikelet loss was measured using two variables, maturity measured by the humidity and harvesting technique (column two). Selection coefficients (using Hillman and Davies' calculation) based on losses during the first year's harvest indicate that domestication would proceed. But if we take into account the quantity harvested in 1991 from spontaneously sown plants, this would seriously reduce selection coefficients.

Plot	Methods	m^2	Date	1989	Hum. (%)	1990	l/m^2	l (%)	s/c	1991	S (%)	1992	SI (%)	1993
A	Shaking	12.5	26.6	0.65	10.36	0.169	0.242	94.5				1.76		0.34*
B	Sickle	25	19.6	1.2		5.5	0.027	10.93	0.114	2.05	37.27	1.55	75.6	
C	Hand	25	21.6	1.2	31.16	1.55	0.088	58.6		2.3	148.38	1.49	64.7	
D	Sickle	12.5	12.6	0.65	50.86	3.3	0.015	5.36	0.106	2.06	31.21†	1.01	49	
d	Sickle	12.5	29.5	0.65	57.40‡									
E	Sickle	25	12.6	1.2	52.68‡	7.5	0.018	5.6	0.105	1.56	20.8			
F	Hand	25	13.6	1.2	53.00‡	5.5	0.057	20.57	0.134	2.25	40.9			
G	Uprooting	12.5	14.6	0.65	49.81	2.55	0.020	8.92	0.110	1.04	18.57†			
g	Uprooting	12.5	19.6	0.65		3.35	0.022	7.58	0.112					
H	Sickle	12.5	13.6	0.65	47.50	2.25	0.018	9.09	0.111	1.97	51.16†			
h	Sickle	12.5	21.6	0.65		1.6	0.031	19.47	0.130					
Poc	Sickle	15	11.6			3	0.011	5.21						
Lf	Sickle	91	21.6		33.59	14.8	0.093	36.8						

Key
1989   = weight sown 1989
Hum. % = percentage of humidity at harvest time
1990   = weight harvested 1990
l/m^2 = loss per square metre
m^2 = area planted in square metres
l (%)   = percentage lost (i.e. fallen after harvest)
s/c   = selection coefficient after Hillman's model <0.1 no domestication
1991   = weight harvested in 1991
S (%)   = percentage of 1991 zero planting harvest compared to the 1990 harvest
1992   = weight of 1992 harvest with no planting
SI (%) = percentage of 1992 zero planting harvest compared to the 1991 harvest
1993   = average of all plots compared for 1993 harvest weight in kilos of hulled grain

Notes
* combined result; † two half plots combined; ‡ estimation.

is harvested then selective pressures in favour of uniform ripening and against uneven ripening would have been minimal.

Self-seeding and its effect on domestication

The domestication experiment was set up in 1989 and continued until 1993. Eight plots, A to H, each measuring 5 × 5 metres, were planted in August with 1.2 kilos of third-generation hulled wild einkorn. The quantity sown may seem high but it must be remembered that the chaff fraction represents well over half of the total weight. The first harvest took place during the last two weeks of June. Two variables were tested: method of reaping (shaking, sickle, hand picking and uprooting) and the degree of maturity, which was measured by the level of humidity. The results, are given in Table 12.2. The main aim of these experiments was to test grain loss through self-seeding under differing conditions and to estimate its effect on the domestication process.

It was found that the combined traits of uneven ripening and brittle rachis resulted in a certain amount of grain falling during harvest regardless of the technique (see Table 12.2). This occurred particularly during the harvest of the last plots, which were riper than those harvested earlier. In theory, loss through fallen spikelets during the harvest results in an increase in selective pressure in favour of solid-rachised domestic plants. Loss was measured by collecting fallen spikelets from a randomly chosen square metre for each twenty-five-metre square. As can be seen, loss is highly variable depending on the conditions of harvesting.

The plots were left fallow and the following year, 1990, a second harvest was obtained and the effects of spontaneous sowing were measured. Harvests were continued through to 1993 by which time competition, essentially from perennial grasses, seriously reduced the yield. As can be seen in Table 12.2, the first year of grow-back in 1991 represents a reasonable harvest. On the one hand, if early farmers opened up new fields, they could hardly ignore the spontaneously sown fallow fields; on the other, if they worked and replanted the same fields, the effects of even short-term dormancy would mean that a reasonable proportion of viable spikelets would in fact survive. Given the results obtained it would appear reasonable to assume that harvests could have contained 25 per cent of self-seeded plants. This 25 per cent could come from continuously cultivated fields, or from fallow fields.

This estimate does not include any spikelets which may have been harvested from natural stands, which is probable during the transition period, because the annual rainfall may not have been reliable. Under the present-day climate the rainfall for the Near East is irregular, particularly in the Euphrates valley, and years with low rainfall are frequent (Traboulsi 1981; Kerbe 1987). This may well have been the case 10,000 years ago. Thus, in poor years, whether due to such climatic abnormalities, disease or social upheaval, gathering from the wild could have supplemented the cultivated harvests. If the gathered cereal became mixed with the seed grain it would have slowed down the rate of domestication. Keeping morphologically identical populations apart would have been difficult. Thus there are at least three factors which would slow selection rates and the process of domestication: (1) supplementary gathering, (2) spontaneous sowing under cultivation, and (3) introgression (Zohary 1969).

We observed the presence of accidentally self-seeded cereals occurring in and around threshing areas at Jalès. This phenomenon must also have occurred during the gathering stage millennia before domestication, when cereals or legumes were displaced for processing, storage or consumption; such unintentional cultivation could have led to the extension of natural stands during the gathering stage.

Problems of identifying morphological domestication

Observations of a wide range of material reveal certain problems when identifying archaeobotanical remains. While it is well known that distortion by carbonization can lead to overlap between einkorn and emmer (this we have confirmed by experimentation), it is less well known that the proportion of single-grained spikelets in twinned-grained einkorn and emmer is extremely variable. This can lead to confusion. In one modern sample of *T. boeoticum thaoudar*, single-grained spikelets considerably out-numbered double-grained ones (Table 12.3). The reduction in number of grains appears to be related to stress caused, for example, by high sowing density or drought. These observations indicate that domestication criteria based on grain morphology alone could be misleading, particularly if based on a limited number of grains.

Table 12.3 The ratio of single- to double-grained spikelets in three wheat species. The variability appears to correlate with varying environmental conditions.

		Double:single
T. b. thaoudar	1987	2.6:1
	1988	3.6:1
	1991 d	1:5.3
	g	1.7:1
	c	1.9:1
T. urartu	1988	1:1
	1987	4.5:1
T. b. aegilopoides	1988	0:1
T. dicoccum	1993	1.2:1

The abscission layer which is formed well before maturity causes the spikelets to dehisce on drying, even when harvested green. The early harvest does not affect the mechanism, which causes the rachis to break up. However, as pointed out by Hillman (1981) and Kislev (1992) and confirmed among our populations, about 10 per cent of wild barley rachis fragments show solid domestic-type fused basal internodes. Thus, 10 per cent or less of domestic types is not necessarily indicative of domestication. If harvesting occurred late, with many of the upper spikelets already fallen, the percentage could be higher.

The distinction between domestic and wild wheats is based on the disarticulation scar. The break occurs in the same place, and in modern material one is rough and the other smooth. However, in ancient carbonized remains the surface is very often too poorly preserved to allow this distinction. The semi-solid rachis in barley has not been recognized archaeologically; however, although not generally known, varieties do exist. The author has collected specimens of semi-solid rachis, two-rowed 'black' barley near Bosra in southern Syria. The disarticulation scar is similar to that of the wild barleys.

Yield

The relevance of crop yield in cultivation (i.e. harvest weight compared to planted area) is likely to have been of limited interest to early farmers, who would have been more concerned with the return from a given amount of grain seed regardless of the planted area (yield ratio). Constant return, despite natural environmental fluctuations, would also have been favoured. Results obtained at Jalès are given by Willcox (1992: 176). Wild einkorn gave variable results in 1986; for example, a plot of 130 square metres gave a yield equivalent to 500 kg per hectare including chaff, but the ratio of harvest to seed corn was 8.6:1. In 1989, 1.2 kg was sown for 25 square metres which in the best plot gave 7.5 kg, which is the equivalent of 3000 kg per hectare but only 6.25:1 for the harvest/seed ratio. According to our cultivation results and results obtained in the field, wild einkorn can give between 0.5 and 1.5 tons of threshed grain per hectare. To take the totally hypothetical example of 200 grams of grain per day per person (72 kilos per annum), one hectare would supply enough grain for 7–21 people. Unfortunately it is not possible to estimate the population of early Neolithic village sites. But one might speculate that a small farming community of fifty people would need between 2.5 and 7 hectares for their cereals.

Conclusions based on experimental data

Traits such as dormancy and uneven ripening are not as disadvantageous as expected when cultivating wild cereals (Zohary 1996). Losses due to spikelets falling before and during the harvest are unavoidable, but these lead to germination and greatly reduce the chances of a mutant solid rachised type being kept back for sowing and increase its chances of ending up on the dinner table, thus diluting selective pressures in favour of a solid ear. In addition, early farmers may have encouraged a system where minimal seed corn gave a maximum return, which would also lead to a higher proportion of lost mutants on the dinner table. In this respect our estimates for the proportion of grain held back for sowing may be too high.

During the initial stages of cultivation, one might expect field size to be relatively small, with a high risk of contact with wild populations at the periphery leading to introgression. In order for selection rates to be high enough to favour a solid rachis population, wild and cultivated populations would have to be separated. In reality this would prove difficult, given the spontaneous germination of fallen spikelets and the probability that gathering from wild populations would be needed in poor years to supplement harvests from cultivated fields which had failed.

The results thus indicate that selective pressures in favour of domestication vary according to the proportions of self-seeded (including wild seed grain) and harvested seed grain from deliberately sown plots. It is clear that once the level of wild seed dropped below 15 or 10 per cent, domestication would advance relatively quickly (Hillman and Davies 1990). For this to occur communities would have to be almost totally reliant on sown crops and have a well-organized farming system; if not, selective tendencies would be too low and cultivation might continue indefinitely without domestication taking place.

Archaeobotanical results compared to observations based on present-day populations

A summary of archaeobotanical results is given in Table 12.4 (on pages 230–231). The earliest evidence for cereal exploitation dates from 19,000 BP at Ohalo II near the sea of Galilee, where wild barley and emmer were recovered (Kislev *et al.* 1992). For the later Epipalaeolithic period (12,000–10,000 BP), there is more information. Small village sites such as Mureybet and Abu Hureyra on the Euphrates in Syria, Hayonim in Israel, Wadi Hammeh in Jordan, Franchthi cave in Greece and Qermez Dere, Nemrik 9 and M'lefaat in northern Iraq indicate that wild cereals were exploited together with a number of edible fruits and pulses. Indirect evidence from glossed tools indicates that plants with high silica contents were harvested at the Epipalaeolithic sites of Nahal Oren, Hatula, and Kebara in Israel, and Beidha in Jordan where plant remains were not recovered (Anderson 1994: 292, and pers. comm.). It is clear that morphologically wild progenitors of Old World cereals and legumes were exploited for several millennia before the appearance of their domestic counterparts. The geographical extent is impressive, stretching from northern Iraq to the southern Levant, and perhaps Western Anatolia, since we have the site of Franchthi in Greece. As was expected from observations of modern distributions, strong regional differences can be seen between Epipalaeolithic sites. Einkorn is dominant at Mureybet and Abu Hureyra (which also has wild oats, rare elsewhere); barley and some emmer are present at Ohalo II. Rye is also present at a number of these sites (Hillman *et al.* 1993).

The Pre-Pottery Neolithic A (PPNA: 10,000–9600 BP) sites are less frequent but the architecture of small round houses is more substantial. No unequivocal morphological evidence for domestication at sites such as Mureybet, Jerf el Ahmar and Netiv Hagdud is forthcoming. For the very earliest levels at Aswad IA and Jericho, remains are numerically too meagre to be certain of domestication, but what is clear for this period is that the plant/crop assemblages vary remarkably between sites. Emmer is dominant at Aswad (van Zeist and Bakker-Heeres 1984b), einkorn at Mureybet and barley at Jerf el Ahmar in northern Syria (Table 12.5). This suggests that the inhabitants of these sites were still gathering local cereals, but this does not exclude small-scale cultivation as described by Harris (1996: 553) using locally available wild cereals as seed stock. Lentils are common on most sites even in the most arid zones.

During the next chronological period (Early PPNB: 9600–9000 BP) architecture is distinctly rectangular. Emmer domestication has been reported for sites such as Cafer Hüyök and Cayönü in eastern Anatolia and for Aswad near Damascus (however, some researchers prefer to rely on the solid rachis in barley and the naked wheats as sure evidence for domestication, especially when sample size is small). At Aswad, between 9730 and 8560 BP (PPNA and early PPNB), 26 per cent of the barley rachis fragments are solid domestic types, but it is not clear if they occur in the earliest levels. At Dja'de (Willcox 1996) preliminary studies indicate that the cereals are not yet domesticated, but indirect evidence of weed associations strongly suggests the presence of cultivation and similar assemblages are seen at Aswad, Cayönü and Cafer Hüyök.

The Middle PPNB (9200–8600 BP) sites are more extensive, more frequent and cover a wider geographical area comprising central Anatolia (Asikli Höyük) and Cyprus (Shillourokambos). Crop evolution and morphological domestication are clearly shown by the appearance of a solid rachis in barley and naked wheat – for example, at Aswad West phase II (van Zeist and Bakker-Heeres 1984b) and at Halula (Willcox 1995, 1996). For the first time there is evidence for the introduction of crop plants into new areas. Domestic emmer was introduced to the middle Euphrates at Abu Hureyra and Halula. But wild types remain at significant frequencies, which are evidenced at Cayönü, Cafer Höyük (wild wheats), Aswad, Ganj Dareh (wild barley), Halula (wild wheats and barley) and also in the Azraq basin (Colledge 1994). These mixed finds could be interpreted in three ways: (1) as evidence of the exploitation of wild stands, (2) as unwanted weeds, and (3) as an integral part of the crop consisting of a mixture of wild and domestic cereals. The relatively high proportion of wild types and the lack of pure finds of domesticates suggest that the wild plants may have been considered as a

Table 12.4 The major cereals, pulses and tree species from sites in the eastern Mediterranean (adapted from Nesbitt and Samuel 1996). There is considerable chronological overlap between sites, particularly for the

Site	Phase	Date BP non cal.	*einkorn* w	*emmer* w	*barley* w	*einkorn* d	*emmer* d	*naked wheat* d	*barley 2r* d
Ohalo II		19,000			O	O			
Franchthi		12,400–9000				O			
Hayonim		12,300–11,900				O			
Wadi Hammeh 27		12,200–11,900				O			
Abu Hureyra		11,000–10,000	O			O			
Hallan Cemi		10,600–9900							
Mureybet I	I–III	10,200–9500	O			O			
Qermez Dere		10,100–9700				O			
Netiv Hagdud		10,000–9400			O	O			
Jerf el Ahmar		9800–9700	O			O			
M'lefaat		9800–9600	?			O			
Tell Aswad	Ia	9700–9600				O	?		?
Dj'ade		9600–9000	O			O	?		
Çayönü rh		9500–9200	?	?					
Jericho	PPNA	9500–9000			?	?	?		?
Mureybet	IV	9400–8500	O			O			
Cafer Höyük	XIII–X	9400–9000	O	O		O	O		
Tell Aswad	Ib	9300–8800				O	O		?
Çayönü	gp bp c	9200–8500	O	O	?	O	O		?
Nevali Cori		9200				O	O		
Ain Ghazal		9000–8500					O		O
Jericho	PPNB	9000–8500				O	O	O	O
Cafer Höyük	IX–VI	9000–8400	O			O	O		
Nahal Hemar		9000–8200					O		O
Bheida		8900–8700				O	O		?
Ganj Dareh		8900–8200			O				O
Ali Kosh	BM	8800–8000	O		O	O	O		O
Jilat 7		8800–8400	O		O	O	O		
Asikli Höyük		8800–8400	O			?	O	O	O
Abu Hureyra PPNB		8800–8000	O		O	O	O	O	O
Tell Aswad	II	8700–8400	O		O	O	O	O	O
Ghoraifé	I	8700–8100				O	O	O	O
Abdul Hosein		8700–7500					O		O
Halula		8700	?	O	O		O	O	O
Magzalia		8600–7800				O	O	O	O
Gritille		8500–7700					O		O
Can Hassan III		8500–7600	O	O		O	O	O	O
Jarmo		8500	O	O	O	O	O		O

Key
w = wild
d = domestic
? = wild and/or domestic

later periods. Note that lentils are very frequent; however, domestication appears over a wide area during the last half of the tenth millennium BP. Lentils are common on most sites. Oak is also well represented.

barley 6r	aegilops	lentil	pea	bitter vetch	oak	almond	pistacia	flax	Reference
d	w	?	?	?	w	w	w	?	Reference
		O			A	O	O		Kislev *et al.* 1992
		O	O	O		O	O		Hansen 1991
		O		O					Hopf and Bar Yosef 1987
		O			W		O		Willcox 1991a; Colledge 1994
		O		O	W	W	O		Hillman *et al.* 1989
		O		O		O	O		Rosenberg *et al.* 1995
		O			W		O		van Zeist and Bakker-Heeres 1984a
	O	O		O			O		Nesbitt 1995
		O							Bar-Yosef *et al.* 1991
	O	O	O	O	W	O	O		Willcox 1996
	O	O		O			O		Nesbitt 1995
		O	O	O		O	O		van Zeist and Bakker-Heeres 1984b
	O	O	O	O	W	O	O		Willcox 1996
		O			W	O	O		van Zeist and de Roller 1994
		O					O		Hopf 1983
		O			W		O		van Zeist and Bakker-Heeres 1984a
		O	O	O	W	O	O		Willcox 1991c; de Moulins 1997
		O	O				O		van Zeist and Bakker-Heeres 1984b
		O	O	O	W	O	O	O	van Zeist and de Roller 1994
	O	O	O	O		O	O		Pasternak 1995
		O	O		W		O	O	Rollefson *et al.* 1985
		O	O				O	O	Hopf 1983
		O			W	W	O		de Moulins 1997
		O			A	O	O		Kislev 1988
	O						O		Helbaek 1966
		O				O	O		van Zeist *et al.* 1986
O					A		O		Helbaek 1969
O			O				O		Colledge 1994
O		O	O	O		O	O		van Zeist and De Roller 1995
	O	O			W		O		de Moulins 1997
		O	O				O	O	van Zeist and Bakker-Heeres 1984b
		O	O				O	O	van Zeist and Bakker-Heeres 1984b
		O				W	O		Hubbard 1990; Willcox 1990
	O	O	O	O	W	W	O	O	Willcox 1996
	O	O							Willcox 1999
		O		O					Voigt 1984
		O		O	W	O	O		French *et al.* 1972
		O			W		O		Braidwood and Braidwood 1983

O = present
? = identification based on a small number of poorly preserved finds
W = identification based on wood
A = acorn

Table 12.5   Comparison of percentages of cereals at four PPNA sites. The differences indicate that the inhabitants were still using local cereals rather than introduced crops, which start to appear in the Middle PPNB.

	Jerf el Ahmar (%)	Mureybet (%)	Aswad 1a (%)	Netiv Hagdud (%)
Einkorn	15.80	96	0	0
Emmer	0	0	89.50	Present
Barley	84.20	4	10.50	Dominant

useful part of the crop, as opposed to unwanted weeds. This suggests cultivation of wild and domestic types together but does not exclude gathering from wild stands in a kind of mixed economy. Even during later periods (Late PPNB: 8600–8000 BP), for example at Ramad between 8210 and 7880 BP, domestic barley rachis fragments are only at 52 per cent. A similar situation was noted at Magzalia (Willcox unpublished report). However, at other contemporary sites such as Bouqras (van Zeist and van Waterbolk 1985) and Ras Shamra (phase Vc) wild types are rare or absent. These sites also contain naked wheat. During the Late PPNB, einkorn becomes a minor component and could be interpreted as a weed for most of the Near East. However, it reappears as a major component later at Jeitun in Central Asia (Harris *et al.* 1992) and at many sites in Europe.

Experimental results indicate that particular agricultural conditions are necessary in order for domestication to occur. As Hillman and Davies (1990: 213) point out, both seed corn from the wild, or that originating from fallen spikelets during the harvest, must be kept apart, and in reality this is not easy. This could explain why significant mixtures occur over a period of at least a millennium and would appear to indicate that selective pressures stayed relatively low. If this interpretation is correct, then it follows that cultivation without domestication would have occurred for some considerable time prior to the appearance of the solid rachis. If this is indeed the case, then archaeobotanists need to look for indirect indicators. Hillman examined the possibility of identifying a weed assemblage from Epipalaeolithic Abu Hureyra (Hillman *et al.* 1989: 253). His results were negative. Preliminary results from a later site, Dja'de, on the Euphrates (Willcox 1996), look more promising. Van Zeist examined the problem for later sites and the possibility of identifying weeds of irrigated fields (van Zeist 1993); he also points out that a number of taxa present at Cayönü are potential field weeds.

Evidence for *in situ* evolution under cultivation

At sites with long sequences such as Aswad and Cayönü it is possible to trace evolutionary trends. At Cayönü wild-type emmer grains are progressively replaced by domestic types (van Zeist and de Roller 1994), whereas at Aswad and near-by Ghoraifé, as already mentioned, wild-type barley rachis internodes are replaced progressively by solid-type domestic rachis fragments (van Zeist and Bakker-Heeres 1984b). The period of time necessary to recognize these changes appears to be about a millennium; that is to say, between the early tenth and early ninth millennia. Other sites such as Mureybet show no evolutionary trends; however taxa which are interpreted as weed assemblages at other sites are present. For example at Cayönü similar taxa are considered by van Zeist to be potential field weeds; these taxa also occur at other PPNA sites, suggesting predomestic agriculture.

Conclusions

Archaeobotanical evidence indicates that wild cereals were exploited in the Near East for several millennia before the appearance of domestic types. Specialized gathering and especially storage of cereals and pulses would have provided a secure subsistence base, making possible a sedentary existence. In the northern Levant it is not clear whether early tenth millennium cereals were domesticated. During the second half of the tenth millennium there is evidence of emmer domestication. However, a millennium after the appearance of domestication wild types still persisted at frequencies which suggest they were part of the crop rather than unwanted weeds. Experimental cultivation indicates that cereal cultivation need not necessarily lead to rapid domestication. Selective pressures were found to be low because wild types continued to propagate under cultivation through spontaneous sowing. Further dilution could occur from occasional gathering from the wild and through crosses with wild populations. However, a number of scholars insist that domestication was a rapid process suggesting that after the appearance of a given mutation the establishment of mutant lines could take place in a few years (McCorriston and Hole 1991; Zohary 1992, 1996). They therefore see the appearance of domestication as simultaneous with the beginnings of cultivation.

The area occupied by these sites is vast, which suggests the possibility that domestication could have occurred independently in different localities. Indeed genetic evidence points to at least two different origins for barley, and according to Zohary emmer and the pulses were taken into cultivation perhaps 'once or at most only very few times' (Zohary 1996: 155). However, still other varieties may have been taken into cultivation but subsequently died out or do not show up because of genetic modifications which have occurred over the last 10,000 years.

The point at which people started to cultivate remains elusive, but small-scale or intermittent cultivation of pulses and perhaps cereals may have occurred over a long period (PPNA and earlier) without leading to domestication, as suggested by Kislev (1992). Not until large-scale cereal cultivation in the Middle PPNB do we see the appearance of domestic barley and naked

wheat and the spread of emmer. As for the identification of predomestic
cultivation the best evidence would appear to come from weed assemblages.

How much can we say about cultural change in subsistence systems from
the observations we have made? It would appear that the transition was
gradual, as there is no evidence for an abrupt change. During the period of
transition there was little need for innovation in material culture. The tools
for processing of gathered and cultivated cereals remain essentially the same.
Storage, and storage structures, could be the same for both economic systems. During the Late Epipalaeolithic one might consider the possibility that
natural wild stands were to some extent managed to avoid over-exploitation.
Then occasional sowing was adopted. As we have seen, inadvertent or acci-
dental sowing around crop processing areas during the collecting stage is
inevitable and could hardly have been totally ignored. Sowing would be
enhanced if the soil was worked, and it is possible that suitable tools already
existed for other activities such as collecting earth for building or digging up
roots and tubers.

The change from a subsistence system to a production economy in the
Near East has also been correlated with climatic change, notably the return
of a cooler, dryer period (Younger Dryas) between 11,000 and 10,000 BP
which, it is suggested, could have been a contributing factor to the subsequent development of agriculture (Moore and Hillman 1992). Movement
of populations into drier areas might have the same effect. Given the steep
gradient in isohyets between the Mediterranean vegetation zone and the
interior steppe zone, even a small climatic change in the marginal areas
would have a profound effect.

The evolution towards and the adaptation to a production economy with
resulting domestication required certain pre-conditions. In other words it
required a combination of complex circumstances leading to an evolutionary
path, which resulted in an economy dependent on cereal cultivation. On the
one hand the plants had to have the right biological attributes (see Zohary
1996), and on the other humans had to have prerequisite behavioural
attributes. They would have to be sedentary gatherers of wild progenitors
with a minimum village size and a storage system. As pointed out by Cauvin,
humans would have to be culturally ready (Cauvin 1994). Once all these
conditions were fulfilled a full-scale farming economy (symbiosis) becomes
inevitable. This would provide a subsistence system where production was
guaranteed to supply demand (and/or surplus) in an expanding economy,
ultimately leading to an irreversible process. We are not in a position to say
whether cultural change played a more important role than climatic change.
To assume that a single factor such as climatic change could have led to the
adoption of plant husbandry is too simplistic.

The archaeobotanical remains, as we have seen, indicate that the change
to a production economy was slow. The biological process of domestication
appears to require that sowing be systematically carried out and that spontaneously sown seed be kept to a minimum. This would require that the soil

be worked rigorously and field systems be carefully managed. Cultivation of pulses and cereals during the early stages, even during the eleventh and tenth millennia, could have been an occasional option, but not necessarily systematically adopted. If occasional domesticates arose they may not have survived in the long term. But ultimately social organization developed to a point where farming became more and more organized, leading to high selective pressures for domestic types. Archaeological evidence during the Middle PPNB indicates the simultaneous emergence of rectilinear architecture, a considerable increase in village size, the consistent appearance of domesticated cereals, and the domestication of sheep and goat. Could these changes be correlated with a more developed and organized sociocultural system which became increasingly reliant on a highly managed agricultural system? This could have coincided with the adoption of rectangular field systems. Ultimately the process led to irreversible domestication combined with a steep rise in population. It appears that these changes were gradual and occurred more or less simultaneously over a wide area; that is to say the Euphrates valley, eastern Anatolia, the southern Levant and the Zagros foothills. Differences in material culture over the area as a whole are slight and contact across the region between geographically widely separated populations has been shown to occur from finds of marine shells and obsidian, which were traded across vast distances. If the area as a whole went through the pre-domestic cultivation stage then it is highly probable that domestication of the so-called founder crops occurred independently in different areas. However, at some sites, for example at Mureybet, only wild cereals were exploited during the Middle PPNB, while at the majority of sites, for this period, domestic cereals were predominant.

Acknowledgements

I would like to thank first and foremost G. Hillman for giving us the original ideas and plan for the experiments at Jalès, and P. Anderson who helped organize the project with me and was of invaluable help in both the theoretical and administrative fields. I would like to express my appreciation and warm thanks to all members of the Antiquities Department of the Syrian Arab Republic from the Damascus, Palmyra and Aleppo museums who during my numerous visits to Syria gave me a warm-hearted welcome, full backing and kind guidance. I would also like to thank J. Valkoun of ICARDA for showing me a large number of wild wheat populations in Syria, and J. Cauvin for his archaeological advice. Finally I am most grateful to W. van Zeist for his numerous publications and his pioneering work on Near Eastern archaeobotany without which much of this chapter would not have been possible.

References

Anderson, P. (1994) 'Insights into plant harvesting and other activities at Hatoula, as revealed by microscopic functional analysis of selected chipped stone tools', in M. Lechevallier and A. Ronen (eds) *Le Gisement de Hatoula en Judée Occidentale, Israël*, Memoires et Travaux du Centre de Recherche Francais de Jerusalem No. 8, Paris: Association Paleorient.

Baruch, U. and Bottema, S. (1991) 'Palynological evidence for climatic changes in the Levant ca. 17,000–9000 B.P.', in O. Bar-Yosef and F. Valla (eds) *The Natufian Culture in the Levant*, International Monographs in Prehistory, Ann Arbor, MI: University of Michigan Press.

Bar-Yosef, O., Gopher, A., Tchernov, E. and Kislev, M. (1991) 'Nativ Hagdud: an early neolithic village site in the Jordan valley', *Journal of Field Archaeology*, 18: 405–26.

Bor, N.L. (1968) 'Gramineae', in C. C. Townsend, E. Guest and A. Al-Rawi (eds) *Flora of Iraq*, vol. 9, Glasgow: University of Glasgow Press, MacLehose.

Braidwood, L. and Braidwood, R. (1983) *Prehistoric Archaeology Along the Hilly Flanks*, Oriental Institute Publications 103, Chicago, IL: University of Chicago Press.

Cauvin, J. (1994) *Naissance des Divinités: naissance de l'agriculture*, Paris: Editions CNRS.

Colledge, S. (1994) 'Plant exploitation on Epipalaeolothic and early Neolithic sites in the Levant', unpublished PhD thesis, Department of Archaeology and Prehistory, University of Sheffield.

Davies, P.H. (1985) *Flora of Turkey and the Aegean Islands*, vol. 9, Edinburgh: Edinburgh University Press.

de Moulins, D. (1997) *Agricultural Changes at Euphrates and Steppe Sites in the Mid-8th to the 6th Millennium B.C.*, Oxford: BAR.

French, D., Hillman, G.C., Payne, S. and Payne, J.R. (1972) Excavations at Can Hassan III 1969–1970', in E. S. Higgs (ed.) *Papers in Economic Prehistory*, Cambridge: Cambridge University Press.

Hansen, J. (1991) *Excavations at Franchthi Cave, Greece*, Fascicule 7: the palaeoethnobotany, Bloomington, IN: Indiana University Press.

Harris, D.R. (1996) 'The origins and spread of agriculture and pastoralism in Eurasia: an overview', in D. R. Harris (ed.) *The Origins and Spread of Agriculture and Pastoralism in Eurasia*, London: UCL Press.

Harris, D.R., Masson, V.M., Berezkin, Y.E., Charles, M.P., Gosden, C., Hillman, G.C., Kasparov, A.K., Korobkova, G.F., Kurbansakhatov, K., Legge, A.J. and Limbrey, S. (1992) 'Investigating early agriculture in Central Asia: new research at Jeitun, Turkmenistan', *Antiquity*, 67: 324–8.

Helbaek, H. (1966) 'Pre-pottery neolithic farming at Bheida: a preliminary report', *Palestine Exploration Quarterly*, 98: 61–6.

Helbaek, H. (1969) 'Plant collecting, dry farming, and irrigation in prehistoric Deh Luran', in F. Hole, K. Flannery and J. Neely (eds) *Prehistory and Human Ecology of the Deh Luran Plain: an early village sequence from Khuzistan, Iran*, Memoirs of the Museum of Anthropology 1, Ann Arbor, MI: University of Michigan Press.

Hillman, G.C. (1981) 'Reconstructing crop husbandry practices from charred remains of crops', in R. Mercer (ed.) *Farming Practices in British Prehistory*, Edinburgh: Edinburgh University Press.

Hillman, G.C. (1996) 'Late Pleistocene changes in wild plant-foods available to hunter-gatherers of the northern Fertile Crescent: possible preludes to cereal cultivation', in D. R. Harris (ed.) *The Origins and Spread of Agriculture and Pastoralism in Eurasia*, London: UCL Press.

Hillman, G.C. and Davies, S. (1990) 'Measured domestication rates in wild wheats and barley under primitive cultivation, and their archaeological implications', *Journal of World Prehistory*, 4: 157–219.

Hillman, G.C., Colledge, S.M. and Harris, D.R. (1989) 'Plant food economy during the Epi-palaeolithic period at Tell Abu Hureyra, Syria: dietary diversity, seasonality and modes of exploitation', in D. R. Harris and G. C. Hillman (eds) *Foraging and Farming: the evolution of plant exploitation*, London: Unwin Hyman.

Hillman, G.C., Wales, S., McLaren, F., Evans, J. and Butler, A. (1993) 'Identifying problematic remains of ancient plant foods: a comparison of the role of chemical, histological and morphological criteria', *World Archaeology*, 25: 94–121.

Hopf, M. (1983) 'Jericho plant remains', in K. Kenyon and T. Holland (eds) *Jericho Vol. V: the pottery phases of the tell and other finds* (Appendix B), London: British School of Archaeology in Jerusalem.

Hopf, M. and Bar-Yosef, O. (1987) 'Plant remains from Hayonim cave, western Galilee', *Paléorient*, 13(1): 117–20.

Hubbard, R.N.L.B. (1990) 'Carbonised seeds from Tepe Abdul Hosein: results of preliminary analyses', in J. Pullar (ed.) *Tepe Abdul Hosein*, Oxford: BAR International Series 562.

Kerbe, J. (1987) *Climat, Hydrologie et Aménagements Hydro-agricoles de Syrie*, Bordeaux: Presses Universitaires de Bordeaux.

Kislev, M. (1988) 'Nahal Hemar cave desiccated plant remains: an interim report', *Atiqot*, 18: 76–81.

Kislev, M. (1989) 'Pre-domesticated cereals in the Pre-Pottery Neolithic A period', in I. Hershkovitz (ed.) *People and Cultural Change*, Oxford: BAR International Series 508 (i).

Kislev, M. (1992) 'Agriculture in the Near East in the VIIth millennium B.C.', in P. Anderson (ed.) *Préhistoire de l'Agriculture*, Monographie du CRA No. 6, Paris: Editions CNRS.

Kislev, M.E., Nadel, D. and Carmi, I. (1992) 'Epipalaeolithic (19,000 bp) cereal and fruit diet at Ohalo II, Sea of Galilee, Israel', *Review of Palaeobotany and Palynology*, 73: 161–6.

Konarev, A.V. and Konarev, V.G. (1993) 'The use of genome-specific antigens and prolamin electrophoresis in the evaluation of wheat and its wild relatives', in A. B. Damania (ed.) *Biodiversity and Wheat Improvement*, Chichester: Wiley.

McCorriston, J. and Hole, F. (1991) 'The ecology of seasonal stress and the origins of agriculture in the Near East', *American Anthropologist*, 93: 46–69.

Mathon, C.-C. (1985) 'La recherche du patrimone sur quelques blés traditionnels du sud-est de la France', *Supplement au Bulletin Mensuel de la Société Linnéenne de Lyon*, 4: 7–34.

Moore, A.M.T. and Hillman, G.C. (1992) 'The Pleistocene to Holocene transition and human economy in southwest Asia: the impact of the Younger Dryas', *American Antiquity*, 57: 482–94.

Mouterde, P. (1966) *Nouvelle Flore du Liban et la Syrie*, vol. I, Beyrouth: Presse Catholique.

Nesbitt, M. (1995) 'Clues to agricultural origins in the northern Fertile Crescent', *Diversity: a news journal for the international genetic resources community*, 11: 142–3.

Nesbitt, M. and Samuel, O. (1996) 'From a staple crop to extinction: the archaeology and history of the hulled wheats', in P. Sadulosi, K. Hammer and J. Heller (eds) *Hulled Wheats. Proceedings of the First International Workshop on Hulled Wheats*, Rome: IPGRI.

Pasternak, R. (1995) 'Die botanischen Funfe aus Nevali Cori, Türkei (Akeramisches Neolithikum) – Ein Vorbericht' in H. Kroll and R. Pasternak (eds) *Res archaeobotanicae: International Workgroup for Palaeoethnobotany. Proceedings of the Ninth Symposium Kiel 1992*, Kiel: Heransgegeben.

Postgate, N.J. (1984) 'The problems of yields in the cuneiform record', *Bulletin on Sumerian Agriculture*, 1: 97–102.

Rollefson, G., Simmons, A., Donaldson, M., Gillespie, W., Kafafi, Z., Kohler-Rollefson, I., McAdam, E., Ralston, S. and Tubb, K. (1985) 'Excavations at the pre-pottery Neolithic B. village of 'Ain Ghazal (Jordan), 1983', *Mitteilugen der Deutschen Orient-Gesellschaft zu Berlin*, 117: 69–116.

Rosenberg, M., Nesbitt, M., Redding, R.W. and Strasser, T.E. (1995) 'Hallen Cemi Tepesi: some preliminary observations concerning early Neolithic subsistence in eastern Anatolia', *Anatolia*, 21: 1–12.

Traboulsi, M. (1981) 'Le climat de la Syrie: exemple de dégradation vers l'aride du climat méditerranéen', thèse du Troisième Cycle, Université de Lyon 2.

Valkoun, J. (1992) 'Exploration mission for wild cereals in Syria', *Genetic Resources Unit Annual Report for 1991*: 16–18. Aleppo: International Center for Agricultural Research in Dry Areas.

van Zeist, W. (1993) 'Archaeobotanical evidence of the bronze age field weed flora of northern Syria', *Festschrift Zoller, Dissertationes Botanicae*, 196: 499–511.

van Zeist, W. and Bakker-Heeres, J.A. (1984a) 'Archaeobotanical studies in the Levant 3. Late Palaeolithic Mureybet', *Palaeohistoria*, 26: 171–99.

van Zeist, W. and Bakker-Heeres, J.A. (1984b) 'Archaeobotanical studies in the Levant 1. Neolithic sites in the Damascus basin: Aswad, Ghoraife, Ramad', *Palaeohistoria*, 24: 165–256.

van Zeist, W. and de Roller, G. (1994) 'The plant husbandry of aceramic Cayönü, SE Turkey', *Palaeohistoria*, 33/34: 65–96.

van Zeist, W. and de Roller, G. (1995) 'Plant remains from Asikli Höyük, a pre-pottery neolithic site in central Anatolia', *Vegetation History and Archaeobotany*, 4: 179–85.

van Zeist, W. and van Waterbolk, R. (1985) 'The palaeobotany of Tell Bouqras', *Paléorient*, 11: 131–47.

van Zeist, W., Smith, P., Palfenier, R., Suwijin, M. and Casparie, W. (1986) 'An archaeobotanical study of Ganj Dareh Tepe, Iran', *Palaeohistoria*, 26: 201–24.

Voigt, M. (1984) 'Village on the Euphrates: excavations at neolithic Gritille in Turkey', *Expedition*, 27: 10–24.

Willcox, G. (1990) 'Charcoal remains from Tepe Abdul Hosein', in J. Pullar (ed.) *Tepe Abdul Hosein: a neolithic site in western Iran. Excavations 1978*, Oxford: BAR.

Willcox, G. (1991a) 'Exploitation des espèces ligneuses au Proche-Orient', *Paléorient*, 17: 117–26.

Willcox, G. (1991b) 'La culture inventée, la domestication inconsciente: le début de l'agriculture au Proche Orient', in M.-C. Cauvin (ed.) *Rites et Rythmes agraires*, Lyon: Travaux de la Maison de L'Orient 20.

Willcox, G. (1991c) 'Cafer Höyük (Turquie): les charbons de bois neolithiques', *Cahiers de l'Euphrate*, 5–6: 139–50, Paris: Editions Recherche sur les Civilisations.

Willcox, G. (1992) 'Archaeobotanical significance of growing Near Eastern progenitors of domestic plants at Jalès (France)', in P. Anderson (ed.) *Préhistoire de l'Agriculture: nouvelles approches expérimentales et ethnographiques*, Monographie du CRA No. 6, Paris: Editions CNRS.

Willcox, G. (1995) 'Wild and domestic cereal cultivation: new evidence from early neolithic sites in the northern Levant and south-eastern Anatolia', *ARX World Journal of Prehistoric and Ancient Studies*, 1: 9–16.

Willcox, G. (1996) 'Evidence for plant exploitation and vegetation history from three early neolithic pre-pottery sites on the Euphrates (Syria)', *Vegetation History and Archaeobotany*, 5: 143–52.

Willcox, G. (1999) 'Charcoal analysis and Holocene vegetation history in southern Syria', *Quaternary Science Reviews*, 18: 711–16.

Zohary, D. (1969) 'The progenitors of wheat and barley in relation to domestication and agricultural dispersals in the Old World', in G. W. Dimbleby and P. Ucko (eds) *The Domestication of Plants and Animals*, London: Duckworth.

Zohary, D. (1992) 'Domestication of the neolithic crop plant assemblage', in P. Anderson (ed.) *Préhistoire de l'Agriculture: nouvelles approches expérimentales et ethnographiques*, Monographie du CRA No. 6, Paris: Editions CNRS.

Zohary , D. (1996) 'The mode of domestication of the founder crops of Southwest Asian agriculture', in D. R. Harris (ed.) *The Origins and Spread of Agriculture and Pastoralism in Eurasia*, London: UCL Press.

Zohary, D. and Hopf, M. (1988) *Domestication of Plants in the Old World*, Oxford: Duckworth.

Update: Rates of domestication assessed

George Willcox

Since the 1999 publication much new archaeobotanical information has become available from early farming sites in the Near East. I cautiously advocated a gradualist domestication model and the possibility of multiple domestication events. New information and new interpretations which support these views have since appeared (Willcox 2002, 2005). The cultivation of morphologically wild cereals prior to their domestication (pre-domestic agriculture) is now accepted by most archaeobotanists for the PPNA in both the northern and southern Levant. Earlier cultivation has been posited for Natufian levels at Abu Hureyra and Khamian levels at Mureybet (Colledge 1998; Hillman *et al.* 2001). This implies that the transformation of shattering wild cereal populations into non-shattering domestic populations was a slow process, because the latter do not appear until the Early PPNB. Indeed, Tanno and Willcox (2006) demonstrate that wild and domestic forms persisted together at relatively high frequencies under cultivation in the Near East for a considerable period of time, further supporting a gradualist model of domestication.

The original article used information from experimental cultivation of wild cereals at Jalès in southern France during 1989–1993. This research has continued and a number of significant observations have been made. In the late 1990s, the wild einkorn population was accidentally contaminated with domestic einkorn. Because the two populations are morphologically similar, neither the exact date nor degree of contamination are known. The separation of a mixture of wild and domestic einkorn is difficult. They continued to be cultivated together. It took less than ten years for the wild population to be almost totally replaced by the domestic non-shattering varieties. This demonstrates that once a small number of present-day domestic plants are introduced, selection will rapidly favour them at the expense of the wild types. However, our cultivation techniques did not simulate the situation of early farmers. During this ten-year period the harvests took place late, well after shattering had started, which would have strongly favoured the domestic varieties. This would not have been the case for early farmers who would have harvested before shattering started, to avoid loss. Under these circumstances non-shattering was far less advantageous.

Furthermore, in the original article I posit that when crops failed, early subsistence farmers would have had to gather from the wild to replenish their seed stock. Poor harvests with low yields occurred occasionally on our plots, but because we were not keeping back grain for consumption we always had enough for sowing, which would not have been the case for early Neolithic farmers. I argue that a combination of early harvests and replenishment from the wild would make the selection of the rare non-shattering mutants highly improbable, implying that a long period would be required for domestic populations to become established (Kislev 2002 gives additional supporting arguments).

Concerning the cultivation of wild two-rowed barley (*Hordeum spontaneum*), we noticed that from the late 1990s the population had some six-rowed specimens. Because they produced more grains, they became dominant at the expense of the two-rowed types in a few years. This can be explained because our original population was collected from an area where domestic barley was cultivated. The appearance of the six-rowed trait was probably due to the fact that the original 'wild' population had grown in close proximity to cultivated barley; either it had introgressed or it was an escape from cultivation (Zohary and Tanno, pers. comm.).

Artificial selection leading to rapid changes, as opposed to (slow) natural selection, was improbable, because domestic traits such as non-shattering and lack of dormancy would not have been readily visible to early farmers. Selection for larger grains in the case of einkorn and barley was slow. This has been established by measurements taken from ancient grains which demonstrate no significant size increase for wheat and barley grains between

9500 and 6500 uncal. BP (Willcox 2004). Selection of large grains is not a straightforward process because grain size depends more upon the position on the ear and environmental conditions than genetic diversity.

Finally, in 2004 we started cultivating wild rye (*Secale vavilovii*) gathered from volcanic soils on Karaça Dag. We had excellent results despite adverse soil conditions, implying that wild rye could have been cultivated on less acidic soils than those found in the Karaça Dag region.

To conclude, the evidence points more and more to slow change in food procuring strategies, crop adaptation and social change at the dawn of farming. Societies may have chosen reliability over the risk of innovation. Small-scale cultivation by 'hunter-gatherers' may well have led to socio-cultural complexity, which has recently been demonstrated by new spectacular finds such as those at the site of Göbekli (Schmidt 2006). This social complexity may have produced incentives to cultivate more intensively, leading to a production economy. A full production economy with systematic domestication did not appear until after the beginning of the Holocene and coincides with the appearance of a stable climate.

References

Colledge, S. (1998) 'Identifying pre-domestication cultivation using multivariate analysis', in A. Damania, J. Valkoun, G. Willcox and C. O. Qualset (eds) *The Origins of Agriculture and Crop Domestication*, Aleppo: ICARDA.

Hillman, G., Hedges, R., Moore, A., Colledge, S. and Pettit, P. (2001) 'New evidence of Late Glacial cereal cultivation at Abu Hureyra on the Euphrates', *Holocene*, 11: 383–93.

Kislev, M. (2002) 'Origin of annual crops by agro-evolution', *Israel Journal of Plant Sciences*, 50: 85–8.

Schmidt, K. (2006) *Sie Bauten die Ersten Tempel*, Munich: C.H. Beck.

Tanno, K. and Willcox, G. (2006) 'How fast was wild wheat domesticated?' *Science*, 311: 1886.

Willcox, G. (2002) 'Geographical variation in major cereal components and evidence for independent domestication events in Western Asia', in R. T. J. Cappers and S. Bottema (eds) *The Dawn of Farming in the Near East*, Studies in Near Eastern Production, Subsistence and Environment 6, Berlin: ex oriente.

Willcox, G. (2004) 'Measuring grain size and identifying Near Eastern cereal domestication: evidence from the Euphrates valley', *Journal of Archaeological Science*, 31: 145–50.

Willcox, G. (2005) 'The distribution, natural habitats and availability of wild cereals in relation to their domestication in the Near East: multiple events, multiple centres', *Vegetation History and Archaeobotany*, 14: 534–41.

13 The beginnings of food production in southwestern Kenya

Peter Robertshaw

The explanation of the origins of agriculture, and by extension the origins of animal domestication, is rightfully regarded as one of the 'Big Questions of Archaeology' (Binford 1983: 26 and see Clutton-Brock 1989, 1993; Harris and Hillman 1989; Harlan 1993). Since east Africa[1] boasts no wild progenitors of either domestic animals or agricultural crops, with the possible exception of finger millet (*Eleusine coracana*) in northern Uganda, the relevant questions in this context are, first, by what process were domesticates introduced into the region; second, how did the earliest food producers adapt to east African environments; and, third, how did these adaptations evolve into those encountered by early European travellers and ethnographers in the last hundred years? East Africa is renowned for its pastoral peoples, who spurn both agriculture and hunting-and-gathering; therefore, the explanation of the evolution of this pastoral adaptation and its socio-cultural framework is an important goal of both archaeological and historical research, which I have attempted to address in other publications (Robertshaw 1982; Robertshaw and Collett 1983). In this chapter I focus upon the adaptations of early food-producing peoples in east Africa, confining myself to an outline of the evidence from southwestern Kenya, where I have been engaged in field research for several years. However, to locate this work within the broader canvas, I shall first outline current thought on the first question – the process by which domesticates were introduced to east Africa.

Domestic animals make their appearance in east Africa as part of what seems to be a 'package deal', which includes new styles of ceramics, lithic artefacts, burial practices and settlement patterns. While the evidence is by no means entirely unequivocal, it thus favours a model of population movement, but on what scale is very difficult to judge, given the sparseness of archaeological research. Pastoralists first entered northern Kenya during the third millennium BC, but their arrival in southern Kenya and northern Tanzania is on present evidence dated only to the end of the second millennium.[2] However, similarities between ceramics from northern Kenya and undated sites in the south suggest that future research will bridge the chronological gap. This early pottery is subsumed within the Olmalenge tradition.[3] There are relatively few sites containing this pottery, an indication perhaps that early pastoral settlement in the region was sparse. From about 1000 BC onwards there are many more sites, the pottery from which is mostly assigned to either the Oldishi or Elmenteitan traditions. Whether the appearance of these traditions is to be tied to further population movements into east Africa is not certain, since so little is known of the earlier parts of the ceramic sequences. Those who have faith in linguistic-archaeological correlations reason that the population movements by which Southern Cushitic and Southern Nilotic languages spread into northern Tanzania are manifested by these ceramic traditions (e.g. Ambrose 1982).

However, the early pastoralists did not enter a depopulated wilderness; rather they encountered hunter-gatherers, who, in the central Rift Valley at least, adapted their lifestyle to take advantage of the new possibilities offered by the presence of domestic animals but without abandoning their hunting-and-gathering existence (Ambrose 1984). While 'post-pastoral' foragers are generally a neglected aspect of archaeological enquiry (Cable n.d.), study of the pastoralists themselves in east Africa has not progressed very far either, being mostly confined to the establishment of culture-stratigraphic sequences, a task not without pitfalls. Efforts to go beyond classification are restricted to a handful of studies (Bower 1978, 1984a, 1984b; Ambrose 1980, 1984; Gifford *et al.* 1980; Robertshaw and Collett 1983; Robertshaw *et al.* 1983; Gifford-Gonzalez 1984; Gifford-Gonzalez and Kimengich 1984; Marshall 1986; Robertshaw 1989).

The environment

Southwestern Kenya (Figure 13.1) is one region where recent research has focused on early food-producing communities and their hunting-and-gathering antecedents. Archaeological fieldwork has been undertaken here in two rather different environmental mosaics. The first of these, in what is now South Nyanza district, begins with the shores of Lake Victoria and climbs eastwards, through a series of impressive ancient volcanoes, into the pre-Cambrian rocks of the Kanyamkago hills (Figure 13.2). Rainfall increases with altitude, from 790 mm per annum on the lakeshores to over 1000 mm in the Kanyamkago hills, the rain falling mostly in two rather indistinct seasons from March to May and October to November. Vegetation varies with altitude and precipitation, shifting from *Euphorbia* and *Acacia* bush and grassland near the lakeshore to *Combretum* and allied broad-leafed savanna species in the hills. Tsetse fly abound in parts of the region carrying both animal, and in some areas human, trypanosomiasis. The present inhabitants of the region are in the main Nilotic-speaking Luo farmers, who keep a few domestic animals. They displaced or assimilated earlier Bantu-speaking groups during the eighteenth and nineteenth centuries (Ogot 1967), though Suba fishermen still live along much of the lakeshore.

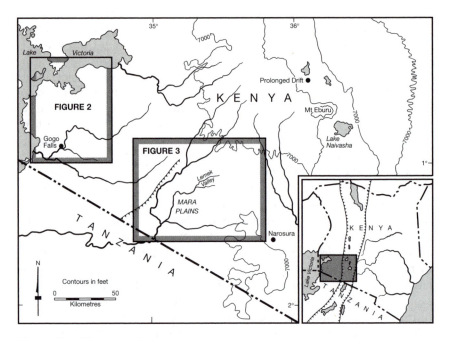

Figure 13.1 The area of research

By contrast the Mara region (Figure 13.3) is in many respects classic pastoralist country inhabited by the pastoralists *par excellence* of east Africa – the Maasai. The Mara is the northern extension of the vast Serengeti ecosystem, in which open, high-elevation grassy plains are interrupted by ranges of quartzitic hills and occasional inselbergs. The archaeological research discussed here was undertaken in the northern part of this region, bounded to the west by the Siria escarpment, to the north by the Amala river and the forests of the Mau and the east by the Loita plains. Here we can contrast two areas – the Lemek valley and the Mara plains. The Lemek valley, with reddish-brown sandy soils derived from the quartzitic hills, receives some 700 mm of rain per annum, mostly in the first half of the year. The presence of springs on the hill slopes and permanent water-holes in the stream-beds makes the valley attractive for year-round settlement. The pastoralists tend to locate their settlements at the bottom of the steep hill slopes, where they have easy access to a range of resources – the bush of the steep slopes for firewood and building materials and browse for goats, the springs for water, and the gentler, lower grassy slopes for grazing their cattle. Rainfall is somewhat higher on the Mara plains, where nutrient-rich black cotton-soils are derived from the underlying volcanic peneplain. The grass plains are interspersed with bush-lined stream courses, where pastoralists locate their settlements on the sandy soils, which flank the streams and are more conducive to the well being of their livestock than the heavy, poorly

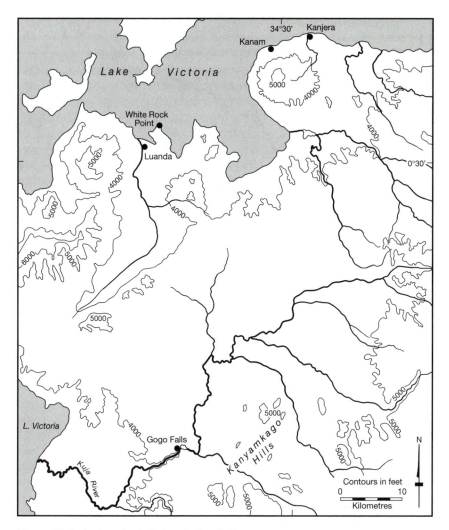

Figure 13.2 Archaeological sites in South Nyanza

drained soils of the plains. The pastoralists compete for grazing, particularly in the dry season (June–October), with vast herds of wildebeests and other ungulates whose numbers have increased enormously since the eradication of rinderpest. At times in the past bush cover was greater and the presence of tsetse fly restricted settlement to the Lemek valley and immediately adjacent areas (Lamprey 1984).

These two regions, South Nyanza and the Mara, with their varied environments promoted rather different adaptations among the early food-producing communities who settled there, despite the fact that they appear to have belonged to a single cultural tradition. We also know something

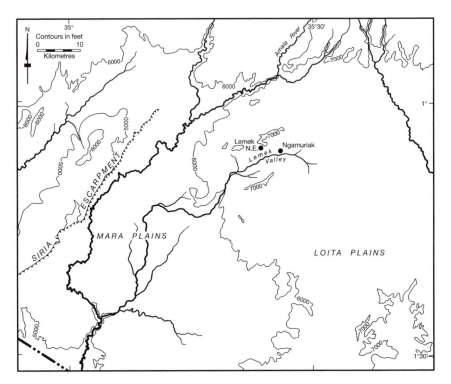

Figure 13.3 The Mara region

of the lifestyle of their hunter-gatherer antecedents in South Nyanza, but the archaeological record of this period in the Mara is elusive.

Later prehistory in South Nyanza

The later prehistoric sequence in South Nyanza begins with the shell middens on the shores of Lake Victoria first investigated by Louis Leakey (1936: 69) and subsequently examined in more detail (Robertshaw *et al.* 1983). The contents of the middens document broad-spectrum hunting-and-gathering subsistence. Shellfish were gathered from the shallows of the lake, where a variety of fish, notably lungfish (*Protopterus aethiopicus*), were also caught, perhaps with the aid of various basket traps. There is a substantial component of mammalian fauna, which is composed exclusively of wild species, mainly medium to very large ungulates. A broad range of species, both gregarious and non-gregarious, was obtained from a wide variety of habitats. Buffalo and hippo are the most commonly represented species, but there are also numerous antelopes, pigs and birds, as well as crocodiles and Nile monitors (*Varanus niloticus*). Gifford has suggested that 'this wide range of animal species taken might reflect a foraging system in which "first choice" animal species were not locally available in sufficient proportions, necessitating expansion of the animal food base to include less energetically rewarding species' (Robertshaw *et al.* 1983: 32). When considered in the light of the evidence from the site of Gogo Falls discussed below, it seems reasonable to infer that the shell middens represent only a part of a region-ally diverse system of subsistence and settlement, much of which may have operated well inland of the lake.

The stone artefact assemblages from the shell middens, like many of their east African later stone age counterparts, are typically nondescript. Backed microliths and scrapers dominate the assemblages, which are manufactured in a variety of raw materials. Obsidian and crypto-crystalline silicas were favoured for the manufacture of shaped tools; the former, present in only small quantities, derives from the central Rift Valley about 230 km to the east (Merrick and Brown 1984), while the latter was probably obtained from hills some 50 km to the east. This again indicates that the middens should be seen as part of a regional system of exploitation of resources. The middens have also yielded highly decorated pottery, now placed within the Kansyore phase of the Oltome tradition (Collett and Robertshaw 1983a), and several barbless bone points (Robertshaw *et al.* 1983).

Similar pottery and stone artefacts have been discovered at Gogo Falls, a large and complex open site located beside the rapids of the same name on the Kuja river 22 km inland from Lake Victoria in the Kanyamkago hills (Collett and Robertshaw 1980). A very small excavation at the site in 1981 yielded cattle remains apparently in association with Oltome pottery; this prompted speculation that the shell middens may have been a lacrustrine-oriented facies of what was for the most part a farming or pastoralist subsistence system (Robertshaw *et al.* 1983: 37). However, more extensive excavations, carried out in 1983, have served to show that domestic animals are not in fact associated with Oltome ceramics at Gogo Falls or, for that matter, anywhere else. The evidence for subsistence during the Oltome occupation of Gogo Falls is in many respects very similar to that from the shell middens. There are shellfish, but in lower densities than in the lakeshore sites; they were collected both from the lakeshore and from the river (P. Kat, pers. comm.). Analyses of the fish and mammalian bones are not yet complete, but preliminary results show the presence of a wide variety of large mam-mals, among which buffalo and hippo again seem to be common. Thus, considered as a whole, Oltome subsistence appears to have varied little spatially or perhaps seasonally. The archaeological evidence suggests a very broad-spectrum, but not internally differentiated, opportunistic foraging adaptation, in which parts of the lakeshore and Gogo Falls may have acted as 'magnet' locations (cf. Binford 1984: 263). In this respect Gogo Falls was renowned historically as a natural weir where fish could be easily collected (Butterman 1979: 103).

The dating of Oltome settlement in South Nyanza is a problem. Apart from some dubious readings on bone apatite, there is a date on shell from one of the middens of 6740 ± 80 bp (Pta-3139), from which at most 100 years should be subtracted, based on a correction factor obtained by dating modern shell from the lake (Robertshaw *et al.* 1983: 7). Recently the Oxford Accelerator Mass Spectrometry laboratory has attempted, generally without success, to extract collagen from several bone samples. However, one date of 5700 ± 100 bp (OxA-828) was obtained from a sample of bone collagen from the shell midden at Kanjera West, but the laboratory comments that this probably represents a minimum age (Gowlett *et al.* 1987: 147). Inland at Gogo Falls the dating of the Oltome occupation is perhaps even less satisfactory, where on the basis of radiocarbon and obsidian hydration dates (Table 13.1) one may choose a 'short' or 'long' chronology. Thus, on the one hand, if one accepts the charcoal date from the Harwell laboratory and the hydration dates, then the ash midden in which the Oltome materials were deposited dates within the last two millennia BC.[4] If, on the other hand, one considers the Oxford AMS date obtained from a charred buffalo tooth as more reliable, then one must argue that the hydration dates are simply wrong and that the charcoal date may be the result of mixing of older and younger charcoal, a real possibility since the sample was composed of scattered fragments of charcoal rather than a single 'lump'.

The dating issue at Gogo Falls is of fundamental importance. If a 'long' chronology is correct, then the Oltome occupation of the site was pene-contemporaneous with that of the lakeshore middens, indicating that they were indeed part of a single subsistence system. The other implication of a 'long' chronology is that there may then have been a substantial hiatus between the period of Oltome settlement and the first appearance of pastoralists in the region, dated to about the beginning of the first millennium AD. However, if a 'short' chronology is correct, then not only would the Oltome settlement of Gogo Falls not be contemporary with that of the shell middens, but also there can have been little or no hiatus between this hunter-

Table 13.1 Radiocarbon and obsidian hydration dates for the Oltome occupation of Gogo Falls

Excavation spit[1]	Radiocarbon date (bp)	Calibrated date (cal)[2]	Hydration date[3]
M3	3020 ± 100	1420–1110 BC	667 BC ± 194
M4	7300 ± 500	6670–c. 5500 BC	
M6			146 BC ± 93
			1663 BC ± 115
M7			524 BC ± 65
M9			16,058 BC ± 383

Notes
1 The deposit was excavated by arbitrary levels (spits) each 10 cm thick and numbered from the bottom of the topsoil (M1) to the base of the deposits (M10).
2 Calibration based on: Pearson and Stuiver (1986); Kromer *et al.* (1986).
3 Dates by MOHLAB.

gatherer settlement and the coming of pastoralism. Therefore, whichever chronology is chosen, there are important consequences for understanding the process of the advent of food production.

The earliest evidence of food production in South Nyanza is also found at Gogo Falls in a rather spectacular manner. An enormous ash midden, 2 m or more thick – almost certainly the burnt dung of livestock – and chock-full of well-preserved bones, potsherds and stone artefacts, partially overlies the Oltome horizons. The majority of the pottery consists of undecorated hemispherical bowls and globular pots with occasional spouts and lugs typical of the Elmenteitan tradition. However, the presence of pots with panels of crudely incised cross-hatching below the rim suggests that this may be a hitherto unrecorded facies of the Elmenteitan in a region well to the west of the previously known distribution of this tradition.[5] What is certain is that this pottery is so vastly different from the Oltome material that there is little alternative but to view the advent of food production in the context of the immigration of new groups of peoples with a different cultural system.

With the advent of the Elmenteitan there are also major changes in the pattern of stone raw material usage at Gogo Falls. In the Oltome horizons quartz predominated and most of the small quantities of obsidian were of a translucent grey colour. In the Elmenteitan midden 80 per cent or more of the artefacts are now made in obsidian, most of which is of a bottle-green colour, shown by chemical analysis to derive from sources on Mt Eburru in the central Rift Valley (Merrick and Brown 1984). A predominance of Mt Eburru obsidian is typical of Elmenteitan assemblages everywhere and demonstrates that the inhabitants of Gogo Falls were part of the wider Elmenteitan world, which succeeded in moving large quantities of obsidian over considerable distances. The location of Gogo Falls at the most distant point from the source of the distribution network, if such a network did indeed exist, meant that obsidian was more highly valued here than else-where. This is manifested by the very small size of most of the artefacts, the abundance of *outils écaillés* and the rarity of the modified blades which are so characteristic of the Elmenteitan industry as a whole (Nelson 1980).

Remains of domestic animals – cattle and caprines – were recovered from all levels of the Elmenteitan midden at Gogo Falls. Caprines dominate the faunal assemblage numerically, followed by cattle and then an array of wild animals, represented in considerable numbers. Topi/hartebeest, oribi, zebra and reedbuck are the most commonly represented species. This faunal assemblage would appear to reflect hunting of local populations of small antelopes and pigs in a variety of habitats, combined with seasonal hunting of larger migratory ungulates (Marshall 1986), as well as some fishing and fowling. The combination of frequent hunting with pastoralism is rare in east Africa both in the ethnographic literature and the archaeological record (see e.g. Horton and Mudida 1993). Only one other site, Prolonged Drift in the central Rift Valley, has produced a similar mixture of abundant wild and domestic animals (Gifford *et al.* 1980). Therefore, the interpretation of these assemblages is a matter of some interest. Gifford-Gonzalez has proposed several alternative models of subsistence and settlement systems to account for the Prolonged Drift assemblage (Gifford *et al.* 1980; Gifford-Gonzalez 1984), while the suggestion has also been made that the site was occupied by poor pastoralists compelled by necessity to hunt while attempting to establish viable domestic herds (Robertshaw and Collett 1983). The latter hypothesis would also fit the Gogo Falls situation (Marshall 1986; Robertshaw 1989), particularly as the abundance of tsetse fly in South Nyanza is likely to have depressed livestock numbers. The alternative suggestion that the Gogo Falls assemblage is the result of hunter-gatherers supplementing the products of the chase by rustling or exchange with pastoralists does not bear detailed scrutiny: first and most cogently, the faunal assemblage was found in an enormous pile of livestock dung; second, the absence of animals with claws, nails and fur is in accord with common taboos among food-producing peoples on the eating of such animals; and, finally, the age profile reconstructed from the cattle teeth is indicative of long-term culling of a pastoral herd rather than opportunistic rustling (Marshall 1986: 169).

Four radiocarbon dates on charcoal samples place the Elmenteitan occupation at Gogo Falls between the first century BC and the end of the fourth century AD. In the topsoil overlying the midden were found considerable quantities of Early Iron Age Urewe pottery, some of which had worked its way down into the upper levels of the midden. Iron bracelets, blades and other objects were found in association with this pottery, but there is no evidence that iron-smelting took place at the site. A single ornament made from marine shell can be attributed to either the Early Iron Age or the latter part of the Elmenteitan occupation. The differences between the Elmenteitan and the Urewe pottery are so radical (cf. Collett 1985, 1993) that, as with the appearance of the Elmenteitan, immigration of new groups of people is the obvious explanation. Indeed, the appearance of Urewe pottery in South Nyanza is undoubtedly part and parcel of the well-documented expansion of Bantu-speaking farmers through eastern and southern Africa (e.g. Phillipson 1977). Thus, major changes in subsistence, settlement and technology in South Nyanza are linked with immigrant populations.

Gogo Falls has provided a fascinating glimpse of the adaptations of stone age food producers in the region, but our understanding is limited by the absence of other contemporary sites in South Nyanza which might permit the recognition of regional patterns of subsistence and settlement. A recent, but brief, survey designed to rectify this situation produced disappointing results (Robertshaw *et al.* 1990). There is clear evidence that the Elmenteitan pastoralists of Gogo Falls combined hunting with herd management, but did they also grow crops? Much effort was expended in the flotation of samples of deposit during the excavations and a good number of carbonized seeds were recovered, but it appears that no cultigens are represented (W. Wetterstrom, pers. comm.). However, it is well to remember that absence of evidence is not the same as evidence of absence.

Later prehistory in the Mara

The Mara region has been subjected to a great deal more archaeological fieldwork than South Nyanza. Thus, some 150 sites have been recorded, though only seven of these have been excavated (Robertshaw *et al.* 1990). Surface collections have been made at several more sites. A considerable suite of obsidian hydration dates has also been processed in order to establish the culture-historical sequence for a region in which virtually every site has only a single occupation horizon.

The later prehistoric sequence in the Mara apparently begins with later stone age (LSA) sites that lack pottery. They occur generally as small, light-density, surface scatters of artefacts found on a broad range of hill slopes. Faunal remains are not preserved at any of these sites. Thus the Mara region presents a marked contrast with South Nyanza with its rich evidence for LSA foraging adaptations. Indeed the absence of LSA sites with faunal remains from the Mara was a shock for we had expected to document prehistorical exploitation of the vast herds of game that roam the Mara plains. Moreover, such evidence has been forthcoming from further south in the Serengeti (Bower and Chadderdon 1986). The obsidian hydration dates for one of the Mara LSA sites fall in the first few centuries AD. Thus we are confronted with the possibility that all these so-called LSA sites may date to the period of pastoralist occupation of the region. Perhaps they are the result of pastoralist activities, for example a casual flaking episode of a group of men out herding cattle and bear no relation to hunting whatsoever. Therefore we have as yet no unequivocal evidence of LSA occupation of the Mara prior to the advent of pastoralism.

On present evidence the earliest sites in the region at which bones of domestic animals – cattle and caprines – are found, contain pottery of the Oldishi tradition similar, but by no means identical, to that from Narosura (Odner 1972). The associated stone artefact assemblages are predominantly made from grey obsidian from the Naivasha region of the central Rift Valley, some 100 km to the east (Merrick and Brown 1984) and chert, the latter being preferred for the manufacture of backed microliths. Oldishi sites have been found only in the Lemek valley, where obsidian hydration dates from several sites indicate occupation between very approximately 800 and 400 BC. The identified faunal remains from the major excavated site, Lemek Northeast, are all domestic, caprines being far more numerous than cattle (Marshall 1986). As at Gogo Falls, there is no evidence of cultivation.

After about 400 BC, possibly somewhat later, sites of the Oldishi tradition disappear from the archaeological record of the Mara to be replaced by other pastoralist sites, the pottery and stone artefacts from which belong without doubt to the Elmenteitan tradition. Again, the implication is that population movements are involved. More than thirty-five Elmenteitan sites have been recorded throughout the region in a distribution pattern closely similar to that of the modern pastoral Maasai settlements (Lamprey and Waller

1990; Robertshaw *et al.* 1990). A histogram of the maximum dimensions, as measured by the extent of the artefact scatters, of these Elmenteitan sites shows something of a bimodal or perhaps trimodal distribution (Figure 13.4). While possible sampling errors, such as differential preservation and exposure of sites, cannot be dismissed, it is clear that the larger sites are not simply the product of greater post-depositional movement of artefacts caused by sheet wash. Two of the six largest sites contain extensive deposits of animal dung indicative of central livestock enclosures. These data raise the possibility of economic differentiation, both between possible pastoral camps and more agriculturally oriented settlements and concomitantly between larger (semi-permanent?) and smaller (seasonal?) settlements. However, with our present knowledge, these are little more than speculations, which may serve to focus future fieldwork priorities.

Large-scale excavations at the Elmenteitan site of Ngamuriak in the Lemek valley have uncovered several middens, dung accumulations, one or two house-floors and vast quantities of artefacts and faunal remains. The last have been the subject of detailed analysis by Marshall (1986, 1990). More than 99 per cent of the identified bones belong to either cattle or ovicaprids. Reconstructions of slaughtering patterns, herd management practices and herd sizes demonstrate that the occupants of Ngamuriak had large herds of cattle compared with small stock by the standards of modern subsistence pastoralists in east Africa. The fact that they allowed their animals to reach maximum meat-weight before slaughtering suggests, too, that ecological and economic constraints on pastoral herd growth were few (Marshall 1990).

In contrast with the abundant evidence for pastoralism, no carbonized seeds of any cultigens have been found at Ngamuriak despite considerable efforts aimed at their recovery. Nor are there many grindstones, though of course grinding equipment need not be made of stone. The large quantities of pottery at the site and the spatial organization of debris is suggestive of long-term occupation, which is arguably incompatible with a subsistence economy based entirely upon pastoral produce.[6] Site catchment analysis has also shown the potential of the Ngamuriak area for farming (Robertshaw and Collett 1983: 70–1). In a wider context, analysis of nitrogen isotope

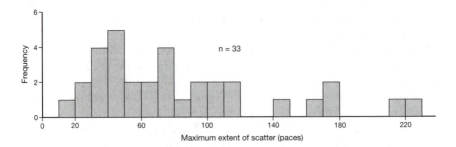

Figure 13.4 The maximum dimensions of Elmenteitan sites in the Mara region

ratios in putative Elmenteitan skeletons, unfortunately not from the Mara region,[7] has revealed a considerable plant-food component in their diet (Ambrose and DeNiro 1986).

Obsidian hydration dates from several sites suggest that Elmenteitan occupation spanned the period from approximately 400 BC to AD 600, possibly even as late as AD 1200 if dates on artefacts collected from the surface of sites and, therefore, in dubious context, are to be credited. There also seems to be some geographical patterning to the dates (Figure 13.5), the Mara plains being first settled by Elmenteitan pastoralists around AD 250, several centuries after their appearance in the Lemek valley. While an explanation invoking sampling errors cannot be discounted, a more exciting alternative would propose that the expansion of settlement onto the Mara plains represents a shift in economic emphasis, following a reduction in cultivation, towards more mobile pastoral strategies aimed at exploiting the rich grasslands of the plains. This would have been facilitated by the spread of iron age farming communities, from whom grain could be traded, into the highlands to the north and west (cf. Robertshaw and Collett 1983).[8] Another alternative hypothesis would suggest that expansion onto the Mara plains may have been facilitated by a reduction in bush cover and hence in the distribution of tsetse fly. This hypothesis is not mutually exclusive with

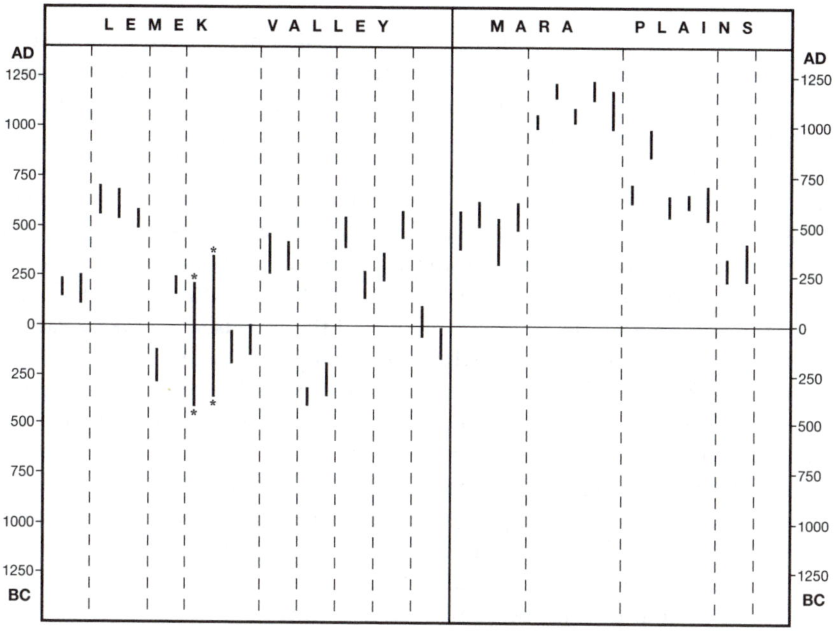

Figure 13.5 Geographical patterning in the dates for Elmenteitan sites in the Mara region. Starred dates are calibrated radiocarbon dates; others are obsidian hydration dates.

the previous one, since the proposed reduction in bush cover may have come about as a result of pastoralist intervention rather than any climatic or environmental changes.

Our knowledge of the later part of the prehistoric sequence in the Mara, that of the present millennium, is in many ways as intractable as that of the pre-pastoralist LSA. A considerable number of sites has been discovered on the Mara plains that defy easy attribution to any of the known cultural traditions. These sites are mostly surface occurrences with stone artefacts made from a variety of obsidians and other raw materials, together with undecorated pottery, which lacks the mica temper characteristic of Elmenteitan ceramics in this region. However, a few sherds with rouletted decoration are a common feature of many of these sites. Since this form of pottery decoration is generally found on sites dating to the middle of the present millennium, there is an indication that the Mara sites may postdate the Elmenteitan. However, we can also not dismiss the possibility that these sites are palimpsests of several occupations, particularly since artefacts from one of them have been dated to around AD 400. What these sites may be documenting is not population replacement but a continuation of Elmenteitan settlement into the period when traditional lithic procurement strategies were breaking down under the impact of the spread of iron tools and weapons, and when new techniques of ceramic decoration were being rapidly diffused.

Several authors have suggested on the basis of either historical linguistics (Ambrose 1982) or ceramic design structure (Collett 1984: 87; Robertshaw n.d.) a link between the Elmenteitan and speakers of Southern Nilotic languages. Therefore, it is of considerable interest to note that Maasai traditions identify the original inhabitants of the Mara region as 'Il Tatua', who are often equated with the Tatoga of northern Tanzania but are perhaps best viewed as an archetype of all earlier Southern Nilotic-speaking inhabitants of what became Maasailand (Lamprey and Waller 1990). Thus, one may posit an equation between the Elmenteitan of the archaeologists, 'Il Tatua' of oral tradition and the Southern Nilotes of the linguists. To take a rather more conservative stance: if further archaeological research confirms the hypothesis that Elmenteitan settlement continued well into the present millennium, then Elmenteitan pastoralists and their descendants occupied the Mara region for the best part of two thousand years. This is a marked difference from the relatively brief episode of Elmenteitan occupation of South Nyanza, where it was perhaps harder to eke out a pastoral existence in the face of tsetse flies. The abundant rainfall and rich agricultural soils of the alluvial floodplain in the vicinity of Gogo Falls also attracted incursions by farmers with hoes and spears with iron blades.

Conclusions

The later prehistoric sequences of the South Nyanza and Mara regions of southwestern Kenya are remarkably different. In South Nyanza a broad-spectrum, gathering-hunting-fishing adaptation is replaced by, or perhaps assimilated into, the Elmenteitan cultural tradition of immigrant pastoralists some two thousand years ago. However, Elmenteitan settlement in South Nyanza is apparently rather short-lived, since radiocarbon dates for other sites in the Lake Victoria basin with Urewe pottery suggest that Early Iron Age farmers probably occupied this region by the middle of the first millennium AD at the latest. In contrast, in the Mara there is little evidence for occupation by foraging peoples prior to the advent of the pastoralists, whose material culture is assigned to the Oldishi tradition. These pioneer herders settled in the Lemek valley, from which they would appear to have been displaced around 400 BC or somewhat later by the makers of Elmenteitan pottery and stone artefacts, who were to occupy the region for the best part of two thousand years.

Not only was the duration of Elmenteitan settlement very different between South Nyanza and the Mara, so also was their subsistence economy. South Nyanza appears to have been ecologically marginal for viable pastoral production, compelling diversification of subsistence into hunting, fishing and possibly cultivation. However, the Mara region was capable of support-ing large numbers of livestock. Thus, hunting was shunned,[9] despite the fact that the herds of the pastoralists had to compete for grazing with large populations of wild herbivores. Whether cultivation was also shunned is a more difficult question, which can only be answered by more fieldwork. However, there is some evidence to suggest that the earlier phases of Elmenteitan settlement were basically restricted to the Lemek valley and that an expansion of settlement onto the Mara plains occurred in the first centuries AD. It has been mooted that this expansion took place within the context of a shift from agro-pastoralism to more mobile pastoralism, with agricultural produce obtained when required through exchange networks. In this shift may lie the origins of the so-called 'pure' pastoral economies which have so enchanted anthropologists.

One might argue that east Africa has little or nothing to offer towards finding the answer to the 'Big Question' of the origins of agriculture, but to do so would be to deny the fact that consideration of the 'where', 'when' and 'how' of food production is really of secondary importance compared to the explanation of the process of the spread of food production across much of the globe and what that involved in terms of human interactions and adaptations – those of farmers, pastoralists and foraging peoples.

Notes

1　By 'east Africa' I refer to Kenya, Uganda and Tanzania.
2　See Collett and Robertshaw (1983b) for a detailed discussion of the dating evidence and a refutation of much earlier 'dates' for domestic animals in southern Kenya.
3　Formerly Nderit ware.
4　The much older hydration date from the base of the deposits presumably represents the chance incorporation into the midden of a much older artefact that does not date the main occupation.
5　Sherds which belong within the rather enigmatic 'Akira ware' were also found. However, discussion of these interesting pots is beyond the scope of this chapter (see Bower 1973; Langdon and Robertshaw 1985).
6　The point has been made elsewhere that no pastoral society can survive indefinitely without access to agricultural produce (Monod 1975: 134). The implications of this statement for our understanding of the subsistence systems of early pastoral communities in east Africa have been discussed by Robertshaw and Collett (1983).
7　No human skeletal remains have been found in the Mara region.
8　The appearance of Iron Age (Urewe) farmers at Gogo Falls may be relevant in this context.
9　Less than 1 per cent of the identifiable faunal remains from Ngamuriak belong to wild animals (Marshall 1986).

References

Ambrose, S.H. (1980) 'Elmenteitan and other late pastoral neolithic adaptations in the central highlands of east Africa', in R. E. Leakey and B. A. Ogot (eds) *Proceedings of the 8th Panafrican Congress of Prehistory and Quaternary Studies*, Nairobi: International Louis Leakey Memorial Institute for African Prehistory.

Ambrose, S.H. (1982) 'Archaeological and linguistic reconstructions of history in east Africa', in C. Ehret and M. Posnansky (eds) *The Archaeological and Linguistic Reconstruction of African History*, Berkeley, CA: University of California Press.

Ambrose, S.H. (1984) 'The introduction of pastoral adaptations to the highlands of east Africa', in J. D. Clark and S. A. Brandt (eds) *From Hunters to Farmers: the causes and consequences of food production in Africa*, Berkeley, CA: University of California Press.

Ambrose, S.H. and DeNiro, M.J. (1986) 'Reconstruction of African human diet using bone collagen carbon and nitrogen isotope ratios', *Nature*, 319: 321–4.

Binford, L.R. (1983) *In Pursuit of the Past*, London: Thames and Hudson.

Binford, L.R. (1984) *Faunal Remains from Klasies River Mouth*, London: Academic Press.

Bower, J.R.F. (1973) 'Seronera: excavations at stone bowl site in the Serengeti National Park', *Azania*, 8: 71–104.

Bower, J.R.F. (1978) 'Culture, environment and technology: preliminary results of an archaeological study in Kenya', *Proceedings of the Iowa Academy of Science*, 85: 41–4.

Bower, J.R.F. (1984a) 'Settlement behaviour of pastoral cultures in East Africa', in J. D. Clark and S. A. Brandt (eds) *From Hunters to Farmers: the causes and consequences of food production in Africa*, Berkeley, CA: University of California Press.

Bower, J.R.F. (1984b) 'Subsistence-settlement systems of the Pastoral Neolithic in east Africa', in L. Krzyzaniak and M. Kobusiewicz (eds) *Origin and Development of Food-producing Cultures in North-Eastern Africa*, Poznan: Polish Academy of Sciences and Poznan Archaeological Museum.

Bower, J.R.F. and Chadderdon T.J. (1986) 'Further excavations of pastoral neolithic sites in Serengeti', *Azania*, 21: 129–33.

Butterman, J.M. (1979) 'Luo social formations in change: Karachuonyo and Kanyamkago, c. 1800–1945', unpublished PhD thesis, Syracuse University.

Cable, C. (n.d.) 'Forager-farmer interactions in Kenyan prehistory or "What happened to the hunters?"', unpublished seminar paper 1987, Department of History, University of Nairobi.

Clutton-Brock, J. (ed.) (1989) *The Walking Larder: patterns of domestication, pastoralism and predation*, London: Unwin Hyman.

Clutton-Brock, J. (ed.) (1993) 'The spread of domestic animals in Africa', in T. Shaw, P. Sinclair, B. Andah and A. Okpoko (eds) *The Archaeology of Africa: food, metals and towns*, London: Routledge.

Collett, D.P. (1984) 'The pottery', *Azania*, 19: 83–7.

Collett, D.P. (1985) 'The spread of early iron-producing communities in eastern and southern Africa', unpublished PhD thesis, University of Cambridge.

Collett, D.P. (1993) 'Metaphors and representations associated with precolonial iron-smelting in eastern and southern Africa', in T. Shaw, P. Sinclair, B. Andah and A. Okpoko (eds) *The Archaeology of Africa: food, metals and towns*, London: Routledge.

Collett, D.P. and Robertshaw, P.T. (1980) 'Early iron age and Kansyore pottery: finds from Gogo Falls, South Nyanza', *Azania*, 15: 133–45.

Collett, D.P. and Robertshaw, P.T. (1983a) 'Pottery traditions of early pastoral communities in Kenya', *Azania*, 18: 107–25.

Collett, D.P. and Robertshaw, P.T. (1983b) 'Problems in the interpretation of radiocarbon dates: the Pastoral Neolithic of east Africa', *African Archaeological Review*, 1: 57–74.

Gifford, D.P., Isaac, G.L. and Nelson, C.M. (1980) 'Evidence for predation and pastoralism at Prolonged Drift: a pastoral Neolithic site in Kenya', *Azania*, 15: 57–8.

Gifford-Gonzalez, D.P. (1984) 'Implications of a faunal assemblage from a pastoral Neolithic site in Kenya: findings and a perspective on research', in J. D. Clark and S. A. Brandt (eds) *From Hunters to Farmers: the causes and consequences of food production in Africa*, Berkeley, CA: University of California Press.

Gifford-Gonzalez, D.P. and Kimengich, J. (1984) 'Faunal evidence for early stock-keeping in the central Rift of Kenya: preliminary findings', in L. Krzyzaniak and M. Kobusiewicz (eds) *Origin and Development of Food-producing Cultures in North-Eastern Africa*, Poznan: Polish Academy of Sciences and Poznan Archaeological Museum.

Gowlett, J.A.J., Hedges, R., Law, I. and Perry, C. (1987) 'Radiocarbon dates from the Oxford AMS system: archaeometry datelist 5', *Archaeometry*, 29: 125–55.

Harlan, J.R. (1993) 'The tropical African cereals', in T. Shaw, P. Sinclair, B. Andah and A. Okpoko (eds) *The Archaeology of Africa: food, metals and towns*, London: Routledge.

Harris, D.R. and Hillman, G.C (eds) (1989) *Foraging and Farming: the evolution of plant exploitation*, London: Unwin Hyman.

Horton, M. and Mudida, N. (1993) 'Exploitation of marine resources: evidence for the origin of the Swahili communities in east Africa', in T. Shaw, P. Sinclair, B. Andah and A. Okpoko (eds) *The Archaeology of Africa: food, metals and towns*, London: Routledge.

Kromer, B., Rhein, M., Bruns, H., Schoch-Fischer, H., Münnich, K., Stuiver, M. and Becker, B. (1986) 'Radiocarbon calibration data for the 6th to 8th millennia BC', *Radiocarbon*, 28: 954–60.

Lamprey, R.H. (1984) 'Masai impact on Kenya savanna vegetation: a remote sensing approach', unpublished PhD thesis, University of Aston in Birmingham.

Lamprey, R.H. and Waller, R. (1990) 'The Loita-Mara region in historic times: patterns of subsistence, settlement and ecological change', in P. T. Robertshaw (ed.) *Early Pastoralists of South-western Kenya*, Nairobi: British Institute in Eastern Africa.

Langdon, J. and Robertshaw, P. T. (1985) 'Petrographic and physico-chemical studies of early pottery from south-western Kenya', *Azania*, 20: 1–28.

Leakey, L.S.B. (1936) *Stone Age Africa*, London: Oxford University Press.

Marshall, F.B. (1986) 'Aspects of the advent of pastoral economies in east Africa', unpublished PhD thesis, University of California, Berkeley.

Marshall, F.B. (1990) 'Cattle herds and caprine flocks: early pastoral strategies in south-western Kenya', in P. T. Robertshaw (ed.) *Early Pastoralists of South-western Kenya*, Nairobi: British Institute in Eastern Africa.

Merrick, H.V. and Brown, F.H. (1984) 'Obsidian sources and patterns of source utilization in Kenya and northern Tanzania: some initial findings', *African Archaeological Review*, 2: 129–52.

Monod, T. (1975) 'Introduction', in T. Monod (ed.) *Pastoralism in Tropical Africa*, London: International African Institute.

Nelson, C.M. (1980) 'The Elmenteitan lithic industry' , in R. E. Leakey and B. A. Ogot (eds) *Proceedings of the 8th Panafrican Congress of Prehistory and Quaternary Studies*, Nairobi: International Louis Leakey Memorial Institute for African Prehistory.

Odner, K. (1972) 'Excavations at Narosura, a stone bowl site in the southern Kenya highands', *Azania*, 7: 25–92.

Ogot, B.A. (1967) *History of the Southern Luo, Vol.1: Migration and settlement 1500–1900*, Nairobi: East African Publishing House.

Pearson, G.W. and Stuiver, M. (1986) 'High precision calibration of the radiocarbon time scale, 500–2500 BC.', *Radiocarbon*, 28: 839–62.

Phillipson, D.W. (1977) *The Later Prehistory of Eastern and Southern Africa*, London: Heinemann.

Robertshaw, P.T. (1982) 'Eastern Equatoria in the context of later eastern African prehistory', in J. Mack and P. T. Robertshaw (eds) *Culture History in the Southern Sudan*, Nairobi: British Institute in Eastern Africa.

Robertshaw, P.T. (1989) 'The development of pastoralism in eastern Africa', in J. Clutton-Brock (ed.) *The Walking Larder: patterns of domestication, pastoralism and predation*, London: Unwin Hyman.

Robertshaw, P.T. (n.d.) 'The prehistory of pastoralism in Kenya', unpublished seminar paper 1984, University of London: School of Oriental and African Studies.

Robertshaw, P.T. and Collett, D.P. (1983) 'The identification of pastoral peoples in the archaeological record: an example from east Africa', *World Archaeology*, 15: 67–78.

Robertshaw, P.T., Collett, D.P., Gifford, D. and Mbae, N.B. (1983) 'Shell middens on the shores of Lake Victoria', *Azania*, 18: 1–43.

Robertshaw, P.T., Pilgram, T., Siiriäinen A. and Marshall, F. (1990) 'The archaeological survey and prehistoric settlement patterns', in P. T. Robertshaw (ed.) *Early Pastoralism in South-western Kenya*, Nairobi: British Institute in Eastern Africa.

Update: Revised interpretations of early agriculture in Africa

Peter Robertshaw

New research has shown that some revisions are required to the original chapter, particularly the argument that domestic animals reached East Africa as part of a package of innovations brought by immigrant pastoralists. In South Nyanza new excavations at Gogo Falls, as well as at other sites in the eastern half of the Lake Victoria basin, have refined our understanding of the Kansyore phase of the Oltome tradition, even though chronological uncertainties remain. New fieldwork in the Mara region has yielded more data but without disturbing the established cultural-stratigraphic framework. Nevertheless, new interpretations suggest avenues for further fieldwork.

The arrival of domestic stock in East Africa

It is now clear that a distinction should be made between the introduction of domestic livestock (primarily cattle, sheep and goats) and the arrival of pastoral communities in many regions of East Africa. The earliest well-dated livestock derive from Dongodien, east of Lake Turkana in northern Kenya at about 4000 uncal. BP (Marshall *et al.* 1984). Though fish bones and wild fauna are present on the site, the predominance of domestic animals suggests that the site was inhabited by pastoralists. However, in southern and western Kenya the first domestic stock occur in very small numbers before 3000 uncal. BP, in what appear to be hunter-gatherer contexts (Karega-Munene 2002; Wright 2003; see Marshall 2000: 200–2 for a review). Thus, diffusion of small numbers of livestock among forager communities may account for the initial spread of cattle and caprines across much of East Africa prior to 3000 uncal. BP. After this date there are numerous sites in the savanna regions of East Africa where domestic animals predominate. Most researchers still assume that these sites reflect the immigration of pastoralist communities. In this way, an initial 'trickle' of domestic animals became a 'splash' of arriving herders (Bower 1991). The reason for this apparent hiatus between the arrival of pastoralist communities and their subsequent southwards dispersal may well lie in the first encounters between pastoralists and several tropical diseases that are often fatal to cattle (Gifford-Gonzalez 2000).

New research in South Nyanza

New excavations and analyses at Gogo Falls (Robertshaw 1991) have yielded more data and prompted new interpretations (Karega-Munene 2002, 2003). Most cogently, these new excavations recovered several cattle and caprine bones associated exclusively with Oltome (Kansyore) pottery. In addition, there is a new AMS date of 3170 ± 70 uncal. BP (OXA-3494) associated with both Oltome pottery and cattle bones, while a date of 3480 ± 75 uncal. BP (OXA-3497) is associated with Oltome pottery and stratified above the earliest caprine remains (Karega-Munene 2002: 100–4). While post-depositional mixing of deposits leading to downward movement of domestic animals from levels containing Elmenteitan pottery is possible, the evidence favours a 'short' chronology for the Oltome occupation, with a few domestic animals occurring in what is otherwise a foraging economy. Recent research on the site of Wadh Lang'o has revealed an ecological setting almost identical to that of Gogo Falls and the same basic stratigraphic sequence of Oltome, Elmenteitan and Urewe occupations (Onjala *et al.* 1999). Although the site is undated, preliminary faunal analysis indicates the presence of caprines associated with well-stratified Oltome pottery (Prendergast, pers. comm.). However, AMS dates from another newly discovered Oltome site in the Lake Victoria basin, Siror, range from 6194 ± 47 uncal. BP (A0316) to 2889 ± 36 uncal. BP (A0318), suggesting that the Oltome may indeed be a long-lived tradition into which domestic animals were introduced in the later phases (Dale *et al.* 2004: 367). Dale *et al.* have also proposed that the Oltome tradition may represent a delayed-return hunter-gatherer economic system.

More extensive analysis of the faunal remains from Gogo Falls has not changed the interpretation of the Elmenteitan occupation of the site, though dogs and donkeys have now been identified (Karega-Munene 2002: 123). Cattle outnumbered caprines in the Gogo herds and both were permitted to reach maturity before being slaughtered (Karega-Munene 2002: 123–5). This undermines the suggestion that the unusual combination of hunting and herding in the Elmenteitan occupation might have resulted from the lower productivity of livestock herds due to disease-bearing tsetse flies (Marshall 1990: 884).

The only potential cultigen recovered during the excavations at Gogo Falls was a single seed of the wild progenitor of finger millet (*Eleusine coracana* subsp. *africana*) (Lange 1991), although edible fruits and weeds associated with livestock enclosures were identified (Wetterstrom 1991). However, following the recent discovery of banana phytoliths in Uganda dated earlier than about 4500 uncal. BP, Lejju *et al.* (2006) have suggested that banana cultivation may have served as the subsistence anchor for Oltome sedentism.

New research in the Mara

Two very large Elmenteitan sites in the Mara region possess central live-stock enclosures. I proposed that these two sites were the settlements of wealthy pastoralists whose success derived from control over the exchange and redistribution of obsidian (Robertshaw 1990: 297). One site, Sugenya, has recently been excavated; while only preliminary results are available, the excavator expresses cautious support for the hypothesis of an Elmenteitan socio-political hierarchy (Simons 2003).

I argued previously that the early pastoral communities of East Africa cultivated cereal crops despite a cultural preoccupation with their livestock. Then, with the advent of iron-working agriculturalists into adjacent regions in the first centuries CE, the pastoral communities were able to shift to an economy based on specialised herd management with grain obtained through trade. Alternatively, Marshall (1990) suggested that the establish-ment of the modern climatic regime with a bimodal pattern of annual rainfall about 3000 uncal. BP permitted an earlier shift to specialised pastoral production. The nexus of this debate has been the interpretation of the Elmenteitan site of Ngamuriak, dated to about 2000 uncal. BP (Robertshaw and Marshall 1990). Was it a settlement of specialised pastoralists (Marshall 1990, 1994) or of people who supplemented the products of their herds with grain cultivation (Robertshaw 1990: 293–302)? However, because flotation techniques are rarely systematically employed on excavations in East Africa, direct archaeological evidence for domesticated cereal crops prior to the late first millennium CE does not exist, despite the predictions of linguistic historians.

References

Bower, J. (1991) 'The pastoral Neolithic of East Africa', *Journal of World Prehistory*, 5: 49–82.

Dale, D., Marshall, F. and Pilgram, T. (2004) 'Delayed-return hunter-gatherers in Africa? Historic perspectives from the Okiek and archaeological perspectives from the Kansyore', in G. M. Crothers (ed.) *Hunters and Gatherers in Theory and in Archaeology*, Carbondale, : Center for Archaeological Investigations.

Gifford-Gonzalez, D. (2000) 'Animal disease challenges to the emergence of pastoralism in sub-Saharan Africa', *African Archaeological Review*, 17: 95–139.

Karega-Munene (2002) *Holocene Foragers, Fishers and Herders of Western Kenya*, BAR International Series 1037, Oxford: Archaeopress.

Karega-Munene (2003) 'The East African Neolithic: a historical perspective', in C. M. Kusimba and S. B. Kusimba (eds) *East African Archaeology: foragers, potters, smiths, and traders*, Philadelphia, PA: University of Pennsylvania Museum of Archaeology and Anthropology.

Lange, G. (1991) 'Appendix V: A seed of wild finger millet from Gogo Falls', *Azania*, 26: 191–2.

Lejju, B.J., Robertshaw, P. and Taylor, D. (2006) 'Africa's earliest bananas?', *Journal of Archaeological Science*, 33: 102–13.

Marshall, F. (1990) 'Origins of specialized pastoralism in East Africa', *American Anthropologist*, 92: 873–94.

Marshall, F. (1994) 'Archaeological perspectives on East African pastoralism', in E. Fratkin, J. Galvin, and E. Roth (eds) *African Pastoralist Systems*, Boulder, CO: Lynn Reiner.

Marshall, F. (2000) 'The origins and spread of domestic animals in East Africa', in R. M. Blench and K. C. MacDonald (eds) *The Origins and Development of African Livestock*, London: UCL Press.

Marshall, F., Stewart, K. and Barthelme, J. (1984) 'Early domestic stock at Dongodien in northern Kenya', *Azania*, 19: 120–7.

Onjala, I., Kibunjia, M., Odede, F. and Oteyo, G. (1999) 'Recent archaeological investigation along the Sondu Miriu River, Kenya', *Azania*, 34: 116–22.

Robertshaw, P. (1990) *Early Pastoralists of South-Western Kenya*, Nairobi: British Institute in Eastern Africa Memoir.

Robertshaw, P. (1991) 'Gogo Falls: a complex site east of Lake Victoria', *Azania*, 26: 63–195.

Robertshaw, P. and Marshall, F. (1990) 'Ngamuriak', in P. Robertshaw (ed.) *Early Pastoralists of South-Western Kenya*, Nairobi: British Institute in Eastern Africa Memoir.

Simons, A. (2003) 'Sugenya: a Pastoral Neolithic site in south-western Kenya', *Azania*, 38: 169–73.

Wetterstrom, W. (1991) 'Appendix IV: plant remains from Gogo Falls', *Azania*, 26: 180–91.

Wright, D.K. (2003) 'Survey, excavation and preliminary analysis of Pastoral Neolithic sites, Tsavo, Kenya', *Nyame Akuma*, 59: 54–61.

Index

Note: page numbers in italics denote figures, tables or illustrations